DOING INTERVIEW RESEARCH

Sara Miller McCune founded SAGE Publishing in 1965 to support the dissemination of usable knowledge and educate a global community. SAGE publishes more than 1000 journals and over 800 new books each year, spanning a wide range of subject areas. Our growing selection of library products includes archives, data, case studies and video. SAGE remains majority owned by our founder and after her lifetime will become owned by a charitable trust that secures the company's continued independence.

Los Angeles | London | New Delhi | Singapore | Washington DC | Melbourne

UWE FLICK

DOING INTERVIEW RESEARCH

The Essential How To Guide

Los Angeles | London | New Delhi
Singapore | Washington DC | Melbourne

Los Angeles | London | New Delhi
Singapore | Washington DC | Melbourne

SAGE Publications Ltd
1 Oliver's Yard
55 City Road
London EC1Y 1SP

SAGE Publications Inc.
2455 Teller Road
Thousand Oaks, California 91320

SAGE Publications India Pvt Ltd
B 1/I 1 Mohan Cooperative Industrial Area
Mathura Road
New Delhi 110 044

SAGE Publications Asia-Pacific Pte Ltd
3 Church Street
#10-04 Samsung Hub
Singapore 049483

Editor: Alysha Owen
Senior assistant editor: Charlotte Bush
Production editor: Victoria Nicholas
Copyeditor: Jane Fricker
Proofreader: Sharon Cawood
Marketing manager: Ben Griffin-Sherwood
Cover design: Shaun Mercier
Typeset by: C&M Digitals (P) Ltd, Chennai, India
Printed in the UK

Library of Congress Control Number: 2021934189

British Library Cataloguing in Publication data

A catalogue record for this book is available from
the British Library

ISBN 978-1-5264-6405-7
ISBN 978-1-5264-6406-4 (pbk)

At SAGE we take sustainability seriously. Most of our products are printed in the UK using responsibly sourced
papers and boards. When we print overseas we ensure sustainable papers are used as measured by the PREPS
grading system. We undertake an annual audit to monitor our sustainability.

CONTENTS

Extended Contents   vii
List of Figures   xii
List of Tables   xiii
About the Author   xiv
Preface   xv
Acknowledgements   xix
Discover the Online Resources   xx

PART I   How to Understand Interview Research   **1**

1   What Doing Interview Research Means   3

2   Theories and Epistemologies of Interviewing   21

3   When to Choose Interviews as a Research Method   39

4   Methods and Formats of Interviewing   59

PART II   Designing Interview Research   **73**

5   Planning and Designing Interview Research   75

6   How Many Interviewees? Sampling and Saturation   101

7   Accessing and Recruiting Participants   121

PART III   How to Conduct Interviews   **137**

8   How to Respect and Protect: Ethics of Interviewing   139

9   Semi-structured Interviews: Working with Questions and Answers   169

10   Interviewing Experts and Elites   199

11   Integrating Narratives in Interviews: Episodic Interviews 219

PART IV   Doing Interviews in Contexts   **235**

12   How to Work with Life Histories: Narrative Interviews   237

13   Working with Focus Groups as Interviews   253

14   Ask (in) the Field: Ethnographic and Mobile Interviewing   271

15   Doing Online Interviews   287

PART V   How to Work with Interview Data   **311**

16   Working with Interview Data   313

17   Credibility and Transparency: Quality and Writing in
     Interview Research   345

18   From Interviewing to an Inner View: Critiques and Reflexivity   369

Glossary   380
References   388
Index   411

EXTENDED CONTENTS

List of Figures   xii
List of Tables   xiii
About the Author   xiv
Preface   xv
Acknowledgements   xix
Discover the Online Resources   xx

PART I   How to Understand Interview Research   **1**

1   What Doing Interview Research Means   **3**
Looking Back: Interviewing in Qualitative Research   4
New Challenges   7
Why Interviews? Purposes and Research Questions   11
Interviewing as Research Built on a Short-term Personal Relationship   14
Interviews as Stand-alone Method or in a Complex Design   15

2   Theories and Epistemologies of Interviewing   **21**
Basic Theoretical Underpinnings of Interviewing   22
Epistemologies of Interviewing   24
Epistemological Concepts of Interviewing   24
Role of the Interviewer   27
Knowledge Produced in the Interview   28
Consequences for Conceiving Interviews   28
Methodological Principles Underlying the Use of Interviews   29
Critical Discussion of Interviewing   31
Doing Interview Research – A Framework   32

3   When to Choose Interviews as a Research Method   **39**
Aims of Interviewing in Various Contexts   40
Research Questions   42
Study Aims   44
When to Choose Qualitative Interviewing   45
Research Strategies   46
Pragmatic Considerations   47
Exploration of Issues   48
Multiplicity of Perspectives   49
Aims of Going Online and Becoming Mobile with Interviewing   50
Participants' Views of Being Interviewed   51
When Not to Choose Interviews as Your Method   54
Doing Interviews despite the Critiques   54

4 Methods and Formats of Interviewing   **59**
General Principles of Interviewing and the Proliferation of Methods   59
Dimensions of Interview Methods   61
Formats of Interviewing   64
Specific Settings of Interviewing in Context   66
Principles and Practices of Interviewing   68
Selecting a Method for Interviewing   68

PART II   Designing Interview Research   **73**

5 Planning and Designing Interview Research   **75**
Designing an Interview Study as Constructing a
        Framework for Listening   75
Designing Qualitative Interview Research – What Does it Mean?   76
The Six F's of Designing Interview Research   77
The Process of Designing Interview Studies   78
Research Questions   80
Case Study Research   83
Comparative Studies   84
Longitudinal Designs   86
Extending the Classical Design of Interviewing   88
Designing Interview Guides   94
Resources   95

6 How Many Interviewees? Sampling and Saturation   **101**
Constructing a Framework for Listening   101
Sampling in the Process   102
How to Sample Interviewees   104
Sampling Criteria Defined in Advance   104
Purposive Sampling   105
Theoretical Sampling   107
Snowball Sampling   109
Sampling in Indigenous Interview Research   110
Planning the Sampling for an Interview Study   111
Sample Size and Saturation: How Many Interviews?   112
Steps, Aims and Criteria in Preparing and Doing the Sampling for
        Interview Studies   115

7 Accessing and Recruiting Participants   **121**
Constructing a Framework for Listening   121
Accessing and Recruiting Interviewees   122
Accessing and Recruiting for Digital Interviews   128
Being Recruited for an Interview: The Participants' Perspectives   130
Steps, Aims and Criteria in Preparing and Gaining Access and
        Recruiting for Interview Studies   132

PART III How to Conduct Interviews   **137**

8 How to Respect and Protect: Ethics of Interviewing   **139**
Ethics of Doing Interviews   139
General Issues of Interview Ethics   140
Data Protection: Regulations in the European Union   141
Participants' Views and Expectations of Interview Research Ethics   145
How to Act Ethically in Doing Interview Research   147
Informed Consent   149
Risk and Harm   152
Dual Role and Over-involvement   153
Politics and Power   153
Doing Justice to Participants in Analysing Data   154
Specific Target Groups of Interviewing   155
Specific Contexts of Interviewing   159
Research Ethics in Constructing a Setting for Listening   161
Steps, Aims and Criteria in Preparing and Doing Ethically
        Sound Interview Studies   163

9 Semi-structured Interviews: Working with Questions and Answers   **169**
Background to Semi-structured Interviewing   170
Constructing a Framework for Listening in Semi-structured Interviews   174
Interview Guides   174
Using Questions and Interview Guides Reflexively   178
Doing Semi-structured Interviewing   179
Using Tools in Interviewing   184
Photo Elicitation   185
Using Vignettes   187
Interviewing with Foreign Languages   188
Interviewing in Different Cultures   190
Steps, Aims and Criteria in Preparing and Doing Semi-structured Interviews   191
How to Select the Appropriate Form of Interviewing   194

10 Interviewing Experts and Elites   **199**
Background to the Expert Interview   200
Expert Interviews in Indigenous Research   202
Constructing a Framework for Listening in Expert Interviews   203
Conducting Expert Interviews   206
Types of Data in Expert Interviews   208
Ways of Using Expert Interviews   209
Elite Interviewing   209
Key Informant Interviewing   210
Planning and Preparing Expert Interviews   211
Being Interviewed: The Participants in Expert Interviews   212
What is Different in Expert Interviews?   212
Steps, Aims and Criteria in Preparing and Doing Expert Interviews   213

11 Integrating Narratives in Interviews: Episodic Interviews   **219**
Background to the Episodic Interview   220
Constructing a Framework for Listening in Episodic Interviews   222
Types of Data in the Episodic Interview   228
Planning and Preparing Episodic Interviews   228
Steps, Aims and Criteria in Preparing and Doing Episodic Interviews   230

PART IV   Doing Interviews in Contexts   **235**

12 How to Work with Life Histories: Narrative Interviews   **237**
Background to the Narrative Interview   238
Constructing a Framework for Listening in Narrative Interviews   240
Conducting a Narrative Interview   240
Types of Data in the Narrative Interview   245
Narrative Interviewing in Critical Research   246
Steps, Aims and Criteria in Preparing and Doing Narrative Interviews   248

13 Working with Focus Groups as Interviews   **253**
Background to Focus Group Interviews   253
Constructing a Framework for Listening in Focus Group Interviews   255
Types of Data in Focus Group Interviews   258
Planning and Preparing Focus Group Interviews   258
Steps, Aims and Criteria in Preparing and Doing Focus Group Interviews   260
Contextualizing Interviews by Focus Groups   262
Doing Focus Group Interviews Online   263
Focus Group Interviewing for Decolonizing Research   265

14 Ask (in) the Field: Ethnographic and Mobile Interviewing   **271**
The Ethnographic Interview   272
Constructing a Framework for Listening in Ethnographic Interviews   276
Extend the Setting: Mobile Interviewing   277
Steps, Aims and Criteria in Preparing and Doing Ethnographic
    and Mobile Interviews   282

15 Doing Online Interviews   **287**
Background to Online Interviewing   287
Constructing a Framework for Listening in Online Interviews   288
Doing Qualitative Telephone Interviews   289
Doing Email Interviews   293
Practicalities of Doing Email Interviews   296
Doing Qualitative Skype Interviews   300
Using Zoom, Webex and Microsoft Teams for Doing Interviews   303
Steps, Aims and Criteria in Preparing and Doing Online Interviews   304
How to Select the Appropriate Form of Interviewing   305
Online Interviews in Indigenous Research   306

PART V   How to Work with Interview Data   311

16   Working with Interview Data   313
  Constructing a Framework for Listening to Interviews as Data   313
  How to Turn Interviews into Data   314
  Secondary Analysis of Interview Data   318
  Data Management and Administration   319
  How to Analyse Interview Data   322
  Coding   323
  Grounded Theory Coding   323
  Thematic Coding   328
  Qualitative Content Analysis   331
  Planning the Analysis of an Interview   333
  Interpretation and Discovery   334
  Comparison and Generalization   337
  Postcolonial Approaches to Analysing Interview Data   338
  Steps, Aims and Criteria in Preparing and Doing the Analysis
      of an Interview   339

**17   Credibility and Transparency: Quality and Writing in
      Interview Research**   **345**
  Approaches to Quality in Qualitative Research   346
  Quality in Doing Qualitative Interview Research   346
  Quality of Interviewing in the Process   348
  Quality Before and After the Interview   348
  Practical Aspects of Advancing Quality in Qualitative Interviews   349
  Validity Concepts in Indigenous Research   353
  Trustworthiness   353
  Credibility and Transparency   354
  Making Interview Research Transparent – Writing Research   356
  Steps, Aims and Criteria in Preparing and Doing the Writing
      Up of Interview Studies   362
  Making Qualitative Research Relevant   363

18   From Interviewing to an Inner View: Critiques and Reflexivity   **369**
  Critiques of Interviewing   369
  Reflexivity   373
  Doing Interviews – Not a Case of Mind-reading but Varieties of
      Talking about an Issue in Context   377

Glossary   380
References   388
Index   411

LIST OF FIGURES

5.1 Levels of triangulation in interview research   89

9.1 Five-degree agreement scale   171
9.2 Street context symbolizing homelessness and stigma for
     a participant   186
9.3 Degrees of interviewees' freedom in using one's own words
     and formulations   194

11.1 Forms of knowledge in the episodic interview   221
11.2 Types of data in the episodic interview   229

16.1 Coding paradigm model   325

LIST OF TABLES

5.1 Questions and tasks in designing research 77
5.2 The six F's of designing interview research 78

6.1 Sampling decisions in the process of working with interviews 103
6.2 Steps, aims and criteria in preparing and doing the sampling for interview studies 115

7.1 Steps, aims and criteria in preparing and doing access and recruiting for interview studies 132

8.1 Steps, aims and criteria in preparing and gaining ethically sound interviews 163

9.1 Steps, aims and criteria in preparing and doing semi-structured interviews 192

10.1 Sample of experts 205
10.2 Steps, aims and criteria in preparing and doing expert interviews 213

11.1 Steps, aims and criteria in preparing and doing episodic interviews 231

12.1 Steps, aims and criteria in preparing and doing narrative interviews 248

13.1 Steps, aims and criteria in preparing and doing focus group interviews 260

14.1 Steps, aims and criteria in preparing and doing ethnographic and mobile interviews 282

15.1 Steps, aims and criteria in preparing and doing online interviews 304

16.1 Steps, aims and criteria in preparing and doing the analysis of an interview 339

17.1 Steps, aims and criteria in preparing and doing the writing up of interview studies 362

ABOUT THE AUTHOR

Uwe Flick is Professor of Qualitative Research in Social Science and Education at the Freie Universität Berlin, Germany. He is a trained psychologist and sociologist and received his PhD from the Free University of Berlin in 1988 and his Habilitation from the Technical University of Berlin in 1994. He has been Professor of Qualitative Research at Alice Salomon University of Applied Sciences in Berlin, Germany and at the University of Vienna, Austria. Previously, he was Adjunct Professor at the Memorial University of Newfoundland in St John's, Canada; a Lecturer in research methodology at the Free University of Berlin; a Reader and Assistant Professor in qualitative methods and evaluation at the Technical University of Berlin; and Associate Professor and Head of the Department of Medical Sociology at the Hannover Medical School. He has held visiting appointments at the London School of Economics, the Ecole des Hautes Etudes en Sciences Sociales in Paris, Cambridge University (UK), Memorial University of St John's (Canada), University of Lisbon (Portugal), Institute of Higher Studies in Vienna (Austria), in Italy and Sweden, and the School of Psychology at Massey University, Auckland (New Zealand). His main research interests are qualitative methods, social representations in the fields of individual and public health, vulnerability in fields like youth homelessness or migration, and technological change in everyday life. He is the editor of *The SAGE Handbook of Qualitative Data Analysis* (Sage, 2014), *The SAGE Qualitative Research Kit* (Sage, 2nd ed., 2018), *A Companion to Qualitative Research* (Sage, 2004) and *Psychology of the Social* (Cambridge University Press, 1998). His most recent publications are the seventh edition of *An Introduction to Qualitative Research* (Sage, 2022), *Doing Grounded Theory* (Sage, 2018), *Doing Triangulation and Mixed Methods* (Sage, 2018), *The SAGE Handbook of Qualitative Data Collection* (editor, Sage, 2018) and the third edition of *Introducing Research Methodology* (Sage, 2020). Currently, he is editing *The SAGE Handbook of Qualitative Research Design* (Sage, 2022). In 2019, Uwe Flick received the Lifetime Award in Qualitative Inquiry at the 15th International Congress of Qualitative Inquiry.

PREFACE

Background to the Book

Doing interview research has become one of the most prominent ways of doing qualitative research and of doing social research in general. We find a broad research practice in several fields which is based on doing interviews, or doing specific interviews. Many methodological papers, book chapters and books about interviewing have been published over the years. We also find critical discussions about research practice and the concept of interviewing. However, between the methodology of interviewing and the doing of interview research, we sometimes find a gap, as a lot of interviewing is done rather pragmatically. Doing interviews can start from several methods that have been developed and which can be selected for a study to be planned and conducted. Both textbooks and research practice often start from a general concept of interviews and interviewing which does not take this proliferation into account.

Aims of the Book

This book on doing interview research pursues several aims. First of all, it provides an introduction to the *process* of doing interview research. Second, it addresses issues of *designing* interview research from several angles, such as sampling interviewees, accessing them, and developing instruments such as interview guides. Third, it treats the methodological alternatives of how to do interviews as a variety of several distinct methods of interviewing, which are presented in detail. Fourth, it sees the analysis of interview data again from several methodological angles but also highlights how interviews have to be turned into data. Fifth, it looks at doing interviews embedded in ethical and epistemological considerations and in issues of quality and presentation. And sixth, it addresses issues of critique and reflexivity. As it has been written mainly during the Covid-19 pandemic, the lockdown and the move to digital teaching and research, it has a broad focus on online interviewing, too.

Overview of the Book

The first part of the book provides a first and general orientation about *how to understand interview research*. Chapter 1 outlines what interviewing is, how it has developed as a method, why it is done and current challenges for doing interview research. In Chapter 2, theoretical and epistemological backgrounds are discussed and a framework of doing interview research as *constructing a framework for listening* is developed for the subsequent chapters. Chapter 3 addresses differences between interviews in research, therapy and journalism before research questions and study aims for research with interviews are treated, as well as when not to use this method. In the fourth chapter, a brief overview of methods and formats of doing interviews concludes this introductory part.

The second part of this book addresses how to *design interview research*. Beginning in Chapter 5 by clarifying what design means in qualitative and particularly in interview research, we will introduce a specific concept of designing interview research as an orientation for the remaining chapters of the book. Here we will also discuss basic designs and research questions. In Chapter 6, the focus is on selecting and sampling participants and on the concept of saturation for defining when to stop. Whereas sampling is the plan, Chapter 7 describes how this will become practical in accessing and recruiting participants.

The third part is about *how to conduct interviews*, first by addressing ethical issues of interviewing in Chapter 8 about how to respect and protect participants. Chapter 9 treats what is mostly associated with interviewing – the use of the semi-structured interview, with an interview guide and by asking the questions to be answered. The methodological proliferation is advanced when we look at what it means to interview experts and elites in Chapter 10, before Chapter 11 turns to the episodic interview as the systematic integration of narratives in interviews.

Part IV puts *doing interviews in context*. The idea is that interviewing about specific issues is also being done in the context of inviting participants to recount their life histories, for example, so that the interview is embedded in a narrative. The method of narrative interviewing is described in Chapter 12. Interviewing can also be pursued in the context of (focus) groups. Chapter 13 is about doing focus group interviews. Ethnography is another context for interviewing, as in the ethnographic interview, and more recently in mobile interviews, which are both the subjects of Chapter 14. The last chapter in Part IV addresses the use of telephone and Skype, Zoom, Webex, email and online interviews – that is, doing interviews in a technological context.

The final Part V is about how to *work with interview data*. Chapter 16 discusses first the need to turn interviews into data, which can then be analysed in several ways. Then, several methods of analysing interview data are presented, not only for one's own interviews but also for secondary analysis of existing or other researchers' interviews. Chapter 17 sees the question of quality and credibility of interview research linked to ways of presenting it. The linking concept here is the transparency of doing interview research. The final chapter briefly addresses some critical discussions about doing interviews, outlines how and where this book provides answers and approaches to respond to them, and clarifies what reflexivity means in this context.

In summary, *Doing Interview Research* aims at giving readers a comprehensive overview of ways of interviewing by introducing the range of alternatives of interview methods. This provides readers with the necessary *background knowledge* about when to use interviews, how to design studies with interviews, and for how to understand and design interview research. It also provides the basis for the core approach in the book:

a very practical, step-by-step guidance for *how to conduct interviews*. The third approach focuses on *how to work with interview data* from analysis to presenting interview research and checking its quality. This book should appeal to a readership including under-graduate and graduate students and younger researchers planning and doing interview studies.

Features of the Book

Every chapter begins with a list of objectives (*How this chapter will help you*), which specify what I hope you will learn from each chapter. A *navigator* through a project of doing interviews is provided for each chapter before the chapter begins so that you can see at a glance how each chapter fits into the whole. To illustrate, the Chapter 1 Navigator is shown on the following page:

Case studies (*Research in the real world*) and other material are provided throughout to illustrate methodological issues. At the end of each chapter, you will find *checklists* for *what you need to ask yourself* and for *what you need to succeed* whilst planning and conducting a research project. These checklists provide readily accessible guidance that can be referred to over and over again as your project progresses. Key points (*What you have learned*), *a number of exercises*, and suggestions for *what's next* to read further conclude each chapter. A *glossary* explaining the most important terms and concepts used in the text is included at the end of the book.

Doing Interview Research Navigator

You are here in your project

How to understand interview research
- What doing interview research means
- Theories and epistemologies of interviewing
- When to choose interviews as a research method
- Methods and formats of interviewing

Designing interview research
- Planning and designing interview research
- How many interviewees: Sampling and saturation
- Accessing and recruiting participants

How to conduct interviews
- How to respect and protect: Ethics of interviewing
- Semi-structured interviews: Working with questions and answers
- Interviewing experts and elites
- Integrating narratives in interviews: Episodic interviews

Doing interviews in context
- How to work with life histories: Narrative interviews
- Working with focus groups as interviews
- Ask (in) the field: Ethnographic and mobile interviewing
- Doing online interviews

How to work with interview data
- Working with interview data
- Credibility and transparency: Quality and writing in interview research
- From interviewing to an inner view: Critiques and reflexivity

ACKNOWLEDGEMENTS

This book has profited considerably from the input of the anonymous reviewers who provided helpful comments in the various stages of preparing and writing it. I want to thank them very much, as well as my very supportive editors at SAGE, Alysha Owen and Charlotte Bush.

DISCOVER THE ONLINE RESOURCES

Get support for doing interview research at: https://study.sagepub.com/flickdir

For students:

Case studies showcase interviews in the real world, including focus groups, narrative research and elite interviews. Each case study comes with critical thinking questions to help you think more deeply about research you consume.

Author Uwe Flick's **annotated interview transcripts** give you best-practice examples of how to do coding and annotation in your own research.

Journal articles and **book chapters** bring interview methods to life, showing you how interview research is done at each step of the process, as well as the opportunities interview research offers.

Videos hand-picked by Uwe give you insight into different aspects of interview research, from understanding research design to assessing research quality and credibility.

Weblinks to research journals, ethical guidelines, qualitative data analysis software and more help you find other people's research, ensure your research adheres to requirements and develop your data analysis skills.

For instructors:

Download **PowerPoint slides** featuring figures and tables from the book, which can be customized for use in your own lectures and presentations.

Check your students' understanding with **multiple-choice questions** for each chapter that can be used in class, as homework or exams.

I

HOW TO UNDERSTAND INTERVIEW RESEARCH

This first part of the book has four aims. First you will receive an overview of what research interviewing is about, how it developed as a method, what role technologies play in this development, what new challenges are linked to interviewing and what interviewing is used for. These are the topics of Chapter 1.

Second, this part seeks to introduce the theoretical, epistemological and methodological underpinnings of interviewing, before a working definition and a framework for the further discussion of interview practices are formulated. This framework sees the interviewer as a 'constructing listener' and interviews as co-constructing knowledge (Chapter 2). In the next step, we will spell out when to choose interviews as a research method and what distinguishes research interviews from interviewing in therapy and journalism (Chapter 3). Following that, Chapter 4 briefly introduces methods and formats of the research interview as an orientation for the detailed presentations in the following chapters.

These four chapters should help you to understand the specific features of research interviewing.

Doing Interview Research Navigator

You are here in your project

How to understand interview research

- What doing interview research means
- Theories and epistemologies of interviewing
- When to choose interviews as a research method
- Methods and formats of interviewing

Designing interview research

- Planning and designing interview research
- How many interviewees: Sampling and saturation
- Accessing and recruiting participants

How to conduct interviews

- How to respect and protect: Ethics of interviewing
- Semi-structured interviews: Working with questions and answers
- Interviewing experts and elites
- Integrating narratives in interviews: Episodic interviews

Doing interviews in context

- How to work with life histories: Narrative interviews
- Working with focus groups as interviews
- Ask (in) the field: Ethnographic and mobile interviewing
- Doing online interviews

How to work with interview data

- Working with interview data
- Credibility and transparency: Quality and writing in interview research
- From interviewing to an inner view: Critiques and reflexivity

WHAT DOING INTERVIEW RESEARCH MEANS

You will:

- learn why interviews are used,
- be introduced to the development of this method,
- be introduced to the epistemologies and theoretical backgrounds of using interviews,
- gain an idea of the current and future developments of interviewing,
- have an initial idea about the debates around interviewing as a method, and
- have an overview of the book.

Doing interview research is a widespread practice in social science and in particular in qualitative research. Collecting data by just talking to people after preparing a number of questions seems attractive, easy and pragmatic for survey institutes as well as for students working on their master's or PhD projects. In most cases, such a 'just do it' approach leads to answers – people are generally happy to say something when asked about their ideas, opinions or feelings. In interviews, statements, answers and **narratives** related to subjective perspectives and experiences are collected. Interviews are conducted with individuals, couples, families and groups. Similar to interviews, **focus groups** are used, but these are more strongly based on stimulating answers in the group than on individual answers or narratives.

However, interviewing has greater potential the more it is taken seriously as a method and as a challenge to ask participants in a sophisticated and focused way – especially if an interview is not solely understood as a number of single questions. If it is seen as a systematic way of developing an approach to the complexity of topics and the, sometimes implicit, issues underlying the participants' relations to such topics, this method has much more potential for uncovering the depth of experiences. If the interview is not just seen as providing a number of answers, statements or insights into inner worlds, but analysed as an interaction between researcher and participant and also for how statements are produced, this method can be taken more seriously than has been done by some critics (see below). Its potential can be fully exploited if we understand that the field of interview research includes several forms of interview methods, which are based on varying aims, differing principles and various practices. Then a major challenge is to ascertain which method of interviewing to choose for answering a specific **research question**. This includes deciding which method is most adequate for doing interviews in a specific study and how to apply this method in the most fruitful way.

This book is designed to help you to take such a decision by giving an overview and a detailed description of the field and various ways of doing interview research. At the same time, it intends to provide a more detailed account of how to apply a specific kind of interviewing. Therefore, it addresses several issues in the context of doing interviews and asking questions. Such issues include whom to select as interviewees and how to approach participants. Ethical concerns around interviewing in general and in specific cases are also detailed as well as how to turn interviews into data and what to do with interview data that have been collected.

This introductory chapter outlines the rationale of interviewing in general and the history of interview research. It also addresses mobile and digital turns and their impact on doing interview research. The aim of this chapter is to give you a first and brief orientation about why interviews are used and about the current developments. A particular focus in the book and in this chapter is on how diversity has become an issue in doing interviews.

Looking Back: Interviewing in Qualitative Research

Interviewing has a long tradition in qualitative research, as Platt's (2012) overview demonstrates. Lee (2004, p. 870) states that in the early 1920s 'the interview in a recognizably modern form, both structured and unstructured, had become established as a data collection method in sociology'. This development paralleled the growing use of interviews in other areas such as psychiatry, therapy or clinical psychology and was influenced by the discussions around '**non-directive counselling**' (Rogers, 1945) as a specific form of interaction. Interviewing has always been based on asking questions or inviting participants to tell stories.

Interviewing as a practice of social research

The very beginning of using interviews in research was dominated by interviewing the knowledgeable and elite rather than by doing interviews with all kinds of people (Holstein and Gubrium, 2003). Later, this limitation was overcome. Interviewees were no longer seen as 'informants' but as respondents, which is a step towards a more reflexive practice of interviewing (2003, p. 7).

In the **Chicago School of Sociology** in the 1920s, interviews were mainly used for collecting the participants' life histories in a rather unstructured form (Lee, 2004, p. 871). The early term 'verbatim interview' used, for example, by Burgess (1928) referred less to interviewees' verbatim statements and more to reporting contents and facial expressions, gestures, and so on, in a rather anecdotal way. In the beginning, using interviews was often based on reconstructing their content from notes, shorthand written protocols during the process or from the memory of the researchers or interviewers. Similar to field research, interviewing was oriented around the idea of **naturalistic research** and a research setting little influenced by any kind of formalization or technologies. Recording devices were not yet available, but writing during the conversation or bringing someone for taking notes and writing a protocol of the conversation between interviewer and interviewee, was some sort of technology in the situation (see below).

Interviewing as a method: origins and developments

Platt (2012) gives a rather detailed account of how the methodological literature covered interviewing as a practice and a method. She refers to a number of textbooks from the 1920s to the beginning of the 21st century and identifies historical patterns starting from works distinguishing interviews from questionnaires in the 1930s and from **participant observation** in the 1950s. Although standardization and experimental approaches became more dominant in the 1940s to the 1960s, Platt holds that by the 1970s 'interviewing was taken for granted as an established practice in the survey world' (2012, p. 23). Critical discussions developed more strongly again in the 1990s with the introduction of the term 'interview society' (Atkinson and Silverman, 1997, and below).

Merton and Kendall's (1946) suggestions were a major step towards developing interview research as a method. They introduced the **focused interview** as their own method (see Merton et al., 1956) and suggested a number of principles to be applied in the preparation of questions to ask in the interview and in doing the interview itself. These principles define the aims of interviewing and the various directions an interview should take and combine at the same time. These principles include 'non-direction' in formulating questions and asking them in the interview. The use of the method should aim at 'specificity' in the issues, aspects and views mentioned by the respondent instead of general and superficial statements. A third criterion is 'range', which refers to the complexity of the interviewees' experiences or standpoints and of the issue that is studied which should be covered in the course of the interview. 'The depth and personal context shown by the interviewee' is the main focus, so that much of the interviewer's activity is directed to **probe** and deepen the way the issue has been addressed so far. These criteria can also give an orientation for other forms of interviewing beyond the focused interview. They show the interviewers' tasks of negotiating in the interview between giving as much freedom as possible to the interviewees for talking about their experiences and views, and the researchers' interest in covering aspects the interviewees do not spontaneously mention.

If we want to take these criteria seriously, we should develop and use several kinds of questions during the same interview. Merton and Kendall linked this idea to the degree of openness and structuration in questions. A second consequence is to think about the best sequence of questions. For example, we should always begin with **open questions** and use more **structured questions** afterwards. A third consequence is to stop seeing interviews merely as a form of open and friendly conversation but also as a well-planned and prepared approach to participants' experiences (see Chapter 5). At the same time, Merton and Kendall's suggestions for doing an interview already show how much successful interviewing is based on the interviewers' reflections (see Chapter 9) and on their decisions within the interview situation. When to add deepening or specifying questions and when to continue with questions extending the range of the aspects addressed so far, can only be decided on in the course of the interview.

This can lead to the idea that we not only need various kinds of questions for doing interviews but also various forms of interviews for different purposes as a fourth consequence. Fifth, such a systematization of qualitative interviewing will include issues of **designing qualitative interview studies** (see Chapter 5). Interviews can be embedded in case studies and they can have a **retrospective design** – requesting the recounting of a process which has happened already – or a longitudinal design – documenting a process in repeated data collection – for example. Finally, such planning of interview studies has been extended to issues of selecting the 'right', 'best' or 'adequate' participants and of how to access them (see Chapters 6 and 7).

Interviewing and technology: developments and impacts

Shorthand writing and field notes as ways of making a transcript of interviews were prominent in the 1940s. They were still sometimes used even after the technologies of phonographic recording became available (see Lee, 2004 for the following summary). One reason was the practical and technical limitations of recording devices, which could not be used in the field, as they needed to be plugged into mains-level voltage. Other reasons were early concerns about interviewees' reluctance to be recorded and the impact of any technology in the room on the interviewees' openness in answering questions. The more easily available and usable recording technologies turned the interview into a more reliable method in social research, in particular after the Second World War. The availability of small (cassette) tape recorders had a major impact on the practicality of interviewing as they could be used with batteries (for some time at least), and made huge machines depending on electric sockets no longer necessary. The new recording devices were not only rather inconspicuous but also became quite common and widespread in everyday life, both of which reduced reactivity to recording in interviews. This also allowed the researcher to go out into the field and to people to interview them and use the recordings as data. The routines of recording also permitted researchers to concentrate more on the conversation with the interviewees. They allowed for more detailed documentation of what the participants said and how they said it exactly. All this made interviewing a much more easy-going method and contributed to the expansion of interviewing as a method. Another effect is that the situation of the interview can be analysed for the way the conversation occurred in detail and what impact it had on what the interviewee said. Finally, this technological development led to critical discussions about interviewing and its role in social and qualitative research (see below). Other technological developments, in particular the Internet, **Skype** and social media as tools impact on doing interviews (see below and Chapter 15).

New Challenges

Practical level: digital and mobile interviewing

The traditional relation between researcher and interviewee as a face-to-face contact in a defined setting, an office for example, and at a specific appointment, has changed and extended in many contexts of current interview research. At this point, only two recent developments will be briefly mentioned.

Online interviewing

In the last decade or so, a trend in **online interviewing** (Salmons, 2015) has attracted a lot of attention. These interviews can be done by email or in chatrooms or by using specific software for group interviews and discussions. The advantages are being able to reach people over big distances without travelling and easier access in general. As a side-effect, relations between interviewer and interviewee are different as the two are no longer meeting face to face. Examples can be found in the literature in which the interviewer for a long time was not sure if the interviewee was male or female or was the assumed person at all. This trend is intensified by the use of social media for qualitative research (see Flick, 2018a, Ch. 22). Here again, getting in touch can be much easier, as can the collection of data, but the relationship between interviewer and participant can remain rather obscure. Other ways of doing interviews online are based on conferencing platforms such as **Zoom, Webex** or MicrosoftTeams, which support online contacts of several people and discussions among them, including recording these discussions.

Skype interviews

A particular trend in interviewing is to use Skype as a medium instead of meeting the interviewee in person. The advantages are that interviews can be organized long distance without travelling, that people can be interviewed in their private or professional context without having to set up a meeting with the interviewer and that a face-to-face contact can be simulated at least on a camera, video and screen basis. This technological version of interviewing has a number of practical advantages, but it should be discussed in more detail for its implications for interviews conducted in this way (see Chapter 15 and Iacono et al., 2016 for more details).

On the role of doing interviews online or via Skype, three aspects should be considered. First of all, many of the methods of interviewing discussed in the later chapters of this book can be used in digital or online contexts: some of them are less easy to transfer, most of them have to be adapted. The impact of such adaptation should be considered. Second, a problem is that interviewing in digital contexts can be reduced again to just asking questions and receiving answers – as it was in the early days of interview research (see above). The challenge is how to maintain the level of methodological development of interviewing as a method in these new contexts. Third, despite the attractiveness of doing research in social media contexts, there are still issues that can best be studied by using classic or more recent forms of (offline) interviewing. Also, in the context of social media research, such offline forms of interviewing – for example, about experiences with social media and decisions not to use it anymore – may be relevant (see the following chapters for more details). However, in the age of the Covid-19 pandemic, these developments in digital and online interviewing have become more relevant – as a way of interviewing still working, as the only way to do interviews during some periods of the pandemic and as an alternative to traditional forms of interviewing.

Mobile methods and interviewing

In the context of ethnographies, there have been specific forms of interviewing for some time already. Terms such as **'ethnographic interviewing'** (Spradley, 1979) have been prominent here for describing interviews that occur informally, spontaneously and in a naturalistic setting rather than in an office or other closed room (see Chapter 14). More recent trends in using **mobile methods** in general or **'go-along' methods** in particular (see Kusenbach, 2018) take the interview out into the fields that are studied and to the participants there. Here again, questions of how to adapt existing forms of interviewing to these new forms and how to combine mobile methods with more traditional forms of interviewing, arise (see Chapter 14).

Both online interviewing and mobile methods come with both new potential and new challenges for the field of interview research in general. These will be addressed in the following chapters in more detail.

Challenges of framing: epistemology and reflexivity

The second set of challenges facing the interviewer comes from two directions. First, we find a critique in the Western (European and Anglo-Saxon) methodological discourse, which sees interviewing as omnipresent and overrated. Key arguments in this debate are that we live in an interview society (Atkinson and Silverman, 1997) and that a naïve use of interviewing would assume a direct approach to meaning, experience and inner views (see also Chapters 2 and 18), which simply have to be collected (Silverman, 2017). For example, in a recent contribution to this debate, Whitaker and Atkinson state that interviews, like other research methods, reflexively construct the phenomena to be described (2019, p. 621). In responding to the challenges coming from this debate, it is necessary to develop a framework of doing interviews which avoids such a naïve approach to asking questions. This framework includes reflecting theories and **epistemologies** of interviewing (see Chapter 2 and 18) and the understanding of several methods of interviewing as various ways of doing interviews with strengths and limits that make them more or less appropriate for a study (see Chapters 4 and 9–15). It also includes the design of interviews in the planning (see Chapter 5), **sampling** (see Chapter 6), and accessing interviewees (Chapter 7). Parts of this framework are the various ways of analysing and interpreting the statements made in an interview (see Chapter 16), which have to be made up as data (see Chapters 16 and 17). Thus, the practice of doing interviews has to be focused not only as a way of producing data and statements but also in the ways different forms of interviewing do this and how we as researchers construct a framework for this practice.

Second, interviewing has been questioned from *outside* this Western discourse of methodology by the discussion on **decolonizing methods**. This discussion does not address interviewing in particular but social science methodologies in general (Chilisa, 2020; Smith, 2012) and has implications for doing interviews as well. The limitations of dominant research methodologies from a decolonizing research perspective are summarized as follows:

- The tendency to ignore the role of imperialism, colonization and globalization in the construction of knowledge
- Academic imperialism – the tendency to denigrate, dismiss and attempt to quash alternative theories, perspectives or methodologies
- Methodological imperialism – a tendency to build a collection of methods, techniques and rules that valorize the dominant culture
- The dominance of Euro-Western languages in the construction of knowledge
- The archives of literature that disseminate theories and knowledge that are unfavourable to former colonized societies and historically oppressed groups. (Chilisa, 2020, pp. 105–6)

The main argument of this discussion is that social science methods have been developed against a background of Western epistemology and of colonization as political tradition, which have an impact if these methods are used in **indigenous research** or in non-Western contexts. We find three consequences of these discussions. (1) Several researchers (e.g. Chilisa, 2020; Cram, 2022; Smith, 2012) claim a stronger role for indigenous people (such as Māori in New Zealand, for example) in indigenous research and other communities beyond being interviewees (i.e. 'Nothing about us without us' – Manokaran et al., 2020 – see Chapter 2). The methodological consequences for how indigenous research is done have been demonstrated in a **systematic review** (see Box 1.1)

Box 1.1   Research in the real world

A systematic review of indigenous research methods

Alexandra Drawson, Elaine Toombs and Christopher Mushquash from clinical psychology and working in Indigenous Mental Health and Addiction at Lakehead University in Canada, carried out a systematic review of indigenous research methods in general based on 64 articles reporting indigenous studies (Drawson et al., 2017). They identified the use of methods such as community-based participatory research (CBPR) as being most prominent in indigenous contexts, which they see as having the following characteristics:

a.   Recognizes community as a unity of identity
b.   Builds on strengths and resources of the community
c.   Facilitates collaborative partnerships in all phases of the research
d.   Integrates knowledge and action for mutual benefits of all partners
e.   Promotes a co-learning and empowering process that attends to all social inequalities
f.   Involves a cyclical and iterative process
g.   Addresses health from both positive and ecological perspectives
h.   Disseminates findings and knowledge gained to all partners. (2017, p. 6)

This list shows that indigenous and decolonized research is often characterized by a specific way of framing the research. But the authors also identified a number of 'methods often used in a Western context' (2017, p. 6) in studies in indigenous research, among them **mixed methods** (see Chapter 5), autoethnography (understood as telling one's story – see Chapter 12), **photovoice** (see Chapter 9 for **photo elicitation**) and interviews in general.

Calls are being made for their involvement in planning and doing the research as well as statements being made that only indigenous people should do research with and about indigenous people (e.g. Smith, 2012). These discussions are prevalent in New Zealand-Māori contexts (see Cram 2022; Moewaka Barnes and McCreanor, 2022; Smith, 2012), and in African (see Chilisa, 2020; Chilisa and Phatshwane, 2022) and Asian contexts (Hsiung, 2012). (2) A discussion about indigenous methodologies (Chilisa, 2020) is developing. At the same time, (3) Western researchers have started to discuss the background assumptions and preconditions of interviewing (Gobo, 2011) or have integrated an approach of a decolonizing interview in their overviews of interviewing (Roulston, 2010a, based on Smith, 2012). And finally we should sound out which role interviewing in such developments can play and how we should conceive the framing and methodologies of interviewing accordingly, as shown in the case study in Box 1.1. This may then become relevant for other communities as contexts of doing interviews such as with vulnerable groups, LGBT communities or in postcolonial studies in European and North American contexts and in interview studies in the Global South (see Schöngut-Grollmus and Energici, 2022).

What does this mean for a contemporary book on doing interviews? Gobo (2018) shows, based on research examples and on Kovach (2009), that several forms of interviewing – ethnographic interviews (see Chapter 14) or group interviews (see Chapter 13) – are used in indigenous research as well.

First, doing interviews should be addressed with *diversity, equity and inclusion* in mind. This means that the doing of interviews should more fully take into account: (1) the diversity of interviewees and their circumstances (see Chapters 6 and 7); (2) the situation created for doing an interview should be constructed in a way that does justice to the interviewee and is characterized by a valuation of the interviewee's person, needs and perhaps discrimination; and (3) interviewing as a method should be constructed and applied in a way that all social groups and communities can be included in the practice of interviewing – as interviewees but also as interviewers (see Chapters 5 and 8).

Second and beyond any technical issues, interviewing will ask for an extended concept of **reflexivity**. This should (1) cover issues of diversity in the meaning outlined above. It should (2) take into account what the discussion about decolonizing methods has pointed out for the designing of interview methods in other communities such as vulnerable groups, LGBT communities and the like. And (3) reflexivity should focus on decentring the interview in two ways: from taking the interviewer out of the centre of the situation to putting the interviewee and the interaction between interviewee and interviewer at centre stage, and from implicit Western concepts of research and interviewing to a more globally reflexive understanding of research. Nevertheless, the potential and limits of interviewing against these backgrounds should remain in focus and should be spelled out in more detail, such as in considering why we do interviews.

Why Interviews? Purposes and Research Questions

Sometimes the decision to do interviews is taken for pragmatic reasons – for example, only one contact per participant is possible or it is not suitable to spend long periods in the field. But there are also a number of positive reasons for using interviews, as the following example may demonstrate. In the field of health care research, we can pursue several aims by using interviews. These aims will be outlined next and illustrated with examples of research questions (see Chapter 3 for more details) linked to each of the aims.

Analysing participants' experiences

First, interviews in this context can aim at analysing participants' experiences – with their treatment, how they decided on a specific treatment and in a particular institution, for example. Interviews may also address how participants' lives changed after their health problem began and they started or finished a specific health care treatment. Finally, research may focus on the experiences which the support participants received (or not) while being at a hospital or in a doctor's surgery. Accounts of these experiences can become the subject of narratives concerning the development (of the illness, life situation and support) or be addressed in open-ended interviews or focus groups of several participants exchanging their views.

Example research questions are:

- How do adolescents with diabetes find the appropriate treatment?
- How do adolescents with diabetes see the professional treatment of their disease?
- How do adolescents with diabetes integrate the disease and its treatment in their everyday lives?

Analysing the needs of hard-to-reach groups

Sometimes the health care system is confronted with groups who are more difficult to reach for services and support than others, although their needs may be even greater than those of the 'average' adolescent, to continue our example. Such **hard-to-reach groups** include migrants, homeless people and people with a specific condition such as chronic illness. In most cases, these groups are hard to reach both for the health care services and for research, so they tend to be underrepresented in surveys, for example. In such cases, interviews can offer a better solution for reaching these groups.

Research questions might include:

- How do homeless adolescents with diabetes find access to an appropriate treatment?
- What are the experiences of homeless girls with doctors in the institutions they attend for help with their health problems?
- How do they cope with their bundle of problems – being homeless and chronically ill?

Analysing professional views and knowledge

The other side of the health relationship can also be studied by doing interviews. Practitioners often have an extensive implicit knowledge about their practice with specific issues or target groups, which can be made explicit – in interviews, for example. They can talk about conditions and contexts that may frame the patients' reports in their interviews. They can also detail their practice and changes in their professional life and working conditions, which may affect social support for the adolescent patients.

Example research questions are:

- What does treating homeless adolescents with a chronic disease require?
- How different is their treatment compared to average patients?

Analysing expert knowledge

In our above examples of hard-to-reach groups, it can be fruitful to approach experts to interview them (see Chapter 10) about where members of this group seek help. Other issues include the following: What happens if they turn to a specific institution to seek help? Which institutions are available to them (or in general for a problem like theirs)? Which institutions collaborate in such cases? How many cases might this group include and what are the deficiencies in the service system if this target group is concerned? Sometimes, for ethical reasons (see Chapter 8), researchers may turn to expert interviews instead of interviewing hard-to-reach groups.

Research questions might be, for example:

- What are the services that homeless adolescents can turn to when they become chronically ill?
- What are the steps in the development of a treatment for a chronic disease when patients live on the street?

Evaluation of services

Finally, interviews (or focus groups) can be useful for evaluating services – by asking clients, staff or public utility providers for their criteria and estimates of success for the specific services.

Example research questions are:

- How far does social work with homeless adolescents help them when they become chronically ill?
- How do health care services adapt their treatment to patients who live on the street?

The case study in Box 1.2 illustrates the use of interviews in this context.

Box 1.2 Research in the real world

Strategies of maintaining health while living on the street

The following example has a slightly different focus on homelessness and health, as it is not about adolescents or chronic illness in particular. Ottilie Stolte and Darrin Hodgetts, two psychologists in New Zealand, did a study with 58 homeless research participants, who were interviewed, some of them repeatedly. In their article 'Being healthy in unhealthy places: Health tactics in a homeless lifeworld' (Stolte and Hodgetts, 2015), they present a case study of Clinton, who was then 47 years old and had been homeless for 12 years. They describe in detail how Clinton engages in health-oriented tactics for maintaining his health and to gain respite while he lives on the streets, which is an unhealthy place in general.

As we will see in later chapters, it depends on the specific research questions to be answered and on the potential participants as to whether interviews in general and which form of interview in particular are most appropriate for a study.

Interviewing as Research Built on a Short-term Personal Relationship

Although **longitudinal studies** (see Chapter 5) with repeated interviews have become common, interviewing is mostly conceived as a one-time encounter of researcher and interviewee and thus as only a short-term personal relation in most cases. In comparison to participant observation, this is discussed as a disadvantage of interviewing (e.g. by Atkinson and Silverman, 1997) as it only permits a very limited insight into the participant's life world. However, on a closer look, this may not be such a disadvantage, in several respects.

In some contexts, it may be helpful that the interviewees have not been and will not be in close or regular contact with the researcher when the interview happens. Robert Weiss's (1994) term of 'learning from strangers' for describing the relation of the interviewer to the interviewee can also be turned around for the interviewee into 'talking to strangers'. Sometimes it may be easier to talk in detail about embarrassing issues, to open up emotionally, to talk about failure or mistakes to a person you will not see regularly and have no personal relation to. At the same time, interviewees will have to provide more detail and context to such professional strangers in order to allow the interviewers to understand what they are talking about. In a longer (or closer) relationship, many aspects may be taken for granted or assumed to be known among the participants. Thus, they do not need to be mentioned. If the relation is based on a certain unfamiliarity, more details may be mentioned explicitly. Therefore, it is suggested not to do interviews with friends and relatives. Hildenbrand warns of the problems linked to this strategy:

> While it is often assumed that access to the field would be facilitated by studying persons well known to the researcher and accordingly finding cases from one's own circle of acquaintances, exactly the opposite is true: the stranger the field, the more easily may researchers appear as strangers, whom the people in the study have something to tell which is new for the researcher. (1995, p. 258)

As a second aspect to consider in this context, we should be aware that the interview itself is only one step in a process, even if it is the most important one of course. Steps to take before the actual interview on the side of the researcher include the decision to include these interviewees in the sample (see Chapter 6), getting in touch with them (see Chapter 7), travelling to the location of the interview, and so on. If these steps are taken in a reflective way, they will provide additional information and insights.

Third, interview research in most cases will be limited to single encounters. However, if the research question asks for it and resources permit, interviews can be conducted in a longitudinal design (see Chapter 5). This means that they are repeated after a period of time in order to document changes and processes in the interviewees' situation; or they are continued with a new focus, new or additional questions and the like.

Fourth, doing interview research successfully is always built on creating a rather close and open personal relationship for and in the interview situation.

Thus, we can combine the strengths of interviews as a short-term relation with a process approach consisting of a series of short-term contacts.

Interviews as Stand-alone Method or in a Complex Design

This book focuses on doing interviews with two aims. First, it wants to support doing research with interviews as the main or only method in a study. Interviews as **stand-alone method** are most prominent in the field of interview research. At the same time, interviews are often embedded in more complex **research designs**, which are the second focus of this book. Ethnographic interviews as part of a broader ethnographic strategy have been mentioned already. Other complex designs including interviews can be found in the context of mixed methods research, which is another current trend. Beyond the combination with quantitative research intended in mixed methods, we still find many examples in which specific methods of interviewing are combined with other qualitative methods, which is known as '**triangulation**' (see Flick, 2018b).

In these contexts of combining interviews with other methods or integrating them into complex designs, we face similar challenges, as mentioned in the preceding sections: How do we plan and do interviews so that they are most effective and conducted methodologically in a sound way? What is it necessary to know about the various ways of doing interview research and how do we link them with the other approaches?

In addition to the above explicit reference to a theoretical perspective in qualitative research and the methodological principles just mentioned, the use of interviews, including the recording of the whole interview, is based on a number of implicit preconditions.

What You Need to Ask Yourself

Knowledge about interviewing is helpful in two respects. It will support you if you want to use interviews in your own empirical study, for example in the context of a master's thesis, PhD or as a professional researcher. And it can help you to understand interview-based research by others – how they proceeded, what came out and what the value of such research is or is not. The questions in Box 1.3 are designed to give you some guidance on the decision whether to use interviews and which form might be best for your research. You may also apply these questions to studies with interviews you read. If you lack the knowledge to make this decision at this point, it will give you some orientation as to what to expect from reading the following chapters of this book.

Box 1.3   What you need to ask yourself

Doing interview research

1. How far can the issue of your research be studied by asking people about it?
2. What is the main focus of your study; what should the main focus of your interviews be?
3. Who should your interview partners be – lay people, professionals, experts, elites?
4. How will you reflect their specific and diverse situation compared to your own background in preparing and doing the interviews?
5. Where and how might you access your interview partners?
6. What good reasons are there, if any, for doing your interviews online or via Skype?
7. How will you document your data – recording and transcription? And if not, why not?
8. What ethical issues might arise in your interviews and how will you manage them?
9. What is it important to document about the context of your interviews as part of the data?

What You Need to Succeed

This chapter should have provided you with an introduction to what interviewing is about. It should help you to understand and contextualize what will be presented in the following chapters in more detail. The following questions (see Box 1.4) will provide you with the key take-home points from this chapter for the next steps discussed in the book.

Box 1.4   What you need to succeed

Basics of doing interview research

1. Do I understand what interview research is about?
2. Am I aware of the development of interviewing as a method of doing research?
3. Do I see the role of decolonizing the interview as a method for my use of it?
4. Am I beginning to understand what interviewing is used for in social research?
5. Do I see the challenges involved in doing online or mobile interviews?
6. Do I see the advantages of interviews as building on short-term relations in the field?

What you have learned

- Doing interviews is more than just asking people. Interviewing has been developed over the years as a method.
- The interview forms that have been developed proceed in different ways towards similar goals. Interviewees should be given as much leeway as possible to reveal their views. At the same time, they should be given a structure for what to talk about.
- Interviews have to be designed in a reflexive way to allow for taking the interviewees' (cultural, social, personal) diversities and those between them and the interviewers into account.
- Interviews can be applied as a stand-alone method or as part of a more complex design.
- Interviews are used as one-shot meetings or in repetition in a longitudinal design. Interviews can be extended to a second meeting with two aims: to document changes since the first meeting and to add new issues.
- Interview research has been extended in two directions: to doing interviewing online and to interviewing using mobile methods.
- The idea of an interview society can be seen positively as providing a context in which being interviewed is something people are used to, thereby increasing their readiness for it.

Exercises

In the following exercises, you are first invited to reflect on some of the main issues in this chapter. Then you are invited to apply the topics of this chapter to the development of a project of your own. Hence, the exercises are a combination of reflection and prospection.

Exercise 1.1

Reflecting on the Chapter: The Use of Interviews in an Existing Study

1. Look through a journal for a qualitative study based on interviews (e.g. Flick et al., 2012). Try to identify which form of interview was used in the study.
2. Consider the study's questions and then improve them by using one or more of the interviewing methods presented in this chapter.

Exercise 1.2

Planning Your Own Research with Interviews

1. Think of your own study and develop a first version of an interview guide for your research question.

What's next

The following article illustrates the use of interviews with vulnerable groups in a case study in New Zealand:

Stolte, O., & Hodgetts, D. (2015). Being Healthy in Unhealthy Places: Health Tactics in a Homeless Lifeworld. *Journal of Health Psychology*, 20(2), 144–53. https://doi.org/10.1177/1359105313500246

This article illustrates the use of interviews in a socio-policy context in a study about migration and inclusion, and gives examples of doing a specific form of interview and the integration into an ethnographic design with mobile methods:

Flick, U., Hans, B., Hirseland, A., Rasche, S., & Röhnsch, G. (2017). Migration, Unemployment, and Lifeworld: Challenges for a New Critical Qualitative Inquiry in Migration. *Qualitative Inquiry*, 23(1), 77–88.

The following article gives a concise overview of the history of interviewing with a focus on the role of using technical devices:

Lee, R.M. (2004). Recording Technologies and the Interview in *Sociology*, 1920–2000. *Sociology*, 38(5), 869–89.

This article summarizes some critical issues from the debate about the interview society. The suggestions made for how to overcome the problems also show that the critical aspects do not mean abandoning interviewing but rather engaging in doing better interviews and more reflective analyses of the data:

Silverman, D. (2017). How Was It for You? The Interview Society and the Irresistible Rise of the (Poorly Analyzed) Interview. *Qualitative Research*, 17(2), 144–58.

This handbook will give you a fuller picture of the variety of methods for collecting qualitative data and help to locate doing interview research in this context:

Flick, U. (Ed.) (2018). *The SAGE Handbook of Qualitative Data Collection*. London: Sage.

Doing Interview Research Navigator

You are here in your project

How to understand interview research

- What doing interview research means
- Theories and epistemologies of interviewing
- When to choose interviews as a research method
- Methods and formats of interviewing

Designing interview research

- Planning and designing interview research
- How many interviewees: Sampling and saturation
- Accessing and recruiting participants

How to conduct interviews

- How to respect and protect: Ethics of interviewing
- Semi-structured interviews: Working with questions and answers
- Interviewing experts and elites
- Integrating narratives in interviews: Episodic interviews

Doing interviews in context

- How to work with life histories: Narrative interviews
- Working with focus groups as interviews
- Ask (in) the field: Ethnographic and mobile interviewing
- Doing online interviews

How to work with interview data

- Working with interview data
- Credibility and transparency: Quality and writing in interview research
- From interviewing to an inner view: Critiques and reflexivity

THEORIES AND EPISTEMOLOGIES OF INTERVIEWING

You will:

- be introduced to the theoretical background to using interviews,
- learn about the epistemologies of interviewing,
- have an initial idea of the interviewer's role,
- see that the debates concerning interviewing as a method are theoretical and epistemological, and
- have a background to help make your way through the practical issues in the book.

The first chapter gave you a brief and initial orientation about what interviewing means and why interviews are used. Its focus was more on a practical level of using interviews and it also gave you a first glimpse of the approach used throughout the book. However, doing interviews is more than just asking questions ('What is it like working in this factory?') or stimulating a narrative ('Can you please tell me how you started working in this factory and how your work has developed over the years?'). Interviews are based on interviewees' statements, answers and narratives related to their subjective perspectives and experiences. Interviewers try to give as much room as possible to the interviewees for presenting and revealing their views in their own personal way, in longer answers, in narratives and in more or less open conversation with the researchers. However, if interviews are done in academic contexts – ranging from students' bachelor, master's or PhD theses to funded research projects with several professional researchers – interviewing is more than just a 'good' conversation. Interviewing is based on specific epistemologies and theoretical backgrounds and should be done referring to an epistemological background, and to the theoretical and methodological concepts of research and interviews. This chapter is intended to provide a more solid grounding in what interviewing is about and to set a framework for the later chapters, elucidating the details of planning, doing and reflecting on interviews and working with the resulting data.

Basic Theoretical Underpinnings of Interviewing

One starting point for a theoretical foundation of interview research is the work of Alfred Schütz. He has argued that facts become relevant only through their selection and **interpretation:** 'Strictly speaking, there are no such things as facts, pure and simple. All facts are from the outset facts selected from a universal context by the activities of our mind' (1962, p. 5). This also means that an immediate access to experience is impossible. Rather, facts are 'always interpreted facts, either facts looked at as detached from their context by an artificial abstraction or facts considered in their particular setting. In either case, they carry their interpretational inner and outer horizons' (1962, p. 5). On a practical level, this means interview research focusing on the concepts and interpretations used by its participants in their everyday lives. For example, if we want to understand why existing social work services are utilized or avoided by a specific social group with a particular problem, we should first find out what the subjective representations of these services and problems are before we simply count how many utilizers or non-utilizers exist, and relate this 'fact' to the number of persons in need who could be utilizers.

A central idea in this context is the distinction Schütz makes between **first-degree constructions** and **second-degree constructions**. According to Schütz, the actors' constructs are first-degree constructs. Thus, he emphasizes that scientific knowledge (second-degree constructions) is always based on actors' everyday knowledge (first-degree constructions): 'the constructs of the social sciences are, so to speak, constructs of the second degree, that is, constructs of the constructs made by the actors on the social scene' (1962, p. 6).

In this sense, Schütz holds that 'the exploration of the general principles according to which man [sic] in daily life organizes his experiences, and especially those of the social world, is the first task of the methodology of the social sciences' (1962, p. 59). In our example, the help-seeking persons' concepts of their problems and of the services would be first-degree constructions, while the typologies developed by the researchers from analysing these concepts are second-degree constructions.

A second basic theoretical underpinning for why it makes sense to collect subjective views and meanings in an open format can be found in Symbolic Interactionism. Herbert Blumer summarizes the basic assumptions of Symbolic Interactionism as 'three simple premises': that people 'act toward things on the basis of the meanings that the things have for them ... that the meaning ... is derived from, or arises out of, the social interaction ... with one's fellows ... and that these meanings are handled in, and modified through, an interpretative process used by the person in dealing with the things he [*sic*] encounters' (1969, p. 2).

What does this mean for interview research and the interview situation? The consequence is that the different ways in which individuals invest objects, events, experiences, and so on, with meaning form the central starting point for research in this approach. The reconstruction of such subjective viewpoints becomes the instrument for analysing social worlds. Another central assumption is the so-called **Thomas's theorem**, which further grounds the methodological premises just mentioned. It claims 'that when a person defines a situation as real, this situation is real in its consequences, leads directly to the fundamental methodological principle of symbolic interactionism: researchers have to see the world from the angle of the subjects they study' (Stryker, 1976, p. 259). The example in Box 2.1 illustrates how these theoretical backgrounds may function as starting points for using interviews for supporting communities to explore meanings of *their* topics for *them*.

Box 2.1 Research in the real world

'Nothing about us without us' – Studying fatness

The following example comes from a group of activists in New Zealand and Scandinavia, who have explored the need to develop the field of 'fat studies' and emphasize the importance of giving fat people a framework to talk about their experiences. They 'argue that social science research on fatness must include fat people in the work, and propose ways for social science scholars to work alongside the fat community in their scholarship' (Manokaran et al., 2020, p. 1). This could be a productive starting point for using interviews to explore the first-order constructions of the phenomenon developed by people in this condition or by activists focusing on it before starting to develop second-order constructions such as typologies or theories of experiencing fatness. Interviews then should be prepared and conducted in a way that gives interviewees as much room as possible to present their views and experiences in dialogue with the researcher(s) or activists doing the interviews (see Chapter 5). Which specific method of interviewing (see Chapters 4 and 9–15) will be most supportive of this disclosure depends on the concrete research question and the issue in focus for the participants (see Chapters 7 and 17). These interviews may also focus on the ways that meanings of fatness are exchanged, negotiated and constructed in the interaction between participants and interviewers.

Beyond such an explicit reference to a theoretical perspective in qualitative research, the use of interviews, including the recording of the whole interview, is based on a number of methodological principles (see below). These again are based on a number of epistemological issues around doing interviews.

Epistemologies of Interviewing

Why do we use interviews? What kind of knowledge or insights do we expect? How should we see the interviewer's role and that of the interviewee? What is the impact of the concrete interview situation on the knowledge we gain? What are data in interview studies? These are some of the major epistemological questions around interviewing.

The term **'epistemology'** refers to theories of knowledge and perception in science. In our context, it refers to how the production of scientific knowledge by using interviews should be conceived and understood. Epistemology has three functions in the context of social research (see Flick, 2020, p. 32):

- To provide a theoretical fundament for conceptualizing the research and procedure
- To provide a basis for critical reflection on methods and the knowledge they produce
- To support, improve and make social research possible and realizable.

In doing interviews, epistemologies refer to the way the method is understood. This includes the roles of the interviewer and the interviewee. Finally, epistemology defines the concept of data coming out of interviewing and the claims for referring from interviews to more general issues.

Several epistemological concepts of interviewing, a number of descriptions for the role of the interviewer, and understandings of interview knowledge are discussed. They can again be illustrated by using the example of studying the health issues of homeless adolescents.

Epistemological Concepts of Interviewing

Alvesson (2003) distinguishes three positions related to interviewing: neopositivist, romantic and localist.

Neopositivist concepts of interviewing

First, neopositivist concepts see that 'the interview conversation is a pipeline for transmitting knowledge' (Holstein and Gubrium, 1997, p. 113). Interviewing accordingly is based on good preparation and a competent, neutral interviewer, who avoids influencing the interviewee. Then the interview provides high quality data and valid findings, which allow reference and **generalization** to other people who have not been interviewed. Qualitative interviewing becomes a technique, which is similar to surveys, but gives more room to the participant than standardized survey questionnaires in order to reveal the interviewees' 'true self' and their experiences. The neopositivist concept of interviewing is seldom applied in a strict and pure sense.

In our example of studying health and homelessness, **structured interviews** with experts (see Chapter 10) from social work and health institutions could aim at collecting information such as: What characterizes the situation of homeless adolescents? How many adolescents are affected by this situation, of what age and gender? Which health problems are they most likely to experience? Which existing institutions could they turn to when they seek help? In this type of interview, the interviewees themselves are less the focus than the information they might give. Several problems linked to this version of interviewing should be reflected upon: for example, that interviewees do not 'necessarily do what they say they do' or tell the truth and that the 'researcher's part in the construction of the data' (Roulston, 2010a, p. 55) is not taken into account in this concept of interviewing.

Romantic conceptions of the interview

Second, Alvesson sees a 'romantic' conception of the interview as the opposite to neopositivist concepts. Interviewing aims at revealing the interviewees' personal views and confessions. The interviewer is expected to support **rapport**, empathy and a trustful relation to the interviewee. Interviewers will facilitate intimate conversations to gain access to interviewees' inner worlds.

In our example, interviewing the adolescents about their experiences with health problems and their attempts at seeking help could be pursued in interviews closer to the romantic concept outlined by Alvesson. Interviewees are asked to recount situations, feelings and experiences in detail and depth.

This concept takes the role of the interviewer much more into account and also the specific realities of the interviewees' situation. However, this understanding of interviewing is not unproblematic, as we should not assume a direct or unfiltered access to interviewees' inner worlds, feelings or experiences in their answers or narratives.

Localist positions on interviewing

Third, Alvesson discusses a localist position on interviewing. Different from the neopositivist understanding, he emphasizes that interviews are not about collecting facts. In distinction to the romantic concept, he denies that the true revelation of inner worlds is possible in interviews. Rather, the concrete circumstances of the social context of the interview situation mainly influence what is said in it and how.

Constructionist conceptions of the interview

Roulston (2010a) extends Alvesson's list by a number of other understandings of the epistemology of interviewing. She develops Alvesson's localist position into a **constructionist** conception of interviewing. Roulston emphasizes that the two participants (interviewer and interviewee) co-construct the contents of the interview in the concrete setting of the conversation. Interviewees' statements are not reports (neither of 'interior states of mind' nor of 'exterior states of the world' – 2010a, p. 60) but accounts in an ongoing conversation. These accounts should be seen and analysed by considering the context of the conversation as part of the data. Then not only does *what* is said become relevant, but also *how* the interviewee said something and in reference to which intervention (question or comment) by the interviewer.

Applied to our example, this means we carefully reflect the interview situation and the interaction between interviewer and homeless adolescent. We analyse the interaction in the interview and do not see the adolescent's statements as pure and true 'facts'. Analysis is based on how something was said, on interpretations of meanings, intentions and the like in the interviewees' statements and narratives.

Transformative and feminist conceptions of interviewing

The epistemological and practical issues around interviewing have been discussed in a critical way in the context of feminist research by Oakley (1981) and, building on the reflections of decolonizing concepts of interviewing, by Harding (1998). The main focus here is how to shape the relation between the participants in terms of reducing social distance between (feminist) researchers and interviewees to establish 'an emotionally emphatic, egalitarian and reciprocal rapport' (Oakley, 1981, p. 55). The language in interviewing and its analysis should be used in a way that ensures that the participants are portrayed rather than categorized (DeVault, 1990, p. 112; see also Roulston, 2010a).

In our example, a particular sensitivity to the specific needs of homeless girls and women and their health issues is necessary. The interviews with them should be carried out by female researchers where possible.

Decolonizing conceptions of interviewing

In more recent discussions, a decolonizing conception of interviewing has attracted specific attention (following Chilisa, 2020; Smith, 2012). It becomes relevant in research with indigenous people but also when researchers and participants come from different social situations, such as in migration studies. Here, a reflection on participants' own research agendas may contribute to revising the effects of colonizing policies. In a decolonizing conception of interviewing, the focus is on cultural diversities between interviewers and interviewees. It reflects and avoids relations of power and inequality between the interviewer and the interviewee. Research reflects how the needs and interests of interviewees with a different cultural or social background may differ from those of the researchers and their studies. Moewaka Barnes and McCreanor (2022) discuss a number of epistemological issues such as reflexivity and positioning of the researchers in the context of decolonization (2022), criticality about research, research questions and methods, identity issues and the orientation towards transformation. Edwards et al. (2005) turn this epistemology into studying the concrete problems of Māoris losing their children, with a focused life-story inter-view (see Chapter 12).

In linking back these discussions to general contexts of interviewing, in our exam-ple, interviewers should be sensitive in the interaction not to reproduce the relations of power and suppression that homeless interviewees may have experienced in other institutional contexts. They should be aware that, for example, 'health' (as the issue of the study) may not be the most important factor in the interviewees' situation of being homeless compared to finding a place to stay overnight.

The epistemologies briefly outlined so far can be useful in three respects for doing interviews: (1) They provide a framework for conceiving and understanding what is going on in interviews. (2) They are starting points for criticizing implicit assumptions in specific forms of interviewing – for example, concerning what 'data' means, what knowledge is gained in interviews, or what the roles of interviewers and interviewees are. And (3) they can provide guidance on how to design interviews with one or the other priority.

Role of the Interviewer

How should we understand the role of the interviewer? We find a number of descrip-tions in the literature – the researcher as *professional stranger* (Agar, 1980), the *learner from strangers* (Weiss, 1994) and the *active listener* (Fujii, 2018), for example. Brinkman and Kvale (2018) take up a widely discussed suggestion made earlier by Kvale (1996). He compared two metaphors for the interviewer, as a miner and as a traveller, for their implications for conceiving interviews. Seeing the interviewer as miner means that 'knowledge is understood as buried metal and the interviewer is a miner who unearths the valuable metal. The knowledge is waiting in the subject's interior to be uncovered, uncontaminated by the miner' (Brinkman and Kvale, 2018, p. 19). The other meta-phor 'understands the interviewer as a traveller on a journey to a distant country that leads to a tale to be told upon returning home' (2018, p. 20). The first metaphor con-ceives knowledge collected in interviews as (objective) *facts* or essential meanings extracted from the data. The second metaphor emphasizes the *exploratory* nature of interviews and the role of the researchers' reports about what they heard as essential for understanding the data. In the first metaphor, the interview is understood as an event for revealing existing knowledge (of the interviewee). In the second metaphor, the interview is seen as 'a construction site of knowledge' (2018, p. 24). What the interviewees mention in the interview is strongly influenced by the situation and the researchers' activities within it. For example, some questions may turn the interview-ees' attention to specific points they were not aware of before. Thus, the interviewer has an active role in constructing the interview situation and a strong impact on the contents and how they are mentioned.

In our above example, the metaphor of the miner is closer to the interviews with the experts. They are asked to report numbers, distributions and diversity in the home-less adolescents' population and their diseases. Kvale's second metaphor, that of the traveller, comes closer to the interviews with the adolescents. After interviewing them and listening to their stories and accounts, the researchers will recount how they explored the living situation of the homeless adolescents and their stories of facing health as an extra challenge of living on the streets.

Knowledge Produced in the Interview

In addition to conceptualizing the interview and the relations in it, a third issue of epistemology refers to how to conceive the knowledge produced in interviews. Following Kvale's idea of the interviewer as traveller and his understanding of the interview situation as a construction site for knowledge, as mentioned above, the knowledge we take home from interviews does not exist in the interviewees' minds and is only presented in the interview. Knowledge becoming thematic in interviews is characterized by 'the conversational, the narrative, the linguistic, the contextual and interrelational nature of knowledge' (Brinkman and Kvale, 2018, p. 24), which Kvale sees as a consequence of **postmodernism** (e.g. Lyotard, 1984). What the interviewers 'know' about the interviewees and their situation, feelings, knowledge, and so on, is the result of a specific conversation between two people. This conversation occurred in a specific context characterized by a time and place and the relation between these two people in a specific situation. What becomes thematic in this situation is presented in specific ways of using language and often in a narrative way. The interviewees construct the knowledge that becomes mentioned in the interview by the actual way they talk about the issue. It is shaped by the words, the formats, the narratives, and in general, by their contributions to the ongoing interview conversation.

In our example, we will construct a framework for listening to the different versions, stories and constructions of the phenomenon 'homelessness and chronic illness' from the perspectives of the adolescents and the experts.

Consequences for Conceiving Interviews

Discussing epistemology can sometimes be rather basic and dry. However, the points briefly discussed here are important background issues for doing interviews in a reflective way and being aware of the potential and limits of using this approach as a method. What does this mean for the practicalities and planning of interviews as outlined later in this book?

All these conceptions and metaphors maintain the basic assumptions behind doing interviews: interviewers (and maybe a research team or institution in the background) are interested in what the interviewees are ready to tell, report or recount about a specific issue. Interviewers create a context and a situation in which the interviewees should have maximum freedom to talk about what is relevant for them concerning this issue and in their own way. What is mentioned in this encounter, and how, is strongly influenced by how this situation is constructed by the interviewers – where and when it takes place, how the conversation is shaped and so on. Furthermore, all that is mentioned comes in the form of language and in specific formats of language, for example a narrative, and is embedded in specific emotional, situational and non-verbal contexts. How informative these conversations will be for the research depends on methodological issues such as selecting interviewees, preparing questions and so on. As the interviewees' perspectives are the relevant ones for the research – that is why they were selected and invited for an interview – the role of the interviewers is mainly that of being *listeners* and not the main speakers. Before and in the actual interview situation, the interviewers construct a setting for the interview as a research encounter. The various tasks and activities for constructing this setting and how to tackle them in the most productive way will be discussed in more detail in the following chapters.

Methodological Principles Underlying the Use of Interviews

If we adapt the features of qualitative research in general developed elsewhere (see Flick, 2018a) to qualitative, **semi-structured interviewing**, we can identify the following methodological principles underlying interview research.

Participants' perspectives and their diversity

Doing interviews is based on the curiosity and interest in what participants have experienced concerning the issue under study and how these experiences differ. Interviewing is also based on the assumption that people are able to reflect and talk about their situation. Finally, interviewing wants to give room for the differences in how people experience the 'same' situations.

Openness to the participants' perspectives

Methods and questions should be formulated in a way that participants are not restricted in their ways of presenting their views of what is studied. Where questions are less adequate for unfolding their views in detail, room for narratives should be given so that the participants can tell their stories about the issue under study. In general, interviews will be a successful way of collecting qualitative data if they combine as much openness for the participant as possible with an orientation on the research topic and question.

Verstehen (understanding) as epistemological principle

Doing interviews in qualitative research aims at understanding the phenomenon or event under study in its complexity from the perspective of the participants. Researchers try to understand the views of one subject or of different subjects. How they put this understanding into specific methodological terms depends on the theoretical position underpinning their research. This is known as **verstehen**.

Reconstructing cases as a starting point

Various approaches of interviewing have in common that the single case is analysed rather extensively before comparative or general statements are made. For instance, statements, answers, narratives are linked to other statements, answers, narratives in the same interview to identify issues running through the case and develop a comprehensive picture of it. Later, other case studies and their results are used in comparison to develop a typology.

Construction of reality as a basis

With interviews we want to understand how participants construct their reality of being students, patients or family members. With their views on a certain phenomenon, subjects construe a part of their reality. In conversations in an interview, phenomena are interactively produced and thus reality is constructed. The reality studied in interviews is not a given reality, but is constructed by different actors including participants and researchers.

Appropriateness of methods

The way we do our interviews and the method of interviewing we apply should be appropriate to the issue that is studied. At the same time, the methods should fit the needs and characteristics of the people we want to apply them to.

Variety of approaches and methods of interviewing

The consequence of the principle of appropriateness of methods is that now a variety of methods for doing interviews exists – ranging from semi-structured (see Chapter 9) to expert interviews (see Chapter 10), from ethnographic (see Chapter 14) to episodic (see Chapter 11) and **narrative interviews** (see Chapter 12), for example. Being aware of this variety will help us to choose the appropriate method for a specific study.

Reflexivity of the researcher and the research

Interviewing strongly builds on the researchers' reflexivity in planning the research but also on the specifics of a particular interview. For example, a decision around when to probe and stick to a specific issue (see Chapter 9) and when to ask a question extending, focusing or changing the issue, is based on reflecting on what has been said so far or at this specific moment.

Reflecting on such implicit assumptions behind interviewing becomes even more relevant due to the new technical and local frameworks in which interviews can be conducted.

Critical Discussion of Interviewing

The various epistemologies of interviewing discussed above are often based on critiques of specific forms of interviewing or can be used for such a critique. Examples are the contexts of feminist interviewing or decolonizing interviews. In addition to these epistemological reflections, some more general approaches for questioning the current interview research have developed, which will be briefly discussed here. The first critique continues the cultural diversity approach driving the discourse about decolonizing interviews. It asks about which implicit conditions of interviewing can be transferred from Western (European) societies to other cultural contexts or to interviewing people from these other contexts without particular reflection. The second asks about the omnipresence of interviewing in Western societies and how far this can impact on the use of interviewing as a method. In consequence, again, the question is how far we can transfer this precondition without particular reflection on interviewing in other cultures and societies.

Implicit preconditions of interviewing

In Western European societies, at least, it is quite common that people are interviewed and it is also quite common to talk about one's own personal history and individual experiences to a professional stranger. It is not uncommon to have such a conversation recorded if certain rules are defined (**anonymization, data protection**, etc.). It may be an irritating idea for the potential interviewee but still quite common that your statements later are analysed and interpreted. Gobo (2011) mentions a number of necessary and taken-for-granted preconditions of using this approach in qualitative research. These include the ability on the part of the interviewees to speak for themselves, and an awareness of themselves as autonomous and independent individuals: an extended concept of public opinion, necessary for communicating opinions and attitudes and describing behaviours considered private in a pre-industrial society, and so on. Debates have begun as to how far these implicit assumptions can be transferred to other cultures or people from countries with a political history which was less liberal than that of Western European countries after the Second World War, for example (see Flick, 2014a).

Interview society or interviewing members of society?

Atkinson and Silverman (1997), drawing on works by Holstein and Gubrium (e.g. 1995), coined a buzzword in the discussion about interviewing, which attracted a lot of attention. In their article, they drew a panorama of issues to illustrate what they called 'the interview society'. This panorama comprised and merged all sorts of interviewing from media (talk shows, journalism) to confessions, therapy and the trend to see illness narratives as a way of talking about and treating the experiences of chronic illness (e.g. Kleinman, 1988). From this overview, they developed the thesis that the over-prominence of interviewing had an influence on images of the (postmodern) self. Finally, they included examples of conceptualizing the research interview in their panorama, ending with a rather fundamental criticism of interviewing, as a research method that 'can take us into the mental world of the individual, to glimpse the categories and logic by which he or she sees the world. It can also take us into the life-world of the individual, to see the content and pattern of daily experience' (McCracken, 1988, p. 9). Their critique mainly addressed a naïve use of the interview as a direct access to experiences and psychological states, which mainly provides interviewees' statements and narratives without taking into account how they were produced in a dialogue between researcher and participant.

In a later article about 'the interview society and the irresistible rise of the (poorly analyzed) interview', Silverman (2017) renews the critique of the over-dominance of the interview. But now the focus is much more on the lack of rigour in transcribing interviews and in analysing the data.

What does this discussion mean for doing interview research? The critical stance towards the 'interview society' should urge the researcher to reflect on:

1. when interviews are the most appropriate method for a specific study (see Chapter 3);
2. their research question for the specific study and how to design interviews (see Chapter 5);
3. thorough selection of participants for an interview study – the questions of sampling, access and recruiting (see Chapters 6 and 7);
4. which specific form of interviewing is most appropriate for their research question and target group (see Chapters 5 and 9–15);
5. how to produce **transparency** through transcription and a rigorous analysis (see Chapter 16);
6. in general how to use the interview in a reflexive way (see Chapters 17 and 18).

Finally, thinking about research interviews should involve keeping in mind the differences from other kinds and contexts of using interviews (such as journalism, media, therapy – see Chapter 3). Then doing interview *research* might make a profit of the familiarity of potential participants being interviewed – maybe this is a positive turn of what is meant by the 'interview society'.

Doing Interview Research – A Framework

As an orientation for the further journey through doing interview research in the remainder of the book, a framework based on the issues discussed so far will conclude this introductory chapter about the theory and epistemology of interviewing. It consists of three elements: a working definition of doing interviews, an understanding of the interviewer's role, and an epistemological position on how knowledge is produced in interviews.

Doing interview research – a working definition

Doing interview research is the use of questions and answers or the stimulation of narratives for collecting data about an issue of research. Research interviews are different from journalistic or **therapeutic interviews**. *The differences include the steps of planning the research and the interview in a systematic way. Doing interview research does not see interviews as direct access to mental states or experiences but will create a situation in which the interviewees are supported in talking about their relation to the topic under study. What is said in a research interview should be seen as the result of an interaction between interviewer and interviewee and of the framework that is created for doing the interview. This framework also includes the research question, the selection of participants and ethical aspects. The purpose is to develop findings from the interviews in a study in a comparative perspective on several interview(ee)s in an analytic perspective which includes the characteristics of the interview situation.*

The elements of this working definition will be spelled out in more detail in the subsequent chapters.

The interviewer as a constructing listener

Coming back to our short review of the epistemologies of interviewing, two conclusions can be drawn for the role of the interviewer, which will guide the more detailed discussions in the following chapters. Starting points are first Back's (2013) idea of seeing qualitative research as the art of listening and the guiding question 'how can we listen more carefully?' (2013, p. 8). Back's book only marginally refers to interviewing but uses the metaphor of 'listening' for discussing all sorts of sociological inquiry. However, it can give some orientation about how to understand the interview as a way of listening, as 'a form of active listening that challenges the listener's preconceptions and position while at the same time it engages critically with the content of what is being said and heard' (2013, p. 23). Fujii (2018) uses this idea of **active listening** in a slightly different way. She first emphasizes that interviewers should be sensitive to all dimensions of the interview situation and its context. Second, interviewers should also notice when the interviewees tend to avoid certain topics, rely on rumours or half-truths as sources for their knowledge, or when they become silent (2018, p. 4). Third, Fujii suggests that the interviewer should become familiar with the interviewees' languages and acquire their lexicons – the words they use for describing their situation rather than the interviewers' vocabulary. How the art of active listening is framed and practised in an interview encounter depends on how the interviewer designs the situation.

Building on the above approaches, we should understand the *interviewer as a constructing listener.* This term refers to listening on two levels.

On the level of dialogic practice in the interview, it means listening to what the interviewee has to say. This emphasizes that the interviewees and their views should be dominant in the interview situation. The interviewers should create a setting that allows this dominance as far as possible and should be active but mainly listen.

On the second level, it refers to Back's very general use of 'the art of listening' for describing sociological research in general as listening to the field under study and its members. For our context, this means that the researchers will be able to listen to the field they study in a more sensitive way, depending on how they select their conversational partners for their interviews – how they sample – and how they create a setting for the conversation in the interview. This takes into account that the interviewers construct this setting by their methodological decisions – about the research question of the study, the method of interviewing that is applied, whom they select, how they interact with interviewees, how they listen and give space, and so on.

How to make these decisions in concrete terms and between which alternatives researchers are able to decide in each step of an interview study, will be outlined in the following chapters of this book. In particular, Chapter 8 on ethics will address the interviewer's role and how to spell it out in creating the interview situation in more detail. In this approach, we transcend Back's concept of *the art* of listening, as the use of the term 'art' may be associated with talent (you have or you don't) and may neglect the aspect of learning – a craft or, in our context, a method and methodological skills.

Interviews as co-constructing knowledge

Interviewers should be listeners to what the participants have to say first and foremost. They construct a setting in which they give maximum leeway for interviewees to express what they want to say and how. Thus and second, interviews should be seen as a *setting of co-constructing knowledge* in which both participants are involved in specific ways. They shape the knowledge that becomes thematic in the interview conversation by participants' ways of asking and answering, narrating and listening, introducing and extending issues and the like. Interviewees are not presenting facts and truths, but talking about their views and images of the issue under study and of their lives (Mills, 1959). Thus, the 'facts' and explanations that are presented are constructions on their part as spectators of their own lives (Back, 2013, p. 10). What is presented in an interview, what the interviewees remember, see as relevant and talk about depend on how the framework of the interview is constructed by the interviewer beforehand and during the interview and in the conversation this framework supports and allows. This approach will be spelled out in more detail for the contributions of methodological decisions in Part II in Chapters 5, 6 and 7, addressing research questions, design, sampling, access and **recruitment** in interviews, and in the chapters in Part III discussing various forms of interviews as an orientation for which one to choose and how to conceive the interaction.

What You Need to Ask Yourself

The questions in Box 2.2 are designed to give you some help in the decision of whether to use interviews and which form might be best for your research. You may also apply these questions to studies using interviews you read. If you lack the knowledge to make this decision at this point, it will give you an indication of what to expect from reading the following chapters of this book.

Box 2.2   What you need to ask yourself

Theory and epistemology of doing interview research

1. How far can the issue of your research be studied by asking people about it?
2. What is the main focus of your study; what should the main focus of your interviews be?
3. What is the epistemological background to using interviews in your study?
4. Who should your interview partners be – lay people, professionals, experts, elites?
5. Where and how can you access your interview partners?
6. What good reasons are there, if any, for doing your interviews online or via Skype?
7. How will you document your data – recording and transcription? If not, why not?
8. What ethical issues might there be in your interviews, and how will you manage them?
9. What is it important to document about the context of your interviews as part of the data?

What You Need to Succeed

This chapter should have given you an understanding of the theoretical background to interviewing and that this method is more than just asking questions.

The following box (Box 2.3) summarizes the main points of this chapter.

Box 2.3   What you need to succeed

Basics of doing interview research

1. Did I understand that several versions of epistemologies of interviewing exist?
2. Do I have an idea of the differences between these epistemologies?
3. Do I see what the framework outlined in this chapter is about in concrete terms of doing interviews?

- A number of theoretical, epistemological and methodological underpinnings can be identified in the background to interviewing.
- The epistemologies of interviewing that have been spelled out lead to proceeding in different ways but towards similar goals.
- The interviewer constructs a framework for listening to the interviewee. This framework should allow as much leeway as possible to reveal their views. At the same time, they should be given a structure for what to talk about.
- There are a number of methodological principles that apply to doing interviews in this framework.
- How this framework becomes concrete for the doing of interviews will depend on the steps that are spelled out in more detail in the following chapters.

Exercises

In the exercises, you are first invited to reflect on some of the main issues of this chapter. Then you are invited to apply the topics of this chapter to the development of a project of your own. Hence, the exercises are a combination of reflection and prospection.

Exercise 2.1

Reflecting on the Chapter: The Use of Interviews in an Existing Study

1. Look through a journal for a qualitative study based on interviews (e.g. Stolte and Hodgetts, 2015). Try to identify which epistemology of interviewing it was based on.
2. Consider the study's questions and then improve them by using one or more of the interviewing methods presented in this chapter.

Exercise 2.2

Planning Your Own Research with Interviews

1. Think of your own study and consider an epistemology of interviewing for planning it.

What's next

This article summarizes some critical issues from the debate about the interview society. The suggestions made for how to overcome the problematic also show that the critical aspects do not mean abandoning interviewing but rather engaging in doing better interviews and more reflective analyses of the data:

Silverman, D. (2017). How Was it for You? The Interview Society and the Irresistible Rise of the (Poorly Analyzed) Interview. *Qualitative Research*, 17(2), 144-58.

These articles present a variety of epistemological stances of interviewing and some suggestions by the authors:

Alvesson, M. (2003). Beyond Neopositivists, Romantics, and Localists: A Reflexive Approach to Interviews in Organizational Research. *The Academy of Management Review*, 28(1), 13-33.

Roulston, K. (2018). Qualitative Interviewing and Epistemics. *Qualitative Research*, 18(3), 322-41. https://doi.org/10.1177/1468794117721738

This article discusses the use of interviewing with a decolonizing approach in the context of research with Māoris in New Zealand:

Edwards, S., McManus, V., & McCreanor, T. (2005). Collaborative Research with Māori on Sensitive Issues: The Application of Tikanga and Kaupapa in Research on Māori Sudden Infant Death Syndrome. *Social Policy Journal of New Zealand*, 25, 88-104.

Doing Interview Research Navigator

You are here in your project

How to understand interview research
- What doing interview research means
- Theories and epistemologies of interviewing
- When to choose interviews as a research method
- Methods and formats of interviewing

Designing interview research
- Planning and designing interview research
- How many interviewees: Sampling and saturation
- Accessing and recruiting participants

How to conduct interviews
- How to respect and protect: Ethics of interviewing
- Semi-structured interviews: Working with questions and answers
- Interviewing experts and elites
- Integrating narratives in interviews: Episodic interviews

Doing interviews in context
- How to work with life histories: Narrative interviews
- Working with focus groups as interviews
- Ask (in) the field: Ethnographic and mobile interviewing
- Doing online interviews

How to work with interview data
- Working with interview data
- Credibility and transparency: Quality and writing in interview research
- From interviewing to an inner view: Critiques and reflexivity

WHEN TO CHOOSE INTERVIEWS AS A RESEARCH METHOD

How this chapter will help you

You will:

- be guided in how to decide when to do interviews,
- see the differences between interviews in research, in therapy and journalism,
- understand what kinds of research questions can be pursued with interviews,
- have an idea of participants' views on being interviewed,
- see when to prefer other methods, and
- understand when to refrain from doing interviews for your research.

At the end of Chapter 2, I outlined a framework for doing interviews. This framework includes a working definition for doing interview research, and a description of the interviewer's role as a constructing listener. It also provides a way of conceiving the interview situation – as co-construction of knowledge. Now we can begin to spell this framework out in more detail by asking why and when researchers should choose interviewing as a method for their studies.

Aims of Interviewing in Various Contexts

To address the main question posed in this chapter, we should keep two distinctions from other forms of interviewing in mind. Different from therapeutic and journalistic interviews, the interviewees in research are approached as representatives. They are interviewed as representatives of other possible participants in a similar situation who could not be interviewed. In most cases, interviewees are not approached as individuals whose specific situations or opinions per se are the main focus of the interviews. They are approached to aid in understanding concepts, impacts or images of a specific issue, institution or situation with which they (and others) are concerned. As a consequence, research interviews are mostly done from a comparative perspective – one example person of a specific group is interviewed in order to compare statements, narratives or information with those mentioned by other example persons.

Interviewing in therapy and qualitative research

In a **therapeutic interview**, the aim is to collect information about the interviewee in order to treat or help with this specific person's problems. Following Weiss (1994, pp. 134–5), there are four differences between a therapeutic and a research interview. (1) The aims and practices are different: in therapy, the 'functioning of the patient' (p. 134) is the concern, whereas in research collecting information about an issue for a study is the aim. (2) In therapy, patients are expected to respond to therapists' questions by revealing their inner states and early life conflicts. In research interviews, respondents are expected to describe scenes, situations and events, and not so much to talk about their current internal states. (3) The relationships are different as well. A therapist is expected to become an 'authoritative figure' (1994, p. 135) in helping the patient, whereas 'the research perspective is defined as one of equals' (1994, p. 135). (4) Therapists are paid by patients (or their health insurance). Researchers are not paid by their interviewees but by a research institute, for example.

Interviewing in journalism and qualitative research

In a journalistic interview, the aim is to garner the opinion of an interviewee (e.g. a politician) about an issue or to understand and throw light on the interviewees' personal situation. The treatment of privacy in journalism is different from research interviews. Journalists may recruit interviewees offering them the chance to tell their story and with the promise: 'Through me you can make your story known' (Weiss, 1994, pp. 65–6). The interviewee in journalism is often approached, interviewed and analysed as an individual in a specific situation. In research interviews, participants are mostly conceived with a 'sample' perspective (see Chapter 6). They are interviewed about their individual situation (e.g. as a patient living with a disease) in order to understand the situation of people affected by such a disease in general.

If interviews are used in **investigative journalism**, the relation is sometimes marked by deception, as the interviewers may refrain from revealing their 'real' aims, which would be seen as unethical in a research interview. In journalism, it is quite common that interviewees will want to see and edit their interviews or the statements drawn from them before the interviewers continue their work by publishing the results. This is seldom done in qualitative research beyond interviewing experts and elites (see Chapter 10).

Brinkman (2013, pp. 128–9) emphasizes the similarities between interviewing in research and journalism in two respects. First, he focuses mainly on writing about the interview and its contents (see Chapter 17), and second on the specific approach of 'intimate journalism' (Harrington, 1997). However, his discussion does not make the difference obsolete. This was discussed above in terms of the relation between the person orientation in journalistic interviews and the sample-oriented understanding of interviewing in research, and as the case study in Box 3.1 illustrates.

Box 3.1   Research in the real world

Interviews in journalism and qualitative research

Three researchers working in social science in Finland with a feminist orientation (Nikunen et al., 2019, p. 489) did a business research study in the area of media work, where they compared researchers and journalists' professional practice in doing interviews and demonstrating their expertise in the interviews. The article is based on a collaborative project of the authors with journalists. By expertise interviews, the authors refer to how questions are asked, to how reflections about the interviews and sensible points are made, what is expected as an outcome of the interviews and how the collected data are framed in the analysis and resulting reports. The main focus is on how these points differ between journalists and researchers. Nikunen et al. see the main differences to research in how journalists use 'news' from interviews or how when they work as freelancers they 'sell' the news to media they work for. Another difference is how journalists maintain control of the communication process (2019, p. 494) and that journalists are 'hunting for surprises' (2019, p. 495) to attract readers in magazines or other media. Researchers look for repetitions, which means that interview statements can be relevant if they occur repeatedly or similarly in a case or across cases, which allows for consolidating patterns or typologies, for example, based on such statements. Thus, differences can be identified in the ways journalists and researchers do the actual interviews and in the ways they report the findings from the interviews. In this case study, we can see the similarities and the differences between journalists' and researchers' uses of interviewing.

In both journalism and therapy, a comparison of the interviewee's statements with other politicians or other patients is not necessarily the central aim of the next steps in the process.

Research Questions

The research question of a study is one of the most important points of reference for deciding whether to use interviews and which kind of interviews. I want to exemplify this with research in the field of social work on adolescents affected by homelessness and chronic illness (see Flick and Röhnsch, 2007; similar research by Stolte and Hodgetts, 2015, has already been discussed in Chapter 1). The starting point was a lack of detailed knowledge about how the two problems (being homeless and chronically ill at the same time) correspond and are experienced in adolescents' everyday lives. It was known, however, that a considerable and growing number of adolescents in the area did not have a regular place to stay. There were assumptions and indicators that chronic illness might occur among these adolescents as it does among adolescents in general. These assumptions came from talking to practitioners in the field. But it was not really known which diseases occur in the target group, how they are experienced and how the homeless adolescents cope with falling ill. In what follows, I want to outline research questions in this context for interviews and reflect about which kind of interviews are adequate. Here, we refer to the research questions for a study and not to **interview questions** participants are asked in a semi-structured interview (see Chapter 9 for this distinction).

Research questions for interviewing

With this example, I want to illustrate several kinds of research questions that can be pursued with interviews. These kinds of questions address several ways of approaching a social problem from different angles.

Perspective 1 – cause: What are the causes of homelessness in our sample? What causes of their situation do the participants see themselves in? What causes do they see for their illness? A first set of research questions addresses why the two problems became part of the adolescents' lives. Here we should first of all do interviews with those adolescents who are living on the street and affected by one chronic disease or several. We will not identify the causes per se (as a physician identifies a specific infection, for example). But we will identify the adolescents' subjective explanations or interpretations about why they became homeless and ill, and classify these perceptions of causes later in a typology, for example. Depending on the concrete focus and aims of the research (see below), we could develop a semi-structured interview (see Chapter 9) or work with narratives (see Chapter 12). Linking this question back to the epistemologies of interviewing (see Chapter 2), we might see this as a case for a romantic concept of interviewing, according to Alvesson (2003), giving the interviewees the chance to explore and present their inner views on their experience of being ill. However, in the way the researchers construct the setting, they influence not only how far they have the chance to listen to these presentations but also the co-construction of the interviewees' presentations. Thus, this research question is an example of turning this epistemology of the interviewer as constructing listener into research and material.

Perspective 2 – strategies: How do the adolescents cope with their disease (neglect, seek help, etc.)? To answer this second kind of question, we should interview the adolescents, asking them to recount situations where the illness became manifest, when symptoms started, and the like. In interviews, we would not be able to access the adolescents' actual practices – this would require (additional) participant observation. But we will receive ideas about the participants' reflections and maybe a rationalization of the disease or irrational reactions to their situation. Again, this research question is embedded in a setting constructed by the researcher to enable them to listen to what the interviewee has to report. In the way in which small or big narratives are stimulated (see Chapter 11 and 12) and the way the interviewee draws a picture of what happens around being ill, a shared process of constructing knowledge is initiated.

Perspective 3 – processes: How do the adolescents seek help once their disease becomes manifest? A third type of research question addresses the participants' views of their reactions and ways of coping with their problems. Here we may again use a more question-oriented form of interviews (see Chapters 9 and 11) or narratives (see Chapter 12). Interviewees should again be the adolescents. If we want to go beyond their specific views and interpretations, either complementary participant observation should be applied to have a more direct access to the practices (of seeking help), or a second extension might be to ask experts such as service providers about their views on such kinds of coping processes with in this target group. This view would go beyond the single adolescents and their experiences, and focus on a variety of ways of coping with the problems. Again, however, this form of addressing the issues is based on interviews but this time expert interviews (see Chapter 10). In the latter case, we could add an interview with a more neopositivist approach to (expert) knowledge referring to context information (numbers, distributions, typical careers) in a co-constructivist understanding of interviewing the adolescents for their versions of the processes.

Perspective 4 – type: What types of coping with a chronic illness can we identify among our participants? Such a research question again would suggest interviewing the participants. But in order to find an answer about *types* of coping, it would be necessary to have a well-selected sample of participants (see Chapter 6) with several diseases and a well-developed comparative perspective on the single interviews. A comparative analysis of several interviews will then allow for identifying types of coping. Here, the researchers' constructions of the situation of listening will begin before the actual interview when selecting participants oriented on varieties of experiences, for example.

Perspective 5 – structure: How can structural problems linked to a specific situation of being influence attempts at coping with the disease? This kind of research question reaches beyond the experience and insights of (most of the) ill individuals or patients. Analysing this bird's eye view would suggest doing expert interviews with service providers (see Chapter 10), who have seen a variety of individual cases and have a view on the structure of the health care system in this context. What is mentioned and related in more detail depends again on the way the researchers construct the

situations of interviewing and listening – from the selection of the (expert) participants, to the questions and their format asked in the actual interview. In addition,
interviews with patients can focus on situations in their everyday life, in which a
structural problem may have affected their coping efforts, e.g. the lack of frequent
and regular public transport in rural areas, which produces barriers in attending
treatment as often as necessary.

*Perspective 6 – frequency: How frequently do specific chronic diseases occur among homeless
adolescents?* Answering such a question with interviews is possible, but this should be
structured expert interviews, and, if available, statistics of treatments as a complementary source. Here we come closer to designing interviews on the basis of a neopositivist
epistemology.

*Perspective 7 – consequences: What consequences can be identified for different forms of
coping with the diseases?* The adolescents might report the consequences they have
experienced when trying to cope with their illness in one way or the other. Expert
interviews with service providers can provide an overview perspective (see
Chapter 10).

In general, we can first distinguish research questions that focus on describing
states or on analysing processes. Both can be answered by using interviews. It is
rather a question of which type of interview is the most appropriate. To analyse
processes, interviews based on narratives (see Chapter 12) or including them in their
focus (see Chapter 11) are suggested. To describe states, semi-structured interviews
(see Chapter 9) are preferable, in which interviewees provide answers to specific
questions.

A second distinction of research questions is that between fact-oriented and
interpretation-oriented questions. To answer questions aiming at interpretations,
interviews are highly recommended, whereas fact-oriented questions should be
answered with other forms of data, as two examples may illustrate. If we are interested in what patients see as the cause of their disease, for example, interviewing
them may be most fruitful – even if they do not reveal the 'real' causes. If we are
interested in causes of an illness, we should use diagnostic approaches. If we want to
understand the legal framework of working with refugees, for example, the analysis
of laws and regulations in legal texts is suggested. To understand how this legal
framework impacts on day-to-day practices in work with refugees, expert interviews
may be the right way.

Study Aims

The decision of when to do interviews should be taken by considering several features
of the study that is planned. The first of these features is the aims of the study. Here
we can distinguish aims that are relevant for doing interviews in general from those
which refer to specific forms of interviewing (e.g. narrative or expert interviews – see
Chapters 10 and 12).

Reasons for conducting interview studies

To answer the question of why interviews should be selected for a study, we find several levels of suggestions. Weiss (1994, pp. 9–11), for example, mentions a number of outcomes that motivate the use of interviews. One type of expectation refers to descriptions as a result of interviewing. This ranges from *developing detailed* and *holistic descriptions* of events, situations or issues that are studied by collecting several participants' perspectives, to *describing process* in detail based on accounts of those people who were part of it.

A second type refers to more analytic aims such as learning *how events are interpreted* by those who were part of them and *integrating multiple perspectives* on these events. A third aim is about *bridging intersubjectivities*. This means allowing the researchers and readers of their reports to grasp a situation from the inside as if they had been there. Another aim on a different level refers to *identifying variables and framing hypotheses for quantitative research.*

These suggestions (in particular the last one) are in some ways rather technical motivations for interviewing, with a focus on what should come out of using interviews. But we also find suggestions which are oriented more towards an attitude of approaching and understanding what is studied.

When to Choose Qualitative Interviewing

Rubin and Rubin (2005, pp. 50–1) give some guidance on the general question of when to choose qualitative interviewing for your study. They have formulated five general questions, which we can use for further consideration of when to do interviews, but they are less technically oriented than Weiss's suggestions. These questions serve as a starting point on which we can elaborate in deciding when to use interviews.

1. 'Are you looking for nuance and subtlety?' (2005, p. 50). If we want to address the subjective experiences or meanings of an event or a situation for our participants, doing interviews will be a better choice than carrying out a standardized survey, for example. It will also be preferable to (participant) observation in which interactions and practices are the focus rather than detailed accounts of meanings and relevance for the individual. In general, this orientation might ask for a dialogue between the interviewer and the participant and thus for a semi-structured interview (see Chapter 9).
2. 'Are you looking for process, steps over time, sequences of causation?' (2005, p. 50). If we want to access such a view on or account of processes, interviewing might be much more fruitful than surveys with rather narrowly focused questions and options for answering them. In such process-oriented research, we can either use repeated interviews in a longitudinal design (see Chapter 5) applied along the process that develops, or we can decide to use a narrative approach and ask the participants about their views on the process and to recount the developments in a story. One method for this is the narrative interview (see Chapter 12).

3. 'Is an entirely fresh view required?' (2005, pp. 50–1). If one of the strategies just mentioned has come to its limits, it might be fruitful to combine them in one method for overcoming the limits of each strategy. An example for such a combination is the **episodic interview** aiming at complementing question–answer strategies with small-scale situation-oriented narratives (see Chapter 11). Another example is to go online with interviewing or to use interviews in the context of social media (see Chapter 15).

4. 'Are you trying to explain the unexpected?' (2005, p. 51). If you are interested in why something works out, contrary to expectations, your strategy might be to interview several of the people involved in this process. One example is a study of how refugees in Germany managed to find a regular job and who was supporting this process, as we are currently studying in an ongoing project (see the case study in Box 7.4 in Chapter 7 and Seidelsohn et al., 2020). Here it might be helpful or necessary to do interviews with several of the protagonists (refugees, employers, and other supporters from NGOs, for example).

5. 'Does puzzling out the research question necessitate layers of discovery?' (2005, p. 51). Interviews can be applied in a repeated or an extended way for revealing more than just one level or one perspective on an issue. This can also be an argument for complementing interviews with other methods or, even more relevant here, other methodological strategies with interviews. For example, several types of interviews can be combined – such as episodic interviews with homeless adolescents about their views on health and illness and expert interviews with service providers about the target group (see Chapters 10 and 11).

As we saw in Chapter 1, the aims of using interviews can range from understanding individuals' stance towards events, situations and processes in their life history to the differences between their stance and those of other actors in the field. Evaluation can be a third aim in doing interviews. In this case, but also in general, we have to take into account the fact that we will obtain subjective views on an issue (to explain or to evaluate) in interviews and should reflect on whether that corresponds to the aims of our research.

Research Strategies

Doing interviews can be embedded in several research strategies. Narrative or bio-graphical semi-structured interviews are mostly embedded in **biographical research**. For example, participants are asked to recount their history of emigrating from their home country (or are asked questions about this emigration). The escape would be seen and become a topic as part of a longer biographical process – which led to the decision to emigrate and which includes the further developments involved after arriving in the new country. Biographical research in most cases is not limited to the single interviewee's experience or fate. It will use the insights from the interviews to also analyse the social process that becomes visible in this case and other interviews. For example, such a biographical study mainly focuses on the question of how a more general social problem – the refugee crisis in Germany after 2015, for instance, or the separation of the two states of Germany after the Second World War – has manifested on the concrete level of everyday life experience of the people concerned.

A second research strategy now puts a strong emphasis on using interviews as well. In her version of **grounded theory research**, Charmaz (2014) relies very much on her concept of '**intensive interviewing**' (see Chapter 9). Data collection was not paid much attention in early grounded theory research (see Flick, 2018c). The new interest in interviewing in this research programme is interesting in our context in a specific way. Interviews are done to obtain participants' views, experiences or life histories, not primarily to understand their view and situation but to collect material for developing a theory of the issue under study. Analysis of statements and narratives in interviews aims at developing concepts as the building blocks of a **grounded theory**. This may in the end be more distant from the participants than in other contexts of using interviews.

A third research strategy employs interviews in a more comprehensive approach of mixed methods research and combines them with quantitative methods (see Flick, 2018b). Here, the role of interviews and the expectations about the insights they will provide are often much more limited than in other research strategies mentioned above, in particular when the quantitative element of the methodological mix is dominant in the study.

Analysing discourses is a fourth strategy in which interviews are used. In the beginning of the boom of discursive psychology in the 1990s – as an approach to studying discourses – this was seen as an alternative to working with interviews. Some of the critical points raised by Potter and Hepburn (2012) against using interviews are still driven by this opposition. However, Willig (e.g. 2014a) demonstrates that interviewing has become a major strategy in analysing discourses. Here again, the single interviews and interviewees are not really the major focus in the analysis. Rather, it is the discourse that is shining through the statements of the interviewees that is analysed and the analysis addresses issues partly 'behind the interviewees' backs'.

Finally, doing interviews can be seen as a research strategy in itself – to collect statements for understanding the participants' situation and for comparing their accounts without any of the wider entanglements discussed above.

Pragmatic Considerations

We find a long discussion in the research literature about qualitative methods concerning the advantages of other methods compared to interviewing, in particular of participant observation. This discussion goes back to Becker and Geer (1957, 1960) and is updated by Lüders (2004a), Jerolmack and Khan (2014), and critically reviewed by Atkinson and Coffey (2001). In some ways, it also influences more current critical discussions of interviewing (e.g. Atkinson and Silverman, 1997; Potter and Hepburn, 2012; Silverman, 2017; and see Chapter 18).

These discussions may be relevant from a methodological point of view. However, Patton (2015) sees the decision for or against interviewing from a more pragmatic angle. First of all, this has to do with the issues we want to study and whether they are accessible through methods other than interviewing:

The issue is not whether observational data are more desirable, valid, or meaningful than self-reported data. The fact of the matter is that we cannot observe everything. We cannot observe feelings, thoughts, and intentions. We cannot observe behaviours that took place at some previous point in time. (2015, p. 426)

Second, the contexts in which phenomena occur are not always accessible to researchers, so that we should try to talk with the 'right' people about these phenomena:

We cannot observe situations that preclude the presence of an observer. We cannot observe how people have organized the world and the meanings they attach to what goes on in the world. We have to ask people questions about it. The purpose of interviewing, then, is to allow us to enter into the other person's perspective. (2015, p. 426)

Other pragmatic considerations for or against interviewing refer to restrictions of time and of other resources in the context of short-term projects such as master's theses. Short-term projects often allow for a limited number of interviews but not to establish an extended field contact. Sometimes it can be dangerous to do ethnographic field research and much less dangerous to work with interviews. In general, we find a number of rather pragmatic reasons to opt for interviewing rather than observation. Other methods can be discussed in a similar way on the advantages and disadvantages compared to doing interviews.

Exploration of Issues

Interviews can be used for exploring issues we do not know much about. This is often mentioned as a reason for working with this method. But what does it mean precisely? The example in the case study in Box 3.2 may illustrate the idea of exploration in some detail.

Box 3.2   Research in the real world

Using interviews to explore an issue

I did my PhD with a study on trust in helping relationships. When I started the project, there was some interest by researchers from clinical psychology about how trust in counselling could be studied and how we could identify where trust is involved in the counselling relationship and where it is not. At that time, the literature offered some rather general reflections on the phenomenon of 'trust', but not much about empirical analyses, in particular in the context of counselling. The original idea of the project, to start from the literature and to develop a set of categories and to analyse counselling protocols with them in a rather standardized way, had to be abandoned as the theoretical grounds for this were lacking. As a consequence, I decided to start from practitioners' experiences of this concept in their own professional work and to interview them. As there were no (scientific) theories available to start from for the analysis, the idea was to reconstruct the practitioners' **subjective theories** on trust. In my study of trust in counselling, I used semi-structured interviews (see Chapter 9) with 15 counsellors from different professional backgrounds (e.g. psychologists, social workers and physicians). The interview focused on topics such as the definition of trust, reasons for trust, its relevance for counselling, and institutional framework conditions and trust. As a response to the question 'Could you please tell me briefly what you relate to the term "trust", if you think of your professional practice?', one interviewee gave as her definition:

> If I think of my professional practice – well ... very many people ask me at the beginning whether they can trust me in the relationship, and – because I am representing a public agency – whether I really keep confidential what they will be telling me. Trust for me is to say at this point quite honestly how I might handle this, that I can keep it all confidential up to a certain point, but if they tell me any jeopardizing facts that I have difficulties with then I will tell them at that point. Well, this is trust for me: to be frank about this and the point of the oath of secrecy, that actually is the main point.

The interviews revealed how the interviewees understood trust and how they identified different types of beginning a counselling session, ideas of good and trust-based situations of counselling and their conditions, and ideas of how at least to approximately produce such conditions in the current situation. Analysing counselling activities showed how counsellors used these ideas in their practical work with clients (see Flick, 1992).

The example of the case study in Box 3.2 demonstrates how the decision to do interviews in this project was taken and how interviews were used for exploring an issue, and thus corresponds to the way Patton defines why we use interviews: 'We interview people to find out from them those things we cannot directly observe and to understand what we observed' (2015, p. 426). However, the use of interviews in this case was not restricted to preparing a quantitative or standardized study. The interviews were one of the main methods in this project and were complemented by **conversation analysis** of counselling interactions and thus by a second qualitative method.

Multiplicity of Perspectives

Many studies are interested in the perspectives of several participants of a social setting – e.g. family members, team members in an institution, professionals and clients, teachers and students. In each of these examples, we might use interactive situations such as focus groups or everyday encounters and communications of the participants to understand how they exchange their views or act in cooperation and conflict.

However, if we really want to go into the details of what an individual thinks and feels, interviews with the members of a field are more fruitful. In a focus group interview (see Chapter 13), a really detailed analysis of individual views is often not possible. Asking a specific participant too many questions would destroy the interaction in the group. The same might be the case in observations. Individual interviews allow us to concentrate on the details of individual views and then to compare them. It may be necessary to use different kinds of interviews in such settings, for example episodic interviews (see Chapter 11) with patients and expert interviews (see Chapter 10) with their physicians. The idea then is not so much to 'correct' one view with the other, but to compare both and to extend the multiplicity of perspectives on a systematic and detailed basis.

Aims of Going Online and Becoming Mobile with Interviewing

Three aspects at least define the classic setting of an interview. The interviewee and the interviewer meet at a mutually arranged, specific time, in an office or another delimited and protected space, and they talk in most cases once and face-to-face. Although we find exceptions in the history of qualitative research (e.g. in the ethnographic interview conducted in the field – see Chapter 14), interview research has been mostly oriented on creating situations that come as close as possible to this classic setting and its three aspects. More recently, two deviations from this setting have become features of specific ways of working with interviews. One trend is to transfer interviewing to the field and to the context of mobile methods (see Chapter 14). The other is to use computer-mediated interaction and to do online interviews (see Chapter 15).

Interviews in mobile research

Decisions for doing interviews in a mobile way are based on intentions to take the interview to the life world of the participants. Jones et al. (2008) see in mobilizing interviews 'a means to take the interviewing process out of the "safe" confines of the interview room and allow the environment and the act of walking itself to move the collection of interview data in productive and sometimes entirely unexpected directions' (2008, p. 8). Mobile interviewing enables the researchers to see what the interviewees are talking about when the interview is embedded in a 'go-along' (Kusenbach, 2018) design. Interviewing then includes observational and participative components. It drives the research into the participants' everyday worlds and allows for an understanding of their use of space and their routines in moving through a city, for instance (see Flick et al., 2017, for an example of this kind of research). More details about this research strategy can be found in Chapter 14.

Online interviewing

There are a number of practical reasons for why online interviewing may be preferred to face-to-face interviews. Among them is a saving both in time and costs as neither interviewer nor participant have to travel to meet for the interview. Other arguments refer to the need to transcribe traditional interviews as part of the data collection as a cost for the researchers before they can analyse the data, which can be saved in online interviews as the answers are provided as text on the screen immediately. Sometimes it is easier to access interviewees online than face-to-face, although online interviewing is limited to participants who have Internet access and use it. Finally, the reasons for deciding to use online interviews can come from the issue or population under study.

Salmons (2015, p. 39) discusses the decision to use information and communication technologies on three levels:

- as a medium for communicating with participants – asking questions and receiving answers online;
- as a setting, when the data collection is embedded in online communities, social media, virtual worlds, etc.;
- and as a phenomenon, when the study refers to online activities, related experiences and behaviours (for more details, see Chapter 15).

Technologies that can be used range from doing interviews as **email interviews** in which questions and answers are exchanged synchronously – the interviewees respond immediately and the interviewers send the next question in turn. The interviews can also be done in an **asynchronous communication** – the interviewee responds some time after receiving the questions (see Salmons, 2015; and Chapter 15 here). An alternative is to use social media such as Facebook or Twitter for doing the actual interview. Closer to the traditional face-to-face interview is the use of Skype instead of meeting the interviewee in person (see Chapter 1 and in particular Chapter 15 for more detail).

Participants' Views of Being Interviewed

When researchers decide to do interviews in a study, they are seldom aware of potential participants' views on this method and whether they want to be interviewed or not or what their view on being interviewed looks like. We can discuss the issue of participants' views on interviewing in three respects: referring (1) to specific methods (or paradigms) of interviewing, (2) to interviewing in general and (3) to interviewing in comparison to other methods.

Views on specific forms of interviewing

In Chapter 2, we discussed several epistemologies of interviewing, according to Alvesson (2003) and Roulston (2010a), which can be turned into specific forms of interviewing on a more practical level.

Box 3.3   Research in the real world

Benefits and risks of being interviewed

A group of researchers in the fields of education, sociology and linguistics coming from various universities in the US (Wolgemuth et al., 2015) have taken Roulston's
overview (such as neopositivist, romantic, transformative and feminist) of 'interviewing
paradigms' for a 'paradigm-driven' analysis of participants' interview experiences.
The authors took their own research studies for a multiple case study approach
according to Stake (2006), which included 'neo-positivist (1), romantic (3), transformative (1), and feminist (1)' interviews with 198 participants across North America,
Southeast Asia and Europe (Wolgemuth et al., 2015, p. 355). From the transcripts, the
authors identified benefits and risks mentioned by the participants. They identified
as benefits of participating: the 'opportunity to: 1) talk to someone; 2) self-reflect;
3) emotionally cleanse; 4) become knowledgeable about a topic of personal/
professional interest; 5) connect with a broader community based on shared experience; 6) advocate for a community/cause; and 7) help someone else down
the road' (p. 358). Complementary to these benefits, the authors identified 'four
risks of participating in our interview projects. They were: 1) being identified;
2) representing voice; 3) causing problems for self and others; and 4) experiencing
emotional pain' (p. 365). In their analysis, they compared these benefits and risks
for each of the paradigms and came to the conclusion that 'the theory of the interview may be less important to participants' experiences than other features' (Wolgemuth et al., 2015, p. 367) such as the interviewers' flexibility to adapt their interview
concept to the interviewees' accounts and needs.

The case study in Box 3.3 suggests shifting the focus on views, benefits and risks on
the level of interviewing in general.

Views on being interviewed in general

In the context of qualitative health research, Corbin and Morse (2003) analyse the
potential risks of participants being interviewed who reveal 'personal, often intimate
aspects of their lives. … One risk is that there might be a break in confidentiality/
anonymity, with possible consequences of a social, financial, legal, or political nature'
(p. 336). Also, in the context of nursing research in the US, Hutchinson et al. (1994)
discuss the benefits of qualitative interviews, which include that interviews (1) serve as
a catharsis, (2) provide self-acknowledgement and validation, (3) contribute to a sense
of purpose, (4) increase self-awareness, (5) grant a sense of empowerment, (6) promote
healing and (7) give voice to the voiceless and disenfranchised (see Corbin and
Morse, 2003; Hutchinson et al., 1994). This balance of benefits and risks of being

interviewed may be strongly influenced by the context of health research, but it also reveals the possible effects of interviews for participants which may be part of possible participants' expectations and views on being interviewed for other contexts of interview research. As already mentioned, concrete ways of doing interviews on a practical level are more important than theoretical or paradigmatic concepts of interviewing.

Being interviewed in comparison to other methods

When people refuse to take part in our studies, in most cases we do not know exactly what triggered that response – the topic, the particular researcher inviting them to participate or the method of interviewing. In the case study in Box 3.4, the study on trust in counselling already referred to is again used as an example. It illustrates how potential participants did not refuse to be part of the study in general, but were not happy to be interviewed.

Box 3.4   Research in the real world

Reluctance to being interviewed

In the study about trust in counselling, I used two methods – interviews and the examination of counselling protocols with conversation analysis. Thus, I approached the individual counsellors with two requests: to agree to be interviewed for one to two hours and to permit the recording of one or more consultations with clients (who had also agreed beforehand). After the counsellors had agreed in general to participate in the study, some of them had reservations about being interviewed whereas they saw the recording of a counselling session as routine. Other counsellors had no problem with being interviewed, but had considerable reservations about allowing someone to delve into their concrete work with clients. Arguments against being interviewed referred to the lack of time for the interview, the fear of 'indiscreet' questions and a general scepticism about reflecting on one's own work with a researcher. Another argument was that it would be difficult to talk about a phenomenon such as trust in relation to clients. These reservations did not refer to participating in the study per se, but against being interviewed in particular (see also Flick, 1992).

The example of the case study in Box 3.4 shows that we also find reservations about being interviewed in contexts where people have been approached as professionals whose work entails talking to people about their problems and enquiring about delicate topics. The prospective participants had also studied at university to become social workers, physicians or psychologists and thus were familiar with the concept of research. And they were used to articulating what they did or didn't want. This example is interesting in two respects.

First, not all the counsellors I approached refused to be interviewed. Some hesitated for a moment and then agreed to participate.

Second, if we transfer such scepticism to other target groups without this professional background and position, we may assume similar reservations in these target groups as well, but may not necessarily be confronted with them explicitly. This suggests reflecting carefully on what it means for potential participants to be interviewed. In this context, an other, sometimes underestimated reason for being reluctant to be interviewed is the research fatigue among over-researched groups (see Clark, 2008). This was the case for some years when HIV was discovered as a new health problem and a new issue for research, and interviews were quite prominent for doing the studies. This is often linked to suspicion of the researchers and their real and assumed motives for doing interviews or for approaching specific individuals for their interviews.

When Not to Choose Interviews as Your Method

Some of the reasons for refraining from using interviews are on an epistemological level. If an evaluation aims at finding out whether something 'really works', a standardized design with measuring effects rather than interviews should be used. In general, measuring effects, intensities or frequencies is not really possible with qualitative interviews. Hypothesis testing is difficult with qualitative research in general and with interviews in particular.

Other reasons for not using interviews have to do with the target groups to be interviewed. If no one has the knowledge needed to answer questions or if the questions are too complex to be answered by single participants, the limits of individual interviewing become evident. And a number of ethical concerns should be considered, which might prevent interviewing from being the best way to analyse people's experiences with an issue (see Chapter 8).

Doing Interviews Despite the Critiques

In Chapters 1 and 2, some critiques of using interviews were discussed, coming from researchers in the West objecting to a naïve concept of collecting and analysing interview data. These critiques may be put in perspective by planning and doing interviews more carefully and by analysing the data more systematically than Silverman (2017) describes the practices he criticizes. The objections against Western methodologies and the call for decolonizing research methodologies also require a more reflexive way of using methods, but within research practice we still find various ways of interviewing. Again, it depends on how the methods are used, how the framework for listening to interviewees is constructed (see Chapter 5) and how appropriate the method selected is for both the issue and participants in the study (see Chapters 4 and 9–15).

What You Need to Ask Yourself

The questions in Box 3.5 are designed to help you to decide whether to use interviews for your research. You may also apply these questions to studies using interviews you read.

Box 3.5 What you need to ask yourself

When to do interviews

1. How far can the issue of your research be studied by asking people about it?
2. What is the main focus of your study?
3. What should the main focus of interviewing your participants be?
4. Where and how can you access interview partners for your interviews?
5. How will you document your data – recording and transcription? If not, why not?
6. What is it important to document about the context of your interviews as part of the data?
7. Would your interviews profit from doing them online or in a mobile design?

What You Need to Succeed

This chapter should have informed you about when (and why) to use interviews in research and how this differs from other contexts of interviewing. It should also make you reflect on what being interviewed means for the participants. The questions in Box 3.6 will help you to see what to take away from this chapter for the next steps in our journey through interview research.

Box 3.6 What you need to succeed

When to use interviews

1. Did I understand the differences between research, therapy and journalism in using interviews?
2. Do I understand what the appropriate types of research questions and reasons for using research interviews are?
3. Am I aware of how interviewees might experience being interviewed in a specific way?

What you have learned

- The decision for doing interviews should be based first and foremost on the research question of a study.
- The focus of the research question should define what kind of interview to apply.
- Decisions around interviews can be embedded in several research strategies.
- Some issues can only be addressed in interviews.
- Exploring issues is a main motivation in the decision to use interviews.
- Single interviews can explore the multiplicity of perspectives in more detail than focus groups permit.
- Doing interviews online or in the context of mobile methods are alternatives to traditional interview settings.
- Participants often have their own reasons to be sceptical about interviews.
- There are also good reasons not to use interviews in a study.

Exercises

The exercises again first invite you to reflect on some of the main issues of this chapter. Then you are invited to apply the topics of this chapter to the development of a project of your own. Hence, the exercises are a combination of reflection and prospection.

Exercise 3.1

Reflecting on the Chapter: The Use of Interviews in an Existing Study

1. Look through a journal for a qualitative study based on interviews (e.g. Clark, 2008). Try to identify how the authors presented their decision to do interviews as part of their project.
2. Reflect on whether the decision to do interviews or a specific form of interviewing was plausible or not.

Exercise 3.2

Planning Your Project Using Interviews

1. Think of your own study and reflect on why you would use interviews in it.
2. Consider the alternatives of online or mobile interviewing for your study and why you might use one of them (or not).

What's next

This chapter addresses issues around interviews:

Hermanns, H. (2004). Interviewing as an Activity. In U. Flick, E. v. Kardorff, & I. Steinke (Eds.), *A Companion to Qualitative Research* (pp. 209–13). London: Sage.

The following article concisely summarizes the issues linked to the decision about a method, including some practical advice:

Wilkerson, J.M., Iantaffi, A., Grey, J.A., Bockting, W.O., & Rosser, B.R.S. (2014). Recommendations for Internet-Based Qualitative Health Research with Hard-to-Reach Populations. *Qualitative Health Research*, 24(4), 561-74.

This book chapter summarizes the methodological approach of mobile methods including interviews in this context:

Kusenbach, M. (2018). Go-Alongs. In U. Flick (Ed.), *The SAGE Handbook of Qualitative Data Collection* (pp. 344-61). London: Sage.

The following article addresses the benefits and risks of being interviewed in health research contexts:

Corbin, J., & Morse, J.M. (2003). The Unstructured Interactive Interview: Issues of Reciprocity and Risks when Dealing with Sensitive Topics. *Qualitative Inquiry*, 9(3), 335-54. https://doi.org/10.1177/1077800403009003001

This chapter describes an example of a specific method in this context:

Flick, U. (2000). Episodic Interviewing. In M. Bauer & G. Gaskell (Eds.), *Qualitative Researching with Text, Image and Sound: A Practical Handbook* (pp. 75-92). London: Sage.

This chapter presents a focused introduction to doing expert and elite interviews for data collection:

Bogner, A., Littig, B., & Menz, W. (2018). Collecting Data with Experts and Elites. In U. Flick (Ed.), *The SAGE Handbook of Qualitative Data Collection* (pp. 652-67). London: Sage.

This article explores the perspective of potential interviewees:

Clark, T. (2008). 'We're Over-Researched Here!': Exploring Accounts of Research Fatigue within Qualitative Research Engagements. *Sociology*, 42(5), 953-70. https://doi.org/10.1177/0038038508094573

This review shows how interviews and which kinds of interviewing are used in indigenous research:

Drawson, A.S., Toombs, E., & Mushquash, C.J. (2017). Indigenous Research Methods: A Systematic Review. *The International Indigenous Policy Journal*, 8(2). doi: 10.18584/iipj.2017.8.2.5

Doing Interview Research Navigator

You are here in your project

How to understand interview research
- What doing interview research means
- Theories and epistemologies of interviewing
- When to choose interviews as a research method
- Methods and formats of interviewing

Designing interview research
- Planning and designing interview research
- How many interviewees: Sampling and saturation
- Accessing and recruiting participants

How to conduct interviews
- How to respect and protect: Ethics of interviewing
- Semi-structured interviews: Working with questions and answers
- Interviewing experts and elites
- Integrating narratives in interviews: Episodic interviews

Doing interviews in context
- How to work with life histories: Narrative interviews
- Working with focus groups as interviews
- Ask (in) the field: Ethnographic and mobile interviewing
- Doing online interviews

How to work with interview data
- Working with interview data
- Credibility and transparency: Quality and writing in interview research
- From interviewing to an inner view: Critiques and reflexivity

METHODS AND FORMATS OF INTERVIEWING

You will:

- be introduced to the general principles of interviewing,
- see that a number of methodological concepts of interviewing are available,
- begin to see the differences between these methods,
- gain an understanding of the principles of these methods, and
- appreciate their consequences for doing interviews.

General Principles of Interviewing and the Proliferation of Methods

In the preceding chapters, I have focused on more general issues of interviewing from the history of interviewing to more recent extensions into the field or the Internet or when to use interviewing as an approach for a study. I also addressed more general issues of theory and epistemology guiding the use of interviewing, also in the light of recent critiques in qualitative methodology and decolonizing methods discourses. So far, I have not addressed specific formats or methods of interviewing in detail. However, in most textbooks the focus is on interviewing as a general method and on specific problems linked to doing interviewing in general, as briefly reviewed below.

A relational approach to interviewing

For example, Josselson (2013) provides an introduction to interviewing which empha-sizes the relation between interviewer and interviewee. Her 'relational approach' is helpful for preparing, building and maintaining the rapport in the interview. However, throughout her book she talks about interviewing as a kind of homogeneous method. She conceives interviewing as eliciting narratives of lived experiences and uses the terms 'narrative' and 'qualitative' research interchangeably (2013, p. vii). Only very occasionally does she allude explicitly to stimulating narratives as a way of interview-ing and to interviewing more based on asking questions. However helpful her examples and advice for creating the relationship in interviewing may be, we do not find a more systematic treatment of various methods of interviewing – or the idea that interviewing has proliferated in various formats which may be more appropriate for some studies than others.

Reflective interviewing

Roulston (2010a) provides an introduction to 'reflective interviewing'. In the first chapter of her book, she briefly mentions some 'interview formats' such as phenom-enological, ethnographic, feminist, oral history, life history, and dialogical and confrontational interviewing (pp. 17–28) of individuals, which basically are distin-guished according to the contents to be studied in the interviews. In the second chapter, she discusses a number of group-related methods such as focus groups. However, the major parts of the book do not discuss these formats in a systematic way but talk basically about the interview as a homogeneous method, with a strong focus on reflecting and analysing the data.

Responsive interviewing

Rubin and Rubin (2005) take a general view of interviewing (in their case seen as in-depth interviewing) for which they suggest and develop a specific style of doing interviews, called **'responsive interviewing'**. They emphasize 'the importance of building a relationship of trust between the interviewer and interviewee that leads to more give-and-take in the conversation' (2005, p. 37). The attitude in ask-ing questions should be 'friendly and gentle, with little confrontation'. A flexible use of questions which responds to the interviewees' statements and aims at creat-ing a space for 'experience and knowledge of each interviewee' (2005, p. 37) should be characteristic for interviewing in general. The attitude outlined by the authors and their suggestions of how to learn and apply it are very helpful for doing interviews in general but they do not differentiate much between specific methods of interviewing.

Intensive interviewing

In the context of grounded theory research, Charmaz (2014) suggests using 'intensive interviewing', defined as 'a gently-guided, one-sided conversation that explores research participants' perspective on their personal experience with the research topic' (2014, p. 56). Charmaz's approach is to outline an attitude for interviewing in general, which can then be used in grounded theory research too, but she does not discuss various methods of doing interviews. Intensive interviewing sits within the framework of semi-structured interviewing (see Chapter 9).

Learning from strangers

Weiss (1994) also gives a helpful orientation about how to see interviewing and interviewees, so that researchers enter a process of 'learning from strangers'. Again, this orientation can be applied to any kind of doing interviews, but does not take any methodological proliferation into account.

Decolonizing interviews

As has been said before, the discourse about decolonizing interview methods has led more to critical discussions than to concrete suggestions for new methods or methodological approaches in interviewing. One exception, also used by Chilisa (2020), is the focused life story interview developed by Edwards et al. (2005):

> Focused life story interviews are very appropriate for sensitive topics as they encourage a reflective, narrative style where the interviewee sets the pace and the interviewer listens, clarifies, probes and possibly brings up topics which need to be covered in the interview that have not arisen spontaneously in the course of the conversation. This particular style allows for a relaxed, almost conversational, approach to data interview. (2005, p. 97)

All these suggestions can be very helpful for developing an attitude about how to do interview research in general. They can support students and researchers in doing interviews. However, these suggestions rather quickly turn to a general understanding of interviewing as a homogeneous method, but do not develop and pursue a methodological approach to the diversity of interview forms. This means they do not really discuss the various methods of doing interviews, of which one or the other can be selected for and applied in a specific study, taking the methodological features and precepts of the specific method into account. In what follows, I will focus on the variety of methods of doing interviews.

Dimensions of Interview Methods

If we want to structure the field of available methods of interviewing, we can start with some broader dimensions first before we subsume existing methods in to these dimensions. In later chapters, I will describe the practices of interviewing with these methods in more detail.

Meanings in their own words

A first dimension is about how far we aim to explore meanings in the interviewees' own words or in the framework of the researchers' scientific worldviews. This means that we should look at how questions, for example, are formulated in a way that supports the interviewees in talking in their own words rather than simply responding using the interviewer's vocabulary. If we want to maximize the scope for interviewees to talk and explore issues in their own words, we should work with open questions rather than questions suggesting specific answers or alternatives in answering (see Chapter 9). Or we should try to stimulate narratives (see Chapter 12) about a specific experience or process.

Experience-near and experience-distant concepts

A second dimension is how far we use concepts in questions and in the interview in general which are **experience-near** or **experience-distant** from interviewees (Geertz, 1974). Hermanns (2004) emphasizes that, *during* the interview, we should not try to discover theoretical concepts, but rather the interviewee's life world. Theoretical concepts can be discovered and elaborated on during the analysis of the interview data. During the interview, for example, we should not ask 'how did you cope with your diagnosis of a chronic illness?' – even if that is our research question – but rather: 'How did you cope with your day-to-day life when you learned that you had a chronic illness?' The second alternative will not necessarily be the interviewees' words but will be closer to the way they experience the problem and support them in responding in their own words. Beyond using open questions or stimulating narratives, this aspect becomes relevant in particular in asking more specific or focused questions, in probing (see Chapter 9) or in stimulating additional narratives (see Chapter 12).

Openness and structuration in the data collection

This leads to the third dimension, which allows for a structuring of the field of interview methods. On the one hand, we are not interested in everything the interviewees might talk about, but in the specific parts of their experience, knowledge or everyday life which are relevant to the research question of our study. However, we are interested in how the interviewees experience and see the issues under study. This means that interviews have to find the appropriate relation of openness (for the interviewees' views) and structuration (towards referring to the research questions).

At the one end of the spectrum are structured interviews similar to a questionnaire, perhaps even presenting ways to answer them. At the other end are interviews which refrain from directing the interviewees in any way by asking specific questions. A successful interview will find the right balance between openness and structuration by asking combinations of questions or by stimulating narratives using specific and focused questions.

Collecting facts or stimulating reflection

We can also differentiate methods of interviewing by how far they are oriented towards collecting facts (How many interviewees see .... as ....?) or towards stimulating the interviewee to reflect on the issues under study. Again, at the one end of this dimension are structured interviews with (or without) presenting ways of answering; at the other end are interviews stimulating narratives about a process related to the issue of the study. For interviews based on **interview guides**, this dimension should be taken into account in how the proportion of open and structured questions is designed or in the decision about working with structured or closed questions at all.

Attitude and method: the interviewer as a constructing listener

The dimensions mentioned so far can be linked to the interviewer's attitude toward the interview and the interviewee. However, they are also relevant in selecting and using a specific method of interviewing and designing a specific way of doing an interview with it. This book pursues an approach to carefully reflecting on whether to do interviews or not, how to prepare the relation to the interviewees and the situation of doing the interview, which format of interview to choose and then how to design the use of that interview format and to tailor it to the issue and the potential participants as far as possible. If we understand the interviewer as a constructing listener as outlined in Chapter 2, the decision to choose a specific method of interviewing is a crucial step in constructing the framework for the interviewees to explore their expectations and knowledge and to formulate them in their own words, and according to what the issue of the interviews means for them and also how it is structured for them. If this framework is closer to the interviewees' words, meanings and experiences, their part in co-constructing the knowledge in the interview will be much stronger than the interviewer expects or thinks. At the same time, methodological formats of interviewing can support interviewers and make the planning of the collection of data easier for them. In the next step, we will briefly outline some of the existing formats of interviewing, which will be described in more detail in later chapters.

Formats of Interviewing

In what follows, I will discuss several interviewing formats to outline the range of alternatives for doing interviews according to (1) their degree of structuring the topic, (2) the relation of asking questions and stimulating narratives in the interview, (3) their orientation towards working with individuals or with groups, and (4) their conceptualization for specific settings and target groups.

Structured interviews

The structured interview is also discussed as the standardized interview. The idea is to develop a set of questions along with a number of answers to select. The aim is to create a research situation in which all interviewees are confronted with the same situation, questions and answers, and to reduce the influence of the individual interviewers on the data (what is said in the interview). Questions are developed from nailing down the issue of the study to specific aspects or from a theoretical model. They are often closed-ended (allowing little choice for the interviewee in how to respond) and consist, for example, of five or seven alternatives in tick-boxes.

This format of interviewing is often used in survey research which refrains from sending out a questionnaire to potential participants. Instead, the questions are asked in interview and the answers are ticked by the interviewee or by the interviewer. The first aim is to increase the response rate, i.e. the number of participants, compared to mailing a questionnaire and waiting for it to be sent back. The second aim is to work with bigger numbers of participants than in other interview studies. And the third aim is to be able to process a statistical analysis of the answers more easily.

Sometimes questions are more open-ended, and the interviewees are given a couple of lines where they can put down some notes or keywords. But most of what is discussed in this book, about how to design the interview situation and the relations to participants in an interview, does not apply directly to structured or standardized interviews. Wordings and meanings in these kinds of interviews are closer to the interviewer's background, and the aim is rather to collect facts than to stimulate reflection on the interviewees' side. Structuring and standardizing the data collection are prioritized over openness for the interviewee (see Chapter 9).

Semi-structured interviews

Turning the issue of the study into a set of questions is also relevant for semi-structured interviews. However, here the idea is mostly that we need several kinds of questions, ranging from open questions, to which interviewees can respond in their own words and without being given a number of specific answers, to, at the other end, structured questions which present a stronger focus on what is relevant and sometimes even a set of possible answers. In between we find semi-structured questions, with a strong focus on what is asked but no predefinitions of how to answer. The aim behind this method is again (1) to break down a complex issue into more simple or easy to grasp questions. (2) The dramaturgy of dealing with the issues is developed in a specific logic of questions and their sequence. (3) For this purpose, an interview guide is prepared for the study, which will also support comparison of the interviews. (4) The main challenge is to make the appropriate choice between various formats of (open, semi-structured, closed) questions and to use the questions developed flexibly in the interview situation. The focused interview developed by Merton and Kendall (1946) is a prototype for this kind of interviewing (see Chapter 9).

The interview formats briefly outlined so far are constructed around using several kinds of questions and vary in the degree of openness and structuration in the questions and in the interview guide that is prepared. Interviewees' reflection on and openness of the situation are prioritized over collecting facts and standardization of the data collection. How far the data collection is driven by the interviewees' meanings and wordings and how open the situation is, depend very much on the way the interviewers use the interview guide and how they probe in the dialogue (see Chapter 9)

Target-group-specific semi-structured interviews

The interviews briefly outlined so far have not been created for specific target groups, but they can be applied to all sorts of people in all sorts of situations. The development of target-group-specific interview methods might be necessary in some areas such as for children or very old people, but we can find examples in other areas too. **Expert and elite interviews** are designed with specific target groups in mind. They are mostly based on semi-structured interviews but adapted to the needs and knowledge of the participants. Often, they are applied in addition to interviews with a different target group for collecting additional information. For example, you may interview homeless adolescents about their life circumstances and experiences on the street and then do complementary expert interviews with social workers about the problems and numbers of adolescents concerned, about responsibilities and support for them and so on. In the expert interviews, you may be interested in collecting facts and figures, but again it is important to meet the interviewees on the level of their own words and concepts and to stimulate some reflection in the interview (see Chapter 10).

Episodic interviews

The narrative interview (see below) focuses on the overall narrative of a longer biographical process, which should be recounted in the interview as a whole. Questions and knowledge beyond processes and narration are not focused in the main part of the interview but at the end (see also Chapter 12). In many studies, the biographical process or the life history as a whole is not necessarily the focus, but rather certain developments and situations in which changes have occurred. Beyond the process, such a study may also focus on the meaning of specific things or events. For such a purpose, the idea of stimulating narratives has been taken up in the episodic interview.

However, the focus is on small-scale narratives (Flick, 1997, 2000) of episodes and situations, in which a change was experienced – for example, a diagnosis was communicated to the interviewee. Different from the narrative interview, questions of meaning are also relevant in the episodic interview – such as: What does 'cancer' mean? What does the interviewee link to this concept? Therefore, such an interview focuses on smaller stories than the narrative interview and combines the narrative approach with a conceptual, question–answer-oriented approach (see Chapter 11 for details). In the narrative parts of the interview in particular, experience-near presentations in the interviewees' words, based on the reflections stimulated in the interview, are in the foreground. Less so are facts and a clear structure of the issues of a study as seen by the interviewer.

Specific Settings of Interviewing in Context

Narrative interviews

The narrative interview (see Chapter 12) goes in a different direction than other interviews. It refers less to the narratives that occur in interviews in general, and more to a methodology originally created by Schütze (1977) in Germany. The narrative interview aims at stimulating a comprehensive narration of a longer period or process (of education, of illness, of migration) and letting the interviewee recount this process without being directed or disturbed by interviewers' questions or comments. Interviewing here is embedded in the context of an overall narrative. The idea is that such a narrative will produce data that are much closer to the interviewee's experiences and meanings. The narration will include more details and relations than a set of questions could (see Chapter 12).

Although the term 'narrative interview' appears in the methodological literature in various ways, the original method is not much discussed in English-language publications (exceptions are Flick, 2018a; Jovchelovitch and Bauer, 2000; Rosenthal, 2004). Here the openness of the interviewees' wordings, meanings and experiences is much more the driving force than the idea that interviewers should structure the interviews. The expectation is that the story develops its own dynamic and structure if we let the interviewees recount their memories and experiences. Telling a story of one's life will make the interviewees reflect about what happened and what it meant for them and their lives. The interviewer's questions should only be part of the final section of the interview, once the narration is finished. In the interview, wordings and meanings can be expressed in the interviewees' own words in an experience-near way. The structure comes from interviewees and the process of narrating they get involved in and less from the researchers' questions. Reflections are more the focus than facts that may be reported but also may be misrepresented (see Chapter 12).

We find three more trends of taking the interview out of the rather closed setting of two people talking in an office about an issue and embedding it in a specific context (see Part IV). In the preceding parts of this chapter, I have discussed interviews with individuals, for which the above methods have been developed.

Individual and group-based interviews

If an individual's statements, narratives or responses are to be more contextualized, it might be helpful to do interviews in groups and to transfer the methods to using them with several participants. Thus, we find suggestions for narratives in families, which are collected with the whole family at once (see Hildenbrand and Jahn, 1988). Merton and Kendall (1946) had originally conceived the focused interview as an individual interview but then transferred it to their concept of focus groups.

As Patton (2015) and Fontana and Frey (2000) emphasize, this led to an approach of doing group interviews. A little later in Germany, the idea of group discussions became prominent. Whereas the group interview is meant to contextualize individual participants' statements, a group discussion is linked to the expectation that the group dynamic will draw the participants out of their shells and make them say things they would conceal in a face-to-face interview. A focus group is currently seen as something in-between – providing a stimulating context but not necessarily provoking participants to say things they would like to keep to themselves.

However, group interviews are less oriented to the individual participants' meanings, wordings and experiences than individual interviews. They may save time compared to doing single interviews with every participant, but research experience shows that the price is a lot of organizational extra effort to bring the group and its members together at the same time and in the same space (see Chapter 13).

In the context of indigenous research methodologies, Chilisa (2020, pp. 255–6) discusses 'indigenous focus group interviews' based on inviting participants into talking circles running through several rounds. Starting from her critiquing traditional focus group (interviews), Chilisa places a strong emphasis on giving all members a chance to be heard.

Interviewing in the field

A second setting is to integrate formal or informal interviewing in ethnographic data collection in the field. Formal interviewing means that you meet someone in the field and arrange an extra appointment for doing an interview with this person (perhaps based on one of the methods discussed above). Informal interviewing means that you do a spontaneous interview on the spot with that person immediately, or integrate it into walking with the person through the field (see Chapter 14).

Online interviewing

The trend of doing interviews in one or other online setting has been advanced in times of lockdown and social distancing, when face-to-face interviews are not possible. Telephone interviews have a longer history, but Skype, Zoom or Webex have become popular digital platforms for doing qualitative interviews as well. Here not only does the lack of direct contact with the interviewee have to be taken into account but also the advantages of it (such as being able to do interviews over long distances, for example). Email interviewing has its limits and advantages, too. In all these contexts, it should be considered carefully whether every or a single specific method of interviewing can be transferred to online contexts (see Chapter 15 for more details).

Principles and Practices of Interviewing

This chapter was intended to give an initial overview of methodological alternatives for doing interviews to support you in choosing an approach and in preparing your interviews. Later chapters will discuss interview methods in more detail for their 'how-to' aspects. Methods such as those mentioned above define the principles for orienting research. They have to be applied in contact with the participants and that means they have to be turned into practice. With each of the principles and formats of interviewing discussed in this chapter, the researcher constructs a specific context for listening to what the interviewee has to say, to answer questions or to recount as experiences.

This means, again, that the issues discussed in the other chapters become relevant for using these methods. First, the more general issues of designing interviews (see Chapter 5), of selecting and finding interviewees (see Chapters 6 and 7), and of working in a reflective and ethically sound way with them (see Chapter 8) require consideration, as do, secondly, aspects of how to fine-tune the use of the selected method of interviewing (see Chapters 9–15) for collecting data and for doing a meaningful analysis of the data (see Chapter 16).

Selecting a Method for Interviewing

A central decision in designing and doing interview research refers to which kind of method you will use or lean on. The most important alternatives are presented in chapters in Parts III and IV in more detail. Here we can frame this later discussion with some guiding questions for selecting a method. These questions should refer to your expectations about what insights a specific method of interviewing will be able to provide into your field of research and how the interviewees will talk about it. With your decision for or against a specific method, you will construct a framework for listening to what the interviewees and the field will have to tell you about your issue.

The first point of reference for this decision should be your research question. You should reflect how far a specific interview type allows the essential aspects of the research question to be addressed. This includes the kinds of questions to be asked, the ways of telling a story the interview aims at, as well as the setting for the interview (face-to-face, Skype, digital or mobile).

A second point of reference for selecting the interview type centres around the potential interviewees and how far the specific way of asking and expectations of how to respond fit their situation and capacities. Is the interview type appropriate to the target group? For example, a specific period of ill health may make it complicated to recount one's life history, and more focused types of questions may be more appropriate. What fears, uncertainties and expectations of (potential) interviewees should be taken into account? How far will the interview type allow the interviewees to present their views within the framework of the questions?

And a third point of reference should be the interviewers and their ability to apply the interview type and to cope with the manner of response in the interview – from long narratives to long periods of silence on the interviewee's side. The details of the decisions briefly mentioned here will be spelled out in chapters referring to ways of conducting interviews in Parts III and IV of this book.

Box 4.1   Research in the real world

Deciding between online and offline designs for interviews

A team of LGBT and health researchers from several universities in the US (Wilkerson et al., 2014) were studying a hard-to-reach population in the field of gay and lesbian studies. Their research focused on (1) how the 'use of sexually explicit media (SEM) influences sexual risk behavior in men who have sex with men (MSM)'; (2) 'the characteristics and sexual behavior of nontransgender men who have sex with transgender persons'; and (3) 'experiences of family among polyamorous parents and their children using personal accounts collected via email-based interviews' (2014, p. 562). Wilkerson et al. offer a helpful list of questions for deciding between online and offline designs for interviews (2014, pp. 569-71). This list includes considerations referring to administrative (e.g. skills in the team, money for travelling and transcription), population (e.g. skills, literacy and access to Internet) and data collection (e.g. barriers to online use, confidence and sampling) issues. Beyond the pragmatic and conceptual reasons, another motivation for doing interviews online is a fascination with using this medium and modern computer technologies for one's research.

What You Need to Ask Yourself

The questions in Box 4.2 are designed to help you in your decision about which form of interviewing might be best for your research. You may also apply these questions to studies with interviews you read. If you lack detailed knowledge at this point, this chapter should have provided you with a taste of what to expect from reading the following chapters in this book.

Box 4.2   What you need to ask yourself

Formats and principles of doing interview research

1.   Do I see the differences between the interview formats presented here?
2.   Have I developed an idea of what these various formats could be applied to?
3.   Do I see any differences in these formats in what they expect from the interviewee?
4.   Do the general principles outlined at the beginning of this chapter apply to all the formats in the same way?

What You Need to Succeed

This chapter should have given you an overview of some general principles of interviewing and of the variety of formats and methods of interviewing. The questions in Box 4.3 should help you to check what you take away from this chapter for the subsequent chapters, in which this overview will be expanded on.

Box 4.3   What you need to succeed

Formats and principles of doing interview research

1.   Do I recognize that there is more than just asking questions to doing interview research?
2.   Do I understand that there are a variety of methods for doing interviews?
3.   Do I have a basic overview of the field of interview methods and their, sometimes, differing principles?

What you have learned

- A variety of interview formats and methods are available for doing interview research.
- They share some common features in principle but differ in their focus and strengths.
- This overview should help you to select a method for your study and to contextualize what is spelled out in later chapters in more detail.

Exercises

In the exercises, you are first invited to reflect on some of the main issues of this chapter. Then you are invited to apply the topics of this chapter to the development of a project of your own. Hence, the exercises are a combination of reflection and prospection.

Exercise 4.1

Reflecting on the Chapter: The Use of Interviews in an Existing Study

1. Try to set up a table for comparing the methods that were covered in this chapter: for example, their target group, their main principles, the weaknesses you see, etc.
2. Try to reflect on what the framework outlined in Chapter 2 means for the methods mentioned in this chapter.

Exercise 4.2

Planning Your Own Research with Interviews

1. Think of your own study and reflect on which of the methods discussed might fit and which will not. What are the reasons for your answers?

What's next

In this article, the idea of experience-near and distant concepts is spelled out:

Geertz, C. (1974). 'From the Native's Point of View': On the Nature of Anthropological Understanding. *Bulletin of the American Academy of Arts and Sciences*, 28(1), 26–45. doi:10.2307/3822971

In this book, the principles of qualitative research are discussed in great detail:

Flick, U. (2018). *An Introduction to Qualitative Research* (6th ed.). London: Sage.

In this article, storytelling as a narrative method in indigenous research is discussed:

Cunsolo Willox, A., Harper, S.L., & Edge, V.L. (2013). Storytelling in a Digital Age: Digital Storytelling as an Emerging Narrative Method for Preserving and Promoting Indigenous Oral Wisdom. *Qualitative Research*, 13(2), 127–47. https://doi.org/10.1177/1468794112446105

II

DESIGNING INTERVIEW RESEARCH

Part I of this book should have given you a sound introduction to the background and foundations of doing interview research. In this second part, we address the phase of planning and designing interview research. First, in Chapter 5, we will address the concept of design in qualitative research and interviewing to construct *a framework for listening* in the planned interviews. Here we will also introduce the *six F's of designing interview research*, which will be the basis for later steps and chapters. In this context, we will also focus on research questions and some basic designs of qualitative (interview) research.

In Chapter 6, we will turn to the steps of selecting and sampling potential interviewees. Several suggestions for how to design the sampling of your study will be addressed as well as the question of when you reach saturation and what this concept means.

In Chapter 7, the focus is on how to find the interviewees you would like to have in your sample. Accessing and recruiting form a practical approach to making your plans for sampling work.

The issues in these chapters are the challenges faced in the planning of your interview study, but they may become relevant too when you are doing your research, for example when sampling and access have to be adapted while you are collecting your data with interviews.

Doing Interview Research Navigator

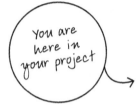

You are here in your project

How to understand interview research

- What doing interview research means
- Theories and epistemologies of interviewing
- When to choose interviews as a research method
- Methods and formats of interviewing

Designing interview research

- Planning and designing interview research
- How many interviewees: Sampling and saturation
- Accessing and recruiting participants

How to conduct interviews

- How to respect and protect: Ethics of interviewing
- Semi-structured interviews: Working with questions and answers
- Interviewing experts and elites
- Integrating narratives in interviews: Episodic interviews

Doing interviews in context

- How to work with life histories: Narrative interviews
- Working with focus groups as interviews
- Ask (in) the field: Ethnographic and mobile interviewing
- Doing online interviews

How to work with interview data

- Working with interview data
- Credibility and transparency: Quality and writing in interview research
- From interviewing to an inner view: Critiques and reflexivity

PLANNING AND DESIGNING INTERVIEW RESEARCH

How this chapter will help you

You will:

- see the role of research questions for doing interviews and for which kinds of questions interviews are appropriate,
- understand how interview studies are designed,
- be introduced to several alternative designs for doing interviews,
- have an idea of the resources you need for doing interview research,
- see how and why the traditional setting of interviewing has been extended, and
- learn how interview guides are designed.

Designing an Interview Study as Constructing a Framework for Listening

Several aspects of your research will be decided by the design of your interview study. In concrete terms, the researchers construct a setting and define who they can listen to and how the interviewees may express their views and experiences, their opinions and their stories. In designing interview studies, the researchers have the chance not only to turn methodological and epistemological criticisms of interviewing into concrete steps but also to attend to improvements in doing interviews, for example by taking diversity or cultural differences among the participants or between interviewer and interviewee into account. In the research design, the interviewer transcends the role of listener, even of active listener, and becomes a constructing listener. That is why the research design in interview research includes much more than just solving technical problems. It is the step which sets the epistemological stage for the interview to unfold and for the interviewer and the interviewees to become the protagonists of the interview story.

Designing Qualitative Interview Research – What Does it Mean?

'Interviewing does not happen by chance but is designed by researchers' (Brinkmann, 2013, p. 45). Brinkmann illustrates the relevance of research designs as an issue in interview research, which highlights the difference with everyday conversations. But what is the meaning of the term research design? Some authors, such as Creswell and Poth (2017), label approaches or research programmes in qualitative research as research designs and see grounded theory or phenomenology, for example, as research designs. The term 'research design' is often associated with quantitative research. In that context, it has often mainly referred to controlling and evaluating research – for example, a control that ensures no external influences raise doubts that the evidence found in a survey or experiment can really be assigned to what was studied. In qualitative research, the term has often been rejected or neglected, but it is now attracting more attention (see Flick, 2018d; Marshall and Rossman, 2016). Here, as well as in more recent discussions in social science in general, the term refers to planning research (not only to controlling it). Ragin sees research design as 'a plan for collecting and analysing evidence that will make it possible for the investigator to answer whatever questions he or she has posed' (1994, p. 191) and emphasizes that 'design' refers to 'almost all aspects of the research'.

This concept of planning a study beforehand is one understanding of research design that is also relevant to interview research. However, we find reports of research showing that plans are often good, but the process of research does not stick to them, as Howard Becker mentioned some time ago:

> No matter how carefully one plans in advance, research is designed in the course of its execution. The finished monograph is the result of hundreds of decisions, large and small, made while the research is under way, and our standard texts do not give us procedures and techniques for making those decisions. (1965, p. 602)

Blaikie and Priest (2019) discuss designing research in a context wider than the one in this book. They suggest a framework which can be helpful for our conceptualization of designing interview research (see Table 5.1).

For Blaikie and Priest (2019, p. 36), a research design will have to answer three basic questions: What will be studied? Why will it be studied? How will it be studied? For the last question, they specify five further questions: What is the logic of inquiry? What are the epistemological questions that are adopted? Where will the data come from?

How will the data be collected and analysed? When will each stage of the research be carried out? Blaikie and Priest develop four research design tasks – *focusing* the purpose of the study (e.g. the problem to be studied, the questions to be answered), *framing* (logics and epistemologies), *selecting* (data types, forms and sources) and *distilling* (the timing and doing of collecting and analysing data and answering the questions).

Table 5.1   Questions and tasks in designing research

Three basic questions a research design will have to answer		Four research design tasks
1. What will be studied?		1. *Focusing* the purpose of the study (e.g. the problem to be studied, the questions to be answered)
2. Why will it be studied?		2. *Framing* (logics and epistemologies)
3. How will it be studied?	Broken down into five further questions:	3. *Selecting* (data types, forms and sources)
	• What is the logic of inquiry? • What are the epistemological questions that are adopted? • Where will the data come from? • How will the data be collected and analysed? • When will each stage of the research be carried out?	4. *Distilling* (the timing and doing of collecting and analysing data and answering the questions)

Based on Blaikie and Priest (2019, p. 36)

The Six F's of Designing Interview Research

In our approach of seeing the interviewer as constructing listener, we can develop this concept of design tasks a bit further with *the six F's of designing interview research*. *Finding* refers to selecting the appropriate participants and sorts of data collection (i.e. the concrete type of interviewing). *Focusing* here means also identifying a topic and questions to be answered. *Framing* means to construct a culturally sensitive and diverse framework in which these questions can be answered and the interviewees have maximum leeway for exploring the issues of the topic in, for them, the most adequate way. *Foreseeing* means that the design construction should be based on anticipating the steps and issues to come up and the decisions to be taken to maximize this leeway. *Foregrounding* means to define the research setting in a way in which aspects are located at the centre of the interview that are most elucidating and also those that the interviewee was not necessarily aware of as being relevant – thus making the implicit explicit. It also refers to the kinds of statements and details that are identified in the data – the answers in the interview, which may lead to second questions, and the statements in the transcripts of the interviews. *Formulating* means, first, the way questions and conversations are formulated in the interview – which type of interview is used, which kinds of questions are asked and how; second, it refers to the way the findings in the material are elaborated, structured and presented in the analysis and the presentation of the research.

Table 5.2   The six F's of designing interview research

The six F's of designing interview research	
Finding	• To select the appropriate participants and sorts of data collection (i.e. concrete type of interviewing).
Focusing	• To identify a topic and questions to be answered.
Framing	• To construct a framework in which these questions can be answered and the interviewees have maximum leeway for exploring the issues of the topic in, for them, the most adequate way.
Foreseeing	• The design construction should be based on anticipating the steps and issues to come up and the decisions to be taken to maximize this leeway.
Foregrounding	• To define the research setting in a way in which those aspects are located in the centre of the interview that are most elucidating and also those the interviewee was not necessarily aware of as being relevant – thus making the implicit explicit. • Which kinds of statements and details are identified in the data – the answers in the interview, which may lead to second questions, and the statements in the transcripts of the interviews?
Formulating	• First, the way questions and conversations are formulated in the interview – which type of interview is used, which kinds of questions are asked and how. • Second, the way the findings in the material are elaborated, structured and presented in the analysis and the presentation of the research.

The aim of this chapter is to provide a solid grounding for planning an interview study and for making the decisions mentioned by Becker before and during a project. For that purpose, we will address issues such as how to formulate a research question, which basic designs can be used in interview studies, how interviews can be integrated into more complex designs, and how to select the appropriate form of interviewing. A final point will be the design of questions for an interview guide. More generally, the chapter will outline the path from research interests to research questions of the interview and, finally, to designing questions for the interview.

The Process of Designing Interview Studies

Designing interview studies is often seen as being embedded in a process of several stages. King and Horrocks (2010), for example, discuss four major steps. The process begins with (1) framing the research question (see below) and continues with (2) choosing the type of interview to use for answering it (see Chapters 9–15 here). The second step was discussed before (see Chapter 4 here). Their third step is to define the sample and recruit the participants (see Chapters 6 and 7 here) and the fourth stage is to develop an interview guide (see below and Chapters 9 and 11). The first and fourth steps will be discussed in some detail later in this chapter, whereas sampling and recruiting are issues of later chapters.

Rubin and Rubin (2015) suggest a more elaborate model of research design, starting from (1) picking a topic (which is interesting) to (2) formulating a research question, and (3) checking whether the project based on it is practical and feasible. Their fourth and fifth stages are to locate where to do the research (4) and with whom (5). The final steps in this model are to decide on the initial questions (6 – the interview guide) and to 'work out ways to ensure the accuracy and thoroughness of the data' (7 – additional questions to ask in subsequent interview if necessary).

What to study? Preparing interviews

What are the stages you will run through on your way to the encounter with your interviewees?

First, you need to identify a topic and a theme you want to study and clarify what the theme is in detail. An example of such a theme could be long-term unemployment. In this step, you should look through the literature to check whether this theme is a topic similar to what has been studied in other projects with interviews. The examples of research questions in the preceding chapters may be helpful.

Second, you should reflect on the relevance of this topic in two respects: (1) why is the topic relevant in general – is there a gap in the literature and in research concerning this topic? For example, what is known about immigrants' long-term unemployment and their situation? (2) Why is this topic relevant for you – relevant enough to invest quite some time and energy in doing a study about it? This second aspect is important to clarify, particularly if the topic is not your own idea but, for example, assigned to you for doing a master's or PhD thesis. In our example, what do you see as relevant enough in the situation of long-term unemployed immigrants to devote your time, energy and inclination for a long period to studying this topic? Clarifying this point is not only important for maintaining your own enthusiasm but also for being able to ask the 'right' questions in the later interviews.

Third, you should reflect on what specifically you will study, for instance by identifying a specific community of immigrants in our example. The fourth step then is to consider what will be relevant from the case and in the case – for instance, what would you like to know about long-term unemployed immigrants with a Russian background? This may include clarifying what the comparative perspective is: for example, to understand this community's particular situation compared to that of the majority of society's members who are unemployed.

Fourth, it would also be helpful beforehand to reflect on whether the topic is something that can be addressed with interviews – by asking individuals to describe their situation. How might this topic and the situation be studied, addressed and expressed by interviewees?

Fifth and finally, who should be interviewed and why? Which competences should be assigned (Holstein and Gubrium, 1995, p. 21) to potential interviewees or which competences should we assume that they have? Assumptions refer to why someone would be the right person to be interviewed – maybe they have had the particular experience you want to address in the interview, and are familiar with the field (the community), the situation (of being unemployed) or the practices under study (of coping with unemployment). These assumptions by the interviewer make someone a candidate for being interviewed. Asking yourself these questions before the interviews and reflecting on them may seem a bit speculative but it will be important for clarifying what you are looking for in your interviews and from whom you expect answers.

Research Questions

Research questions are the most important aspect of a research design. We have already addressed research questions for interview studies in the first few chapters. There, however, the focus was on giving you an idea of what kinds of research questions there are and how they might be pursued in interview research. Now we will give you some advice on how to develop a research question as part of the design of your interview study. Generally speaking, the precise formulation of the research question is a central step when you conceptualize your research design. Research questions often have their source in the background of the researchers' personal biographies or their social contexts. Sometimes a personal experience leads researchers to decide to study a topic. One example is provided by the observations that Arlie Hochschild made of interactions in her childhood, when visitors with various cultural backgrounds came to her parents' house: this led to Hochschild later developing an interest in studying the management of emotions empirically (Hochschild, 1983).

One of the most important aspects of research questions is whether you manage to translate a general or personal interest in a topic into a question that can be studied and answered empirically. In our context of interview research, this means whether you have a question that can be answered by asking and responding or by telling a story, for example. If you decide on a concrete research question, certain aspects of your field will be brought to the fore, whilst others will be regarded as less important and (at least for the time being) left in the background or excluded. For instance, the decision over the research question will be crucial in the case of data collection through single interviews. Research questions should be examined critically as to their origins (what has led to the actual research question?). They are points of reference for checking the soundness of your research design and the appropriateness of the methods you intend to use for collecting and interpreting your data. The case study in Box 5.1 looks at existing studies and where their research questions came from.

Box 5.1   Research in the real world

Constructing research questions: Spotting gaps or problems

More generally, but empirically, Sandberg and Alvesson (2011), two organizational researchers in the field of business working in Australia and Sweden have analysed ways of constructing research questions and found two major alternatives – gap-spotting or problematization. They analysed 52 published studies in the field of organization research. In their analysis, they show that gap-spotting is a major source for formulating research questions for new studies. Gap-spotting means that gaps in the literature or in research are identified. Three basic modes of gap-spotting were found. 'Confusion spotting' means that competing explanations for the same phenomenon coexist and further empirical clarification is needed. 'Neglect spotting' refers to overlooked areas in research, under-researched fields or lack of empirical support for some explanations. 'Application spotting' refers to the extension or complementation of a theory to other fields. Sandberg and Alvesson see gap-spotting as the dominant way of identifying a research question for further studies, but see their second mode of identification as the more promising alternative. Problematization means that not only is a lack of research taken as a starting point but also a questioning of what is taken for granted: 'A central goal in such problematization is to try to disrupt the reproduction and continuation of an institutionalized line of reasoning. It means taking something that is commonly seen as good or natural, and turning it into something problematic' (2011, p. 32). So, with reference to their own area (organization studies), they demonstrate the emergence of new research questions between lacks and gaps, on the one hand, and raising problems in what seems to be evident on the other hand. This study is interesting for elucidating the sources and motivations for research questions but does not clarify how research questions are nailed down as questions that can be empirically pursued.

How are research questions constructed? In the case study in Box 5.2, a number of research questions that were pursued in semi-structured interviews are developed in concrete terms.

Box 5.2   Research in the real world

Construction of research questions

Agata Vitale and Judy Ryde, two researchers in clinical psychology at Bath University in the UK, present a study (Vitale and Ryde, 2018) in which they intended to

(Continued)

understand how to conduct in-depth, semi-structured interviews with male refugees regarding their mental health and integration after they have been granted their refugee status. They started from the observation that research in this area was either too broad in its focus on refugees or only addressed women or children. They 'used the small amount of existing literature in this field to start developing our research questions' (2018, p. 3). Pragmatic reasons for focusing on male refugees' mental health soon after they receive their status resulted from one of the authors' impression from her practical work that 'male refugees, more than females, struggle with mental health issues'. They see their study as an exploratory one with the aim to develop community intervention for improving 'male refugees' mental health and integration after they receive their status' (p. 3). They summarize their research questions in the following list: (1) What are male refugees' immediate experiences having been granted their status? (2) How does this affect their mental health and their integration in the host country? (3) What type of support is available to them? (4) What are their suggestions regarding the type of interventions needed to promote their mental health and integration? In this case study, the research questions were constructed after identifying a gap (male refugees being under-researched) and with a practical purpose in mind (improving their mental health support). The research questions were focused on the participants' views and thus formulated with interviewing them in mind.

Good and bad research questions for interviewing

What characterizes a good research question for interview studies? First of all, you need an actual *question*. For example 'The living situation of homeless adolescents in a West European country' is an interesting issue, but is not a (good) research question, as it is too broad and non-specific for orienting a research project. Implicitly, it addresses a variety of subgroups – and supposes that homeless adolescents in the UK and Germany, for example, are in the same situation. Also, the term 'living situation' is too broad; it would be better to focus on a specific aspect of the living situation – for example, their health problems and the use of professional services. Accordingly, it would be better to formulate a research quest such as: 'What characterizes the health problems and the use of professional services of adolescents in a West European country like Germany?' Here, we have a real question (What characterizes ... ?), a focus on two topics (health problems and use of services) and a clear local focus (Germany). Thus, the issue has been turned into a research question.

Neuman (2000, p. 144) identifies five types of 'bad research questions': (1) questions that are non-scientific questions, for example: 'Should adolescents live on the streets?'; (2) statements that include general topics, but not a research question, for example: 'Treatment of drug and alcohol abuse of homeless adolescents'; (3) statements that include a set of variables but no questions, for example: 'Homelessness and health'; (4) questions that are too vague or ambitious: 'How to prevent homelessness among adolescents?'; (5) questions that still need to be more specific, for example: 'Has the health situation of homeless adolescents become worse from their point of view?' King and Horrocks (2010, pp. 26–7) emphasize that the scope of a research question for an interview study should not be too broad, and should also have an eye on the resources available for the project. They also problematize 'in-built presuppositions' in research questions. For example, a research question such as 'What are the feelings of immigrants after experiencing daily racism practices?' has built in two presuppositions: that immigrants experience racism and that this racism consists of daily practices. It would be better to pursue the research question: 'How do immigrants experience reactions to their new life circumstances?' for example. Here, the above presuppositions are not built into the question.

These examples show the importance of having a research question that is really a question (not a statement) that can indeed be answered in interviews. It should be as focused and specific as possible instead of being vague and non-specific. All the elements of a research question should be clearly spelled out instead of remaining broad and full of implicit assumptions. To test your research question before you do your study, reflect on what the possible answers to that question would look like. Once you have formulated your research question, you will turn it into a concrete research design. However, as King and Horrocks (2010, pp. 26–7) discuss, the research question of a study may shift during the project. Maxwell (2012), with an eye on research design, distinguishes between generalizing and particularizing research questions. The first are extending an issue and the knowledge existing about it (e.g. does a finding from one group of participants also apply to another group?), whereas the second take a narrowing focus (e.g. what is the specific role of a specific aspect?) Maxwell also argues that the design of a study is not necessarily the consequence of a research question, but the result of an interaction between the purposes, research questions, methods, concepts and validity claims of a study.

In the next step, we will look at the basic research designs (see also Flick, 2018a, 2018d) which can be used for this purpose. We will mainly address case and comparative studies and longitudinal and multimodal designs for their role and potential in doing interview research.

Case Study Research

What is a case? This question is still debated after Ragin and Becker's (1992) collection of articles presenting various versions answering it. Argumentations on a methodological level move between case studies (consisting of one case – see Stake, 1995) and case-oriented research (Sandelowski, 1996). Case studies can consist of one case that is studied – ranging from one life history (of one person) to one institution or community or city. Case-oriented research can consist of several cases of people being interviewed but stresses maintaining the focus on each of the people as cases in their own right. Then the structure and particularity of each case is focused on before taking a comparative perspective on single aspects across participants. For example, we might focus on chronic illness in the context of the single interviewee's biography and recon-struct developments in their life and illness before comparing such reconstructions or interviewees. Or we may focus on specific aspects of chronic illness in a comparative perspective right away – for example, several participants' illness concepts or coping strategies. The first alternative – illness in the context of biography – is a case-oriented approach.

For our discussion on designing interview research, the concept of the 'case' becomes relevant in two respects. A major view is that cases are found and sampled in a population. Say, for example, Mr X is a case in our sample and is characterized by specific features – his age, his living situation, his experiences and so on. He is sampled together with other cases characterized by the same or different features – variation in gender, age, living situation, etc. In such an understanding, we refer to cases that *exist* and are only found, picked and collected by researchers for a study.

The second understanding starts from assuming that cases are *made* by the research and for it. By defining our research interest – e.g. a specific chronic illness in a spe-cific age range (say 20–30 years) and a specific living situation (say without a flat, without a job) – we construct and turn someone into a case. We also turn a number of people with these features into a more general case for the research – although the individuals themselves perhaps would not see much in common among them. In our practices, starting from formulating research questions to decisions about the nature of the phenomenon under study and methodological choices of how we design the study and the methods of collecting data, we define, create and construct the cases that we study. This process is described as 'casing' in the literature, follow-ing Ragin (1992) and Sandelowski (2011). Ragin sees casing as a 'research tactic' in which researchers 'concoct' (1992, p. 217) cases for managing complexity. Cases are not found by researchers but delimited and declared (1992, p. 217) and thus made or constructed. This process of casing also includes the fact that cases can be in a state of 'shifting' in the research process and over time, so that researchers may have a clear understanding of what their case is only at the end of their study or maybe have a different understanding of it once they have run through their study.

Comparative Studies

Interviewers often aim at listening to a variety of views or experiences of the issue under study. The seeds of comparison in interviewing are first of all set in the com-position of the participants who will be interviewed. Comparison can be planned in several ways. First of all, we can aim at comparing interviews for specific content (statements, descriptions, accounts) given by all or most of the interviewees (see Chapter 16). This would imply a cross-sectional approach to the material and a focus on having statements in the interviews that are rather similarly collected. On a meth-odological level, this would be realized with an interview guide and questions that are asked in a similar way and in every interview. The focus for analysing the material would then be on comparing statements from each interview and on **coding** (see Chapter 16) these statements.

According to Lewis and McNaughton Nichols (2014, p. 65), comparison can help to identify the presence or absence of topics in interviews from several groups, the difference in how people from various groups mention or explain specific phenomena or the differences in which a topic emerges or is experienced. In the case study in Box 5.3, the comparison of interviewees focused on one aspect, supported by sampling participants in two groups who were very similar in other respects.

Box 5.3   Research in the real world

Designing a comparative interview study of women's health concepts

This study was conducted by two psychology students, Beate Hoose and Petra Sitta, for their diploma thesis, and pursued the research question of whether concepts of health and illness are cultural phenomena or not. To answer this question, they looked for cultural differences in the views of health among Portuguese and German women. Therefore, they selected interview partners from both cultures. To be able to trace differences in the interviewees' health concepts, they kept as many other conditions in the cases as similar as possible; for example, participants had similar living conditions in as many respects as possible (big-city life, professions, income and education), so that any differences might be related to the comparative dimension of 'culture'. The study was planned as an exploratory one, so that the number of cases in each subgroup might be limited. The design of the study was a comparative one: two groups of women were compared for a specific feature – their health and illness concepts. The planning of the interviews focused on the development of current health and illness concepts in the interviewees' biographies. (See Flick, Hoose and Sitta, 1998)

In the case study in Box 5.3, comparison was made over a distance – interviewees in several locations were included and compared. Comparative studies can also be based on a series of case studies (see above), which are analysed one after the other and then compared. Then, keeping the cases as similar as possible, as described in the above example, is not necessary. Rather than comparing participants for their features (such as living conditions, for example), the results from analysing the cases will be the material for comparison. Finally, comparing cases can be oriented on comparison over time – how views and experiences change or have changed in a process. One way to realize this kind of comparison is located within the single interviews, when researchers look for similarities and differences in how an issue is mentioned by the interviewee referring to different periods or situations.

Longitudinal Designs

The most consistent way to analyse comparison in interviews is to plan this right away and to use a longitudinal design. Here we can again distinguish two forms. Prospective longitudinal designs are applied in parallel to a development or process. Their main feature is the repeated collection of data, in our case repeated or multiple interviews with the same interviewees over time. Retrospective longitudinal designs focus on developments or processes that have already occurred. In most cases, this design is realized in one interview, based on asking the interviewee for one longer or several shorter narratives and to recount a process – of migrating, for example. Finally, combinations of both forms can be designed, starting with a retrospective (narrative – see Chapter 12 – or episodic interviewing – see Chapter 11) and continuing with one or more additional interviews after a lapse in time.

Prospective longitudinal designs

The great strengths of a prospective **longitudinal study** are that (1) researchers are able to document changes of views or actions through repeated data collection cycles; and (2) the initial state of a process of change can be recorded without looking at it from the perspective of the situation at the end of the process (see Box 5.4).

The central feature of prospective longitudinal designs is that they include more than one episode of research (see Lewis and McNaughton Nichols, 2014, p. 64), for example several interviews or several follow-up contacts after the first interview. How many of these episodes are necessary and whether the methods in each episode have to be the same depend on the concrete issue and target group of the study. In many cases, the second interview will be adapted and focus on developments since the first interview. In the initial sampling (see here Chapter 6), a bigger number of participants should be included than in a single episode study for two reasons. First, a loss of participants between the first and following interviews may occur for several reasons. For example, participants may lose interest – research fatigue – may move or their contact details may change without them giving notice to the researcher. Second, not all first interviews may be interesting to follow up, or not all interviewees may fit as much as expected into the study, so that the researchers may decide to reduce the number of interviews for follow-ups. A major challenge in prospective longitudinal research is maintaining contact with the participants. Schedules for calling them that are too tight and with too frequent follow-ups may lead to aversive reactions, while schedules that are too loose increase the risk of losing contact.

Neale (2019, p. 5) distinguishes the timeframe of a longitudinal study – i.e. the overall time span in which it is conducted – from its tempo – i.e. the number, duration and frequency of field contacts. The author (2019, p. 47) emphasizes that a 'clear set of research questions at the outset' will help to navigate the process over time. The questions should focus on temporal processes, change or how events mentioned in the first interview have developed over time and influenced later circumstances. To understand a process, it will be helpful to have some kind of baseline, an event or a change (such as becoming a refugee) and a process building on it (e.g. transitioning into regular work in the new country). Neale (2019, p. 48) gives examples of research questions from a longitudinal study of young fatherhood: 'How and why do young men enter into early parenthood? How is young fatherhood constituted, practised, and understood in varied socio-economic and personal circumstances? How is young fatherhood "worked out" over time?' (2019, p. 48). Read (2018) uses the term of 'serial interviews' with the same interviewees over time for better understanding participants' life histories and changing perceptions (2018, p. 1).

Box 5.4   Research in the real world

Researching homelessness in a longitudinal design

In a study about transition through homelessness in Scotland (McNaughton, 2008), '30 participants were re-interviewed at 6 month intervals for 18 months after the first interview for exploring changes in their situation and the factors they attributed to them' (Lewis and McNaughton Nichols, 2014, p. 63). To keep in touch with the participants, the researchers collected different types of contact details (email, telephone, etc.), 'obtained consent to contact significant others in the participants' lives' (p. 63), and kept a low-level (telephone) contact between the interviews, for example. In the end, they were able to successfully re-interview 28 of the 30 participants after 18 months.

Biographical retrospective designs

The turn to qualitative longitudinal research is rather recent and not common in the mainstream of designing interview studies. More prominent has been the use of retrospective designs focusing on biographical and life-history approaches. Here, the process under study is mostly covered in one interview, in which the interviewee is asked to recount how their life has developed as a patient, as an immigrant, as a teacher. The perspective is retrospective from today to earlier events. Well-developed methods in this context are the narrative interview created by Schütze (1977 – see Chapter 12) and the episodic interview (Flick, 2000, 2018d; see Chapter 11). In both types of interview, narratives are central (in the narrative interview) or a major part of treating an issue. For the success of this kind of retrospective research, the formulation of good narrative stimuli and questions is decisive (see for details Chapter 11). It is also important to consider whether the process in focus can be revealed in biographical or situation-related narratives and if the interviewees have access to the knowledge and experience necessary to recount the processes.

So far we have considered a number of basic designs of qualitative research which are relevant and can be used for doing interview research in a classical design with interviews as stand-alone methods. In the next step, we will look at current extensions of this classical design and ways of integrating interviews in wider and new contexts.

Extending the Classical Design of Interviewing

The classical design of interviewing can be characterized as an interviewer and interviewee meeting face-to-face, on the one occasion, in a confined room such as an office, and where the study methodology consists of interviews only. Longitudinal research with repeated or serial interviews has been discussed above as a first extension of the classical design of interviewing. A second way of extending the classical design is to combine interviewing with other methods in the context of triangulation and mixed methods.

Triangulating interviews with other qualitative methods

Triangulation means using several approaches in the study of a phenomenon, for example several methods, various types of data or theories (see Flick, 2018b). In the beginning, triangulation was seen as a strategy of confirming what was found with one method by the results of a second method, for example interview findings with survey outcomes. Although this understanding is sometimes still used, the discussion about triangulation has advanced to seeing it as a strategy for extending the knowledge coming from a study by using several approaches to a phenomenon under study. We find triangulation of interviews with other qualitative approaches like **ethnography** (where interviewing becomes embedded in the 'master' strategy of ethnography – see Chapter 14) or with methods like participant observation or focus groups. Fielding (2018) and Flick (2018a) address specific issues of triangulating online data with physical data, for instance online and face-to-face interviews (see Chapter 15). In general, these examples illustrate that triangulation has become an issue beyond assessing the quality of results and rather an element of designing qualitative studies.

For example, you can use interviews in triangulation with observation in several ways. In a study about developing gendered identities, researchers could start with observations in classroom situations at school for episodes in which gendered identities become visible. Then the study continues with interviewing some of the participating students for their concept of gender differences and gender-specific ways of building relationships, for example. Observations can be pursued in parallel or recommence after the interviews. This brief example illustrates some of the design issues around triangulating interviews. First of all, there is the sequence and connection of the methodological approaches. Starting with observations allows exploring the field for an orientation for developing the questions and the interview guide.

Second, in the observation, ideas about whom to select for an interview can be developed. The selection (see Chapter 6) might focus on students among those who were observed or go beyond that group – in other classes or beyond school. If the students for the interviews are selected from the observation participants, the triangulation of data and results can be made on the level of the single case (see Figure 5.1). This allows relating the same individuals' statements in interviews to observed practices. Sometimes this direct link is not possible for all cases, for example because some interviewees could not be observed or not all participants in the observations could be interviewed. In this case, we can apply the triangulation to the level of the data sets and link the trends we found in the interviews to those resulting from the observations. Of course, we can combine both forms of triangulation in studies in which we can link the single cases and look at the links on the level of the data sets as well.

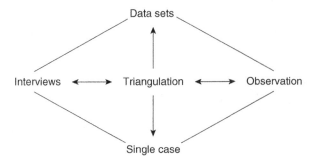

Figure 5.1   Levels of triangulation in interview research

As said before, we can use the insights from the observations for developing or refining the interview guides. We can also use the findings from the interviews as an orientation for the observation – what, whom, when, which situations, and so on. to observe. Our brief example can be modified for using other 'second' methods instead of observation, for example by analysing documents as a data source. But what has been said for interviews and observation would be relevant for using triangulation as well.

Interviews in mixed methods research

Triangulation refers to combining all sorts of methods (depending on the issue and the study), for example several qualitative methods. Mixed methods is used as a label for the same idea but confined to combining qualitative with quantitative methods. In the literature on designing mixed methods research, we find suggestions for the parallel use of qualitative and quantitative research, for example interviews and questionnaires being applied at the same time. A second suggestion is to use 'phase designs' (Creswell, 2003), in which qualitative and quantitative methods are applied separately one after the other, no matter in which sequence. In our context, this means beginning with interviewing and continuing with questionnaires or turning the sequence the other way round. An extensive discussion can be found about which method should be dominant or less dominant: is the central method of a study a specific kind of interviewing with questionnaires only applied in addition, or are some interviews conducted in the context of a mainly quantitative study? More elaborate mixed methods designs link both kinds of research in all phases of the research process.

If interviews are the first method, a quantitative survey could be the second. Basically, all that has been said before about designing triangulation with interviews can be transferred to using them in the context of mixed methods – the mutual inspiration of what to ask in each of the methods, the sequence of using the methods and the links on the single case or on the data set level. Which of these suggestions should be applied, and how, depends on the research question of the study. The example in Box 5.5 links mixing interviews with quantitative methods in a longitudinal design.

Box 5.5   Research in the real world

Studying attention deficit/hyperactivity disorder (ADHD) with interviews in a longitudinal mixed methods design

Mirka Koro-Ljungberg and Regina Bussing did the following study while they were working in the field of human development and organizational studies in education, at the University of Florida in the US. Their article (Koro-Ljungberg and Bussing, 2013) is based on their study entitled 'ADHD detection and service use'. It employed mixed methods with a qualitative longitudinal part based on interviews and was 'designed to describe elements and experiences that have helped or hindered help-seeking for ADHD for two underserved groups: girls and African American youth with ADHD' (2013, p. 427). The qualitative part of the 10-year study ran for five years. The authors discuss, on the one hand, methodological adaptations in the qualitative part along the way and the need for methodological continuities, on the other. They see the need for 'unique methodological solutions and iterative uses of methods that suit particular research situations. These methodological solutions are often results of processes in which methods and data, purposes, and practices inform each other.' The study used mixed methods in a parallel mixed methods design including quantitative and qualitative research cores: 'Typical of parallel mixed methods studies, our qualitative research core was independent yet linked with the quantitative core.' The authors describe how the longitudinal design of using interviews had to be adapted also because of the needs and progress of the quantitative part of the study. It was based on the ADHD Treatment Perception Survey, which was informed by the insights gleaned from the interviews.

Mixed methods: opportunities for decolonizing methodologies

In the context of decolonizing methodologies and indigenous research, the concept of mixed methods has been taken up as well (see Chilisa, 2020, Chs 7 and 8). Moewaka Barnes and McCreanor (2022) discuss the decolonizing of qualitative research in general. Cram (2022) focuses on designing indigenous qualitative research for policy implementation. Adamson (2022) discusses specific aspects for designing qualitative research for studies in Asian contexts, and Schöngut-Grollmus and Energici (2022) in Latin American contexts.

So far, we have addressed extensions of the classical interview design on methodological levels – longitudinal designs with interviewing over time and repeatedly, triangulation of interviewing with other qualitative methods, and mixed methods designs of qualitative interviewing and quantitative methods. Next, we will discuss extensions of the interview setting – first, to the world 'out there' and then to digital realms.

Designing mobile interview research

This extension attracts attention and means taking the interview out of a defined local setting (a room, an office, the interviewees' homes) and accompanying the interviewees on a walk through their neighbourhoods or an area relevant for them and the topic of the study. The interview is conducted while walking through this area:

> Various kinds of mobile conversation ('go-along,' 'bimble,' and walking interview) … provide a means to take the interviewing process out of the 'safe' confines of the interview room and allow the environment and the act of walking itself to move the collection of interview data in productive and sometimes entirely unexpected directions. (Jones et al., 2008. p. 6)

Carpiano (2009) uses neighbourhood-walking tours in two neighbourhoods with residents to study the role of local areas in shaping health outcomes. He mentions that go-along can be used with different formats of interviewing, mainly open-ended formats, letting the participants comment on whatever they see fit, or in a semi-structured format, which can be potentially more conversational in nature. The method will be discussed in more detail in Chapter 14 as part of interviewing in the field, but some of the design-oriented decisions will be mentioned here. First, on choosing the setting, Evans and Jones mention: 'The most important choice that researchers must make when designing walking interviews is whether the route is set by the interviewer or the interviewee' (2011, p. 850). In the first alternative, the interviewer has more influence on where the interview is conducted, and what it refers to, whereas the second alternative, leads more into the interviewees' life worlds.

Finally, we find a number of combinations of mobile and other methods: Pawlowski et al. (2016) triangulated go-along interviews with qualitative observations, GPS tracking and accelerometer data for recording the speed of walking. Stals et al. (2014) combine go-alongs with photography, GPS tracking, emotion mapping and EPR (Emotional Route Planning). And Flick et al. (2017) triangulated go-along interviews with interviewing the same participants with more traditional methods and more common settings such as offices (see Box 5.6 for another example).

These examples (see more in Kusenbach, 2018) illustrate some of the design challenges resulting from this mobility turn in interviewing. They also show the flexibility in using such an approach for developing the scope of doing interview research (see Chapter 14).

Box 5.6   Research in the real world

Studying students' perceptions of sexual health resources in a walking interview design

This becomes evident in a study carried out by a research group from the University of Minnesota, US. Garcia et al. (2012) used this kind of interviewing to obtain college students' contextualized perceptions of sexual health resources: 'Seventy-eight undergraduate students showed and described the resources on and near five campuses in a Midwestern state' (2012, p. 1395). Their study demonstrated:

> The dynamic nature of the interview was also demonstrated in the diversity of routes participants chose and the amount of movement that took place within the interview. The loosely structured interview guide was designed to encourage this open-ended, iterative process while maintaining the focus of the interview on sexual health resources. (2012, p. 1398)

Designing digital interview research

As we saw in Chapter 1, the development of interviewing as a social science method has always been influenced by technological progress. One of the more recent developments is to do interviews in the context of digital research. Here we can distinguish several forms of digital interview research.

The first form is doing interviews online (see Salmons, 2015). Here only some design issues are discussed, while more details will be outlined in Chapter 15. Online interviewing (see O'Connor and Madge, 2017) can be organized in a synchronous form, which means that you get in touch with your participant, for example in a chatroom, and directly exchange questions and answers while you and the interviewee are both online at the same time. This comes closest to the face-to-face interview. But online interviews can also be organized in an asynchronous form, which means that you send your questions to the participants and they send their answers back after some time and you are not necessarily online at the same time. In both cases, you can do interviews by email. Where do you find your participants for an email interview? The easiest way is to contact people whose email address you already have or whose email address you are able to retrieve (from their own website or from that of their institution, such as a university). You can also use snowballing techniques (see Chapter 6), which means that you ask your first participants for the contact details of other potential participants for your study.

However, you will face several problems in pursuing these methods. First, using these ways, in some cases, will mean you have only limited information, such as people's email address or the nickname they use in discussion groups or chatrooms. In some cases, you will know no more about them, or have to rely on the information they give you about their gender, age, location, and so on. This may raise questions of reliability of such demographic information and lead to problems of contextualizing the statements in the later interview. Markham (2004) discusses doing interviews online but without seeing the interviewee and being unclear about the interviewee's gender. In contrast to face-to-face interviews, in online interviews the supposed interviewee may have delegated the task of answering to someone else or run the draft responses past someone else for approval before sending them to you. This may contradict one of the major aims of interviewing – to elicit the spontaneous and subjective views of the interviewee – without giving the interviewer the chance to become aware of this. The more recently available conferencing platforms (Zoom, Webex, Microsoft Teams) provide a visual level in doing the interview, but the main problem – that there is no personal contact with the interviewee – remains (see Chapter 15).

The second form of digital interviewing is via social media (see Flick, 2018a, Ch. 22). This can range from finding your participants via Facebook, Twitter or blogs to actually doing the interview in the context of Facebook (see Chapter 15). We can distinguish three basic ways of doing social media research on the level of designing interviews. (1) We might study social media, the use and the consequences and experiences related to them. Using interviews developed in other contexts would be the choice for such research. Social media are then the issue of research or part of what the issue of the study is. For example, you could do interviews with users of a social media platform, asking about experiences and evaluations of social network building with social media. The interviews are then conceived as in other contexts and the research design is linked to what we have to take into account in other areas. (2) Social media can be used as a tool for analysing practices in their use, and to design a methodological approach for this kind of study, also by doing interviews with users. (3) We can use social media as a tool for analysing wider social problems. We also find examples in the literature about using Twitter for doing interviews (see the case study in Box 5.7).

The third form of digital interviewing is less principally and more pragmatically motivated, for example with the aim of reaching participants over longer distances without traveling. Using telephones, mobiles or Skype for doing the interview raises a number of questions (see Chapter 15 for details).

Box 5.7   Research in the real world

Using Twitter as a research tool

Bonnie Stewart is a social media researcher at the University of Windsor in Ontario, Canada. She sees her study in the context of 'traditional ethnographic methods adapted for a geographically distributed digital-communications-based study' (Stewart, 2017, p. 254). Her interest was in her participants' academic use of Twitter. The focus was first on using social media for inviting potential participants, with a call for volunteers distributed on several social network sites, mainly Twitter. Stewart describes Twitter as a 'valuable platform for research into decentralized non-gate kept professional cultures' (2017, p. 254). From the respondents to her call, she selected 14 participants from the US, Canada, Europe, Latin America, Africa and Australia and 'eight "exemplar" identities' (p. 256) who were ready to have their Twitter profiles assessed by the participants. Her participants also agreed to be openly identified in the research by their public Twitter use. Stewart applied participant observation for which she created a specific Twitter account for observation, from which she observed several times per day how 'participants presented themselves, engaged with others and shared their work and that of other people' (2017, p. 257). Stewart tweeted in a limited way but used Twitter as a performative space. Participants were in addition asked to select a 'representative 24-hour period' of their network activities and inform the researcher when this period was going on or had just finished. In studying these 24-hour reflections, Stewart extended her focus to other platforms on which the participants were active (such as Instagram). The participants made available some short reflective documents with screen captures of their activities within that period. Furthermore, the study includes 'profile assessments' of the eight exemplary identities concerning the assumed influence of the persons described in these identities. Finally, Stewart did 10 Skype interviews with participants (not on Twitter) during the process of participant observation after a few weeks. The transcripts of the interviews were collated with the reflective documents provided by the participants and analysed by coding.

Designing Interview Guides

After deciding to use one specific type of interview (see Chapter 4), the next step in designing interview research is to design the interview guide or more generally the instrument to work with. Most interviews are based on guides and questions (see Chapter 9), but some methods of interviewing are based only on one question aiming at stimulating a life history narrative (see Chapter 12), for example. How to design these questions in detail depends on the specific method and will be outlined in more detail in the later chapters. Here, I will discuss some more general principles for designing questions and an instrument for interviewing. First of all, research questions are not the questions you will ask in the interview. A research question such as 'How do adolescents cope with the diagnosis of a chronic disease?' will have to be broken down into concrete interview questions to ask (e.g. 'how was the situation for you when the doctor told you that you have asthma?') and areas to cover with concrete interview questions for answering the research question. For this purpose and if you work with an interview guide, you will identify areas (e.g. diagnosis, treatments, fears, consequences) for which you will formulate concrete questions. Even if the interview does not necessarily develop according to your guide and its structure, you should develop a guide beforehand. It should be based on some kind of logic, for example oriented on the process of finding out (e.g. about a diagnosis), the reactions to it (e.g. fears), consequences for daily life (e.g. attending school), evaluations, strategies of coping, plans for the future, and so on. This will help orient you to the topic and the situations you will be confronted with in the interviewees' accounts. If you work with a 'one question' narrative interview, you should develop such a question.

In both cases – working with interview guides or with the one question – you should prepare for the situation that your questions in the interview guide or the narrative fail to lead to the answers you require, because they lack detail, involvement, and such like. For this purpose, it is helpful to develop 'second questions' for directing the interviewees' account into more detail and so on. You should also make provision for probing, to push for details and clarification, if the treatment of the issue remains too superficial.

The preparations mentioned so far refer to the questions and interview guide and need to be adapted to the specific type of interviewing you plan to apply in your study. In general, however, you should prepare a framework for the interview, including how to begin the interview and how to end it. You should reflect on what information to give the interviewee at the beginning, how to welcome the interviewee, how to start the conversation and how to transition from small talk into the actual interview. In ending the interview, give the interviewee the chance to add things omitted in your questions. It is also helpful to prepare your goodbye and your request to re-contact the interviewee if necessary.

Resources

Any calculation of the resources you need for doing your interview project strongly depends on the concrete circumstances of your study, such as the type of interview, the features of the interviewees, travel requirements, and so on. The following suggestions can only give a rather rough guideline, but they should raise your awareness around reflecting on your available resources and planning your study accordingly. For a realistic plan for an interview project, I recommend making a calculation of the activities involved which assumes, for example, that an interview of around 90 minutes will need as much time again for locating interview partners, organizing appointments, and travel (see Chapter 6). For calculating the time for transcribing interviews (see Chapter 16), the estimates will diverge depending on the precision of the system of transcription in place. Morse (1998, pp. 81–2) suggests that for transcribers who write quickly, the length of the tape containing the interview recording should be multiplied by a factor of four. If checking the finished transcript against the tape is also included, the length of the tape should be multiplied by a factor of six. For the complete calculation of the project, Morse advises doubling the time allowed for unforeseen difficulties and 'catastrophes'. If you plan a project that will work with transcribed interviews, you should use a high-quality device for the recordings.

In this chapter, we have discussed the major issues involved in planning and designing interview studies. In the step of designing the study, the interview and the use of the method in it, you construct a framework that will allow you to listen to the interviewees in an adequate way and will give them the leeway to unleash their views on the issue and their situation. Staller and Chen (2022) give some advice on how to choose a qualitative research design in general, which is helpful for doing interview studies as well. In the following chapters, we will address the issues of selecting potential interviewees (see Chapter 6) and of how to find and win them over to participation (see Chapter 7) in your study.

What You Need to Ask Yourself

The questions in Box 5.8 are designed to give you some guidance on the decisions to take in designing interview research. If you feel you lack sufficient knowledge for making these decisions at this point, they will at least orient you on what to expect from reading the following chapters in this book.

Box 5.8 What you need to ask yourself

Designing interview research

1. What is your research topic and why is it relevant (for you or in general)?
2. What are your research questions and how did you construct them?
3. What is the role of single cases in using interviews in your study?
4. How will you undertake comparison in your study?
5. How will you take time and process into account in designing your interviews?
6. Will you use interviews as a stand-alone method or in combination with other methods?

7. Where and how will you do your interviews, in a mobile context for example?
8. What good reasons are there, if any, for doing your interviews online or via Skype?
9. How did you decide on the specific way of doing interviews (method, context) in your study?
10. How did you develop your interview guide and questions from your research questions?
11. Did you reflect on whether your resources fit your plans for doing interviews?

What You Need to Succeed

This chapter has spelled out the concept of designing qualitative interview research as a major step in constructing a framework for listening in the actual interview and the idea of the six F's of designing qualitative interview research as a guideline. The following box (Box 5.9) summarizes the main points of this chapter about designing interview research.

Box 5.9   What you need to succeed

Designing interview research

1. Do I understand why designing interview research is a major step for doing it successfully?
2. Am I aware of the role of research questions for doing interview research?
3. Do I understand the basics of designing an interview guide?

What you have learned

- Doing interviews is based on a process of planning and designing interviews.
- This includes preparations such as clarifying the topic and its relevance on several levels.
- The most important step is to construct and clarify a research question.
- Interviews can be used in case studies or case-oriented research.

(Continued)

- Longitudinal designs are increasingly used in interview studies.
- Interviews can be applied as a stand-alone method or as part of a more complex design.
- Interview research has been extended in two directions: to doing interviewing online and to interviewing in the context of mobile methods.
- Designing interview research also includes deciding on a specific method and developing an interview guide and questions for the interview.

Exercises

In the exercises, you are first invited to reflect on some of the main issues of this chapter. Then you are invited to apply the topics of this chapter to the development of a project of your own. Hence, the exercises are a combination of reflection and prospection.

Exercise 5.1

Reflecting on the Chapter: The Use of Interviews in an Existing Study

1. Look through a journal for a qualitative study based on interviews (e.g. Wood et al., 2020). Try to identify which form of interview was used in it and how the authors designed their study.
2. Consider the study's questions and then improve them by using one or more of the interviewing methods presented in this chapter.

Exercise 5.2

Designing Your Own Research with Interviews

1. Think of your own study. Formulate a research question and develop a design for the study.
2. Design a first version of an interview guide for your research question.

What's next

This short book is focused on the practical issues of how to design qualitative research:

Flick, U. (2018). *Designing Qualitative Research* (2nd ed.). London: Sage.

This article addresses the issue of research design for the area of qualitative social work research:

Shaw, I., Ramatowski, A., & Ruckdeschel, R. (2013). Patterns, Designs and Developments in Qualitative Research in Social Work: A Research Note. *Qualitative Social Work*, 12(6), 732–49.

This article addresses the design of mobile interviews in health research:

Garcia, C.M., Eisenberg, M.E., Frerich, E.A., Lechner, K.E., & Lust, K. (2012). Conducting Go-along Interviews to Understand Context and Promote Health. *Qualitative Health Research*, 22(10), 1395–403.

This article gives some advice on selecting research designs:

Staller, K., & Chen, Y. (2022). Choosing a Research Design for Qualitative Research: A Ferris Wheel of Approaches. In U. Flick (Ed.), *The SAGE Handbook of Qualitative Research Design*. London: Sage.

The following articles discuss specific aspects of designing qualitative research in Asia and Latin America:

Adamson, J. (2022). Designing Qualitative Research for Studies in Asia: Decentering Research Practices for Local Norms of Relevance. In U. Flick (Ed.), *The SAGE Handbook of Qualitative Research Design*. London: Sage.

Schöngut-Grollmus, N., & Energici, N.-A. (2022) Designing Qualitative Research for Studies in Latin America. In U. Flick (Ed.), *The SAGE Handbook of Qualitative Research Design*. London: Sage.

This chapter discusses research design in the context of indigenous research:

Moewaka Barnes, H., & McCreanor, T. (2022). Decolonising Qualitative Research Design. In U. Flick (Ed.), *The SAGE Handbook of Qualitative Research Design*. London: Sage.

Doing Interview Research Navigator

How to understand interview research
- What doing interview research means
- Theories and epistemologies of interviewing
- When to choose interviews as a research method
- Methods and formats of interviewing

Designing interview research

- Planning and designing interview research
- How many interviewees? Sampling and saturation
- Accessing and recruiting participants

How to conduct interviews
- How to respect and protect: Ethics of interviewing
- Semi-structured interviews: Working with questions and answers
- Interviewing experts and elites
- Integrating narratives in interviews: Episodic interviews

Doing interviews in context
- How to work with life histories: Narrative interviews
- Working with focus groups as interviews
- Ask (in) the field: Ethnographic and mobile interviewing
- Doing online interviews

How to work with interview data
- Working with interview data
- Credibility and transparency: Quality and writing in interview research
- From interviewing to an inner view: Critiques and reflexivity

HOW MANY INTERVIEWEES? SAMPLING AND SATURATION

You will:

- see the difference between selection and sampling,
- understand the close link between sampling and access,
- deal with sampling and saturation in several contexts of doing interviews in general,
- see the various forms of purposive and theoretical sampling,
- understand snowball sampling,
- see the steps between having an idea through to sampling and having the right participants,
- understand that ideas about the perfect number of participants are relative.

Constructing a Framework for Listening

In this chapter, we continue to spell out the framework for doing interviews outlined in Chapter 2. Here we address how researchers construct the variety of voices from the field to listen to in their interviews by sampling participants. Selecting the 'right' participants is important for listening to the 'best' versions of experiences or knowledge from the field for understanding and analysing the issue under study and for answering the research question. At the same time, researchers organize their access to the voices they need for understanding the complexity of their issue and their field. For the principles of designing interview studies (*the six F's of designing interview research*; see Chapter 5), sampling is the way to *finding* participants, to *focusing* on the central aspects and views, as well as to *foregrounding* relevant experiences and knowledge for the analysis. It also provides the basis for *framing* the analysis in an elucidating comparative approach. One issue to keep in mind here is how to take the individual, social and cultural diversity of perspectives in the sample of a study into account and how to do justice to integrating diverse perspectives in a study. At the same time, sampling builds on *foreseeing* who or which groups may be most instructive for the study and its findings, before we *formulate* the principle behind our sampling strategy. In the next chapter (Chapter 7), we will focus on how to recruit people for interviews and what it means to be recruited as a participant. This current chapter begins with an orientation about the various locations in the research process where sampling becomes relevant beyond selecting participants for interviews.

Sampling in the Process

Sampling will become relevant at different stages in the research process of an interview study in a number of decisions you will take (see Table 6.1). Sampling refers to the decision about which persons you will interview (case sampling) and from which groups these should come (sampling groups of cases). Furthermore, it is related to deciding with which of the interviews you should continue to work – that is, which ones you will transcribe and analyse (material sampling). During your interpretation of the data, sampling becomes relevant again when you decide which parts of a text you should select for interpretation in general or for a particularly detailed interpretation (sampling within the material). Sampling becomes an issue yet again when you present your findings: which cases or excerpts from transcripts are best for demonstrating or illustrating what you found in your study (presentational sampling)? Finally, sampling is also an issue for the transferability of results: which fields are selected for checking and demonstrating how far the findings of a study work.

Table 6.1 illustrates these sampling decisions for interviews. The understanding behind these illustrations is that sampling for interviews focuses on the persons you want to work with, whereas in observations it is rather situations you will look for as 'material units'.

In this chapter, we focus on the first part of the sampling process outlined in Table 6.1. The second, third and fourth steps will be discussed later (in Chapter 16 on analysing and Chapter 17 on presenting and transferring findings from interviews).

Table 6.1 Sampling decisions in the process of working with interviews

Stage in research	Sampling decisions	Example for interviews
While collecting data	Case sampling	Selecting an interviewee
	Sampling groups of cases	Selecting a group whose members you should interview about your issue
While analysing the data	Sampling material	Selecting an interview for (beginning) the analysis
	Sampling within the material	Selecting statements or excerpts from the interview to analyse in more detail
While presenting the findings	Presentational sampling	Selecting statements and interpretations for illustration or evidence
While transferring the findings	Transferability sampling	Selecting fields for applying the results and for checking if they work

Selection and sampling

In most studies, sampling to find interviewees consists of two steps. First, a group of people is *selected* relevant to the topic under study. Coming back to our earlier example (see Chapter 1), the health problems of marginalized and vulnerable people can be studied for a number of groups, for instance people who are long-term unemployed, or migrants, very old, very poor or homeless. The first decision is to select a group for your study, for example homeless people, as in the study of Stolte and Hodgetts (2015). This kind of selection can also refer to choosing a field for the study, for example homeless people in London. Then the next step is to *sample* cases from this selected group who will be interviewed. At the end, one or two of these cases will be selected again for the presentation of findings in an article (Stolte and Hodgetts, 2015 – see the case study in Box 1.2). Thus, we can distinguish selection (of a group, etc.) from the sampling of cases for interview.

Selecting groups or fields and sampling cases in the end determine not only whom you will have spoken to during your interview process; they are also an issue that is relevant for assessing the quality of your study. Here we may think of generalization and representation – what can you infer from your findings for other people in similar conditions whom you did not interview, or for a population in general? These questions are mainly driven by a quantitative logic of research. More interesting in qualitative studies in most cases is the question of how far you managed to talk to the 'right' people – in extreme cases to the 'right' person for answering your question and your research question in general. It will also be relevant how you manage to take the social and cultural diversity (of migrant or indigenous communities, for example, compared to majority perspectives) into account when analysing a social phenomenon.

How to Sample Interviewees

We find a number of attempts at clarifying the concept of sampling in qualitative research. One line of distinction is sampling in quantitative research versus sampling in qualitative research based on the logic of research behind the two approaches. A second line is to distinguish selection and sampling as above, although these terms are sometimes used as synonyms. Here, a distinction between the two concepts will be suggested. For a first clarification, let's use an example. If an interview study is pursued with the aim of understanding how people live with a chronic illness, we first of all will not pursue the idea that the findings will be representative on a demographic level – all people, all people in Canada or all people with an illness. Rather, we are interested only in people with a *chronic* illness. Either the focus is on those people in general (e.g. suffering from different diseases, such as diabetes and chronic fatigue syndrome) or on those with a specific disease – a type of diabetes, for example. Such a distinction is based on the specific research question pursued in the study and is not (yet) a question of sampling. If our interest is in chronic illness in general, the first is decision is to define a specific case, which means at this point selecting one (or several kinds of) chronic disease and people living with it. We will define what counts as a chronic disease for our study, and what characterizes people who would be interesting as participants. We would also delimit such characteristics – for example, only people living in a city or only those living in rural contexts. Also, we would define how long someone should have suffered from the disease in order to be of interest to our study. Perhaps we would define other demographic features (having a family or living alone, age groups, professions, etc.). Finally, we might define the practical conditions of how to reach the potential participants in the context of our research project and resources. Should our interviewees live in the same city as we do, in towns we can reach by using public transportation or in our country, and should they speak our language, for example? Should participants come from the same communities as the researchers or how should diversity be taken into account in the sampling process? These decisions are based on practical issues. They do not yet address who will be part of the interviewees in the end. But they refer to selecting a population for the study, from which participants can be sampled, chosen and asked for participation. There are a number of basic strategies that can be distinguished. Many interview studies start by defining a sampling plan in advance.

Sampling Criteria Defined in Advance

For instance, we want to compare members of two groups for their experiences with a specific issue, such as palliative care. For this purpose, we interview social workers and nurses for their concept of end-of-life treatment. Then the *primary* sampling criterion is membership of one of the two groups. In such a case, often a number of *secondary* criteria are defined, for example the need to have *male and female* interviewees or specific institutional backgrounds in each group. In such a study, we have set criteria for searching and integrating concrete interviewees. These criteria have been defined before we begin to search cases and before we start interviewing. This approach can be complemented by two extreme situations: a complete collection or a single case study.

A complete collection

Sometimes the criteria defined in advance will allow us to interview all people meeting these criteria, so that we can apply a **complete collection** (see Flick, 2018a) or comprehensive collection (LeCompte and Preissle, 1993, p. 70) of all possible cases without drawing a sample from them. But then we should define the inclusion criteria (who is in the group) and the exclusion criteria (who is not in this group) carefully enough that the number of possible interviewees remains manageable.

In this context, another distinction made by LeCompte and Preissle (1993) may be relevant. They refer to **naturally bound groups**, for example all people with a certain characteristic (e.g. a university degree) living in one community. An **artificially bound group**, for example, consists of all physicians who are characterized by a certain specialization but live across the country. In artificially bound groups, it is much more difficult to include their members in a comprehensive sample than in naturally bound groups, where the boundaries are defined much more clearly.

A single case study

The other extreme is to select *only one interviewee* for the study, as in the case of Stolte and Hodgetts (2015 – see Box 1.2 in Chapter 1), because he or she is the only person who is able to provide the specific information aimed at in the interview study. This is often the case in studies based on doing expert and elite interviews (see Chapter 10). Perhaps here you only require one participant for your study. Sometimes there is only one of a kind if a number of expert cases with varying backgrounds are to be included. LeCompte and Preissle refer to this as 'unique-case selection' (1993, p. 75).

Purposive Sampling

In general, we can distinguish between sampling according to formal criteria (driven by the idea of representativeness, for example) and that in relation to substantial criteria (focusing on specific cases or groups). Qualitative research and interviewing in particular are mostly based on sampling according to substantial criteria (e.g. who has had a particular experience and should be interviewed about it?). In most cases, **purposive (or purposeful) sampling**, according to Patton's (2015) suggestions, is applied, which he defines as 'strategically selecting information-rich cases to study cases that by their nature and substance will illustrate the inquiry question being investigated' (2015, p. 265).

Extreme case sampling

Patton has made some concrete suggestions for purposive sampling strategies. The first is to approach the field under study from its margins, aiming at better understanding it as a whole. One strategy is to purposively sample *extreme cases*. In order to analyse the process of transition from one type of school to a different one, for example, particularly successful examples of such a transition are chosen and analysed. Or cases of failing transitions are selected and analysed for reasons of this failure. If you plan interviews with teachers about their perceptions of such success and failure, for example, you may sample interviewees with the longest experience in the field of teaching and those who have just recently started working within it.

In the context of management research, a group of researchers from the US (Bell et al., 2018) worked with a sample of extreme teams, such as disaster relief teams, special operations teams and astronaut crews (p. 2740), in order to analyse management challenges and processes in this specific context.

Typical case sampling

In a second strategy, we can approach the field from inside and from its centre. For example, we could select particularly *typical* cases (i.e. those cases in which success and failure are particularly typical for the average or the majority of cases). To return to our example, here you would try to find out how long people typically work in this field of teaching, and you would try to find interviewees meeting this criterion.

Variation sampling

The third strategy starts from the *assumed variation* in the field. For example, you could aim at the maximal variation in the sample. Then you would integrate only a few cases, but those which are as different as possible, in order to disclose the range of variation and differentiation in the field. In our example, you would look for people with very different lengths of service in the field, try to vary their professional backgrounds and the types of school where they work, for instance, or their gender if possible, or according to other criteria relevant to your study.

Intensity sampling

In the fourth strategy, we define a specific feature and look for cases according to the *intensity* of that feature (e.g. experiences, processes, and so on) that can be assumed for them. Either you choose cases with the greatest intensity or cases with different intensities and systematically integrate them into your sample and compare them. In our example, you could try to find those people who identify themselves most clearly with their work and those who view the work just as a job (as part-time teachers or teaching assistants, for example).

Sampling critical cases

The strategies described so far aim at identifying cases according to a structure in the field. Patton also suggests more case-specific approaches. The selection of *critical* cases aims at those cases in which the relations to be studied become especially clear (e.g. according to the opinion of experts in the field) or which are particularly important, in our example, for facilitating students' successful transition from one to another school. Here you would ask experts at which institutions or with whom you should do your interviews.

Convenience sampling

Patton also mentions **convenience sampling**, which means to select those cases that are the easiest to access. Sometimes this may be the only way to do a study with limited resources of time and people. Then you give up specific criteria for choosing interviewees in a field and do your interviews with those people ready to help you out. This may not be seen as the most valuable strategy of finding research participants but sometimes is the only one that works. Convenience sampling 'can be defined as reliance on participants who are readily available and accessible to the researcher', as Abrams (2010, p. 542), a researcher at the University of California, did for her study at the intersection of criminology and social work. But you should turn to convenience sampling only after other, more criterion-oriented strategies have not worked, or in addition to those strategies. Abrams discusses, for example, how her decision to study a specific hard-to-reach group (incarcerated youth) was theoretically well defined, but also how she turned to convenience sampling when the specific study participants were selected (2010, p. 545).

Patton's suggestions can be applied both before the interviews and the study take off the ground and during the process of the study, which is more often the case.

Theoretical Sampling

Theoretical sampling has been quite prominent in qualitative research as 'the' genuine sampling strategy. It has been developed in the context of grounded theory research by Glaser and Strauss (1967). Theoretical sampling is characterized by developing criteria for sampling and knowledge about the population the sample refers to in the process of research and theory development. It is driven by the state of analysing the data so far available and what is missing so far for (further) developing the theory. The original description of the strategy sees theoretical sampling as 'the process of data collection for generating theory whereby the analyst jointly collects, codes, and analyses his [sic] data and decides what data to collect next and where to find them, in order to develop his theory as it emerges' (1967, p. 45).

This description shows that 'theoretical sampling' originally meant the whole approach to collecting data and not only a way of selecting interviewees, for example (see Flick, 2018c for more details). In the further development of grounded theory research, the understanding of theoretical sampling has been specified. Morse (2007, pp. 234–41) suggests a model consisting of four steps, integrating theoretical sampling as one step. As the first step, she sees convenience sampling (see above), which means that (first) participants or situations are selected on the basis of accessibility. The second step consists of the purposeful sampling (see above) of participants who are selected as indicated by the initial analysis of the first interviews. The third step in Morse's (2007) model then refers to theoretical sampling, when participants are selected according to the descriptive or explanatory needs for further developing the emerging concepts and theory. As a fourth stage, Morse suggests doing theoretical group interviews for expanding and verifying the emerging model.

In a similar way Charmaz (2014, p. 197) has defined what theoretical sampling is not: sampling for addressing initial research questions, for reflecting population distributions, for finding negative cases, or until no new data emerge. According to these understandings, theoretical sampling becomes relevant only in the later stages of (grounded theory) research – when first cases have already been selected, first data collected and analysed and further cases and data are to be selected for refining the first set of categories and their properties. Thus, theoretical sampling is one strategy of sampling in a sequence of other strategies and it would be worth reflecting on whether it should be transferred to other studies using interviews while not aiming at developing a theory.

Theoretical saturation

The endpoint of theoretical sampling is when **theoretical saturation** has been reached. Theoretical saturation means that integrating more cases (such as further interviews) will not contribute new insights to the developing theory. It does not mean that there are no more people who could be interviewed, for example, but that there will no new knowledge for the theory result from interviewing them. Sometimes 'saturation' is used more generally, meaning that no new insights in general are expected from continuing with sampling and interviewing (see the case study in Box 6.1).

Box 6.1 Research in the real world

Sample construction as a process

Tim Rapley (2014) has presented an illustrative case study in medical sociology in the UK and describes a process of sampling in several rounds with varying aims. He studied families with children suffering from Juvenile Idiopathic Arthritis (JIA) and the question of why diagnosis is delayed in such cases. He had the chance to familiarize himself with the issue on the basis of several existing data sets (case notes) for preparing his own interview study. He began with an 'initial round of sampling (n=3)' (p. 53) in order to try and understand a first variety of different processes in dealing with this disease. Sampling focused on three typical cases. The second phase of sampling was a sort of convenience sampling in no particular order (p. 55), which led to interviews with eight families and in parallel with health practitioners, which means he had another 14 interviews. In the next step, he turned from new patients who were so far in the focus to established patients. These were suggested to him for interview by clinics' teams, which led to another six families and five health professionals. Sampling included 'intensity sampling' and 'critical sampling', in particular in a case where the parents were told the diagnosis but at the same time that nothing could be done in terms of treatment (p. 56).

In the fourth round, sampling 'shifted towards more conceptual development as well as focusing on some specific criteria' (p. 57). These criteria focused mainly on the link of the family to the NHS or on earlier significant diagnoses of the child, which led to another 17 cases. Finally, although thinking that theoretical saturation had been reached with the cases included, Rapley integrated a 'few more for luck' as he came across another two 'really interesting' cases suggested by the clinic staff. He summarizes the outcome of his sampling procedures:

> Over the life of the project, I conducted 36 interviews with families. I'd spoken to mothers (n=34), fathers (n=9), teenage patients (n=5), grandmothers (n=2) and an aunt (n=1). I'd also undertaken 11 interviews with professionals involved in the care pathway of these JIA patients: orthopaedic surgeons (n=4), paediatricians (n=3), a paediatric immunologist (n=1), a GP (n=1), a nurse (n=1) and one non-health professional (n=1) – a primary school teacher. (2014, p. 60)

This example is interesting as it shows how sampling develops and changes focus over the process and how a multifaceted perspective on the phenomenon under study is built along the way.

Snowball Sampling

Similar to what was discussed above as convenience sampling, the construction of samples is often part and result of the data collection process. **Snowball sampling** is a metaphor for describing how the researchers advance by asking interviewees to suggest the next interviewees to address.

Box 6.2   Research in the real world

Sample construction through snowball sampling

Christine Brickmann Bhutta, a researcher in religious studies from the Orange University in the US, discusses this technique for her studies using Facebook (see Chapter 15) as a sampling frame (for finding interviewees or examples) based on her definition: 'Snowball sampling is a chain-referral technique that accumulates data through existing social structures. The researcher begins with a small sample from the target subpopulation and then extends the sample by asking those individuals to recommend others for the study' (Brickmann Bhutta, 2012, p. 59).

Different from convenience sampling, snowball sampling is often based on defining criteria for the potential participants and only refers to finding people meeting these criteria, whereas convenience sampling is often driven by pragmatic criteria such as accessibility. However, for practical reasons, these two sampling strategies are very common in interview research.

Sampling in Indigenous Interview Research

The sampling strategies discussed here are also discussed in the context of indigenous research. Chilisa (2020, p. 212) mainly suggests reflecting on your sampling procedures in terms of how the 'ethnophilosophy, philosophic sagacity, cultural artifacts, and decolonization of interviews' are underlying your sampling decisions. However, she also suggests the following for the role of sampling in the context of transferability of the research and its results:

> *Dense Description.* Sampling alone does not provide enough information
> for those who read the research study to decide if findings are applicable to
> other settings. The researcher must provide dense background information
> about the research participants, research context, and setting so that
> those reading the study can determine if there are similar settings
> to which findings of the study can be applicable or transferable.
> (2020, p. 217)

This means you should write a description of the cases and the sample throughout your research – from selecting participants, to formulating a sampling strategy and also based on your findings – to allow your readers to locate your research with in its social and cultural context and the diversity covered in it.

Planning the Sampling for an Interview Study

The various ways of sampling interviewees discussed so far can be used in planning and doing an interview study, as outlined in Box 6.3. This use includes constructing a sampling framework which defines whom the researchers will be able to listen to as part of their study and the organization of the sampling process.

Box 6.3   Research in the real world

Planning the sampling for an interview study

Planning the sampling for an interview study includes suggestions for preparing (1) the sampling framework (kinds of data, general guidelines on sampling decisions and on the number of participants and saturation) and (2) how to proceed with the sampling for the interview study.

Steps involved in sampling for an interview study	Six F's of designing interview research
Reflect in advance again	
1. What is the research question behind the interviews?	Focusing
2. What kind of persons will be relevant as potential interviewees?	Foreseeing
Steps for preparing the framework for listening through sampling interviewees	
3. Reflect on what potential interviewees should know in advance before being ready to join your study. Start from what interviewees will perhaps already have experienced when contacted first.	Framing
4. Prepare to write a detailed description of the sample and of the single cases: Which information and dimensions should be covered to give rich detail on the (social and cultural) diversity in your study?	Finding and Formulating
5. Frame (in keywords) how to ask an interviewee for suggestions for other interviewees.	Framing
Steps for preparing how to proceed with the sampling	
6. Who would be the best person(s) to be interviewed?	Foreseeing

(Continued)

(Continued)

Steps involved in sampling for an interview study	Six F's of designing interview research
7. Which experiences of the interviewees would be of central interest?	Foreseeing
8. Which biographical events might provide information on the central topic(s) in the interviewees' cases?	Foregrounding
9. Phrase the criteria that interviewees should fulfil.	Formulating
10. Which comparative perspective would you take on interviewees?	Focusing
11. Which dimensions of social and cultural diversity should be represented in the sample?	Foreseeing
12. Note keywords about where you might find the 'ideal interviewees'.	Finding

On a practical level, the process outlined in Box 6.3 culminates in a question asked of most interview studies: How many interviews do I have to do and how many do I need to answer the research questions in my study?

Sample Size and Saturation: How Many Interviews?

The question of how many interviews you need is raised quite often, and discussed in the literature. One of the most intriguing questions for students doing their first project or doing their PhD research is how many interviews are enough for a project. A second question is what is the best, the adequate or the minimum sample size in a qualitative study with interviews. And a third question is, when we can talk about saturation of a sample, so that no more data need to be collected. We find a number of reflections in the literature on these questions.

Sample size

Ritchie et al. (2014, pp. 117–18) discuss seven issues that will help to determine sample size, such as the population's heterogeneity, how many selection criteria have been defined, how far 'nesting' of criteria is needed, which means how far criteria are combined. Other issues are centred around whether the research addresses 'groups of special interest that require intensive study' or asks for multiple samples within one study, and which types of data collection methods are used. A final issue is the available budget and resources for the study. The authors' discussion of these issues already demonstrates that size of samples in qualitative research in general and interview studies in particular depends very much on the concrete study.

Box 6.4   Research in the real world

Planning the sample size for a PhD study with interviews

Policy research analyst Mark Mason from Oxford Brookes University addressed the question of how big a sample should be in qualitative research from the angle of PhD students. He did a data bank survey of qualitative dissertation projects from several disciplines and pursued as a research question: 'How many participants are used in PhD studies utilising qualitative interviews? And do these numbers vary depending on the methodological approach?' (Mason, 2010, para. 23). As a result, he found that the average and also the expected numbers of participants in a qualitative dissertation project depend very much on which method was applied and on the disciplinary and institutional contexts in which the dissertation was done.

How many interviews are enough?

Baker and Edwards (2012) invited a number of experts on qualitative research from several fields and also some early career reflections to answer the question 'How many interviews are enough?'

The first answer found in most of the contributions is 'it depends' and that there is no rule of thumb (Brannen, 2012).

The second answer is that it depends in particular on the resources of the project and the researcher (Flick, 2012, 2018a), which means time, travel funds, maybe money (for transcription or incentives).

Third, the answer to the 'how many' question depends on the formal or structural conditions of the research. Many departments have regulations or an implicit agreement on how many interviews a master's thesis should be built on and how many more a PhD study should include.

Saturation of samples in interview research

Fourth, the concept of saturation is often the point of reference for answering the above question. But here, it is often forgotten that 'saturation' became prominent in qualitative research as 'theoretical saturation'. This kind of saturation does not mean that there are no more people to interview (or data to collect), but that further interviews (or data) will not add any substantial knowledge to a theory that has been developed on the basis of the data collected so far. This kind of saturation is not linked to the number of interviews but to the wealth and depth of insights provided by the data collected and analysed so far. Ryan and Bernard (2004) mention that when and how saturation is reached depends on a number of things: (1) the number and complexity of data, (2) investigator experience and fatigue, and (3) the number of analysts reviewing the data (see also Guest et al., 2006, p. 77). To clarify the sometimes rather vague concept of saturation, Guest et al. (2006) did an analysis of one of their own projects with interviews (see the case study in Box 6.5), which provides some arguments for a rather limited number of cases needed for reaching saturation.

Box 6.5   Research in the real world

Saturation in interview studies

A team of family health researchers in the US did a study using semi-structured, open-ended interviews for analysing how women 'talk about sex and their perceptions of self-report accuracy in two West African countries – Nigeria and Ghana' (Guest et al., 2006, p. 62). They interviewed women who met at least three basic criteria: '(1) were eighteen years of age or older, (2) had vaginal sex with more than one male partner in the past three months, and (3) had vaginal sex three or more times in an average week' (p. 62). The sample in their study consisted of 30 women in each country, which means 60 cases in total. The authors analysed their data by developing a code scheme in the process of the analysis moving from case to case. In our context, this case study is interesting, because Guest et al. used their research for critically examining the idea of 'saturation'. They looked at the process of coding and in which phase of analysing their interviews the codes were developed and when a saturation could be identified – that fewer and hardly any new codes were developed from analysing more interviews. Their conclusion is: 'Based on our analysis, we posit that data saturation had for the most part occurred by the time we had analyzed twelve interviews. After twelve interviews, we had created 92% (100) of the total number of codes developed for all thirty of the Ghanaian transcripts (109) and 88% (114) of the total number of codes developed across two countries and sixty interviews' (Guest et al., 2006, p. 74).

Problems of the concept of saturation

Michelle O'Reilly from Child Psychiatry at Leicester University in the UK and Nicola Parker from the Solihull Mental Health Foundation Trust in Birmingham critically discuss the concept of saturation in two respects. One argument is that the general attraction of this concept has led to a more fuzzy understanding – from theoretical saturation to data saturation (e.g. in Guest et al., 2006) or thematic saturation or saturation in general. The authors 'challenge the unquestioned acceptance of the concept of saturation and consider its plausibility and transferability across all qualitative approaches' (O'Reilly and Parker, 2013, p. 190) when discussing the aspect of 'data saturation' (p. 190). They emphasize that this extension of the concept has made it almost meaningless and unclear, and refer to Caelli et al. (2003, p. 9), who stated: 'While saturation has a distinct theoretically embedded meaning in grounded theory, its ubiquitous and non-selective use risks rendering the term meaningless to the qualitative research community.' While the original concept was based on a clear explanation, why we should expect a point of saturation – that new data would not advance the theory developed from the already existing data – the extended understanding of saturation gives the impression that there are no cases which could be collected and integrated in the sample or new data that could be produced – which is rather unlikely.

Steps, Aims and Criteria in Preparing and Doing the Sampling for Interview Studies

Table 6.2 summarizes the steps in preparing sampling for interviews and the criteria for evaluating their outcome.

Table 6.2 Steps, aims and criteria in preparing and doing the sampling for interview studies

Six F's of designing interview research	Steps	Aims and actions	Criteria
Framing	1. Preparing the sampling process	• Clarify the research question • Prepare a documentation sheet for the information about the interviewee (demographic data, etc.)	• Does the initial concept of sampling cover the area under study? • Does the documentation sheet cover the information relevant for the research question?
Foreseeing	2. Clarifying your expectations about participants	• Reflect on the relevance of your criteria for choosing participants for your study	• Do such people exist and are they likely to be found?

(Continued)

Table 6.2 (Continued)

Six F's of designing interview research	Steps	Aims and actions	Criteria
Formulating	3. The sampling plan	• Prepare steps in which you will decide whom to involve in your study and where to find these participants	• Are there any dimensions of purposive sampling in your sampling (plan)? • Are these relevant for answering your research question?
Foregrounding	4. The central cases in your sample	• Try to think about cases that cover relevant areas of the field of your study	• Are these cases characterized by diversity?
Focusing	5. The dimensions of comparison in your sample	• Try to get into the detail of the central parts of the issue under study • Try to increase the depth and richness of the experiences becoming visible in the interviews	• Are there main and secondary dimensions of comparison? • Are these leading to new insights?
Foreseeing	6. Socio-demographic characteristics and data	• Develop a checklist for this purpose • Apply the documentation sheet and extend it if necessary	• Is all information included that is necessary for contextualizing the interviewees' statements and narratives?
Framing	7. Saturation of your sampling	• Consider what you expect to see when saturation is reached	• What are good reasons to see saturation has been reached?
Finding and Formulating	8. Making your sampling transparent	• Think about what would be covered in a description of cases and of the sample	• Does this description provide insights into the social and cultural diversity in the sample?

What You Need to Ask Yourself

The questions in Box 6.6 are designed to give you guidance in how to recruit participants for your interviews and what to consider. You may also apply these questions to studies with interviews you read.

Box 6.6   What you need to ask yourself

Sampling in interview research

1.   What is the target group of your study?
2.   Will there be enough people to identify and recruit?
3.   How far can the issue of your research be studied by asking people about it?
4.   Who should your interview partners be – lay people, professionals, experts, elites?
5.   Have you included the relevant cases (e.g. people, groups, institutions) you need for research?
6.   What are your criteria for selecting participants?
7.   If you are applying convenience sampling, have you tried a more systematic way first?
8.   Which dimensions are covered by your sample?
9.   What was your reason for stopping sampling or limiting the sample to a concrete number of cases?

In this chapter, the focus was on planning the selection of participants and on constructing the range of voices you will be able to listen to in your study. This chapter should raise your awareness, that there is no one right way in designing a sample, in determining the number of participants in a study, in defining saturation in a general way for a concrete study and in finding access to the participants you want to recruit. Rather, it is a process consisting of trade-offs and decisions, of negotiations and reflections, in which you will set up who is in your sample and how far you can listen to the diversity within your field of study, relevant to your issue. This process does not only consist of technical and practical issues but is mainly dependent on your sensitivity towards your participants' needs and situation and thus linked to ethical issues (see Chapter 8). It also depends on how you develop reflexivity in doing interviews and in listening to your respondents and to the field you study (see Chapter 8). As outlined in Table 6.1, we will return to the issue of sampling in later chapters, in the context of analysing data (Chapters 16) and of writing about your research (Chapter 17). In the context of discussing specific methods, we will refer to specific problems of sampling as well. The following chapter will address in more detail the two steps that will make your sampling plan work in the field (or not). First, you will have to find access to fields and people in them and second, you will have to convince potential participants to take part in your study, so that you can successfully recruit them for interview.

What You Need to Succeed

The following box (6.7) lists the main points you should have understood after reading this chapter.

Box 6.7   What you need to succeed

Sampling in interview research

1.   Do I understand what sampling in interview research is about?
2.   Am I aware of the various alternatives for sampling for interviews?
3.   Do I know what saturation means in this context?
4.   Have I understood how this contributes to constructing a framework for listening?

What you have learned

- Sampling is a process of making decisions, regarding what/whom to look for and why.
- These decisions constitute the sample and are important for what is covered in the study.
- The rationales for sampling can be different depending on the selected sampling strategy.
- Sampling decisions in interview studies (who or which group next?) are often taken during and as a result of data collection and analysis.
- In sampling, you will construct the cases you study in your research.
- Sampling decisions in interview research are often taken on a substantive level rather than on a formal level: they may be based on purposeful decisions for a specific case rather than random sampling.
- Sampling should contribute to integrating diversity in the study.
- Whether sampling strategies 'work' depends on whether the researchers gain access to the sampling 'units' (people, fields, institutions; see Chapter 7).

Exercises

In the exercises, you are first invited to reflect on some of the main issues in this chapter. Then you are invited to apply the topics of this chapter to the development of a project of your own. Hence, the exercises are a combination of reflection and prospection.

Exercise 6.1

Reflecting on the Chapter: The Use of Interviews in an Existing Study

1.   Take a qualitative study from the literature (e.g. Coltart and Henwood, 2012). First (a) describe how the authors did their sampling and then (b) define the rationale or plan visible in the presentation of the study.

2. Choose a study with qualitative methods from the literature (e.g. Reeves, 2010). Try to identify from the text which problems of access the researcher mentions. In addition, try to imagine which problems arose when the researcher attempted to enter the field.

Exercise 6.2

Planning Your Own Research with Interviews

1. Consider your own research. How would you plan your sampling? How would you proceed?
2. Think about your own study and plan how to access the field you want to study. From whom do you have to seek permission? What is the best way to approach those people you want to include in your study?

What's next

In this book, the author describes several strategies of purposive sampling:

Patton, M.Q. (2015). *Qualitative Research and Evaluation Methods* (4th ed.). London: Sage.

This chapter has a focus on sampling in the light of data analysis:

Rapley, T. (2014). Sampling Strategies. In U. Flick (Ed.), *The SAGE Handbook of Qualitative Data Analysis* (pp. 49–63). London: Sage.

This article gives a concise and systematic overview of sampling in interview research:

Robinson, O.C. (2014). Sampling in Interview-Based Qualitative Research: A Theoretical and Practical Guide. *Qualitative Research in Psychology*, 11(1), 25–41.

In this book, the issue of sampling is discussed from several angles but referring to indigenous and decolonizing research methodologies:

Chilisa, B. (2020). *Indigenous Research Methodologies* (2nd ed.). London: Sage.

This article discusses sample size in interview research and in qualitative research in general:

Sandelowski, M. (1995). Sample Size in Qualitative Research. *Research in Nursing & Health*, 18, 179–83.

This last paper gives an overview of the discussion concerning sample size in interviewing:

Baker, S.E., & Edwards, R. (2012). *How Many Qualitative Interviews is Enough? Discussion Paper*. National Centre of Research Methods. http://eprints.ncrm.ac.uk/2273

Doing Interview Research Navigator

How to understand interview research
- What doing interview research means
- Theories and epistemologies of interviewing
- When to choose interviews as a research method
- Methods and formats of interviewing

Designing interview research
- Planning and designing interview research
- How many interviewees: Sampling and saturation
- Accessing and recruiting participants

You are here in your project

How to conduct interviews
- How to respect and protect: Ethics of interviewing
- Semi-structured interviews: Working with questions and answers
- Interviewing experts and elites
- Integrating narratives in interviews: Episodic interviews

Doing interviews in context
- How to work with life histories: Narrative interviews
- Working with focus groups as interviews
- Ask (in) the field: Ethnographic and mobile interviewing
- Doing online interviews

How to work with interview data
- Working with interview data
- Credibility and transparency: Quality and writing in interview research
- From interviewing to an inner view: Critiques and reflexivity

ACCESSING AND RECRUITING PARTICIPANTS

You will:

- further understand the close link between sampling and access,
- deal with access and recruitment in several contexts of doing interviews in general,
- manage access and recruitment in interviewing hard-to-reach groups,
- cope with both issues in interviewing experts, elites and professionals,
- find your way from ideas about a research issue to participants in an interview study,
- see participants' interviews and data in context, and
- further understand that ideas about the perfect number of participants become relative in the process of finding access.

Constructing a Framework for Listening

In this chapter, we take the next step in spelling out the framework for doing interviews outlined in Chapters 2, 5 and 6. Now we address how the researchers manage to integrate the variety and diversity of voices from the field into the interviews they constructed in designing a sample of participants. Finding access to the 'right' participants is important for listening to the 'best' versions of experiences or knowledge in the field, for understanding and analysing the issue under study and for answering the research question. In recruiting participants, the researchers practically organize the access to voices they need for understanding the complexity of their issue and their field. For the principles of designing interview studies (*the six F's of designing interview research*, see Chapter 5), access is the way to *finding* participants for the study, to *focusing* on the central aspects and views for the issue under research, as well as to *foregrounding* relevant people's experience and knowledge for the analysis. It also provides the basis for *framing* the analysis in an elucidating comparative approach. At the same time, access builds on *foreseeing*, who or which groups may be most instructive for the study and its findings and where to find them, before *formulating* your strategy in finding access on your way into the field and to interviewees. Finally, in this step, it will become evident how far the researchers are (1) open to the diversity of perspectives in the field and (2) how far they avoid simply an 'at first glance' **credibility** of their data but (3) take a critical perspective towards the voices in the field.

Accessing and Recruiting Interviewees

On your way to finding the interviewees you should have according to your sampling plan, you will have to master two steps. 'Accessing' basically means to *find* the potential interviewees you seek, while 'recruiting' means to '*get them on board*' for doing an interview and participating in your study.

Accessing interviewees

Access is not (only) a technical problem, as the case study in Box 7.1 may illustrate.

Box 7.1   Research in the real world

Access in interview studies

A business researcher from Østfold University College in Norway, Juliane Riese, did 'research on the organizational dynamics behind the Greenpeace campaign against Norwegian whaling' (Riese, 2019, p. 669). Against this background, she emphasizes that access is a 'relational process', which means that it depends on, sometimes multiple, relations the researcher manages to build up and maintain in the process. This sometimes continues throughout the whole research process and refers to the potential interviewee but also to intermediary actors such as '**gatekeepers**' or participants that have been interviewed already. The success of this process 'depends on the researcher's ability to access' (2019, p. 674) and on the 'researcher's and the research's accessibility' (2019, p. 674). Riese summarizes her way to finding access: 'I "got" excellent access for my research project because I had worked [as a] volunteer for Greenpeace Nordic for a year. Thus even Greenpeacers who had had very negative experiences with the anti-whaling campaign trusted me and granted me open-hearted interviews. However, it took years before I was able to view the case from certain perspectives that were relevant to my project, but difficult for me' (2019, p. 674).

In many cases, endorsements by other people in the field may be helpful, while in other cases material incentives are needed. It may be helpful or even necessary to offer people a certain sum of money or a voucher for participating in a study, but also for facilitating the contact to potential interviewees. Rugkåsa and Canvin (2011; see Box 7.3 below) discuss the use of paid recruiters, who were given money for identifying and locating potential interviewees and for establishing the contact with them.

Accessing interviewees in institutions

If your research is planned in institutions (e.g. schools), the problem of access becomes relevant and sometimes complicated. In most cases, several levels of authority might be involved in regulating the researchers' access. There are not only those to be interviewed, who will be investing their time and willingness, but also the people responsible for authorizing the research. In case of difficulties, they are held responsible for this authorization by external authorities.

Two researchers from Germany working in organizational research, Lau and Wolff (1983, p. 419) have outlined the process for research in administrations. Institutions such as social administrations tend to see researchers with their research interests as clients. Researchers are expected to make their requests for participation in formal terms like clients formulate their request for help. The researchers as persons, their request and its implications (research question, methods, time needed) are submitted for an 'official examination'. The treatment of a researcher's requests is 'pre-structured' if those requests have been sent by other (higher level) authorities. The researcher's means of support for the request may produce distrust in the people to be interviewed (why is this superior authority supporting this research?). Endorsements by other people (e.g. colleagues from another institution), however, may also facilitate access. In the end, the researcher's request is fitted into administrative routines and treated using institutionally familiar procedures.

This process can be seen as 'work of agreement' and a 'joint product, in some cases an explicit working problem for both sides'. A main task might be to negotiate common language regulations between researchers and practitioners. Analysing the process of access as a constructive one and, more importantly, analysing any failures in this process, allow the researchers to reveal the central processes of negotiation and to develop routines in the field in an exemplary manner (e.g. with 'real' clients).

Once you have gained access to the field or institution relevant for your research, you will face the problem of how to reach those people within it who are the most interesting interviewees. For example, how might you recruit experienced and practising teachers for participation in the study and not simply interns with very limited practical experience but more time to participate in the research? How might you access the central actors in a setting and not merely the peripheral or marginal ones? Here again, processes of negotiation, strategies of reference in the sense of snowballing and, above all, skills in establishing relationships play a major part.

In our research in nursing homes, we had to contact the various levels of directors (of the whole institution, of the single ward, etc.) to get permission to approach people in the field. Then we had to get in touch with the nurses, both to ask them to take part in the study themselves and for their support in approaching residents. For the latter, in many cases we had to ask the residents' relatives to consent to their participation in the study.

How to find interviewees outside institutions

If you plan to work with individuals whom you cannot approach in the context of an institution, the problem of how to find and access them sometimes becomes more challenging. For the study of individuals who cannot be approached as employees or clients in an institution or in a particular setting, the main problem is how to find them. We can take the example of a biographical study about the subjective evaluation of one's own professional career in retrospection. In such a study, it might be interesting to interview individuals following retirement, who live by themselves. This raises the question of how and where to find this kind of person. Strategies could be to use the media (advertisements in newspapers, announcements on radio programmes, social media) or to post notices on the blackboards of institutions (education centres, meeting points) that these people might frequent. Once the first cases have been found, snowballing from one case to the next may be a fruitful strategy. In using this strategy, often friends of friends are chosen and thus you would look for people from your own broader environment. Hildenbrand (1995, p. 258) warns of the problems linked to this strategy (see also Chapter 1), in that you will not be told many (new) details if you are too familiar with the interviewees and their personal situations. For observation in organizational research, Cassell (1988) distinguishes between physical and social access to field settings. Physical access means one's capacity to enter a field and get in touch with potential research subjects, groups and gatekeepers. Social access means to establish field relations that make the process of collecting research data easier. Gaining physical access to a setting does not necessarily imply social access to the individuals or groups that occupy it and are needed for an interview study (Clark, 2011).

Box 7.2   Research in the real world

Recruiting in interview studies

Valerie Wigfall et al., a group of educational and social science researchers from the Institute of Education, University of London, did a study (Wigfall et al., 2013) with intergenerational families. They wanted to interview chains of grandfathers, fathers and grandsons in three different ethnic groups. This may be an unusually over-complex design and challenge for recruiting participants, as recruitment was only successful when all three generations from one family could be won for the interviews. However, the problems and strategies the authors discuss for making recruitment work are also interesting for 'simpler' designs. In many cases, they built up a relationship with a father, for example, who then had to be asked to find and convince his son and his own father. To access the first member of these chains, Wigfall et al. (2013, p. 595) employed methods such as presentations in community groups, visits to pubs and churches, and flyers distributed at or sent out to bus stations, dentists and schools. They displayed posters at libraries and tried email and telephone contacts at job centres, put advertisements in journals, sent out email newsletters and used snowballing and Internet searches for relevant organizations. The authors discuss their strategies for their three ethnic groups – White British, Irish and Polish men. Interesting for our more general context is their experience that 'The white British had no defined overall community we could tap into' (2013, p. 600). Different from the other ethnic minority groups, the majority group could not be approached via existing ethnic communities and the researchers had to use their own personal networks for recruiting. This can be seen as a more general problem. The more 'average' a target group is, the more difficult it may be to identify communities or networks for recruiting them, compared to minority groups. The authors discuss some methodological issues in the background of their experiences: 'A key issue was about defining ethnicity and according to whose definitions' (2013, p. 601). So it could have been that people define themselves as Irish, British or both, which might complicate their allocation to the subsamples and comparison among them. Another issue was gender, as in this project with men only, the researchers were all female. Finally, working with ethnic minorities may raise issues of understanding, trust and power in terms of the relations between researchers and a majority group. This study may be specific to its target group, but the insights into problems of recruitment and strategies for solving them make it interesting in other contexts, too.

How to find interviewees from hard-to-reach groups

In Chapter 1, I mentioned studies with hard-to-reach people as a particular reason for doing interviews. In this case, access and recruitment can be real challenges. In our study with homeless adolescents, we tried to gain access to potential interviewees by hanging out at the meeting spots of the adolescents to become familiar with them and giving them a chance to become familiar with the person of the interviewer. This was a time-consuming way of obtaining access, although the time could be used for observations of the field, the participants, their activities and communication as well. A second form of approach was to get in touch with the adolescents through the support of people working in the field, in particular social workers offering food and counselling to the adolescents. And finally, we used the strategy of snowballing – asking our way from one adolescent or interviewee to the next.

Box 7.3   Research in the real world

Recruiting hard-to-reach groups in interview studies

Jorun Rugkåsa, a student of political science and a social anthropologist, and Krysia Canvin, a health researcher from Westminster University in London, did a research study on mental health in minority ethnic groups. They conducted two related studies of experiences of mental health problems in Black and minority ethnic communities in the United Kingdom (Rugkåsa and Canvin, 2011). Their research focused on participants who are seen as hard to reach for two reasons – being mentally ill and part of an ethnic minority. The authors used 'three main strategies: the employment of bicultural recruiters, intensive information sharing about the studies, and work through local community groups' (2011, p. 132). They discuss their experiences around issues that might have affected the results of recruitment, such as gatekeepers' attitudes, whether to reward participants or not, and reciprocal arrangements with local community groups. The last point may be difficult, as researchers should refrain from promising immediate benefits to participants. Payment of participants has become more accepted now, as it is in many contexts the only way to convince hard-to-reach groups to participate in research (interestingly enough, the same applies to general practitioners, for example, in my own experience). Being ready to do interviews in the participants' language may facilitate recruitment but has cost implications in transcribing and translating the interviews later (see Chapters 9 and 16), as the authors have experienced.

Multi-angle case construction in sampling and recruiting to access a phenomenon

We find strong arguments for case studies (consisting of one case – see Stake, 1995; Tight, 2022) but also for case-oriented research (Sandelowski, 1996). Here one question is whether a 'case' means a single interview or consists of a number of people involved because of their role in the case, or consists of a number of repeated interviews, as in the case study in Box 7.4.

Box 7.4   Research in the real world

Multi-angle case construction in sampling and recruiting

Our ongoing study on the integration of refugees from Syria, Eritrea and Iraq into the regular labour market in Germany (see Seidelsohn et al., 2020) is based on interviews. Our research group of sociologists, education researchers and social psychologists focuses theoretically on the concept of transition and doing interviews with the several stakeholders involved in the process of the refugees' transition into regular work. We pursue rather complex sampling and recruiting strategies. We first of all defined what 'refugee' means (e.g. coming from Iraq, Eritrea or Syria to Germany after 2015). Then we defined what transition to work means (a regular job, without support by the state – not training or an internship, for example). Furthermore, we defined several 'sampling points', which means selected areas across Germany covering the diversity of refugees' experiences. These sampling points include bigger and smaller cities, and rural areas, both from the south and north and – in particular – from the west and east of Germany. At these sampling points, we take a triangular approach to cases, consisting of (1) the refugee, who found work, (2) the employer who hired the refugee and (3) job centre employees or other actors (facilitators) who put the two sides in contact. The refugees are the core group in the focus of the study and the aim is to cover a broad variety of professional qualifications and of current job situations. Once we have interviewed single refugees, we try to identify the other people involved – their employer, and their contact persons in the job centre. Sometimes the process is the other way around – we interview job centre employees first and ask them for cases of refugees' transition they worked with and whom we can interview. In terms of sampling, this example is relevant in several respects. First, the idea that a case consists of three components (refugee, employer, facilitators) and that this triangle defines the sampling unit. Second, we first defined a population (refugees who found work coming from a number of countries). Third, we defined sampling points across Germany for covering a maximum variation of cases and their experiences. Fourth, we then sample interviewees and cases from the populations at the sampling points. Fifth, we approach the cases starting from each of the three angles – starting with the refugee and complementing the other perspectives, or starting with the facilitator and trying to locate a refugee, and so on. Finally, the idea behind this sampling strategy is to have a maximum variation in several aspects – professional education, current work situation, age, country of origin, current locale, gender, etc. It is also interesting how much of this variation was realized in the actual sample – for example, we found limited access to women working in regular jobs or, in general, highly qualified participants working in adequate jobs. Often, the degrees were not (yet) accepted as fully equivalent to a degree in Germany so that participants were having to work in jobs at a lower level. As a sampling strategy, we used purposive sampling on all levels. We repeatedly returned to sampling decisions in the process.

In the example in Box 7.4, the number of cases was about 60, but as some of them were to be interviewed repeatedly in a longitudinal perspective and as the cases included not only the refugees but also their employers and those who were in involved in organizing or mediating the employment, the 60 cases consisted of around 200 interviews in total. As Miles and Huberman (1994) note, in relation to complex cases: 'You are sampling people to get at characteristics of settings, events, and processes. Conceptually, the people themselves are secondary' (1994, p. 33). Thus, the number of interviews necessary for a study first depends on conceptual issues – what is a case? This may also include conceptual issues related to the topic of the study and the expected diversity in the topic and in the field. In the example in Box 7.4, the case is not an individual human being, but a phenomenon – cases of successful transition of a refugee into gainful work and the regular labour market. It includes several human beings (refugee, employer, job centre staff, NGO activists, for example).

How to access and recruit experts and elites

Interviewing experts and elites (see Chapter 10) is confronted with a number of the issues of sampling and access discussed so far in a nutshell. You should identify, find and access the 'right' interviewees and their number is often rather limited, sometimes even to one case, who could be the best or only interviewee about a specific topic. Bogner et al. (2014, 2018) outline a multi-step process of sampling and access. First, you should use the literature in the field, media publications or informal conversations with people familiar with the field for finding out who are or are seen as the relevant experts in a field. It is rather important in this context to gain an overview of the relevant experts in the field and to include them in the sample for the interviews (2014, p. 35). This initial sample should be extended in the course of the interviews by asking every interviewee for suggestions for further participants. Such a snowballing should take into account that contradicting positions are also integrated in the sampling. After identifying the potential interviewees, a number of barriers in accessing them have to be taken into account. Barriers can consist of secretaries, assistants or public relations departments prepared to prevent the expert from being contacted directly. Lack of time on the side of the potential interviewees can also be a barrier, which may force them to strictly distinguish between important and less important activities when asked for an interview, for example. Once you have managed to get in touch briefly at least, on first contact the importance of the research should be demonstrated succinctly. It should also be highlighted that the interview will be rather short (maybe only 30–45 minutes) to allow the expert to squeeze in an appointment into a maybe very tight agenda (2014, p. 39).

Accessing and Recruiting for Digital Interviews

In general, sampling for online interviews can be done in the same ways as purposive or theoretical sampling, which were discussed in Chapter 6, as Salmons's overview demonstrates (2015, pp. 121–3). Some specifications come from a number of questions that should be reflected on for accessing and finding interviewees.

First, does the target group or population you want to study use the Internet or social media platform you want to use for recruiting interviewees?

Second, do you want to do your interviews online or in the context of social media, or do you intend to do traditional face-to-face interviews and use the digital context only to find participants?

Third is the role of trust in interviews in the digital context: Markham (2004) reports a case in which she found out, after a longer exchange in an online interview, that she did not know if her interviewee was male or female. So there is an extended amount of trust in the relationship – the interviewer has to trust the interviewees that they are what they said they are and what they were selected for. At the same time, the interviewee has to trust that the interviewer is what they are said to be. In both cases, the lack of 'face validity' is missing which is typical for a face-to-face interview (see Chapter 15). There are number of suggestions for how to solidify a basic trust in social media research (see Flick, 2018a, Ch. 22).

Fourth, sampling and access consist of three levels – for example in using blogs for research: first the decision to use blogs instead of other social media, second which blogs to use for the study and third which contributors or contributions to select as data.

Box 7.5 Research in the real world

Planning access and recruiting for an interview study

Planning access and recruitment for an interview study includes suggestions for preparing (1) the framework of access (kinds of people to contact, general guidelines on decisions in the process and on the number and kinds of participants to work with) and (2) how to proceed with getting in touch and entering the field for the interview study.

Steps for access and recruitment for an interview study	Six F's of designing interview research
Reflect in advance again	
1. What is the research question behind the interviews?	Focusing
2. What kind of persons will be relevant as potential interviewees and where do you expect to find them?	Foreseeing
Steps for preparing a framework for listening through accessing interviewees	
3. What institutional agreements do you need?	Foreseeing
4. Reflect on what potential interviewees should know in advance of being ready to join your study. Start from what interviewees will perhaps already have experienced when hearing about the interview study.	Framing

(Continued)

(Continued)

Steps for access and recruitment for an interview study	Six F's of designing interview research
5. Prepare to write a detailed description of the recruitment process leading you to the single cases: What information and dimensions should be covered to give rich detail on the (social and cultural) diversity in your study?	Finding and Formulating
6. Prepare to reflect on and write about which of the (potential) interviewees you have lost in the process and what that means for your study.	Formulating
7. Frame (in keywords) how to ask interviewees for suggestions for other interviewees.	Framing
Steps for preparing how to proceed with access and recruitment	
8. Who would be the best person(s) to be interviewed first?	Foreseeing
9. Who could help you to get in touch with such interviewees?	Foreseeing
10. What experiences of the interviewees would be of central interest?	Foregrounding
11. What experiences of the interviewees provide information about the central topic(s) in the interviewees' cases?	Foregrounding
12. Phrase the criteria that interviewees should fulfil.	Formulating
13. Which dimensions of social and cultural diversity should be represented in the sample you want to address and how will you access the appropriate people for this?	Foreseeing
14. Note keywords about where you might find the 'ideal interviewees'.	Finding

Being Recruited for an Interview: The Participants' Perspectives

In a survey, participants are selected and recruited randomly (or according to other, rather formal criteria). Sampling for qualitative interviews is often much more directed at the individual. It has to be assumed that the participants are aware of this focused interest in their situation. This may be perceived as an appreciation of a specific competence, knowledge or experience in an expert interview, for example. It can also be seen as an acknowledgement of the particular experience of someone who has lived with a particular disease for some time, for instance. Beyond such a positive feeling of being valued by the researchers' interest, we have repeatedly seen other reactions. For example, I was sometimes asked 'Are you sure that I am the right person to answer your questions?' when I invited people to take part in an interview study (before they knew the interview questions). This kind of person-focused selection in some cases also produced feelings of being responsible for good contributions, or of being over-charged by the researchers and their expectations concerning the interview. Being selected as an individual in a specific situation may also make it more difficult to refuse to participate, even when the potential interviewee has good reasons not to join the sample. These kinds of thoughts may be intensified when the potential inter-viewee is recruited as part of an institution and sees that other members of the team have not been asked to participate. Therefore, researchers should be sensitive to any ambivalence on the part of their potential participants that may come across in the invitation to be part of the study. The important question is not only the number of cases we have in total, but also which ones we have in our sample and which not (see the case study in Box 7.6).

Box 7.6   Research in the real world

The voices heard and the voices silenced

Kristensen and Ravn (2015) put the problem in a nutshell in the title of their paper: recruitment processes in qualitative interview studies define the voices heard and the voices silenced in a concrete study. The two researchers, social anthropologists and gender researchers from the Norwegian University of Science and Technology, use several of their studies as examples, among them: (1) '"One body: Two lives. Pregnancy, the fetus and the pregnant body – an anthropological analysis" (Ravn) was a longitudinal study of pregnant women's understandings of pregnancy, their experiences with their pregnant body and their perceptions of their fetus. Eight women were interviewed – each up to six times – throughout their pregnancy and the year after their baby was born' (2015, p. 725); and (2) '"Family planning – behind the numbers. Narratives on family planning among immigrants in contemporary Nor-way" (Kristensen) was a qualitative research project in which a total of 21 women and men from Iran and Iraq who were living in Norway were each interviewed once or twice. The interviews centred on their understandings of the ideal family and on fer-tility decisions' (p. 726). In relation to these and a number of their other studies, the authors discuss the meanings and effects of the research topics, of the (predefined) sampling procedures of mediators and of the researchers' positionality for finding and maintaining access over time. They summarize their research experience with recruitment as follows: 'Recruitment to some research projects shows clear gender and class distinctions; in our particular cases, we had easy access to middle class women, while both men and those in the working class – particularly working class men – were left (or left themselves) in silence. The result was a reinforcement of the middle class as the main voice in society and women as the main voices on fertility and domestic affairs' (2015, pp. 734-5). This example shows influences on the process of finding access, the difficulties of maintaining access over time and the danger that people that are lost in this process reduce the diversity of the voices that are heard in such a study.

Steps, Aims and Criteria in Preparing and Gaining Access and Recruiting for Interview Studies

Table 7.1 summarizes the steps in preparing access and recruiting for interviews, and the criteria for evaluating their outcome.

Table 7.1   Steps, aims and criteria in preparing and gaining access and recruiting for interview studies

Six F's of designing interview research	Steps	Aims and actions	Criteria
Framing	1. Preparing the process of access	• Clarify the research question • Reflect on your sampling goals • Prepare a documentation sheet of information on steps to finding interviewees (in institutional or everyday fields)	• Does the initial concept of sampling cover the area under study? • Does the way recruiting proceeds lead to the intended sample? • Does the documentation of the steps cover the information relevant to analysing the process?
Foreseeing	2. Clarifying your expectations about participants	• Reflect on the criteria for being a relevant participant for your study	• Do such people exist and where are they likely to be found?
Formulating	3. The plan of accessing participants	• Prepare steps in which you will decide whom to involve in your study and where to find these participants	• Are there any dimensions in your plan for accessing interviewees? • Are these relevant to answering your research question?
Foregrounding	4. The central cases in your sample	• Try to get in touch with cases that cover relevant areas of the field of your study	• Are these cases characterized by diversity?
Focusing	5. The dimensions of comparison in your sample	• Try to get into the detail of the variety and diversity concerning the issue of your study • Try to advance the depth and richness of the experiences becoming visible in the interviewees	• Are there main and secondary dimensions of comparison? • Are these leading to new insights?

Six F's of designing interview research	Steps	Aims and actions	Criteria
Foreseeing	6. Socio-demographic characteristics and data	• Develop a checklist for this purpose • Apply the documentation sheet and extend it if necessary	• Is all information included that is necessary for contextualizing the interviewees' statements and narratives?
Framing	7. Saturation of your sampling	• What do you expect to see when saturation is reached?	• What are the reasons to see saturation has been reached?
Finding and Formulating	8. Making your sampling transparent	• Think about what should be covered in a description of cases, of the sample and of access to them	• Does this description provide insights into the social and cultural diversity in the sample?

The above examples of case studies and the general discussion in this chapter have illustrated that sampling, access and recruitment are interwoven in the process. Advancing in the recruitment process and overcoming problems along the way may lead to changes in and adaptation of the original sampling plan.

What You Need to Ask Yourself

This chapter's topics are challenges for the researcher, but also issues to manage in the process. The questions in Box 7.7 are designed to guide you in recruiting participants for your interviews and in what to consider. You may also apply these questions to studies with interviews that you read.

Box 7.7 What you need to ask yourself

Access and recruitment in interview research

1. What is the target group of your study?
2. Will there be enough people to identify and recruit?
3. How far can your research topic be studied by asking people about it?
4. Who should your interview partners be – lay people, professionals, experts, elites?

(Continued)

---

5. Have you managed to reach the relevant cases (e.g. people, groups, institutions) you need for the research?
6. Which criteria relevant to selecting participants might you meet in access?
7. If you are applying convenience sampling, have you tried a more systematic way of accessing people as well?
8. Which dimensions are covered by the sample you recruited in the end?
9. Where and how might you access your interview partners?
10. Have you spoken to all the relevant people you need to give you access (e.g. not only the children you want to interview, but also their parents)?
11. What obstacles have come up for recruiting interviewees?
12. What ambivalence could the invitation to join the study have produced on the participants' side?

What You Need to Succeed

This chapter has outlined the practical challenges and issues you will meet on your way to constructing the specificity and diversity of the voices you will need to listen to in your interviews and in your study in general. This chapter should show two things: (1) Sampling is theory and methodology for defining the number of participants and for defining saturation in general. (2) Whether you meet your criteria of sampling and saturation depends on whether you have access to fields and the participants you want to recruit. This is a process consisting of trade-offs and decisions, of negotiations and reflections, in which you will set up who is in your sample and how far you can listen to the diversity in your field of study, related to your topic. This process not only consists of technical and practical issues but also mainly depends on your sensitivity towards your participants' needs and situation, and is thus linked to ethical issues (see Chapter 8). It also depends on how you develop reflexivity in doing interviews and in listening to your respondents and to the field you are studying (see Chapter 18). The questions in the following box (7.8) will help you to check what to take away from this chapter before proceeding to the next steps.

Box 7.8 What you need to succeed

Access and recruitment in doing interview research

1. Do I understand what access means in this context?
2. Am I aware that sampling plans only work if I gain access to interviewees?
3. Do I recognize the possible difficulties of finding participants inside and outside institutions?

What you have learned

- Entering the field entails more than just being there: it involves a complex process of locating yourself and being located in the field.
- When researching individuals, you should try to include people you do not know personally in order to glean fruitful insights.
- Access to a field or to people does not necessarily mean that they can be recruited for interview.
- Possible participants may have good reasons as to why they do not want to be interviewed.
- Whether sampling strategies 'work' depends on whether the researchers gain access to the sampling 'units' (people, fields, institutions).

Exercises

In the exercises, you are first invited to reflect on some of the main issues in this chapter. Then you are invited to apply the topics of this chapter to the development of a project of your own. Hence, the exercises are a combination of reflection and prospection.

Exercise 7.1

Reflecting on the Chapter: The Use of Interviews in an Existing Study

1. Take a qualitative study from the literature (e.g. Coltart and Henwood, 2012). First (a) describe how the authors turned their sampling plan into a strategy for access and then (b) define the rationale or plan visible in the presentation of the study.
2. Choose a study with qualitative methods from the literature (e.g. Reeves, 2010). Try to identify from the text which problems of access the researcher mentions. In addition, try to imagine which problems arose when the researcher attempted to enter the field.

Exercise 7.2

Planning Your Own Research with Interviews

1. Think about your own study and plan how to access the field you want to study. From whom do you have to seek permission? What is the best way to approach those people you want to include in your study?

What's next

This book chapter deals with concrete problems and examples of entering a field and taking a role and position in it:

Bengry, A. (2018). Accessing the Research Field. In U. Flick (Ed.), *The SAGE Handbook of Qualitative Data Collection* (pp. 99–117). London: Sage.

This article describes the process of access to field sites and gives some practical advice:

Bondy, C. (2013). How Did I Get Here? The Social Process of Accessing Field Sites. *Qualitative Research*, 13(5), 578–90.

This article shows strategies and impacts for the process of finding and maintaining access in a study with (repeated) interviews and how the samples may change in the process and what the results of these changes may be:

Kristensen, G.K., & Ravn, M.N. (2015). The Voices Heard and the Voices Silenced: Recruitment Processes in Qualitative Interview Studies. *Qualitative Research*, 15(6), 722–37. https://doi.org/10.1177/1468794114567496

HOW TO CONDUCT
INTERVIEWS

Part I of this book was designed to help you understand the basics and background to doing interview research. Part II turned to more practical issues of planning and designing such an interview study. Part III focuses on how to conduct interviews in four respects:

Ethics of interviewing can be seen as an aspect of planning a study, but ultimately it is a case of doing an interview in a reflexive and ethically sound way. That is why Chapter 8 is the first chapter in this part of the book.

Interviewing is often associated with an interviewer asking questions the interviewee is expected to answer. The most common way of doing such an interview is the topic of Chapter 9, which focuses on semi-structured interviews. This is the first of specific methods of interviewing treated in this book.

Chapter 10 addresses the use of this approach for interviewing specialists, experts and elites as a second method of interviewing and discusses the challenges of such interviews.

In Chapter 11, the use of questions in interviews is complemented by integrating narrative approaches in an interview as a third method, where the episodic interview is presented in some detail.

In the subsequent Part IV, interviewing will be discussed in some specific contexts.

Doing Interview Research Navigator

How to understand interview research

- What doing interview research means
- Theories and epistemologies of interviewing
- When to choose interviews as a research method
- Methods and formats of interviewing

Designing interview research

- Planning and designing interview research
- How many interviewees: Sampling and saturation
- Accessing and recruiting participants

You are here in your project

How to conduct interviews

- How to respect and protect: Ethics of interviewing
- Semi-structured interviews: Working with questions and answers
- Interviewing experts and elites
- Integrating narratives in interviews: Episodic interviews

Doing interviews in context

- How to work with life histories: Narrative interviews
- Working with focus groups as interviews
- Ask (in) the field: Ethnographic and mobile interviewing
- Doing online interviews

How to work with interview data

- Working with interview data
- Credibility and transparency: Quality and writing in interview research
- From interviewing to an inner view: Critiques and reflexivity

HOW TO RESPECT AND PROTECT

ETHICS OF INTERVIEWING

How this chapter will help you

You will:

- be introduced to the ethical challenges of doing interview research,
- understand and apply the principle of informed consent,
- see its limits and challenges,
- learn how to work in an ethically sound way in interviewing children and the elderly, and
- understand the ethical issues of mobile and digital interviewing.

In this chapter, we will focus on constructing a framework for doing interview research as a constructing listener by addressing major issues concerning the researchers' attitudes towards interviewing and interviewees. We will take a theoretically and even more practically oriented look at research ethics in interviewing.

Ethics of Doing Interviews

Ethical issues in research are discussed and become relevant to our context on several levels: for research in general, for social research in particular (see Flick, 2020, Ch. 3), for qualitative research in general (see Flick, 2018a, Ch. 9) and for doing interviews especially. Research ethics can be seen as a rather abstract set of theoretical principles and moral issues. This topic can also be perceived as a chore or a strategic need – in being allowed to do a study or to publish a paper in a journal that insists on ethical approval of the research. New regulations also see research ethics and data protection as a legal issue with rules to keep and penalties imposed in the case of not doing so. Most relevant to our context and the real challenge is how to turn general principles into concrete practices before, during and after doing interviews. On this practical level, there is a strong link of ethics to reflexivity in doing interviews, which is the subject of the later part of this chapter.

General Issues of Interview Ethics

Research ethics for social research are discussed as a concept on four levels – in definitions, in a theory of research ethics, in regulations, and in principles. We will address these four levels before we turn to the practice of ethical research.

Definitions of research ethics

Ethical issues have a special relevance in health and nursing research, where we find the following definition of research ethics, which can be transferred to other research areas as well: 'Research ethics addresses the question, which ethically relevant influences the researchers' interventions could bear on the people with or about whom the researchers do their research. In addition, it is concerned with the procedures that should be applied for protecting those who participate in the research, if this seems necessary' (Schnell and Heinritz, 2006, p. 17). Although the term 'interventions' may be associated with medical interventions such as treatments, every kind of research activity in a field can be seen as an intervention – for example, the invitation to recount one's life can be an intervention in the interviewee's situation by reactivating unpleasant memories.

Ethical theory

A theory of research ethics is often formulated around the four issues Murphy and Dingwall (2001, p. 339) discuss: *Non-maleficence* means that researchers should avoid any harm for people resulting from participating in a study. *Beneficence* means that research involving human subjects should not simply be carried out for its own sake but it should promise or produce some positive and identifiable benefit. *Autonomy or self-determination*: research participants' values and decisions should be respected. *Justice* means all people should be treated equally in the study. Thus, protection of participants and reflection on the necessity and usefulness of a study determine such a theory.

Data protection: regulations in the European Union

Data protection has become a major concern in Europe in the context of social media and Big Data and the use of both for commercial and research interests. The European Union (EU) has passed new regulations for data protection and has discussed this as an issue of ethics in research and beyond: 'Data protection is both a central issue for research ethics in Europe and a fundamental human right' (EU, 2018, p. 3). The regulations passed in the EU parliament in 2016 and have implications for research in the EU, in every country in the EU and beyond, where countries or subjects from EU countries are involved. For research, the EU (2018) has published a document on ethics and data protection, which was developed by a panel of experts, and underlines the fact that in 'research settings, data protection imposes obligations on researchers to provide research subjects with detailed information about what will happen to the personal data that they collect. It also requires the organisations processing the data to ensure the data are properly protected, minimised, and destroyed when no longer needed' (EU, 2018, p. 3).

This document highlights the responsibilities of the researchers or their institutions for providing sufficient information to participants as a result of the EU's 2016 General Data Protection Regulation (GDPR). The focus is on data whose processing entails a *high risk* for the participants, because of the kinds of data or information that are used (e.g. political opinion, religious beliefs), or due to specific subjects that are involved (e.g. children, vulnerable people, people who have not given their consent), to specific data collection or processing techniques (which are privacy-invasive, for example, or based on data mining) or the involvement of non-EU countries (see 2018, p. 6). In such cases of higher-risk data processing, researchers have to *provide a detailed analysis* of ethics issues raised by their project, including:

- an overview of all planned data collection and processing operations;
- an identification and analysis of the ethics issues that these raise; and
- an explanation of how you will mitigate these issues in practice. (EU, 2018, p. 7)

Data protection is specified around three concepts. References to research subjects should be based on **pseudonymization**, in which all personal information (e.g. individuals' names) is substituted by unique identifiers that are not connected to their real-world identity. *Anonymization* converts personal data into anonymized data without identifiers. *Re-identification* is the process of turning pseudonymized or anonymized data back into personal data (EU, 2018, p. 8). This may be necessary if you want to do a longitudinal study with the same participants and need to contact them again (see Chapter 5). Otherwise, this is discussed as a risk to minimize or avoid – in that other people might be able to re-identify participants of a study too. A further issue is the need to restrict the data that are collected to what is absolutely necessary: 'Data processing must be lawful, fair and transparent. It should involve only data that are necessary and proportionate to achieve the specific task or purpose for which they were collected (Article 5(1) GDPR)' (EU, 2018, p. 10).

What are the key changes in the GDPR compared to earlier regulations and practices? A first change is the extended territorial scope that also applies to companies and researchers from outside the EU. If the research involves EU citizens or, vice versa, if EU researchers work with people outside the EU, the GDPR applies as well. Other changes concern the (high) penalties for breaching GDPR rules that have been defined, the new rights for data subjects – to be notified in case of a breach of GDPR regulations within 72 hours, the rights to access one's own data and to be forgotten (i.e. to have that data erased) – and the fact that privacy of participants has to be a major concern of research design. Finally, research institutes should have Data Protection Officers appointed according to their professional qualifications as staff members or external officers, who should be given the appropriate resources for protecting rights and data and should report to the highest levels of management (see www.trunomi.com/blogs/cmo-dpo-data-protection).

The United Kingdom Research Institute (UKRI, 2018) has published a helpful overview (*GDPR and Research – An Overview for Researchers*). It summarizes the lawful bases for data processing set out in Article 6 of the GDPR for any research, of which at least one will apply to legitimizing a research study. Either (a) the individual's consent or (b) a contract with the individual, (c) a legal obligation to process the data, (d) vital interests (to protect someone's life), (e) a public task performed by the research or (f) legitimate interests of the researcher or a third party, should be provided to legitimize a study.

As a consequence, many universities have produced informative material to instruct their researchers on how to act according to the new EU regulations and following country-specific laws. For example, University College of London (UCL, 2018) has formulated a document called 'Guidance Paper for Researchers on the Implications of the General Data Protection Regulation and the Data Protection Act 2018'. It summarizes the treatment of personal data, **informed consent**, data protection, fairness and transparency at EU and UK levels. If you are planning your research, consider beginning by consulting this guidance or, even better, check with your university whether a similar document and guidance are available.

Country-specific ethics cultures

The research foundations in the member countries of the EU have formulated rules and guidance for doing research according to the new EU law. In Germany, the German Research Council (DFG, 2018) has set up an information document integrating GDPR and the German data protection law. For the Nordic countries (that are not members of the EU), NordForsk (2017) has provided an overview of the treatment of ethical reviews, data protection and biomedical research in Denmark, Finland, Iceland, Norway and Sweden, especially in light of the new GDPR requirements in and by the EU and their consequences for Scandinavian countries. Also, beyond research ethics, we find discussions that in Germany, for example, sensitivity towards data protection in general is relatively high compared to other countries (Dot.magazine, 2017).

Principles of research ethics

The rather abstract theoretical reflections and legal regulations have been substantiated in formulating principles of research ethics, which should be taken into account when planning a project or applying for funding, for example. In the UK, the Economic and Social Research Council (ESRC, 2019) has formulated six key (or core) principles for ethical research in its Gateway to Research:

- Research should aim to maximize benefit for individuals and society and minimize risk and harm
- The rights and dignity of individuals and groups should be respected
- Wherever possible, participation should be voluntary and appropriately informed
- Research should be conducted with integrity and transparency
- Lines of responsibility and accountability should be clearly defined
- Independence of research should be maintained and where conflicts of interest cannot be avoided, they should be made explicit. (ESRC, 2019)

These principles define general preconditions, such as respecting the individuals involved, basing the research on informed consent, i.e. that people know that they are (voluntarily) taking part in a study, what it is about and what level of participation will be expected of them. Avoidance of harm, transparency and independence of the research are other guiding principles.

In the context of health sciences, Schnell and Heinritz (2006, pp. 21–4) have developed a more comprehensive set of eight principles specifically concerning the ethics of research. These principles include the notions that researchers (1) can justify why their research is necessary, (2) explain what its aims are and (3) the circumstances under which subjects participate. Researchers should also (4) be able to make their procedures comprehensible to non-experts and to (5) estimate the positive or negative consequences for participants, as well as (6) the possible violations and damages and (7) how to prevent these. (8) False statements about the usefulness of the research have to be avoided and data protection rules respected. These principles are influenced by the context of health research in which they were formulated but they can be transferred to guiding other areas of social research too.

Hammersley (2015) critically discusses ethical principles, for which he sees two roles (following Homan, 1991, pp. 39–40) – 'whether they ought to provide specific prescriptions and proscriptions or should be framed instead as general principles'. Hammersley states that: 'Many ethics codes and frameworks mix the two, this no doubt partly reflecting the fact that they have usually been developed by committees and/or through consultation – so that consistency in formulation has been hard to maintain' (2015, p. 433).

Codes of ethics

Professional associations such as the British Psychological Society give themselves **codes of ethics**. These are formulated to regulate the relations of researchers to the people and fields they intend to study. Principles of research ethics require that researchers avoid harming the participants involved in the process by respecting and taking into account their needs and interests. Here are a few examples of codes of ethics found on the Internet (accessed 23 April 2019):

- The British Psychological Society (BPS) has published a Code of Conduct, Ethical Principles and Guidelines (www.bps.org.uk/news-and-policy/bps-code-ethics-and-conduct)
- The British Sociological Association (BSA) has formulated a Statement of Ethical Practice (www.britsoc.co.uk/media/24310/bsa_statement_of_ethical_practice.pdf)
- The British Educational Research Association (BERA) has published ethical guidelines for educational research: British Educational Research Association [BERA] (2018) *Ethical Guidelines for Educational Research* (4th ed.), London (www.bera.ac.uk/researchers-resources/publications/ethical-guidelines-for-educational-research-2018)
- The American Sociological Association (ASA) refers to its Code of Ethics (www.asanet.org/code-ethics)
- The Social Research Association (SRA) has formulated Ethical Guidelines (the-sra.org.uk/research-ethics/ethics-guidelines).

Codes of ethics require that research should be based on *informed consent* (i.e. the study's participants have agreed to partake on the basis of information given to them by the researchers – see below). Research should also *avoid harming* the participants; this requirement includes the need to *avoid invading their privacy* or deceiving them about the research's aims.

Ethics committees

Many universities and professional associations have established **ethics committees** for ensuring that ethical standards are maintained. For this purpose, the committees examine the research design and methods of a study before they can be applied. Good ethical research practice is then based on two conditions: that the researchers will conduct their research in accordance with ethical codes; and that research proposals have been reviewed by ethics committees for their ethical soundness. Reviewing by ethical soundness focuses on three aspects (see Allmark, 2002, p. 9): scientific quality; the welfare of participants; and respect for the dignity and rights of participants.

Scientific quality: Any research which is only duplicating existing research, or which is not of a quality to contribute new knowledge to the existing knowledge, can be seen as unethical (see e.g. Department of Health, 2001, and see above on the GDPR). This can already be a source of conflict. To judge the quality of research, the members of the ethics committee should have the methodological knowledge for assessing a research proposal. Therefore, the members, or at least some of the members of the committees, should be researchers themselves. Researchers often complain about how a research proposal was rejected because the members did not understand its premise, or because they had a methodological background different from that of the applicant and the proposal, or they simply disliked the research and rejected it for scientific rather than ethical reasons. This reveals a problem with ethics committees: there are many reasons why a committee may decide to reject or block a research proposal, which are not always ethical ones.

Welfare of participants is often linked to weighing the risks (for the participants) against the benefits (of new knowledge and insights about a problem or of finding a new solution to an existing problem). Again, we find a difficulty here: weighing the risks and benefits is often relative rather than absolute and clear.

Dignity and rights of participants are linked to consent given by the participants, to sufficient and adequate information provided as a basis for giving that consent, and the consent is given voluntarily (Allmark, 2002, p. 13). Beyond this, researchers need to guarantee participants' confidentiality: that information about them will be used only in such a way that it is impossible for other people to identify the participants or for any institution to use it against the interest of the participants.

Ethics committees review and canonize these general principles (for a detailed discussion of such principles, see Hopf, 2004; Murphy and Dingwall, 2001). These principles are not necessarily a clear-cut answer to ethical questions but more a general orientation about how to act ethically within the research process (Hammersley, 2015).

Participants' Views and Expectations of Interview Research Ethics

Ritchie et al. (2014, p. 83) emphasize that ethics in interview research is more than just obtaining approval from an ethics committee, or documenting informed consent by the participants (see below). The case study in Box 8.1 illustrates what participants of interview studies see as research ethics and expect from an ethically sound interview research study.

Box 8.1   Research in the real world

Participants' expectations of research ethics

Jenny Graham, Ini Grewal and Jane Lewis, from NatCen in the UK, did a study (Graham et al., 2007) for the Government Social Research, Department of Analysis for Policy. In this study, they asked participants of surveys and interviews about their understanding of research ethics. They received statements such as: 'Ethics to me is,

(Continued)

I suppose, similar to being politically correct, being – just being correct in the way you do things in respect of all sorts of different ideals like race, like age, like religion, and kind of things like that. Ethics is making sure that you don't offend people unnecessarily. I think that's what it means to me' (Male, 31–40, survey participant). The authors also found what participants expect from being interviewed in an ethically sound way: 'Conducting the interview as I would assume that you've been trained and so on, yeah, just carrying out the interview as they were trained and correctly, and following procedures' (Female, 31–40, qualitative participant). They found that 'the interview interaction, and in particular the relationship with the interviewer, was central to participants' experiences. People looked to interviewers to help them to feel "comfortable". Being interviewed was an unfamiliar experience and people had little sense of what to expect. Being at ease was also important for the quality of data – it helped people answer honestly and influenced how much information was shared. It was also important to participants to feel that they and their input were valued by the interviewer, that the pace of the interview was unhurried and that interviewers were non-judgemental. Participants generally constructed a somewhat passive and circumscribed role for themselves' (2007, p. 7).

The authors also developed as a result of their interviews a three-step map of interview research ethics in the view of participants. Before the interview, the issues include unpressurized decision-making about taking part, knowing why one was selected to be approached, or knowing what to expect and being able to prepare, especially in terms of coverage and questioning style. During the interview, participants referred to the right not to answer a question or to say more than they want to, time to think about questions and answers, clear, relevant and non-repetitive questions. After the interview, they expected to have the right to privacy and anonymity respected in the storage, access and reporting of the research, unbiased and accurate research and reporting, or the opportunity for feedback on findings and use – what will be made of the research for wider social benefit (2007, p. 18). Finally, for highlighting the role of ethics in planning interviews, the following finding in this study may be helpful: 'Alongside the interviewer's behaviour and characteristics, reactions to questions and questioning style were an important component of the interaction. Key issues were the extent to which the interview gave scope for self expression, and the relevance of the questions asked. More negative reactions to questions and style could be mediated by a skilful interviewer' (2007, p. 7).

The case study in Box 8.1 shows some rather concrete expectations on the participants' side about how interviewing should be done in an ethical way. It demonstrates, at the same time, that ethics is not only a question of preparing interviews but also refers to doing interviews and to reflecting what is going on during interviews and how we move on after collecting the data.

How to Act Ethically in Doing Interview Research

So far, we have addressed research ethics mainly on the level of theory, regulations, principles, codes and committees. However, whether research is ethically sound depends on the way the researchers do their study. In our context, this means going beyond approval by committees and the orientation on rules and principles; it is the practices in contact with the interviewee and the conduct in the interview which make research ethical – or not. Northway (2002, p. 5) outlines the overall ethical involvement of any research study: 'However, all aspects of the research process, from deciding upon the topic through to identifying a sample, conducting the research and disseminating the findings, have ethical implications.' You will be confronted with ethical issues at every step of the research. The way you enter a field and address and select your participants raises the issue of how you inform your participants and whom you inform about your research, its purposes and your expectations.

Ritchie et al. list a number of methods-specific ethical issues for interviews:

- Particularly intimate and disclosive environment: how to help participants manage the extent of disclosure?
- Detailed personal accounts raise issues about potential identifiability in reporting
- Common method for very intimate or personal subject matter: how to leave the participants feeling well?
- Managing any expectations that the researcher will be able to help the participant with the particular issue the research is exploring. (2014, p. 86)

Allmark et al. (2009) did a literature review on the topic of ethical issues in in-depth interviews. To understand how the issue of ethics in interview studies is treated in the literature, the authors analysed three types of articles: general discussions, issues in particular studies, and studies of interview-based research ethics. They identified five major topics in their results (privacy and confidentiality; informed consent; harm; dual role and over-involvement; politics and power), which we will take as an orientation here to structure the field of practices and challenges in acting ethically in interview research.

Privacy and confidentiality

Privacy is a most delicate issue in interviews and research ethics, as interviews are mainly preferred over other forms of data collection as they access private and personal experiences. The main challenge is how to guarantee the participants' privacy toward other (third) parties. Privacy and confidentiality become issues in four major steps of interviewing:

1. In *preparing* questions that are not overcoming the borders of privacy by asking too much or too deeply about issues that are not necessary or essential for the study.

2. As the interview may extend to areas and topics but also layers of the problem under study that were not anticipated by the researchers or the participants, in *doing* the interview, privacy and confidentiality become an issue in the process. Allmark et al. (2009) mention studies in which a form of voyeurism and sensationalism became a problem in the interview.
3. In documenting the data and the information about the interviewee, in particular in transcription and in managing the issue of anonymization.
4. In reporting, writing and publishing the research. These issues are challenges in all kinds of interviews but they become even more relevant in dyad interviews with several family members or team members in an organization, who may have differing needs over an issue being kept private. Suggestions for managing privacy are to use pseudonyms, and to clearly define the possible limits of confidentiality with the participants (Ensign, 2003), for example.

Confidentiality in writing about your research

It should be beyond doubt that researchers need to guarantee participants' confidentiality: that information about them will be used only in such a way that it is impossible for other people to identify the participants or for any institution to use it against the interest of the participants. Issues of confidentiality or anonymity may become problematic in research with several members of a specific setting. Interviewing several people in the same company, or several members of a family, turns the need for confidentiality into an issue that is not only relevant in relation to a public outside this setting. Readers of reports or publications should not be able to identify which company or which persons took part in your research. For this purpose, you should encrypt the specific details (names, addresses, company names, etc.) to protect participants' identities. Try to guarantee that colleagues cannot identify participants from information about the study. For example, when interviewing children, you may often find that parents want to know what their children said in the interview. To avoid this problem, you should inform the parents right at the beginning of your research that this will not be possible (see Allmark, 2002, p. 17). Finally, it is very important that you store your data (i.e. recordings and transcripts) in a safe and completely secure container, so that no one will be able to access these data who is not meant to (see Lüders, 2004b). Hammersley (2015, p. 441) discusses examples in which participants may have an interest in their names and identities not being concealed but rather mentioned openly. For example, institutions may want to be mentioned openly because the teams are proud of their work, or to advertise their services. On the other hand, hospitals and their staff may have an interest in remaining anonymous to be safe from any prosecution in case of lapses in care. Hammersley discusses these examples to show that ethical principles such as anonymization can be relative and that they have to be negotiated in the single case of a study with the participants.

At this point, the specific concepts of research ethics become relevant, which are discussed, for example, by Chilisa (2020, p. 83): 'The questions to ask are, Can there be universal research ethics? Can they be value free and inclusive of all knowledge systems?' An example of differing views in this context can be found in Box 8.2.

Box 8.2   Research in the real world

Ethics in postcolonial indigenous methodologies

In postcolonial indigenous methodologies, research ethics are discussed in a specific way. Here, 'ethics protocols that are informed by the value systems of the researched' are called for (Chilisa, 2020, p. 41). A specific topic is the anonymization of participants in writing about research done in an indigenous context, as Shawn Wilson (2008) explains in the context of indigenous research in Australia and Canada:

> The ethics involved in an Indigenous research paradigm sometimes differs from the dominant academic way of doing things. I would like to use the real names of everyone I worked with on this research, so that you will know exactly who I am talking about. This goes against the rules of most university ethical research policies. However, how can I be held accountable to the relationships I have with the people if I don't name them? How can they be held accountable to their own teachers if their words and relationships are deprived of names? What I will do is write using the real names of everyone who has given me explicit permission to do so. I will use pseudonyms for anyone who I couldn't get in touch with to talk about it or who had any misgivings about the use of names. (2008, p. 63)

But this desire to talk openly about the participants is not only on the researchers' side, but also seen in the participants themselves, when Wilson highlights that 'participants did not want anonymity because they understood that the information imparted, or story offered, would lose its power without knowledge of the teller. The entire notion of relational accountability would have been lost had I not honored the co-researchers by using their names' (2008, p. 130).

I would suggest carefully checking such a need for openness with every participant of your study.

Such a desire to be identified in the writing about the research one has participated in, as in the example in Box 8.2, can also be found in other contexts when expert interviews are used (see Chapter 10).

Informed Consent

A key theme of principles and practices of research ethics is that participation should be based on informed consent, which means people know that they are part of a study, have agreed to be studied and had the necessary knowledge to decide for or against participating. Informed consent is defined as follows: 'The term informed consent implies that subjects know and understand the risks and benefits of participation in the research. They must also understand their participation is completely voluntary' (Flynn and Goldsmith, 2013, p. 10). In taking this principle as a precondition for participation, we find in the literature a number of criteria for informed consent (see e.g. Allmark, 2002, p. 13). The consent should be given (1) by someone competent to do so after (2) being adequately informed about the research and what participation would mean. The consent is given (3) voluntarily.

Practical issues of informed consent

If you want to put the participants' consent on a solid ground of information and agreement, you can use a form like the one in Box 8.3 as a practical means.

Box 8.3   Research in the real world

Agreement about informed consent and data protection in interviews

Agreement about data protection for scientific interviews

- Participation in the interview is voluntary. It has the following purpose

[Issue of the study: ...]

- Responsible for doing the interview and analysing it are:

Interviewer: ....

[Name of the institution: ....]

Supervisor of the project:

[Name ....]

[Name and address of the institution: ....]

The responsible persons will ensure that all data will be treated confidentially and only for the purpose agreed upon herewith:

The interviewee agrees that the interview will be recorded and scientifically analysed. After finishing the recording, he or she can request that single parts of the interview are erased from the recording.

To assure data protection, the following agreements are made (please delete what is not accepted):

The material will be processed according to the following agreement about data protection:

Recording

1. The recording of the interview will be stored in a locked cabinet and in password-protected storage media by the interviewers or supervisors and erased after the end of the study or after two years at the latest.
2. Only the interviewer and members of the project team will have access to the recording for analysing the data.
3. In addition, the recording can be used for teaching purposes. All participants in the seminar will be obliged to maintain data protection.

Analysis and archiving

1. For the analysis, the recording will be transcribed. Names and locations mentioned by the interviewee will be anonymized in the transcript as far as necessary.
2. In publications, it is guaranteed that identification of the interviewee will not be possible.

The interviewer or the supervisor of the project holds the copyright for the interviews.

The interviewee may take back his or her declaration of consent completely or in part within 14 days.

[Location, date]: ....

Interviewer: ....   Interviewee: ....

In case of an oral agreement

I confirm that I have informed the interviewee about the purpose of the data collection, explained the details of this agreement about data protection, and obtained his or her agreement.

[Location, date]: ....   Interviewer: ....

Both the interviewee and the researcher should talk about the contents of this form, sign the document and receive a copy of it. It should provide the researcher with a basis for continuing with the participants' interview, and the interviewees a framework for agreeing to take part and – if necessary – to withdraw their agreement.

Critical issues of informed consent

In their review, Allmark et al. (2009) discuss several studies referring to problems linked to the idea of informed consent – at least as something to be guaranteed or entirely assured without problems. Information about the issues to be addressed in the interview should be given in advance, so that the interviewees can give their consent on the basis of that information. In most cases, informed consent is an issue before the interview begins. However, in semi-structured interviews a broader range of topics can emerge that are addressed by the interviewee answering a question or by the interviewer probing (see Chapter 9) at some points and mentioning unexpected details or topics. In narratives (see Chapter 12) as well, the interviewee may come up with details or topics that neither the interviewer nor the interviewee had anticipated when clarifying the informed consent before hand. Thus, it may become necessary to clarify the consent again or continuously when new topics are mentioned by asking: 'Is it alright if we talk a little more about that?' (2009, p. 49). Other topics linked to informed consent are related to vulnerable groups not really being ready to understand all the information given and necessary to build the consent on. The informed consent may become problematic if several people are interviewed at the same time, such as couples or patients and carers or children and parents, and one party begins to feel uneasy with certain topics. This may have consequences for privacy and confidentiality.

Risk and Harm

Corbin and Morse (2003) mention as a risk 'that there might be a break in confidentiality/anonymity, with possible consequences of a social, financial, legal, or political nature' (2003, p. 336) and 'the risk that interviews on certain topics might arouse powerful emotions' (2003, p. 337). Ritchie et al. discuss the need to manage risks before, during and after the interviews (2014, p. 105) in order to avoid harm for any of the participants. Although in interviews, different from some forms of health research, the interventions of research mentioned above are limited to verbal interventions, the issue of producing harm with questions or invitations to tell a life story should not be underestimated. Confrontation with sensitive topics – for example, when an educational path was irreversibly terminated by failing in school or when a disease turned terminal – can be harmful for the interviewee but also for the interviewer when seeing the other's suffering. Linked to this is the need to manage any expectations that the researcher will be able to help the participant with the particular issue the research is exploring (2014, p. 86). An issue linked to this is the need to avoid any negative consequences for the participants from doing the interview – for instance, an intensification of the disease (2014, p. 94). In their literature review, Allmark et al. (2009) mention discussions of interviews that are about sensitive issues which can make interviews emotionally intense and might harm both interviewees and interviewers, in some cases (violence studies or homeless youth) also on a physical level. Another issue discussed in the literature is the potential harm resulting from confronting interviewees with self-perceived failures in what they are talking about. Allmark et al. discuss the strategy of 'consoling refrains' mentioned in several articles – if the interviewer does not switch into a therapist's role, some issues are best avoided in the interview. In several of the articles, they summarize ways of 'Minimizing the risk of researcher burn-out and safety issues are addressed in some detail and may be summarized under the themes of personal and group support, education and training and addressing practical concerns' (2009, p. 52). These are discussed as a support for the researchers but also for avoiding harm done to the participants. They are a means of foreseeing possible sources of and ways of dealing with harm. These suggestions include supervision, ongoing research training, and in the case of researching home-less people, the option to gain experiences of working with them voluntarily (Ensign, 2003). Also, any signs of distress on the participants' side should lead to some reflec-tion on whether or not the interview should be continued.

King and Horrocks (2010, p. 122) address the other side in more detail – how to avoid harm for the researcher in doing interviews, including on the level of physical safety. If you go somewhere the interviewee suggested to do the interview, you should always have a mobile phone with you, inform someone that you are going to that place for the interview and where that is, and contact them again once the interview is finished. During the interview, you should reflect on whether you feel safe and if there are any safety issues coming up. This does not mean that you should generally suspect interviewees to be dangerous, but in many cases with spe-cific target groups it might be helpful to be aware and reflexive.

Dual Role and Over-involvement

In Chapter 3, we discussed the similarities and differences between research and therapeutic interviews, which result from the relative proximities of the two contexts of interviewing. This proximity also has implications on an ethical level in two direc-tions: the interviewee may develop inadequate expectations (about being helped by the researcher) and the interviewer has to be aware when these expectations become visible and to react adequately. In the other direction, the researcher has to take care not to become over-involved with the interviewee on a personal level, creating a friendship or taking on a responsibility, and such like. The literature Allmark et al. analysed does not offer much in the way of suggestions for how to manage this issue except to be clear about the researcher's professional background.

Politics and Power

Researchers should be able to sense situations where an interviewee feels obliged to take part in an interview and they should not overly determine what can be mentioned in the interview itself. In particular, if more than one person is interviewed in a (dyadic) interview, the researcher has to be careful not to take sides with one of the interviewees – for instance, of the parent versus the child, if both are interviewed at the same time (Allmark et al., 2009, p. 50). An issue often discussed on an ethical level is whether to pay interviewees for their participation or not. Here we suggest three concerns:

1. Is payment in general justifiable or not? In my experience, for many social groups such as homeless adolescents, long-term unemployed immigrants, or refugees, a small amount of money can be an essential support for them and a precondition for doing the interview. Groups such as physicians with their own surgery ask for compensation for their time spent on the interview instead of treating patients and being paid for this.
2. If in a study with both these groups, e.g. refugees and physicians, the question of differences in the payment of interviewees (higher sums for the physicians, or for the refugees?) may be an ethical issue.
3. And finally, this may be seen as an issue of power in relation to the interviewee.

In many contexts, interviewers have the experience of interviewees talking about the relevant issues 'off the record(ing)', which means before and after the actual interview and recording. Or they ask for the recorder to be turned off for a moment to talk about sensitive issues. The resulting question is whether interviewers should accept this, whether they have a chance to avoid this and how they treat the information from such off-the-record conversation – how they document and how they analyse the information in addition to the transcript of the recorded parts – or whether they should ignore such information for the analysis.

Another issue in the context of power and politics in interviews is who owns the data following the interview – the interviewee, the interviewer or a funding institution, for example? This may become concrete in questions such as having the right to withdraw from the research – which should always be a possibility for the participant but should be limited to a specific time period to give the researcher the chance to continue working with the data (see Box 8.2). Or should the interviewees receive a copy of the transcript of their interview? – which may produce a lot of irritation when they read what they said and thus should be avoided if possible. Should the interviewees have the right to edit the transcript? – which could again be seen as a question of ownership ('my data') but may have negative implications for the usability of the data for the researchers.

Doing Justice to Participants in Analysing Data

Analysing and writing about data implies making judgements. For example, in analysing coping with a specific problem, a person can be allocated to types of coping skills while other persons are allocated to other forms of coping behaviours. If your participants read this, they may find it embarrassing to be compared (and equated) to other people and they may also see themselves in a different way. Beyond such discrepancies in classifying oneself and being classified, 'doing justice to participants in analysing data' means that interpretations are really grounded in the data (e.g. interview statements). Also, they should not include judgements on a personal level and should not make the participants subject to a diagnostic assessment (of their personality, for example). Mertens (2014) and Wertz et al. (2011) discuss general issues of ethics in using qualitative data and their analysis. So far, we have addressed ethical issues around interviewing people in a more general way in two respects – in what concerns the target group and in the context of interviewing. Now we will turn for both to more specific cases.

Specific Target Groups of Interviewing

When we now focus on specific target groups and the ethical issues around interviewing them, all that has been said about research ethics, data protection, informed consent, and so on. should be seen as applying to these groups, too. The aim is rather to add the specific extra challenges to the issues to keep in mind when doing interviews with these groups.

Interviewing children and young people

Doing interviews with children has a long tradition in qualitative research. We can first distinguish whether the children will be interviewed in the context of a family interview or together with a parent (or some other grown-up) or alone. Second, we should clarify what 'child' means in our context. Distinctions are made according to the age of the potential interviewees, with a common classification distinguishing between 'preschoolers' (4–6 years old), 'middle childhood/preadolescence' (10–12 years old) and 'adolescents' (14–16 years old) (Garcia and Fine, 2018, p. 378). A threshold is often linked to the age of 16, when children are seen as having the capacity to make their own decisions. This legal distinction is not always compatible with the development of a specific child, who may be cognitively able to decide under the age of 16, while another cannot do so who is that age or older.

Box 8.4 Research in the real world

Interviewing children classified as learners with profound and multiple learning difficulties: Ethical precautions

Cathal Butler from the University of Bedfordshire, UK, did a study in the context of special education on how to recognize the capabilities of children classified as

(Continued)

learners with profound and multiple learning difficulties, and used interviews as part of it (https://core.ac.uk/download/pdf/161941324.pdf). In her report (Butler, 2018, p. 21) she discusses a number of precautions that have to be taken in collecting the data: 'The use of video recordings, which is considered intrusive in relation to anonymity also required careful consideration. The researcher and staff (particularly the head teacher) had a number of discussions before selecting the students who would be part of this research, to ensure that their participation was, in their judgement, in the students' best interests. Parents were provided with detailed informed consent letters, informing them of their rights and the rights of the student in relation to participation. While video recordings/photos are not uncommon as a means of collecting general assessment data in the context of special schools, it was made very clear in the consent letter to parents that these videos would not be used or accessible outside the parameters of the research. Members of staff were also consulted extensively, and ensured that the video data was being used solely to look at the developmental milestones of the learner. Staff also discussed with the researcher the sensitivities around making recordings, and were given freedom of judgement in relation to when to record and not record individual learners, if they judged that the recordings would be detrimental to the learner, or that they were demonstrating behaviour that could be deemed a withdrawal of consent.' The author also discusses ethical issues around storing and using the data: 'The data collected was kept securely at all times. When not in use, the video camera was kept in a secure, locked cabinet. Data from the camera was regularly transferred from the camera to a password protected computer/online drive, and then deleted from the camera. The videos were only accessible to the researchers, and no permissions [were] granted for their use outside of the current research. Upon completion of this research, video files will be deleted. Anonymity of participants is guaranteed through the use of pseudonyms, and the removal of potentially identifying information in publications' (2018, p. 21).

Another distinction refers to the role of children in research – whether as an object under study, as subjects whose subjective perspectives are being studied, as a social actor, who is (already) consciously and reflexively partaking in social processes, or as a participant or even co-researcher, who is actively involved in doing the research (Christensen and Prout, 2002). In each of these cases, the ethical question is about informed consent – who gives it (the child or the parent, or both)? If obtaining consent is not possible for capacity reasons (the child isn't able to oversee the questions in a consent form or cannot yet sign it), the alternative concept is 'assent', i.e. the agreement of someone who is not able to give legal consent to participate, for example because they are too young (Garcia and Fine, 2018, p. 369). In most cases, assent is not sufficient, and a gatekeeper's or an institution's consent has to be obtained as well (p. 369). The issue of consent highlights a more general ethical issue in interviewing children – can we assume that a parent's consent really represents the child's will? What is the power relation between child and parent but also between researcher and child? Christensen and Prout (2002) discuss the need to consider and establish 'ethical symmetry' between researcher and child. When holding biographical interviews with children, an extra issue may be children's lack of life experience to deal with the expectation to narrate their illness trajectory, for example (Duncan et al., 2009). If we do the interviews with parents and children together, what does this imply for confidentiality and conflicting views between parent and child? This question is also relevant if we only interview the children – can we guarantee to them that we do not (have to) talk to their parents about what we heard in the interviews? Pyer and Campbell (2013) discuss the role and impact of significant adults (parents or teachers) in the room when children are interviewed. First of all, they mention that this presence can be desired by the child, by the adult or by the researchers, and give examples in which the adults' presence had positive effects on the child and the interview. The authors also discuss how to deal with the involvement of significant adults in research with children and see two issues the researcher should focus on. First, they need to 'balance the agendas of all those involved' (2013, p. 160) – what are the parents' interests versus those of the child? Second, they emphasize the reflexivity on the researchers' side before, during and after the interview and the need to plan how to define the boundaries of the adults' involvement in the interview.

And, finally, we have to be reflexive about how far our instruments, such as the questions in an interview, are appropriate for the children we want to interview, and also must take the diversity in our target group into account if they vary in age.

Box 8.5   Research in the real world

Interviewing vulnerable younger people: Ethical dilemmas

This study (Röhnsch and Flick, 2015) addresses the health problems of a group of young adult, Russian-speaking immigrants and in particular their experiences with health services in Germany. First, with regard to the design of the study: the instruments for data collection and the information given to possible participants were presented to our university's ethics committee for approval. This implied that such information had to be produced for all possible groups of participants who were to be interviewed – in this case, the immigrants themselves and the service providers. We also needed to produce information sheets for institutions, which might support us in gaining access (see Chapter 7) to our participants (social services, meeting points, drop-in centres, etc.). For participants who might be younger than 18 years, it was necessary to obtain their parents' consent if possible. We also had to define the rules of data protection in the process, for example, in transcription, and so on. As some of the interviews would require

(Continued)

translators, we also needed to define the rules of data protection for this step. In a case where participants were not willing to sign an agreement like the one in Box 8.2, we had to find a way of documenting that they had given their informed consent before the interviews.

The case study in Box 8.5 demonstrates ethical concerns and issues related to working with younger people who are on the threshold between child and adult.

Interviewing the elderly

At the other end of the age spectrum, we may face similar issues on an ethical level. Not all research with the elderly is about illness, frailness and cognitive limitations (Stephens et al., 2018), but we have to adapt our procedures to old and maybe very old participants. Again, we face the problem of age and classification. If someone is 70 years old, the person might be seen as old but is maybe mentally, cognitively and capacity-wise younger than someone of 60 years with a greater cognitive loss. This can become relevant for answering the question of who may give the consent for participation in the study. Beyond any assumptions of cognitive degeneration, we have to be sensitive as to how we formulate information materials and consent forms for elderly participants (see also Poland and Birt, 2018; Szala-Meneok, 2009).

Box 8.6   Research in the real world

Interviewing a vulnerable group of older people

Wolfram Herrmann did his PhD in the context of a larger study on residents' sleep disorders in nursing homes. His study focuses on the residents' views of the issue of sleep, their subjective perceptions and subjective explanation of why they did not sleep well, and on how they deal with this problem. Herrmann interviewed 30 residents in five nursing homes and used the episodic interview as a method of data collection, after the research was approved by the ethics committee of a large medical university in Berlin. Ethical issues concerned how to obtain the informed consent of the potential interviewees, how to find out whether they were (still) able to give such consent, and how to give an interview. As a large part of the nursing home population in Germany suffers from cognitive restrictions, the participants had to be selected according to criteria as to whether they were oriented in 'person and place' for being included in the interviews. To ignore such a selection criterion would have meant conducting interviews with people unable to give informed consent, while applying it would exclude a major group of residents (and potential interviewees) beforehand. Taking such a criterion seriously may produce limitations when applying the results to the target group in general (nursing home residents), while ignoring the criterion may make the quality of the data questionable not only on an ethical but also on a methodological level. Being confronted with the need to apply such a selection criterion may also produce an ethical dilemma in the step of sampling (see Chapter 6).

Specific Contexts of Interviewing

In the next step, we will address specific ethical issues that come up when the classic setting of interviews – two people meet face-to-face in a specific room at a defined time and talk about an issue defined in advance, with informed consent also given in advance – is transcended.

Formal and informal interviews

Most of what has been said so far has been developed for the classic interview situation. Participants are recruited in advance and give their consent after ethical approval has been obtained. Interviews are conducted at a specific location and an appointment is made with the interviewee beforehand. Questions and an interview schedule have been developed and approved. Conditions such as recording and anonymization have been defined in advance. However, in many contexts, interview research is not only based on such formal interviews and designs. Often, more informal interviews are added to formal interviews or are the only way to do interviews in a field. In doing formal interviews, the researcher may meet other people who seem interesting and are interested in being interviewed. Or in an ethnographic study, ad hoc interviews are an option or may be the only way to talk to homeless people, for example. Sometimes, such informal interviews cannot be recorded but have to be documented in protocols. Formalized procedures of informed consent are difficult to manage, and so on. In such a case, the researchers have the obligation to adapt their work in the field and with interviewees as much as possible to the rules and suggestions discussed above. For example, interviewees should be informed that they will be speaking to a researcher in the context of a study and that their privacy will be respected. The interviewer should construct a setting in which the interviewees have maximum leeway for presenting their views and experiences. In context descriptions, researchers should try to avoid giving any details that are not necessary for their research, but might do harm to the participants; and always aim to be fair and neutral towards the interviewees.

Mobile interviewing

In Chapter 14 we will address a new trend in interviewing which extends the traditional setting of interviewing (just talking in a room, etc.) by transferring the interview into a more mobile approach. In walking or go-along interviews, the participants take the researcher on a walk through an area which is relevant for them or the research (see Chapter 14 for methodological details). Sometimes media such as taking photographs are used in addition (see Chapter 9 for details). Here new ethical dilemmas emerge, as the case study in Box 8.7 illustrates.

Box 8.7   Research in the real world

Ethical dilemmas in mobile interviewing

Penelope Kinney is a researcher at the School of Occupational Therapy at the Otago Polytech in New Zealand. She uses a study of her own (Kinney, 2018) on the transition of forensic psychiatric clients from hospital to living in the community to discuss walking interviews (see Chapter 14) including photo elicitation (see Chapter 9 for details). Kinney describes her problems in gaining ethics approval as several institutions (university, hospital, community services) were involved whose ethics committees had to approve the study. She describes eight ethical dilemmas (2018, pp. 182–4): (1) The likelihood in walking in public spaces of meeting someone who was known to the interviewee or the researcher which might lead to questions and answers endangering the interviewee's privacy. (2) Members of the public passing by who might overhear the interview conversation or end up with their own conversation and voices on the recording. (3) Using the camera in public spaces where other people were around and could end up in the photo (e.g. children) without consenting. (4) How to transport the interviewee from home to the walking interview location – especially if no funds are available for public transportation. (5) The researcher's safety if the interviewee starts to feel mentally unwell and perhaps becomes aggressive or if they take the researcher to dangerous areas the researcher is not familiar with. In such cases, the researcher should carry a mobile phone and let someone know where they are going as a backup. (6) Whether or not giving a personal mobile number to the participants for making arrangements may produce privacy issues for the researcher. (7) Avoiding hours of darkness or isolated locations might be necessary to protect the researcher. (8) Conflicts of interest may arise if the researcher checks (e.g. with staff members) about the mental state or circumstances of the participant beforehand in order to calculate risks and to prepare for the interview.

Some of the dilemmas mentioned in the case study in Box 8.7 may occur in other forms of interviewing as well, but are more relevant here, while others are specific to this kind of research. They show the need to plan research on an ethical level as well.

Interviewing with digital technologies

When interviews are done online (see Chapter 15), most of the general issues around research ethics in interviewing apply as well. Salmons (2015) discusses research ethics in general, but also some specific issues for online interviewing. Informed consent, for example, should include the technological side of being interviewed – for instance, do participants have to wear headsets to answer the questions, and do they need to be adept in using a computer (2015, p. 151)? Interviewees' privacy should be kept as in other contexts, even if the participants have exposed much of the information in social media already. Data protection should also focus on the ways the data are produced online, by email, for example, and ensure that they cannot be accessed by someone else. Gaiser and Schreiner (2009, p. 14) have listed a number of questions to consider from an ethical point of view when planning an online study. They include questions such as: Can participant security be guaranteed? Anonymity? Protection of the data? Can someone ever really be anonymous online? And if not, how might this impact on the overall study design? Can someone 'see' a participant's information, when s/he participates? Can someone not associated with the study access data on a hard drive? Is it ever OK to deceive online? What constitutes online deception? These questions show how general issues of research ethics are relevant for online as well as traditional research.

Research Ethics in Constructing a Setting for Listening

In this chapter, we have addressed the frameworks relevant to carrying out interview research in an ethically sound way. Doing so has advanced from an originally moral approach – that is, conditions of acceptable research respecting and protecting the participants – to a formal and legal obligation – for example, working with informed consent and approval by ethics committees and solid ways of ensuring data protection. On a practical level, this has also advanced to a consideration of how to plan a study with interviews (see Box 8.8).

Box 8.8   Research in the real world

Planning an interview study in an ethically sound way

Designing an interview study in an ethically sound way includes suggestions for preparing (1) the framework of doing the interview (information, consent, documentation and setting) and (2) how to develop the actual interview (questions, attitude towards the interviewees).

(Continued)

Steps involved in planning ethically sound interviews	Six F's of designing interview research
Reflect in advance again	
1. What is the research question behind the interviews?	Focusing
2. What kind of people will be relevant as interviewees and which specific issues in research ethics relate to them?	Foreseeing
3. What might be some ethically problematic aspects of the research?	Foreseeing
Steps involved in ethically preparing a framework for listening in the interview	
1. What institutional agreements do you need?	Framing
2. Reflect on what potential interviewees should know in advance in order to be ready to join your study. Start from what the interviewees will perhaps already have experienced about the conditions of the study when making the appointment for an interview.	Foreseeing
3. Which issues should you inform the participants about?	Focusing
4. What should you take care of in obtaining informed consent?	Focusing
5. Prepare to write a detailed description of how the interview went in the single cases: What problems or unclear situations occurred on the level of interview ethics?	Formulating
6. Prepare to reflect on and write about the (potential) interviewees you have lost in the process and what that means from an ethical perspective for your study.	Finding and Formulating
7. Frame (in keywords) how to ask interviewees from an ethical perspective for feedback on being interviewed.	Framing
Steps involved in preparing the conduct and content of interviews in an ethically sound way	
8. How might your main questions stress out your interviewees?	Foreseeing
9. What are the ethical issues in interviewees' experiences that provide information about the central topic(s)?	Foregrounding
10. Phrase the criteria that your interviews should meet ethically.	Formulating
11. How do you take social and cultural diversity in your interview(ee)s into account in an ethically sensitive way?	Foregrounding
12. Note down some keywords about what is important in asking your questions and conducting the interview.	Formulating

However, in our approach, constructing the ethical soundness of research is also a practical concern in building a solid ground for the interviewees, allowing them to reveal their views and the interviewers to listen to an interviewee's unrestricted presentation. By giving sufficient information and by making consent explicit for both sides, by clarifying issues of privacy and data protection as well as by creating a respectful and harm-free climate with in the dialogue, the researchers will be able to reduce the reservations on the interviewees' side and permit – for both sides – a fruitful and open-minded dialogue in the interview. Research ethics are also a matter of designing interview research (see Chapter 5) and the design elements (the six F's) are relevant here as well. *Framing* means here to set up a framework that allows the interviewee to trust the researcher and the interview situation. *Finding* means that the researcher will identify the ethically relevant aspects of this particular research study and for this particular participant. *Focusing* means that the researcher has an eye on the single interviewee's needs and what might stress them out in the interview situation. *Foreseeing* refers to reflecting on what could be harmful or stressful for interviewees or for some of them. *Formulating* means that questions and comments have to be worded in a respectful way, and that findings from the interviews are treated carefully and respectfully. *Foregrounding* refers to how much the interview creates a space for the interviewee's individual experience and situation and not just for what the interviewer had in mind theoretically regarding the issue and the interviewees beforehand. Research ethics, however, are not something to think about once, clarify and tick off. Rather, it is an issue that runs through the whole process of an interview study, from formulating a research question to selecting and approaching participants. It continues through the development of instruments to doing interviews, analysing the data and publishing the findings of the process.

Steps, Aims and Criteria in Preparing and Doing Ethically Sound Interview Studies

How exactly a study is conducted in an ethical way depends on the researcher's reflexivity in preparing, developing and using instruments and in creating relationships and encounters with participants. This will be addressed in subsequent chapters.

Table 8.1 Steps, aims and criteria in preparing and doing ethically sound interviews

Six F's of designing interview research	Steps	Aims and actions	Criteria
Framing	1. Preparing information for interviewees to enable them to give their consent	• Clarify the research question • Prepare an information sheet for interviewees about what they will agree to in the consent form	• Is your information material adequate for the area under study? • Does the documentation of the interview cover the information relevant to analysing the process ethically?

(Continued)

Table 8.1 (Continued)

Six F's of designing interview research	Steps	Aims and actions	Criteria
Foreseeing	2. Clarifying what is ethically relevant in the case of your participants	• Reflect on the criteria for being relevant as a participant for your study	• Do you take into account specific conditions, e.g. vulnerability, very young or very old age?
Formulating	3. Preparing how to obtain informed consent	• Prepare steps in which you will check what your participants need to know in deciding to participate	• Are there any dimensions in your obtaining informed consent? • Which of these are relevant to answering your research question?
Foregrounding	4. The central aspects in your ethics check	• Try to reflect on areas of the field of your study and your participants' situation	• Do these aspects cover cultural specificity and diversity?
Focusing	5. Comparison and ethical implications	• Try to get into the detail of the variety and diversity concerning the issue of your study • Try to advance the depth and richness of the experiences becoming visible in the interviews	• Are there main and secondary dimensions of comparison? • Are these leading to new insights? • What are the ethical implications of your comparison plan?
Foreseeing	6. Socio-demographic characteristics and data	• Develop a checklist for this purpose • Apply the documentation sheet and extend it if necessary	• Is all necessary information included for contextualizing interviewees' statements and narratives for ethical aspects?
Framing	7. Saturation and stopping data collection	• Reflect on what saturation means in your study and what it means to stop interviewing and leave out potential participants	• What are good reasons to see saturation has been reached? • Has everyone ready but not yet interviewed been adequately informed?
Finding and Formulating	8. Making your treatment of ethical questions transparent	• Think about what should be covered in a description of the interviews and of the cases	• Does this description cover social and cultural diversity aspects in your interviewing?

What You Need to Ask Yourself

The questions in Box 8.9 are designed to guide you in how to use interviews in an ethically sound way. You may also apply these questions to studies with interviews you read. If you lack the knowledge to make the decision at this point, these questions can be taken into consideration as you read the following chapters of this book.

Box 8.9 What you need to ask yourself

Ethics and interviewing

1. What might the ethical issues in your interviews be and how will you manage them?
2. How will you inform all participants who are taking part in your study or are involved in it?
3. How will you put the principle of informed consent into practice?
4. How will you ensure that participants are not harmed in any way by the study or by taking part in your interviews?
5. How will you guarantee the voluntariness of the participation?
6. What is it important to document about the context of your interviews as part of the data?
7. How will you organize the anonymization of the data and the issues of data protection in the study?
8. Have you checked your method of proceeding against the relevant ethical code(s)?
9. If so, what problems became evident here?
10. Is a statement from an ethics committee necessary for your study and, if so, have you obtained it?
11. What is the novelty in the expected results which justifies doing your project?

What You Need to Succeed

In this chapter, some conceptual and practical issues around how to conduct interview research in an ethically sound way have been addressed, which also apply to the methods discussed in the later parts of the book and refer to the steps involved in interview research mentioned in earlier parts. The questions in Box 8.10 may help you plan and conduct your study while respecting and protecting its potential participants.

Box 8.10   What you need to succeed

Ethics and interviewing

1. Do I understand the importance of reflecting on research ethics for interview research?
2. Am I aware of how to take the ethical principles and challenges involved in doing interviewing research into account?
3. Do I see the necessity of informed consent and of data protection?

What you have learned

- Finding solutions to ethical dilemmas is essential to legitimate interview research.
- In interview research, ethical dilemmas are sometimes particularly difficult to resolve.
- Codes of ethics regulate the treatment of ethical issues generally. Ethics committees can be important in assessing research proposals and the rights and interests of the participants.
- The dynamics of ethical dilemmas reveal themselves in the field and in contact with people or institutions.
- Many ethical dilemmas arise from the need to weigh the research interest (better knowledge, new solutions for existing problems, and so on) against the interest of participants (confidentiality, avoidance of any harm, and the like).
- Specific target groups (e.g. children or the elderly) raise additional ethical issues that need to be taken into account.
- Specific methodological developments (e.g. mobile or digital interviewing) come with additional ethical issues.
- Data protection becomes more and more an issue for careful consideration.
- Research ethics are an issue of regulation and committees.
- But the decisive point is how to act ethically in a study and before, during and after holding interviews.

Exercises

In the exercises, you are first invited to reflect on some of the main issues in this chapter. Then you are invited to apply the topics of this chapter to the development of a project of your own. Hence, the exercises are a combination of reflection and prospection.

Exercise 8.1

Reflecting on the Chapter: Ethical Issues in an Existing Study Using Interviews

1. Take a qualitative study (like Taylor, 2012) and determine whether the author(s) addressed ethical issues. How did they deal with them? What other issues around research ethics might be expected in such a study?
2. What are the ethical issues relevant to that study (even if they are not mentioned by the author(s)?

Exercise 8.2

Planning Your Own Research with Interviews

1. For your own study, identify and reflect on the ethical issues, establish guidelines and create a plan for participants.

What's next

This article illustrates the practice of doing ethics in interviews:

Allmark, P., Boote, J., Chambers, E., Clarke, A., McDonnell, A., Thompson, A., & Tod, A.M. (2009). Ethical Issues in the Use of In-Depth Interviews: Literature Review and Discussion. *Research Ethics*, 5(2), 48-54. https://doi.org/10.1177/174701610900500203

In this article, ethical and methodological issues around work with participants' statements in publications are discussed in detail:

Taylor, S. (2012). 'One Participant Said ...': The Implications of Quotations from Biographical Talk. *Qualitative Research*, 12(4), 388-401.

This chapter illustrates the problems seen when applying Western concepts of research ethics to indigenous and decolonizing research:

Chilisa, B. (2009). Indigenous African-Centered Ethics: Contesting and Complementing Dominant Models. In D.M. Mertens & P.E. Ginsberg (Eds.), *The Handbook of Social Research Ethics* (pp. 407-25). Thousand Oaks, CA: Sage.

Doing Interview Research Navigator

How to understand interview research

- What doing interview research means
- Theories and epistemologies of interviewing
- When to choose interviews as a research method
- Methods and formats of interviewing

Designing interview research

- Planning and designing interview research
- How many interviewees: Sampling and saturation
- Accessing and recruiting participants

You are here in your project

How to conduct interviews

- How to respect and protect: Ethics of interviewing
- Semi-structured interviews: Working with questions and answers
- Interviewing experts and elites
- Integrating narratives in interviews: Episodic interviews

Doing interviews in context

- How to work with life histories: Narrative interviews
- Working with focus groups as interviews
- Ask (in) the field: Ethnographic and mobile interviewing
- Doing online interviews

How to work with interview data

- Working with interview data
- Credibility and transparency: Quality and writing in interview research
- From interviewing to an inner view: Critiques and reflexivity

SEMI-STRUCTURED INTERVIEWS: WORKING WITH QUESTIONS AND ANSWERS

How this chapter will help you

You will:

- understand the use of questions in doing interviews,
- be introduced to the various types of questions used in interviews,
- learn what interview guides are about,
- understand the role of tools in interviewing,
- be introduced to the challenges of working with interviews in different or foreign languages, and
- learn how to construct a framework for listening in semi-structured interviewing.

In this chapter, the most common form of doing interviews and of being interviewed is our focus. Interviewers ask questions and hope to receive answers about their research topic, about the participants' attitudes towards it, and to identify the variety and variability in these attitudes. Questions can be formulated in different ways and the number of people studied with them may also vary. This rather stereotypical image of doing an interview can also be found in many of the standard textbooks on interviewing. They mainly focus on *the* qualitative interview, sometimes labelled with a new name or a specific aspect of interviewing, for example the relationship to the interviewee, the aspect of reflexivity, and so on. Sometimes the focus is on one concept of interviewing, in other cases interviewing is discussed in relation to the various epistemological backgrounds it can be based on. Rather seldom, we find an approach presenting several methods of interviewing in a differentiating way, amongst which the semi-structured interview is only one of the available alternatives. In this chapter, this first way of constructing a framework for listening to the participant and for doing interviews is discussed in some detail, before the succeeding chapters discuss several other ways of interviewing for their backgrounds, principles and purposes as alternative methods of constructing such a framework.

Background to Semi-structured Interviewing

Types of questions

At one end of the range of using questions in interviewing, the structuration and standardization of questions become relevant, in particular when bigger samples are studied and maybe even by several interviewers. Then often the possible answers are limited to five or seven alternatives, which means the interview comes close to some kind of questionnaire study. At the other end of the scale, various kinds of open questions are discussed and used. In-between we find several suggestions for semi-structured or semi-standardized questions. Thus, we can distinguish several ways of formulating questions for interviews from closed to open questions.

At the same time, several functions for questions can be distinguished. We find *main questions* and *sub-questions* as parts of a prepared interview guide. Questions for *probing* what was said in response to a question can also be formulated in advance, but mainly need to be developed in the course of the interview. This also applies to **follow-up questions**, which come back to the topic raised in an earlier question in the interview and what was said about it. *Explorative* questions are asked to start the dialogue about the topic in general before more focused questions follow. Finally, *generative* questions aim, for example, at stimulating a *narrative* about a process or period (see Chapter 12) or at starting a *discussion* about the issue in a group interview or a focus group (see Chapter 13).

Structured and semi-structured interviewing

The use of questions with smaller samples and in qualitative research in general is often embedded in what is called semi-structured interviews. To clarify the specific potential and challenges of developing semi-structured interviews, we will first briefly address its opposite – what characterizes a structured interview?

Structured interviews: wording and sequence of questions

Structured interviews have a neopositivist understanding of interviewing as an epistemological background (see Chapter 2). In structured interviews, the main challenge is to formulate questions in advance, which can be used with several interviewees and by several interviewers without biasing the answers or the individual interviewees. Therefore, questions have to be constructed in a precise way and so that they represent as exactly as possible what they should cover regarding the topic of the study. At the same time, questions should be easy to understand and clear, so that the interviewee doesn't have to think too hard about what they mean. Finally, questions should be arranged in a sequence which is logical and at the same time free of any influence from one question to another. Thus, the literature is full of rules and suggestions for how to organize an interview schedule in an optimal way. Although not all the suggestions made in this context can be covered here, some examples will be discussed.

Suggestions refer first to question wording. For surveys and standardized interviews, Porst (2014) has formulated '10 commandments' of question wording, starting from the notion that 'bad questions lead to bad data and no procedure of weighing and no method of analysing the data can make good results from bad data' (2014, p. 118). Porst's commandments are designed to ensure that questions are clearly formulated and do not over-challenge or confuse respondents. Questions for structured interviewing and surveys should be based on 'simple unambiguous concepts which are understood by all respondents in the same way'; interviewers should 'avoid long and complex, … [or] hypothetical questions, … double stimuli and negotiations, … presumptions and suggestive questions or aiming at information many respondents presumably will not have'; they should 'use questions with a clear temporal reference, … answer categories which are exhaustive and … free of overlap … ensure that the context of a question does not impact on answering it … [and] … define unclear concepts' (2014, pp. 99–100). Although the aim is to have clear, unambiguous and standardized questions presented to each and every interviewee in the same way, Porst admits that these rules should be understood only as an orientation as 'most of the rules leave room for interpretation and sometimes … are even in competition with each other and thus cannot be applied a hundred per cent at the same time' (2014, p. 118). When answering questions according to this way of thinking about interviews in surveys, options for answering are often reduced to a very limited range, such as that shown in Figure 9.1 (a five-degree agreement scale).

Answers given in such a format are easy to transfer into numbers, which can be processed for statistical analysis.

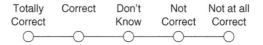

Figure 9.1   Five-degree agreement scale

A second issue in this context is the structure of an interview schedule. In order to avoid any overloading of an interview schedule, Bortz and Döring (2006, pp. 244–6) suggest using a checklist for assessing standardized oral questions including guiding points such as:

- Are all the questions necessary?
- Are redundant questions included?
- Which questions are superfluous?

They also address the effect of the position of questions and the framing of an interview schedule:

- Might the result be influenced by the position of the questions?
- Are the opening questions adequately formulated and has the interview a properly reflected end?

Finally, they suggest reflecting the adequacy of the questions to the potential interviewees:

- Are questions formulated in a suggestive way?
- Will the interviewee be potentially able to answer the questions?
- Is there a risk that the questions will be embarrassing for the interviewee?

The main purpose of these suggestions for how to formulate questions and how to construct an interview schedule is to increase the clarity of the instrument, to reduce its influences on the data by reducing vagueness of formulations and differences between the interviews done with them. The aim of the above suggestions is less to develop a framework for the interviewees for exploring their individual experiences and perspectives and more to reduce any bias in the answers stemming from the way the questions and the interview schedule are constructed. In the context of structured interviewing, the interviewees' specific perspectives and the leeway for making their subjectivity heard are not relevant in constructing the instrument – as long as the questions are formulated in such a way that the interviewee is able to answer them.

The framework constructed for listening to what participants have to say about their experience or attitude is strongly determined by the researcher's thematic and methodological interests and leaves much room for the individual interviewee's particular situation, views or expressions.

The focused interview as a prototype of semi-structured interviewing

As an early version of semi-structured interviewing as a method, the focused interview was developed by Robert Merton and his team (Merton and Kendall, 1946; Merton et al., 1956). Its epistemological background is a localist position (see Chapter 2).

When constructing interview guides and doing interviews, four criteria are helpful, which were initially developed for focused interviews. These criteria are: (1) *Range*, meaning the interview should cover a broad range of meanings the issue might have for the participant. (2) *Specificity* refers to interviewees' view and definition of the situation and should characterize the answers stimulated by the questions. (3) *Depth* means that the 'interview should help interviewees to describe the affective, cognitive, and evaluative meanings of the situation and their involvement in it' (Merton et al., 1956, p. 12). (4) *Personal context* should become visible in the interviewees' answers, so that the issue's meanings for them should be transparent. In addition to these criteria, Merton et al. emphasize two principles of conceiving interviews: first, that the interview should be characterized by no *non-direction* in relations with the interviewees, similar to how a good therapist explores patients' situations; second, *retrospection* is a central feature of the interview situation: 'The primary objective of the focused interview is to elicit as complete a report as possible of what was involved in the experience of a particular situation' (1956, p. 21). This method and the methodological discussion of criteria and aims are still relevant for what has since been developed as methods of semi-structured interviewing. The means for meeting the above criteria and aims in the focused interview are mainly to use various types of questions, including unstructured, semi-structured and structured questions. Originally, the focused interview was developed to understand the effect of propaganda materials in the Second World War and interviewees were asked about the perception of contents of films, for example, and their reactions to them. These materials (films or sometimes texts) were presented to the participants before or during the interview and then questions referred to the content of the materials. As the materials had been content analysed before, the researchers had a clearer idea what the interviewees were talking about or responding to. In this context, unstructured questions are very open, not asking for specific detail in the film or for a specific kind of reaction (e.g. 'What impressed you most about this film?'). Semi-structured questions either define the concrete issue (e.g. a certain scene in a film) and leave the response to it open (e.g. 'How did you feel about the part describing Jo's discharge from the army as a psychoneurotic?'), or define the reaction and leave the concrete issue open (e.g. 'What did you learn from this pamphlet which you hadn't known before?'). In structured questions, both parts are defined (e.g. 'As you listened to Chamberlain's speech, did you feel it was propagandistic or informative?'). Interviewers should ask unstructured questions first and introduce increased structuring only later during the interview; this prevents the interviewer's frame of reference being imposed on the interviewee's viewpoints.

Although current research with the focused interview in its original format is hard to find, the ideas behind this method have influenced the use of semi-structured interviews (and still do) in four respects. First, the four criteria mentioned above (range, specificity, depth and personal context) describe quite well how an interview should be planned and conducted so that we know more about the interviewees' stance on an issue than a questionnaire study could reveal. Second, the attitude outlined in the two principles (retrospection and non-direction) makes the interviewer sensitive to how the interviewees see and interpret situations, objects or their experiences with them. A third heritage of the focused interview for current uses of semi-structured interviewing is the use of various types of question, including open and more focused and structured questions. This idea can be found in various types of qualitative interviewing. And fourth, the idea of developing an interview guide that refers to the important aspects of the issue under study and of using it in a flexible way adapted to the dialogue with the interviewee, is the defining principle in semi-structured interviewing. The focused interview was the first method of interviewing in which visual or textual materials were employed as tools for eliciting reflections and answers on the interviewees' side (see later in this chapter for this extension of interviewing). And finally, as we saw in Chapter 4, the concept has been taken up as focused life-story interviews by Edwards et al. (2005) in the context of indigenous research (see also Chapter 12).

Constructing a Framework for Listening in Semi-structured Interviews

Preparing the interview

The idea of designing interviews in a semi-structured way has been developed as distinct from a more methods-oriented, rather than participant-oriented, way of interviewing in a survey. For semi-structured interviews as well, a number of questions are prepared that are supposed to address the intended scope of the interview. For this purpose, an interview *guide* is developed as an orientation for the interviewers and not an interview *schedule*. However, the above list of guiding points developed for structured interviews may be applied to semi-structured interviewing as well for checking whether questions are clearly formulated or redundant. In contrast to structured interviewing, interviewers can alter the sequence of questions and also do not necessarily stick to the exact wording of the questions when asking them. The aim of interviewing is to get as close as possible to the interviewees' individual views on an issue. Therefore, questions should rather stimulate a dialogue between interviewer and interviewee than realize a kind of exact measurement. Again, in contrast to structured interviews and questionnaires, the interviewer will not present a list of possible answers to the interviewees. Rather, the participants are expected to reply as freely and as extensively as they wish. If their answers are not detailed enough, the interviewer should probe further.

Interview Guides

Aims of using interview guides

Interview guides for semi-structured interviewing are less strictly planned and organized than interview schedules in structured interviewing. They are intended to guide both the interviewer and the interviewee through the topical landscape of the interview and of the study issue. They are organized aiming at being open to the individual participants' particular views and experience and oriented to the issue of the study and to addressing its relevant aspects. Finally, they should contribute to making interviews comparable among the various participants and across the various topics coming up in the interviews.

Research question and interview questions

It is important in doing qualitative interviews to understand the distinction between *research questions* and *interview questions*. The research question is developed from a researcher's general or scientific interest in a topic. The wording of a research question is often mainly characterized by scientific concepts and terms and their relations (does vulnerability increase the risk of becoming mentally ill?). If the way to research this interest is to use a semi-structured interview, then the challenge is to translate the content, concepts and elements of the research question into questions that ask interviewees about their situation, their views and experiences. The term 'vulnerability', for example, has to be transformed into questions about the living situation, stresses and social, economic and other conditions. The challenge is to find expressions and wordings that refer to the interviewees' life worlds, mundane ways of thinking and talking about these issues, and which stimulate participants to reflect and answer in detail and in a personal way.

What kinds of questions can be asked in interviews?

Patton (2015, p. 445) lists six kinds of questions that can be asked in interviews. Questions can refer to interviewees' (1) experiences and behaviours; (2) opinions and values; (3) feelings; (4) knowledge; (5) sensory perceptions; and (6) personal background and demographic situation. First of all, this list is interesting as it gives you an idea as to what interviews can refer to and normally do. It can also give you an orientation as to what to look for in doing interviews. The list also shows that in a qualitative interview you will mostly ask less about how something 'really' was or happened, and more for interviewees' experiences with that something. Or you will not so much ask about how a hospital is designed, but about the sensory perceptions of it (e.g. 'How did it smell when you went there for the first time?'; 'What was your impression of the colour of the corridors?'; 'What was your first (or strongest) impression on entering this building?'). Patton's list also does not mean that all the kinds of questions in it have to be asked in every interview, but it gives an orientation about *how* questions can be asked and on what level (subjective impressions, for example, rather than facts). You can ask what someone knows about an issue, but of course this is not a knowledge test or exam.

How to construct an interview guide

Interview guides consist of questions. Mostly they include several kinds of questions, for example more open ones and those that are more focused on a specific aspect. In most cases, both questions and the guide refer to several areas of the topic (e.g. reasons, features, consequences of a phenomenon being studied), or of interviewees' (everyday or professional) lives, in which the phenomenon might be relevant or experienced. This means that an interview guide is often constructed around single questions but also with a structure that connects the questions. Finally, an interview should have a beginning and an ending, which should be planned in a way that supports the dialogue about the issues of the interview, that allows the interviewees to feel safe and well in the interview situation and that gives them the impression that the interviewers know what they are doing.

Preparing several kinds of questions

Depending on your research question, on the issue you want to study, and on the type of interview you want to conduct, it may be helpful to prepare several kinds of questions. More open ones about the issue can be complemented by more focused ones (addressing specific aspects of it). Sometimes questions are purposefully formulated in a confrontational way after a number of open questions have been asked. Some interviews (see Chapter 11 for the episodic interview) include narrative invitations to recount a specific situation, for example. Asking for descriptions can be complemented by more explanatory questions. Thus, it makes sense not only to plan the topics of the single questions but also the format or features of how the question should be asked and to vary this across the interview guide.

Main and follow-up questions

When preparing the interview guide, it is helpful not only to include the questions that should be answered in any case. These are the main questions that ideally cover the topic of the interview and what the interviewee has to say about it. It is also helpful to prepare follow-up questions that should be asked if the response to one of the main questions is not as comprehensive as expected or if one or more aspects are not mentioned. Even if it is only within the interview situation itself that we can ascertain what these missing aspects are, it is helpful to reflect in advance and prepare questions for deepening, extending or completing the dialogue about the issues in the interview. Box 9.1 presents some ideas of what to reflect on and prepare in constructing an interview guide for a semi-structured interview. Each step is linked to the six F's of designing interview research discussed in Chapter 5.

Box 9.1   Research in the real world

Planning a semi-structured interview

Planning an interview includes suggestions for preparing (1) the framework for listening in the interview (data protection, general guidelines on questions and on the length and type of the conversation) and (2) the conduct of the interview (bringing in the subject, question areas, questions, etc.).

Steps involved in planning a semi-structured interview	Six F's of designing interview research
Reflect in advance again	
1. Who will be relevant as a potential interviewee?	Finding
2. What is the research question behind the interview?	Focusing
Steps involved in preparing a framework for listening in semi-structured interviews	
1. Reflect on what the interviewees should know in advance in order to be well prepared for the interview and understand what it is about and what their role should be. Start from what the interviewee has perhaps already learned about your study when making the appointment for the interview.	Framing
2. Phrase (in keywords) an appropriate introduction to the interview for the following aspects: the purpose of the interview, recording and data protection. (After agreement, turn on the recording device). Frame an explanation of what the interview will be about, e.g. a very personal view; and give an explanation of how the conversation will proceed and how long it will probably take. (The actual interview starts at this point.)	Framing
3. Frame (in keywords) how to conclude the interview, including asking if they have anything to add and for their feedback.	Framing
Steps involved in preparing the conduct and content of semi-structured interviews	
4. Overview of subjects of interest for the interview.	Foreseeing
5. What themes are of central interest?	Foreseeing
6. What area of the interviewees' professional, everyday life, for example, can provide information about the central topic(s)?	Foreseeing
7. For every area, frame an open question that might motivate the interviewee, as clearly and unambiguously as possible, to provide, for every topic under point 6, examples related to the main themes (e.g. if you look back, what do you link to ...? Could you give me an example of this in some detail?)	Foregrounding
8. For every area, phrase some questions about relationships, etc. that might stimulate the interviewees, as clearly and unambiguously as possible, to express their views of these relationships or concepts (e.g. what is .... for you? What do you associate with this term?).	Formulating
9. Note down some keywords for probing central aspects, which you would like to return to if the interviewee does not spontaneously mention them.	Foreseeing

Using Questions and Interview Guides Reflexively

Whatever type of interview has been selected and whichever questions you prepared, the success of an interview depends on the reflexive use of both in the dialogue with the interviewees. Interviewing is something that can be learned and well prepared for.

Learning to interview

A first step is to read about interviews – in textbooks, methodological articles, case studies, reflections, and if possible interview transcripts. However, such a more theoretical approach is just one step. Experience shows that interviewing can be learned best by actually doing interviews. Seminars teaching interview skills should include the practical parts of doing interviews, from developing research questions to interview questions and guides to interviewing real people, transcribing and analysing the interviews. Small group work and workshops are good approaches that allow trainees to get into the practical challenges.

Learning from mistakes and failures

Several authors have suggested having a closer look at mistakes made in interviews and analysing interview failures. Roulston (2011b, p. 81) discusses in some detail four interview 'problems' as a source for improving interviewers' skills. She sees a (1) tendency to use the interview guide as a spoken survey, which means simply reading the questions out to the interviewee as they are formulated in the interview guide. (2) Questions that are asked in the actual interview tend to be closed rather than open questions, so that exploration is rather blocked and the interviewers find their assumptions confirmed. (3) The same applies when questions provide possible responses already or (4) include assumptions about participants' life worlds. Roulston's way of dealing with such problems is to do a conversation analysis of interview interaction (see Briggs, 1986; Rapley, 2012, for extended approaches to such an analysis).

Preparing interviews and interview training

For semi-structured interviews, detailed **interview training** has proved helpful. Here, the application of the interview guide is learned in role-plays among the participants in simulated interviews, which should be recorded or videotaped. The recording is discussed with all the interviewers involved in a study (or students participating in a seminar). Issues are how the interview guide was used, procedures and problems in introducing and changing topics, interview mistakes, the interviewers' non-verbal behaviour and their reactions to the interviewees. This discussion aims at making different interviewers' interventions and their steering of the interviews more comparable. This allows to take up 'technical' problems (how to design and conduct interviews) and to discuss solutions for further supporting and improving interviewing, the use of questions and the guide and the interaction with the interviewees. Ultimately, this may lead to a revision of questions, their wording and the interview guide as well.

The successful conduct of such interviews depends essentially on the interviewer's situational competence. This competence may be increased by having practical experience of making the necessary decisions in interview situations, in rehearsal interviews and in interview training, in which interview situations are simulated and analysed afterwards, with a view to providing trainee interviewers with some experience. Some examples are given of typical needs for decisions between more depth (obtained by probing) and guaranteeing the range (by introducing new topics or the next question in the interview guide), with the different solutions at each point. This makes the difficulties of pursuing contradictory targets easier to handle, although they cannot be completely resolved.

Doing Semi-structured Interviewing

Beginning an interview appropriately

The important step of beginning an interview in an appropriate way includes several challenges: to welcome the interviewees, to produce a comfortable situation for them, and to explain again what the interviewees should expect from the interview situation and what is expected of them. Interviewees should receive all the information about the study and the interview that is necessary for their participation – so that they know what they have agreed to do. A crucial step is to have a consent form filled in and signed which also clarifies the researcher's responsibility for protecting the data and privacy of the interviewee. It is also important to highlight again that the interview will be recorded and transcribed in an anonymous form, to reiterate who is allowed to read it (see Chapter 8, Box 8.3) and to obtain the interviewee's agreement to these points. The most important challenge is to establish a rapport between the interviewee and the interviewer. It is helpful to offer water or coffee to the interviewee. At the same time, it is important to keep in mind that this is not a meeting among friends to chat about an issue, but rather the interviewer has some personal (e.g. writing a thesis) or professional (e.g. working on a research project) interest and the interviewee is in a position to share knowledge, insights or experiences the interviewer does not have. The real challenge in this part of the interview is to establish a relation on both levels – a professional one and a personal one – so that the exchange is open but without giving a wrong impression or producing false expectations. Of similar importance is that the researchers should be aware that their research questions are not the same as the interview questions. Thus, they should try to use everyday language instead of scientific concepts with in the questions. Discovering theoretical concepts and using scientific concepts is something for the data analysis process; using concrete everyday wording is what, in contrast, should happen in the questions and the interview, as Hermanns (2004, pp. 212–13) holds. Most crucial in his suggestions (in my experience) is that during the interview you should try to discover not theoretical concepts, but rather the life world of the interviewees.

Asking questions

This is the central aspect of the semi-structured interview – how to ask questions in an appropriate way. It is based on a translation process in two respects. As mentioned above, first the research question of the study has to be translated into several questions in the interview guide – which means nailing it down into some kind of everyday language and into experience-near concepts. Brinkmann and Kvale demonstrate this in the following example: a research question ('Which form of learning motivation dominates in high school?') is translated into three interviewer questions: 'Do you find the subjects you are learning important?', 'Do you find learning interesting in itself?', 'What is your main purpose in going to high school?' (2018, p. 66). This step is located in preparing the interview guide. The second step is to translate this question from the interview guide into a question in the conversation with the interviewee. This means (1) asking it at a point when it fits into the issues the conversation is addressing and (2) in a way that fits into this conversation without losing the point that is behind the question. To achieve this, it may be necessary to adapt the wording of the question to the interview situation. And it means that the interviewer should continue to explore a subject until the interviewees have said what is important for them on this point.

In general, questions in an interview should be open and explorative. Questions should always be asked in a way that addresses interviewees' personal concerns, views, thoughts or opinions about the issue in question. Brinkmann and Kvale suggest a number of linguistic forms for questions, such as:

> Can you describe it to me?; What happened?; What did you do? How do you remember it?; How did you experience it? What do you feel about it?; How was your emotional reaction to this event? What do you think about it? How do you conceive of this issue?; What is your opinion of what happened? How do you judge it today? (2018, p. 69)

In later chapters in this book, you will find more examples of interview questions for the other methods discussed there. However, in most cases, the interviewees' response to such questions or interview questions in general will not be exhaustive in at least two respects: (1) in what the interviewees (would) have to say about the topic in question and about their relation to it; (2) in what the interviewer has expected as aspects that are relevant for the interviewee but also for answering the research question. In both cases, it may be necessary to ask again before moving on to the next question or part of the interview guide.

Probing

The term 'probing' means to ask for more or deeper aspects of what the interviewee has said in answering a question. Probing questions should not predefine what exactly should be added, but invite the interviewees to explore the issue and their views on it further. Brinkmann and Kvale give some examples of probing questions: 'Could you say something more about that?'; 'Can you give a more detailed description of what happened?'; 'Do you have further examples of this?' (2018, p. 67). The art of probing does not only include the basic decisions around when to probe and how to do it, but also sufficient awareness to know when to stop asking another question of this kind without annoying the interviewee. Thus, there has to be a balance between the further interest of the research(er), the assumed additional contribution of the interviewee and the interactional adequacy of the conversational process and relationship of the two participants. This interactional adequacy also depends on the point reached in the interview process. In the first part of the interview, it may be helpful to probe more extensively in order to adjust levels of exploring the issue and of the comprehensiveness required in answering a question on the interviewee's part. When the interview has run for quite some time and comes close to what the planned timeframe was and when the interviewee shows some exhaustion of the topic and the situation, it may be necessary to probe in a more limited way.

Active listening

Both when asking questions and when probing, interviewers should do and demonstrate active listening. This concept comes originally from (non-directive) therapy, but is also relevant in contexts such as management, as McNaughton et al. show: 'The goal in active listening is to develop a clear understanding of the speaker's concern and also to clearly communicate the listener's interest in the speaker's message' (2008, p. 224). For interviewing, this means interviewers should demonstrate their attention and encourage the interviewees to continue with what they are saying. According to Ayres (2008), this includes non-verbal communication, such as being relaxed but turned to the interviewees, orienting one's body to the speaker and focusing on the face, for example. Verbal communication includes 'paraphrasing, reflecting, interpreting, summarizing and checking perceptions' (2008, p. 8). In all these cases, the interviewers should be careful not to alter the meaning of what was said, when paraphrasing it in their own words, for example. To wait and be silent can also be a way of communicating that there is interest in and space for more of what the interviewee has to say. The art of active listening is about managing and demonstrating attention without intervention. Active listening includes three essential elements: the listener's non-verbal involvement, reflecting back the speaker's message and encouraging the speaker to provide elaboration and further details (see Weger et al., 2010). Active listeners avoid making judgement on the speaker (see Spataro and Bloch, 2018).

Box 9.2   Research in the real world

Interview extract

Rebecca Dimond from Cardiff University did research with families with a child with genetic syndromes as a social scientist doing a PhD at the Economic and Social Research Council (ESRC) Centre for Economic and Social Aspects of Genomics (Cesagen), Cardiff University, and thus working in an interdisciplinary research environment. The following extract comes from an interview about the construction of responsibility in families with a child with a genetic syndrome:

Dataset exemplar, extract 1

Researcher: Do you remember telling your family that it might be a family genetic syndrome?

Mother: Yes. And that's when sort it sort of came out, well, 'it's not from my side'.

Researcher: Who says that?

Mother: Husband's side, yeah.

Researcher: How did you cope with that?

Mother: Er, it was quite hard really because, you know, because there was no proof either way to be sort of accuit was almost as if we were accused. You know, it's my – from my side and it's my fault. You know, so that was very hard. So it was obviously, like I said it was a relief when we knew that it wasn't from either side.

Researcher: How did you feel about being tested at the time?

Mother: I think it sort of was a relief really because everybody's – there was a lot of – from my husband's side of the family, well, it's not our side, it hasn't come from our side you know, and I was, you know, I was quite open-minded. I didn't know where it had come from and why she had it.

[Fam10 Interview with the mother of April, diagnosed at one month old] (Dimond, 2015; see more about the project and analysis in Dimond, 2014)

Bureaucratic use of the interview guide

Using the term 'interview guide' instead of 'interview schedule' or questionnaire refers to a flexible use of questions, their sequence or that of areas and topics in the interview situation. It also implies that questions do not need to be asked in the exact wording in the guide, but can be adapted to what the interviewee said before, for example. It is important that the message of a question should be maintained in any rewording. In the ideal case, the interviewer has internalized the questions and the structure of the interview guide as much as is necessary to use both spontaneously and flexibly without forgetting the intention behind them. The aim is still to have statements that can be compared in the analysis, in which differences that become visible result from differences in the interviewees' views and not from those in how the interviewer asked the questions. When analysing interviews not for their content or interviewees' statements, we often find that interviewers stick too much to the interview guide, sometimes even cutting some possible statements that could be made by the interviewer in order to move on to the next question in the guide. Then the results are a problem of mediating between the input of the interview guide and the aims of the research question on the one hand, and the interviewee's style of presentation on the other. Thus, the interviewer can and must decide during the interview when and in what sequence to ask the questions. Whether a question has already been answered in passing and may be left out can only be decided ad hoc. Interviewers will also face the question of whether and when to probe in greater detail and to support the interviewee, or when to return to the interview guide when the interviewee is digressing. The term 'semi-structured interview' is also used with respect to choice in the actual conduct of the interview. You will have to choose between trying to mention certain topics given in the interview guide and being open to the interviewee's individual way of talking about these topics and other topics relevant for the interviewee. These decisions, which can only be taken in the interview situation itself, require a high degree of sensitivity to the concrete course of the interview and the interviewee. Additionally, they require a great deal of overview of what has already been said and its relevance for the research question in the study. Here a continuous mediation between the course of the interview and the interview guide is necessary.

Hopf (1978) has coined the term 'interview guide bureaucracy' for cases in which interviewers stick too rigidly to the interview guide, the sequence and the wording of the questions in it and thus rather impede than support the interviewees' presentation of their views. According to Hopf (1978, p. 101), there may be several reasons for this, which include the protective function of the interview guide for coping with the uncertainty due to the open and indeterminate conversational situation. Another reason may be that the interviewers fear being disloyal to the targets of the research (e.g. because of skipping a question), and there is a dilemma between time pressure (due to the interviewees' limited time) and the researchers' interest in information. Again, this problem can be addressed in interview training with excerpts of interviews in which it occurred.

Mistakes in interviewing

General mistakes in doing interviews on the levels of asking questions or probing can occur during the interview, when, for example, a question is formulated for which only a 'yes' or 'no' answer is suggested or possible. A second mistake can result from interrupting the interviewee with a new question or by asking for clarification. Questions and probes referring to the interviewees' knowledge about an issue should not become exam questions. Interviewers should avoid providing the answer to their questions themselves. Interviewers may misunderstand the interviewees' answers and thus probe in the wrong direction, which will be less likely the more the interviewers are familiar with their topic and the ways other people might experience it.

Box 9.3   Research in the real world

Interviewers' race influencing the doing of and the relation in the interview

In the context of psychiatric rehabilitation and clinical psychology in the US in Boston and Los Angeles and in the UK in Suffolk, Lauren Mizock, Debra Harkins and Renee Moran analysed how the researchers' race may influence the relationship within the interview (Mizock et al., 2011b). They analysed 40 qualitative interviews between Black- and white-identified researchers and participants to assess the influence of researcher race in deviations from the interview script. They compared interviews in the four possible conditions ('Black researcher–white participants', vice versa or same race for both). They found in their analysis that in each of these constellations, differences in treating topics related to racism could be identified.

Ending an interview appropriately

Interviews approach their end when both participants have the impression that all has been said about the topic. They can also come to an end when the interviewer has asked all the questions prepared in the interview guide. And they come to a stop when the time slot given by the interviewee is exhausted. However, in all these cases, the interviewer should transition to the finishing of the interview in an appropriate way. This means giving the interviewee the chance to make any additional, relevant points that sit outside the questioning, to give their critique of the questions or the interview in general. In the case of sensitive or emotionally stressful issues, the interviewer should ask whether the interviewee feels OK. If necessary, the interviewer should provide contact information for professionals whom the interviewee could turn to for support.

Using Tools in Interviewing

So far we have looked at the semi-structured interview as the basic setting linked to interviewing generally and historically. We did so by focusing on the core of this setting – an interviewer constructs a room for listening to interviewees by asking questions that the interviewees are expected to answer so that their views, experiences, knowledge or practices become topics of the conversation. Later, we will address some special variations of this setting – by adapting it to target groups (Chapter 10), specific forms of knowledge

(Chapter 11) and contextualizing it in specific approaches (Chapter 12), groups (Chapter 13), fields (Chapter 14) and online research (Chapter 15). Now we will consider the use of specific tools, which has become an issue in the methodological literature. These tools are discussed along with their use for facilitating or deepening conversation on the topics of an interview. The interview guide as the first of these tools, which has been discussed in some detail already and it plays a role again in the chapters on expert, episodic and focus group interviews (Chapters 10, 11 and 13). Other tools that will be discussed now can be applied in all sorts of interview situations and the discussion should be transferred to subsequent chapters.

Photo Elicitation

The idea behind photo elicitation in interviews is rather simple and has a long tradition: 'Photo elicitation is based on the simple idea of inserting a photograph into a research interview' (Harper, 2002, p. 13). Photos (sometimes films or videos) are used in several ways in this context and a main distinction is whose photos are used and who brings them to the research situation. The first way is to present one or more photos to the interviewees and to ask them about what they see, how they evaluate this and what their response to it is. This goes back to the focused interview of Merton and Kendall (see above), in which films were presented to the interviewees who were asked about their reactions to the material. The second way is to ask the interviewees to bring their own photos relevant to the issue of the study to the interview session. Questions will then refer to these photos. The third option is to ask the participants before the interview to take pictures of their everyday life (relevant to the topic of the interview) and bring them to the interview, or to give them cameras and ask them to take photos in preparation for the interview, as in the example in Box 9.4 (see also Flick, 2018a).

Box 9.4   Research in the real world

Photo elicitation interviewing

In this study from New Zealand (Hodgetts et al., 2007), photos are used to explore how homeless people make use of and represent public space in a major city in Europe. Participants were given cameras and asked to take pictures of their everyday life and then interviewed about the pictures and their day-to-day experiences. For example, in the following extract, a participant, Jean, discusses the photograph in Figure 9.2 which depicts a back street in which she links stress and stigma to a loss of self, associated with being reduced to an abandoned physical object:

(Continued)

Jean: I live and eat and work with it and I haven't had a break for years …
                And the street, can claim you … It has various ways of claiming you.
                That's why this … photograph I feel epitomises completely my view.
                That street, just one back alley will claim you as a homeless person.

Interviewer: How does the street keep you?

Jean: Well, how does a car, end up being parked in one street for a very long
                time? I've often seen cars like this, has been abandoned, right. Now
                if a car could speak, the car would say I've got no choice. My driver's
                gone; I've run out of petrol … I'm stuck in this street and there are lots
                of time[s] when you think, I'm not human anymore. (Hodgetts et al.,
                2007, pp. 714-15)

Figure 9.2   Street context symbolizing homelessness and stigma for a participant

Source: Hodgetts et al. (2007, p. 715)

Copes et al. (2018) use photo elicitation in the context of analysing personal narratives
(see Chapter 12) with 52 participants living in rural Alabama who use methampheta-
mine. In most studies using photo elicitation, this addition to the core interview
setting is not so much seen as a technical strategy for advancing the collection of
interview data but as a way of extending the participation and involvement of the
interviewees. Crilly et al. (2006) have transferred this idea to graphic elicitation using
diagrams in interviews for similar purposes. Woodward (2020) extends the use of
elicitation to an approach of material methods using all sorts of objects brought in by
the researcher or the participants. She suggests asking interview questions such as:
'What does that object mean to you? What is the significance of it? In what way does

it matter to you? How does that object make you feel? ... Tell me about how your relationship to the object has changed over your life-course? ... What are the main activities you use the object for?' (2020, p. 42).

Using Vignettes

Vignettes have been used in quantitative methods for a while but are now employed in qualitative and focus group interviewing, too. Bloor and Wood (2006, p. 184) define vignettes as 'sketches of fictional (or fictionalized) scenarios. The respondent is then invited to imagine, drawing on his or her own experience, how the central character in the scenario will behave. Vignettes thus collect situated data on group values, group beliefs, and group norms of behaviour. ... vignettes act as stimulus to extended discussion of the scenario in question.' Jeffries and Maeder define vignettes as 'incomplete short stories that are written to reflect, in a less complex way, real-life situations in order to encourage discussions and potential solutions to problems where multiple solutions are possible' (2005, p. 20).

Different from the use of self-experienced situations the interviewee is asked to recount in the episodic interview, the use of vignettes is based on the researchers' construction of those sketches and aims at stimulating the interviewees to orient themselves to the story and to how they think it will develop.

Box 9.5   Research in the real world

Using vignettes in education research

Karen Skilling and Gabriel Stylianides (2020) of the University of Oxford, UK, used vignettes in educational research, in a study on eliciting teacher beliefs and understandings as value-laden constructs for seeing how these constructs influence teacher practices. They have suggested a framework for constructing vignettes including three basic key elements: conception (content, portrayals of actors and purpose/function of the vignette), design (presentation, length, settings and terminology, open or closed questioning, participant perspectives) and administration (instructions, timing and responses, delivery mode and frequency), which is very helpful for planning what the vignette will include and how it is to be used in the interview.

They show in a case study how Louise, an 18-year-old White British young woman who cared for her disabled mother, reacted to the vignette, to the protagonist Mary and to what that means in terms of reflecting her own situation as a carer. O'Dell et al. discuss issues of interpretation in the use of vignettes, in particular 'how to interpret the responses when participants shift between discussing the vignettes as themselves, taking the perspective of the character in the vignette and commenting on what "ought"

(Continued)

to happen' (2012, p. 702). The authors argue that such shifts should be seen as a further source for understanding how the participants locate themselves in the field under study. So Louise first identified herself with Mary in the vignette, before she moved to herself and her own situation, which she reflected on starting from the vignette, before she took another step in relating herself to the generalized other, when she started talking in the 'you' mode in the sense of 'one'. So the case study shows examples of positioning on the side of the interviewee, which reveal her feelings and understanding of the relationship between help and identity that in her own case were also stimulated by the vignette. Hughes emphasizes the tool character of vignettes and that their fruitfulness depends on the way they are used: 'There can be little doubt that vignette-based experiences are different from real-life but whether this in itself makes it an unsuitable research tool depends on the rationale for using it' (1998, p. 384).

The use of vignettes is mostly less confrontational than it may sound, but more an indirect way of talking about embarrassing issues or those the interviewees are not immediately aware of in the context of the interview topic. Vignettes are constructions created by the researcher which might also direct the interviewees' perception and presentation of their experience or situation. At the same time, they allow the researchers to 'know' what the interviewees are referring to when they are referring to the vignette. So far only text-based vignettes have been discussed, but as the study of Khanolainen and Semenova (2020) shows, unfinished graphic stories (comic strips) can also be used as graphic vignettes. Then the participants are asked to complete these stories also on a graphic level and are interviewed with the finished vignettes used as prompts.

Interviewing with Foreign Languages

At the beginning of this chapter, we mentioned that the interview guide is already a kind of tool for doing an interview. If interviewing can be seen in general as 'learning from strangers', as Weiss (1994) has put it, language can become a crucial point if researchers work with interviewees who have a different language or a limited command of the researcher's language. The use of interpreters or translators can be a solution here, but, as a growing body of literature about this shows, this becomes a methodological issue in itself (e.g. Edwards, 1998; Edwards and Temple, 2002; Littig and Pöchhacker, 2014; Resch and Enzenhofer, 2018). Questions here are how far translation is a practical issue that should be controlled and made 'invisible' as far as possible by reducing its impact in the interview situation. Or does the need for translation constitute a different research situation, which involves a third major actor – the interviewer, the interviewee and the translator, whose contributions have to be analysed as well? This also raises the question of whether translation and translators' impacts should be seen only as an issue in data collection. Or should translators also be involved in the analysis of the (translated) data (see Littig and Pöchhacker, 2014)?

Box 9.6 Research in the real world

Interviewing Russian-speaking immigrants in Germany

The following is based on our study of Russian-speaking immigrants in Germany with addiction problems. One challenge refers to how to do the interviews. The first point here is the language used in the interview. This decision should take into account the symbolic meaning of language, which is linked to an expression of power, status, identity and personal influence. Doing the interview in Russian means that we need to work with interpreters or translators (see Edwards, 1998; Edwards and Temple, 2002). Expectations of interpreters/translators include that they have very good skills in both the original and target language (Russian and German). They also need culture-specific skills like knowledge about symbolic codes and rules of behaviour, which allow them to be sensitive to the latent structures of meaning in the process of interpretation and translation. This means that they may be potentially over-challenged by the double role of being interviewer (responsible for the content) and interpreter. Coming from the same culture as the interviewees and sharing their language is not necessarily sufficient for sharing a life-world reference between interviewers and interviewees due to differences in age, gender, social status, belief systems and the like. At the beginning of the interview, it is necessary to give detailed information about the procedure and to emphasize that there is no wrong or right in the interviewees' views. In the case of our study, interviewees are invited to recount situations relevant to them in the context of the study's topic – e.g. about how they started taking drugs, their decision to quit them, seeking professional help or their experience with therapists, or how they learned that they have a disease following their addiction. Questions refer to the interviewees' representations of addiction or of hepatitis, for example. The main areas covered in the interviews are addiction and hepatitis-related illness experiences and practices; risk awareness; help-seeking behaviour experiences with the health care system; and expectations around help. The interviews lasted 60 minutes on average and were all audio-recorded: 28 interviews were done in German, 18 were consecutively translated in German–Russian/Russian–German, or completely done and transcribed in Russian and then verbatim translated to German.

Once the interviewees had accepted the interview situation, the migrants in our study were generally ready to reflect on and talk about their situation. One major exception was questions about the family, which is sacrosanct in the Former Soviet Union-area, where family problems tend to be concealed. This was also a trend in our interviews. During the interview, the interviewer often fed back what had been said so far. This feedback aimed at avoiding any feelings on the participants' part of being interrogated. The interpreters and translators were native Russian-speaking students with a

(Continued)

social science background, who received training before the interviews. Edwards (1998) underlines how important it is to work with 'suitable interpreters' (1998, p. 199), who have been trained for their role in the current project (1998, p. 203). In our project, it was necessary to translate information letters and interview guides into Russian, and to ensure their accuracy through back translation. That we let the interviewees always choose the language for their interviews had the result that most interviews were done in German as they referred to their good language skills. However, 18 interviews were done in Russian. This means these interviews involved three persons: the researcher (who directs the contents of the conversation), the interpreter and the interviewee. These interviews were based on consecutive interpretation during the interviews. This was followed by a complete transcription of the interview and verbatim translation of this text into German, which was overseen by a second interpreter/translator. In general, the interviews done in Russian were less yielding than those in German.

Interviewing in Different Cultures

A more general aspect is how far the research in examples such as in Box 9.6 is complicated by the role of different languages or of different cultures and how to take this into account. One way again is to use interpreters as mediators of culture (Kluge, 2011). That means to integrate native speakers in analysing the data, for example for checking back the meaning of words and idioms, of words or phrases. As a basis for such an extended understanding of the contents of interviews in different languages, Inhetveen (2012) suggests not only doing oral translations during the interview but also a written translation of the transcript after the interview and comparing the two for differences. For this purpose, Schröer (2009) suggests integrating culture-native co-interpreters to bridge the gaps between the researchers and their 'foreign objects'. Both suggestions are applied in the above example.

The question of which language to use in an interview comes up at several points in the process – in contacting potential interviewees, in doing the actual interview, in transcribing it, in analysing the data and finally in presenting and perhaps publishing the results. This question can be seen as a practical problem and decided by the researchers in a pragmatic way. However, it can be seen as a more general problem linked to making visible the culture of the interviewees and then it can be made a decision to be taken by the interviewees, as is discussed in indigenous postcolonial research (e.g. Chilisa, 2020).

Box 9.7   Research in the real world

Taking the different languages into account in presenting interview data and findings

Bagele Chilisa (2020, p. 205) from Botswana refers to an example discussed by education researcher Yvonna Lincoln from Texas A&M University and Elsa M. González y González, a researcher from Mexico with a business administration background, in their article on language in the context of emerging decolonizing methodologies in qualitative research (Lincoln and Gonzalez, 2008). Aroztegui Massera (2006) did her PhD at Texas A&M University in the US on 'The Calabozo: Virtual reconstruction of a prison cell based on personal accounts' and conducted her interviews in Spanish and worked with translations:

> The personal accounts this dissertation is based upon were collected in Spanish. The general criteria I used for translation is that, whenever possible, I translated the original word or sentence into English inside a parenthesis. However, the act of translation always implies the loss of information. Therefore, every time a testimony is recalled, I place the original Spanish transcript and the translation into English, together within the document. The purpose for this is to allow the reader who knows Spanish to read the original version. The difficulty in translating is mostly a cultural problem. Some words that are essential to understanding the meaning of the narratives have a specific meaning within the context of the group interviewed: Uruguayan female former political prisoners. Such words, although they might have a standard English translation, would lose an important part of their meaning because these meanings are created by the context within which they are used. For very frequently used words, I use the original word in Spanish, in italics, and clarify the meaning only once, in this appendix. (Aroztegui Massera, 2006, cited in Lincoln and Gonzalez, 2008, pp. 787–8)

In such a study, the researchers have to connect with two language worlds – with the interviewees and the own language – here Spanish – and with the scientific community in their language – here English.

Steps, Aims and Criteria in Preparing and Doing Semi-structured Interviews

Table 9.1 summarizes the steps of preparing and doing a semi-structured interview, including the aims and actions for each step as well as the criteria for judging if these steps have been successfully planned and realized.

Table 9.1 Steps, aims and criteria in preparing and doing semi-structured interviews

Six F's of designing interview research	Steps	Aims and actions	Criteria
Framing	1. Preparing the interview	• Prepare an interview guide based on a pre-analysis of the field under study • Run test interviews and interview training • Prepare a documentation sheet for the context of the interview	• Does the interview guide cover the area under study? • Did the interviewer(s) internalize the principle of the interview? • Does the documentation sheet cover the context information relevant for the research question?
Framing	2. Introducing the interview principle	• Prepare a good introduction for the interviewee, and make sure it is clear	• Did the interviewee understand and accept the principle of the interview?
Formulating	3. The interviewee's concept of the issue and his/her biography in relation to the issue	• Prepare questions for subjective definitions of relevant concepts • Prepare questions covering relevant steps in the interviewee's personal history to the issue or the field under study • Pay attention to any point where a deeper inquiry is needed	• Do the questions encompass relevant aspects of the subjective meanings for the interviewee? • Did the interviewer ask additional questions to bring more depth to the interview?
Foregrounding	4. The meaning of the issue for the interviewee's everyday life	• Try to cover relevant areas of the interviewee's everyday life	• Are questions heading towards the interviewee's special situation? • Are they open to the unexpected?
Focusing	5. Focusing the central parts of the issue under study	• Try to get into the detail of the central parts of the issue under study • Try to increase the depth and richness of the interviewee's responses by additional inquiries	• Has the interviewee gone into detail and depth? • Has the interviewer been sensitive to any extra depth on which to focus?
Foreseeing	6. More general topics referring to the issue under study	• Try to avoid overly general argumentation without any personal or situational reference in the interviewee's responses	• Has the interviewer managed to lead the interviewee's responses back to the level of personal concerns?

Six F's of designing interview research	Steps	Aims and actions	Criteria
Framing	7. Evaluation and small-talk	• Make room for some conversation • Make room for critique and additional aspects	• Were additional aspects mentioned?
Foreseeing	8. Documentation	• Use the documentation sheet • Ensure a good recording and a detailed transcription	• Is all additional information (not on the recording) documented?
Finding and Formulating	9. Analysing semi-structured interviews	• Choose an appropriate method for coding and interpreting the answers	• Does the method take the quality of the data into account (e.g. the explanatory structure of accounts)?

Box 9.8   Research in the real world

Where should critically ill adolescents be treated? Interviews with staff members

Wood et al. (2020), an interdisciplinary team at the Bristol Royal Hospital for Children, did a study about where and how best to care for critically ill adolescents – in adult or in paediatric intensive care units (ICU) (mainly for little children)? This study was based on semi-structured interviews with 12 members of staff from four intensive care units. The interview guide comprises 11 questions such as: '1. What proportion of your time is spent looking after adolescents?, 2. In what circumstances would an adolescent come to ICU (adult or child) for care? – Are there any specific circumstances? 3. Are there specific policies relating to care of adolescents on the ward? – E.g., visiting times. ... 11. What is your view on adolescent being cared for in a pediatric vs. adult ICU? What are the issues associated – Are there any?' Main findings were that a central topic (what do interviewees understand as 'adolescent') is connected to two other topics ('Needs of the critically ill adolescent' and 'Implications for staff'), which tend to support the conclusion that critically ill adolescents should be treated in adult intensive care as experience shows that they are better suited here, but that decisions should reflect the individual circumstances such as medial situation and their condition.

How to Select the Appropriate Form of Interviewing

Much of what has been discussed in this chapter can be applied to other forms of qualitative interviewing, too. However, as mentioned at the beginning of this chapter, this book treats semi-structured interviews as one format of interviewing and will present other formats as methodological alternatives in the following chapters. Some of the details that will be discussed there might be inspiring for doing semi-structured interviewing as well. Qualitative interviewing is not just a matter of asking the right questions to the right people, as we should select the most appropriate method for an interview study too. Points of reference for this selection have already been mentioned in Chapter 4. In the following chapters, we will first discuss a method which is tailored to interviewing specific target groups (expert and elite interviews – Chapter 10). Then we will address the use of narrative approaches as a different format to integrate in interviews (episodic interviews – Chapter 11). After that we will discuss interviewing in context – using narratives as an alternative to interviews but as a context to reach the aims linked to interviewing (narrative interviewing – Chapter 12). A second context is to work with groups instead of individual interviewees and to do interviews in focus groups (Chapter 13). A third context is to take the interview to the field out there (ethnographic and mobile interviewing – Chapter 14) or to the field 'up there' (online interviewing – Chapter 15). All these methods and contexts are closer or less close to interviewees' ways of talking about their experiences, feelings, values, perceptions and so on and provide more room or less space for expressing these. As Figure 9.3 shows,

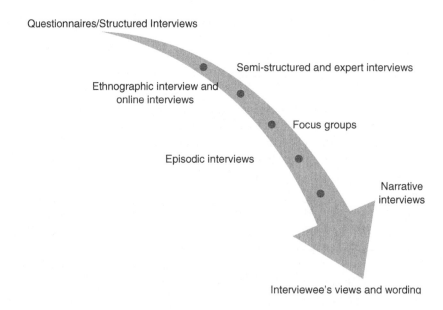

Figure 9.3 Degrees of interviewees' freedom in using one's own words and formulations

these methods vary in how different or similar they are to the setting of the question-naire and the structured interview.

To select the appropriate method of interviewing from these alternatives, we can take several points of reference: the research question defines whether statements (as in semi-structured interviews) or smaller narratives (in the episodic interview – see Chapter 11) are appropriate or if we should do our interviews in the specific contexts mentioned above. The second point of reference is the target group to be interviewed – can they only be reached online or in the field and will they be ready to recount their life histories or to participate in a group? A third point is the inter-viewers' experience and readiness for doing one or the other kind of interviewing. And, finally, the planned analysis of the data should be a point of reference in this decision. If I know already that I will only do a very rough categorization of the data (see Chapter 16), I should save the interviewee and the researcher from the extra efforts and challenges linked to a narrative interview. If I want to do a very detailed interpretation of the data, I should not do a semi-structured interview with very brief and maybe general questions, but think about a narrative interview if it fits the research question. I should also try and find some example studies with the specific method I have in mind, if possible even in my area of research, and look how far the method has worked in a way that it will be likely to meet my expectations.

What You Need to Ask Yourself

Semi-structured interviewing is more than just asking some questions. It needs prepa-ration and reflection if the interview is to be a good one. The questions in Box 9.9 will help you here.

Box 9.9   What you need to ask yourself

Doing semi-structured interviews

1. How far can your research topic be studied by asking people questions about it?
2. How will you prepare probes and additional questions?
3. Will your participants be able to understand and answer your questions?
4. Can the participants and the interview be supported by using tools?
5. If relevant, how will you manage the problem of (foreign) languages?
6. Would a different method of interviewing be more appropriate perhaps?
7. Are your questions open enough for exploring the interviewees' views?
8. Have you used several types of questions?

What You Need to Succeed

This chapter has provided you with a good grounding in what interviewing with open or more focused questions is about. It should help you to understand and contextualize what semi-structured interviewing is before the following chapters present some alternative methods in more detail. The following questions (see Box 9.10) help set out what you will take home from this chapter for the next steps discussed in the book.

Box 9.10   What you need to succeed

Doing semi-structured interviews

1.   Do I understand what interview research with questions and semi-structured interviews is about?
2.   Do I understand the challenges of working with interview guides?
3.   Do I know how to construct a framework for listening in the semi-structured interview?
4.   Do I understand how the design principles outlined in this book apply to semi-structured interviews?

What you have learned

- Doing semi-structured interviews is more than just asking people. This kind of interviewing has been further developed over the years as a method as well.
- It is based on developing a well-reflected interview guide and then on using it in a flexible way.
- Using several kinds of questions can be helpful.
- The art of semi-structured interviewing consists of probing at the right moment and in the right way.
- Semi-structured interviewing can and should be learned.
- A number of tools such as photos or vignettes, but also good means of translating in the interview situation in the case of foreign languages, can contribute to improving interviews.

Exercises

In the exercises, you are first invited to reflect on some of the main issues in this chapter. Then you are invited to apply the topics of this chapter to the development of a project of your own. Hence, the exercises are a combination of reflection and prospection.

Exercise 9.1

Reflecting on the Chapter: The Use of Interviews in an Existing Study

1. Look through a journal for a qualitative study based on interviews (e.g. Wood et al., 2020). Try to identify which form of interview was used in it and how the authors designed their use of semi-structured interviewing.

Exercise 9.2

Planning Your Own Research with Interviews

1. Think of your own study and develop an interview guide with several kinds of questions and probes set out below your overall research question.

What's next

The following book gives an overview of interviewing, adding a specific stance to this book:

Brinkmann, S., & Kvale, S. (2018). *Doing Interviews* (2nd ed.). London: Sage.

Here the use of photo elicitation in interviews is illustrated:

Copes, H., Tchoula, W., Brookman, F., & Ragland, J. (2018). Photo-Elicitation Interviews with Vulnerable Populations: Practical and Ethical Considerations. *Deviant Behavior*, 39(4), 475–94. doi:10.1080/01639625.2017.1407109

This book chapter gives a more detailed review of some of the issues in this chapter:

Hopf, C. (2004). Qualitative Interviews: An Overview. In U. Flick, E. v. Kardorff, & I. Steinke (Eds.), *A Companion to Qualitative Research* (pp. 203–8). London: Sage.

Here the use of vignettes in interviews is illustrated and detailed:

Jenkins, N., Bloor, M., Fischer, J., et al. (2010). Putting it in Context: The Use of Vignettes in Qualitative Interviewing. *Qualitative Research*, 10(2), 175–98.

This article addresses the choice and use of languages in qualitative studies in the context of intercultural and indigenous research:

Lincoln, Y.S., & Gonzalez, G. (2008). The Search for Emerging Decolonizing Methodologies in Qualitative Research: Further Strategies for Liberatory and Democratic Inquiry. *Qualitative Inquiry*, 14(5), 784–805.

Doing Interview Research Navigator

How to understand interview research

- What doing interview research means
- Theories and epistemologies of interviewing
- When to choose interviews as a research method
- Methods and formats of interviewing

Designing interview research

- Planning and designing interview research
- How many interviewees: Sampling and saturation
- Accessing and recruiting participants

How to conduct interviews

You are here in your project

- How to respect and protect: Ethics of interviewing
- Semi-structured interviews: Working with questions and answers
- Interviewing experts and elites
- Integrating narratives in interviews: Episodic interviews

Doing interviews in context

- How to work with life histories: Narrative interviews
- Working with focus groups as interviews
- Ask (in) the field: Ethnographic and mobile interviewing
- Doing online interviews

How to work with interview data

- Working with interview data
- Credibility and transparency: Quality and writing in interview research
- From interviewing to an inner view: Critiques and reflexivity

INTERVIEWING EXPERTS
AND ELITES

You will:

- be introduced to the various ways of using the term 'expert interview',
- learn the various aims of using this method,
- be able to plan and conduct expert interviews,
- become familiar with the ideas of using this method as a stand-alone method or a complementary way of collecting data,
- recognize the particular challenges, the benefits and limits of doing expert interviews,
- appreciate that expert interviews can be complementary to other interviews, in some cases being held instead of interviewing the (e.g. vulnerable) target group of the study, and
- see the similarities and differences in interviewing elites and key informants from other interviewees.

In the preceding chapter, we addressed the holding of semi-structured interviews in general. This chapter will focus on specific target groups in doing such interviews. Experts, elites and key informants are interviewed for their specialist knowledge and experience. Second, such interviews can be used as a complementary resource in several ways or as the main approach in a study. After reading this chapter, you should be familiar with the particular challenges, benefits and limits of doing this kind of interview.

Background to the Expert Interview

Doing interviews with experts is a common practice in qualitative research. Most forms of interviewing can be adapted and applied to research with experts. On the methodological level, the use of expert interviews is often not really spelled out but remains rather vague or pragmatic. This vagueness may also result from the fact that, in English-language literature on qualitative research, the term 'expert interview' is often not explicitly used or the term 'elite interviews' (see Littig, 2009) is used instead. In German-speaking areas, the term 'expert interviews' is more common, and a methodological discussion about this method has developed. Attempts at transferring this discussion to English-language discourse on elite interviewing should take into account the fact that experts are not necessarily part of some kind of elite, but that there are different ways of conceiving what is understood as being an expert. We will first address expert interviews in some detail.

What and who are experts?

Experts are defined as people who are 'particularly competent as authorities on a certain matter of facts' (Deeke, 1995, pp. 7–8). That someone is (seen as) an expert is also a kind of construction. The term 'expert' is used as a relational term (Bogner and Menz, 2009). To take an example: someone is an expert at playing chess, but not necessarily an expert in tennis or other forms of sport. People are (seen as) experts because of their specific knowledge, skills or their specific position in an institution or a field, for example. In research contexts, it depends, first of all, on the topic of the study and its theoretical background who is seen as expert. Second, experts 'have technical process-oriented and interpretive knowledge referring to their specific professional sphere of activity. Thus, expert knowledge does not only consist of systematized and reflexively accessible specialist knowledge, but, in big parts, it has the character of practical knowledge.' **Expert knowledge** can 'become hegemonic' and structure 'the practical conditions of other actors in their professional field' (Bogner and Menz, 2009, p. 54).

People as experts of their own lives

Sometimes, the term 'expert' is also used for people who have developed a specific form of experiential knowledge in their everyday life – for example, people suffering from a chronic disease for a very long time may have become experts of living with this disease, at least in their individual case. In the methodology of the narrative interview (see Chapter 12), interviewees are seen as 'experts of themselves', who may not only tell the story of their illness, for example, but can also present their views on the causes, processes and consequences of their disease.

People as subjective theorists

In research about everyday knowledge, a research programme, in Germany in particular, sees everyday knowledge in analogy to scientific or expert knowledge. Here, subjective theories are studied, sometimes in the context of professional practice. For example, I have studied counsellors' subjective theories of trust in their work with clients. The term '**subjective theory**' refers to the fact that the interviewees have a complex knowledge about the topic under study. For example, people have a subjective theory of cancer: what cancer is; what the different types of cancer are; why they think people fall ill with cancer; what the possible consequences of cancer will be; how it might be treated; and so on. This knowledge includes assumptions that are explicit and immediate, and which interviewees can express spontaneously in answering an open question. These are complemented by implicit assumptions.

However, both – interviewees as experts of themselves and as subjective theorists – are rather particular understandings of the concept of 'expert' in the context of interviewing. The more general discussion about expert interviewing (e.g. in Bogner et al., 2009) conceives expert in a different way, as outlined at the beginning of this chapter.

Aims of doing expert interviews

Expert interviews can be employed with different aims. Bogner and Menz (2009, p. 46) distinguish three aims in using expert interviews. *Theory-generating* expert interviews are applied to developing a typology or a theory about an issue from reconstructing the knowledge of various experts – for example, about contents and gaps in the knowledge of people working in certain institutions concerning the needs of a specific target group. *Explorative* expert interviews are used for exploring and finding an orientation in a new area, for understanding the field for which a study is planned, for developing a thematic structure and to generate hypotheses. Expert interviews can be helpful for developing or refining the main instrument in a study for other target groups (e.g. patients). *Systematizing* expert interviews aim at collecting context information complementing insights coming from applying other methods (e.g. interviews with patients). Bogner et al. (2018) also mention *grounding* expert interviews, which are used for further substantiating, contextualizing or validating insights from other interviews. For example, when homeless adolescents complain about the lack of services available for access in the case of health problems, expert interviews may contribute to checking back this statement.

Sometimes, expert interviews are used in the study of vulnerable or hard-to-reach groups, for three reasons: first, when the members of these groups cannot be reached to interview them, expert interviews can reveal at least some information about them; second, when for ethical reasons interviewing these groups might not be appropriate; and third, they can be used as a complementary perspective on the more general situation of these groups in addition to interviewing them directly.

Knowledge in expert interviews

A distinction becomes relevant in doing expert interviews (see Meuser and Nagel, 2002, p. 76) as both **process knowledge** and context knowledge can be reconstructed with this method. Either the aim is to have information about a specific process in the field of study, for example how does the introduction of a quality management instrument in a hospital proceed? What problems have occurred in concrete examples? How were they addressed? What happens if people in a specific situation (e.g. being homeless) become chronically ill; who do they address first; what barriers do they meet; how does the typical patient career develop? From such process knowledge, we can distinguish context knowledge: how many of these cases can be noted; which institutions are responsible for helping them; what role is played by health insurance or by the lack of insurance, and so on?

Box 10.1   Research in the real world

Problem-centred expert interviews

Stefanie Döringer is a PhD candidate in Vienna, at the Austrian Academy of Sciences, Institute for Urban and Regional Research. She describes her use of expert interviews as being influenced by the idea of the problem-centred interview (see Witzel, 2000). Her interest is focused on the implicit, interpretative expert knowledge of the background to her own empirical study in human geography in the context of her PhD thesis. She did several case studies with local gatekeepers and experts (Döringer, 2020).

Bogner and Menz (2009, p. 52) further distinguish between technical knowledge (1), which 'contains information about operations and events governed by rules, application routines that are specific for a field, bureaucratic competences and so on', and process knowledge (2). This knowledge is instructive for understanding 'sequences of actions and interaction routines, organizational constellations, and past or current events'. The third type is interpretive knowledge (3), that is, 'the expert's subjective orientations, rules, points of view and interpretations', which can be accessed in expert interviews to be seen 'as a heterogeneous conglomeration' (p. 52).

Expert Interviews in Indigenous Research

The terms expert interviews and elite interviews (see below) are not unproblematic in the context of indigenous and decolonizing research as they may be (mis-)understood as referring to experts from Western societies meeting lay people from indigenous cultures. However, as examples such as Mji (2019) show, terms such as expert and elite can refer to, for example, older women in a cultural community and their knowledge, and interviewing them as experts can be a way to secure their knowledge and make it available for later generations (see Box 10.2).

Box 10.2   Research in the real world

Expert interviews in indigenous research

Gubela Mji, the director of the Centre for Rehabilitation Studies, Faculty of Medicine and Health Sciences, Stellenbosch University, Cape Town, South Africa, did a study on 'Searching for indigenous health knowledge in a rural context in South Africa' (Mji, 2019), in which she included 'all the older Xhosa women above the age of 60 years and (2) family members of all the older Xhosa women above the age of 60 years from the 18 villages of Elliotdale' (2019, p. 112). The women participated in focus groups (see Chapter 13) and were interviewed as 'elite older women' in an in-depth interview for their 'indigenous health knowledge: In this study, the IHK carried by the older Xhosa women in their care of health problems within the home situation is described, and most importantly an attempt is made to present the interpretation of these practices through the eyes of the older Xhosa women' (2019, p. 110).

The research in Box 10.2 can also be seen as an example of bridging indigenous and Western sciences in advancing research methodologies for traditional, complementary and alternative medicine systems, as Amy Massey and Ray Kirk discuss for the case of health care research in New Zealand (Massey and Kirk, 2015). In a Russian context, Libakova and Sertakova (2015) discuss using expert interviews for studying indigenous people.

Constructing a Framework for Listening in Expert Interviews

A framework for listening in expert interviews will be constructed in several steps.

Identify who might be experts for your topic

The first step is to clarify whom you see as experts to be interviewed. It is important to identify the right people in the proper positions as being relevant for expert interviewing. This means you should do some research about who your interview partners might be, what they do, what background they might have, if they are working with the people or fields you are interested in, and so on. This kind of preparation also helps to position yourself in the interview, if the experts are in a situation which is substantially different from yours in seniority, professional experience, age, position, and so on.

Research questions for expert interviews

What are typical research questions that can be pursued with expert interviews? For example, detailed insights into institutional routines with a specific problem or target group could be the focus: What happens if someone living on the street falls chronically ill, whom could this person turn to and what would be the routine and process of finding access to help that starts in this case? A second type of research question refers to overviews of a field: How many adolescents – maybe roughly estimated – are now living on the streets of a specific city and how has this changed? What are the relevant characteristics of people in this situation? A third type of research question may be focused on the structure of an institutional network: What institutions exist in a city that a homeless adolescent could turn to and what has changed here in the last few decades? These are only examples of research questions, which would then be honed into detailed questions within the expert interview (see also Chapter 9).

The case study in Box 10.3 illustrates the use of expert interviews.

Box 10.3 Research in the real world

Research question and sampling in expert interviews

The study (Migala and Flick, 2020) builds on earlier research focusing on patients and relatives with a migration background and their experiences with the palliative health care system. The current study aims at reconstructing the significance of cultural diversity within an ageing society in scientific and health policy discourses from a critical perspective on power relations and organizational ethics. The project is part of a wider programme of research addressing ethical issues of social justice in an ageing society. Our problem – justice in the access to and accessibility of health care services against the background of migration – is a specific issue of intergenerational justice in the health care system. The main research questions address the conceptual framework of interculturality and the practical consequences:

- How can interculturality as a normative concept contribute to good and just care at the end of life in a society that as a whole is ageing in diversity? Which interventions can be derived from interculturality for alternative solutions to health policy discourses, taking ethical approaches into account?

- How do organizations in the health care system and the protagonists in these organizations perceive their responsibility for implementing interculturally sensitive end-of-life care? What concepts of care in hospices and nursing prove relevant in this context? What are the users' expectations of these organizations in relation to such concepts?

Expert interviews (Bogner et al., 2018) are conducted with various actors in the health care system. The interviews focus on the social representations (Flick, 1998) of ethical responsibility shared by the experts, and on their role within the organization of care.

The originally planned sampling for the expert interviews with scientists from various backgrounds in the health care system was complemented by religious study scholars, nursing scientists or sociologists working on issues of Islam in practical contexts of health care for covering practices and routines in this context (see Table 10.1).

The interview guide for the expert interviews with executives and senior managers who are involved in implementing statutory provisions in the practices in organizational structures in hospices and nursing, and also significantly involved in health policy and societal discourse, includes questions about:

Table 10.1 Sample of experts

Feature		Number
Gender	Female	20
	Male	10
Religion	Protestant	11
	Roman Catholic	4
	Islam	4
	None	11
Profession	Nursing	20
	Social work	10
Provider	Confessional	14
	Non-profit	9
	Private	7
Home care	Support of nursing in the family	8
	Nursing services	5
	Hospices	4
In-patient care	Nursing home	5
	Geriatric ward	4
	Hospice and palliative ward	5

(Continued)

- Their ideas concerning ethical responsibility in their organization
- Their view on the role of organizations in designing good health care
- Their individual appraisal of what good intercultural health care is like
- Their self-perceptions as ethically responsible protagonists
- Their individual positioning towards the norms, values and ideologies of the organization they work in
- Their positioning vis-a-vis superior structures of legal and political frameworks.

Conducting Expert Interviews

The success of doing expert interviews mainly depends on three phases. First, identifying experts for your study (see Chapter 6) who are really experts in the issue of the study and successfully accessing them (see Chapter 7). Second, success depends on good preparation and, third, on establishing a good working relationship in the interview situation. Good preparation mainly means that the interviewers familiarize themselves with the issue and the practices in the field of study. Reading the literature is important here, maybe even more than in other kinds of interview research. Here, this does not only mean knowing about other studies and scientific publications but also familiarizing yourself with media coverage of the issue you want to study. If your study refers to a currently relevant issue or event, you should be familiar with its press and TV coverage in the last half year, maybe last one or two years. If the main focus is on an event in the past, you should try to read the press reports of that period relating to the issue.

Introducing the idea of the expert interview

The quality of the preparation manifests itself in the quality of the interview guide you prepare for the interview. Most expert interviews are based on an interview guide for several reasons. Interview guides have a double function in the preparation and situation of the interview. Their preparation should help to avoid researchers 'present[ing] themselves as incompetent interlocutors. ... The orientation to an interview guide also ensures that the interview does not get lost in topics that are of no relevance and permits the expert to extemporize his or her issue and view on matters' (Meuser and Nagel, 2002, p. 77). Box 10.4 presents an excerpt from an interview guide for an expert interview.

Box 10.4   Research in the real world

Excerpts from an interview guide for an expert interview

This excerpt comes from the interview guide for interviewing experts in the health care system about their concept of ethically sound health care for immigrants in their institutions and the health care system (see Case study 10.3 and Migala and Flick, 2020):

- To begin, I would like to ask you to tell me what your task here in this institution/organization is and what your professional background is.
- Now, I would like to ask you to explain briefly what the mandate of your institution/organization is in health care. Which aims are pursued by your institution/organization?
- What does it mean with in your institution to provide good (and fair) care for your clients at the end of life? Could you please illustrate this for me with an example?
  - o Where do you think this understanding comes from?
    - A specific worldview or religious orientation?
    - A specific position in social policy?
    - Statutory provisions?
  - o Do your institution's views correspond with your personal views?
- If you consider your professional background: What makes nursing/social work with clients good practice? Could you please illustrate this for me with an example?
- What in your institution contributes to implementing such good care?
- What are the restrictions for you or your colleagues in making that work? Where do you think such restrictions come from?

A second function of the interview guide is to make the interview as focused as possible, particularly if the time slot reserved by the expert for doing the interview is rather short.

Avoiding failure in the expert interview

Expert interviews may fail. Every kind of interview can do this, but here some specific challenges become relevant. Forms of failure in the expert interview include the following:

- The expert blocks the interview in its course, because he or she proves not to be an expert on this topic, as previously assumed.
- The expert tries to involve the interviewer in ongoing conflicts in the field and talks about internal matters and intrigues in his or her work instead of talking about the topic of the interview.
- He or she often changes between the roles of expert and private person, so that more information results about him or her as a person than about his or her expert knowledge.
- As an intermediate form between success and failure, the 'rhetoric interview' is mentioned. In this, the expert gives a lecture on his or her knowledge instead of joining the question–answer game of the interview. If the lecture hits the topic

of the interview, the latter may nevertheless be useful. If the expert misses the topic, this form of interaction makes it more difficult to return to the actual relevant topic.

These kinds of problems and failures often only become visible during the actual interaction in the interview situation.

Interaction in expert interviews

Conversations in interviews with experts are different from other forms of interviewing other target groups. Here, researchers talk to people who know about their area of expertise and are aware of their pre-eminent social position. These interviewees are used to being asked for their perspective, knowledge and expertise and listened to by others. Trinczek (2009), for example, suggests interviewers planning to conduct expert interviews with managers successfully should have expert status as well – at least they should appear reasonably comparable to the interviewee concerning their age and qualifications:

> The interviewer is indeed required to be an expert himself: the more an interviewer demonstrates knowledgeability during the interview by giving competent assessments, stating reasons, and raising counterarguments, the more managers in turn will be willing to offer their own knowledge and take a stance on issues, thus disclosing their subjective structures of relevance and patterns of orientation in absence of strategic considerations. (2009, p. 211)

Planning and conducting expert interviews in this respect can be tricky, because there is no '"best practice" concerning the interaction structure in interviews', as Bogner et al. (2018, p. 661) emphasize: 'Different forms of knowledge and different functions of the interview within the research design make different interaction situations more preferable than others.' This means that questions for process knowledge should be framed with a focus on development and timescales of institutional processes, for example (e.g. 'What happens if a homeless person needs medical help? Whom would they address first?'). Questions on technical knowledge would address the facts more (e.g. 'How many homeless persons live in Berlin? How many are in need of medical help?'). If interpretive knowledge is the focus, questions should address the interviewees' evaluation of a situation (e.g. 'Do you think the existing health care system is adequate for homeless people with chronic diseases?').

Types of Data in Expert Interviews

The data resulting from expert interviews comprise process descriptions, additional information, estimations (of health care needs, for example), or background information about a target group or institutional routines. Compared to other interviews, the data are less about the interviewees' subjective situations or feelings, but of course are also based on their personal experiences and interpretations in relation to their professional practice or a target group.

Ways of Using Expert Interviews

In many studies, the expert interview is used as a stand-alone method. If a study aims at a comparison of contents and differences of expert knowledge in a field, which is held by representatives of different institutions, expert interviews are the method of choice. Then the relevant people are selected and enough interviews in a sufficient variety are done and analysed.

But, more often, expert interviews are used to complement other methods in a study. You can use them beforehand for developing the main instrument or for orientation in the field. They can be applied in parallel to rounding up information from other interviews and complement views on the issues with a second perspective. Finally, they can also be used after the main data collection, for example in an expert validation of findings resulting from interviews. In such cases, the expert interview is not used as a single, but rather as a complementary, method. Both can be seen as an example of triangulation of different perspectives on an issue under study.

Box 10.5   Research in the real world

Expert interviews and focus groups

An interdisciplinary group of health researchers from Hannover and Bielefeld in Germany, led by Christin Walter, used expert interviews with seven caregivers to complement focus groups with 15 patients on the use of telemonitoring in heart failure therapy (Walter et al., 2020). The data were analysed with qualitative content analysis (Mayring, 2000) with the categories '(1) benefits for patients, (2) benefits for hospitals and the healthcare system, (3) acceptance and causative factors and (4) infrastructural implementation' (Walter, 2020, p. 385). The study showed the expectations and evaluations of using telemonitoring technology in home care therapy and the differences between the patients' and caregivers' perspectives documented in the expert interviews.

Elite Interviewing

As mentioned before, expert interviews as an approach and term are more prominent in the German-speaking context than in the Anglo-Saxon discussion. However, we find a number of approaches with similar aims.

Littig (2009) compares the approach of interviewing experts to the Anglo-Saxon tradition of interviewing elites. Here, elites are defined by privileged positions in society and as having a greater influence on political processes than other people (Richards, 1996, p. 199). For elite interviews, it is more the interviewees' top positions in the hierarchies of institutional or public life that are the focus. The experts mentioned in the previous sections are often located in middle-range positions and have more of an insight into institutional routines and processes than a top-down perspective. The potential target person for an **elite interview** is described as 'an informant (usually male) who occupies a senior or middle management position', often a long tenure with the company or institution in focus, with developed personal networks and 'considerable international exposure' (Welch et al., 2002, p. 613).

Harvey (2011) gives some advice on strategies for conducting elite interviews, whereas Mikecz (2012) addresses the methodological and practical issues, such as how to gain access to and the trust of potential interviewees. He mentions the influence of doing the interview in the interviewee's office, of the problem of getting 'the respondents' honest opinions, however subjective or emotional they are' (p. 484) and the major question of the researcher's positionality. Referring to Welch et al. (2002), he suggests that researchers should attempt to take the position of the 'informed outsider', which again – as in the expert interview – underlines the importance of being informed and a competent dialogue partner as expectations to be fulfilled by the interviewer. As the first problem often is to define and identify the 'right' people as the elites who are relevant for the study, and then the second is that the interviewer has to manage to be taken seriously as a competent exchange partner, Mikecz draws the conclusion that elite interviewing 'is not determined on an "insider/outsider" dichotomy but is on an "insider/outsider" continuum that can be positively influenced by the researcher through preparation' (2012, pp. 491–2). These brief remarks may illustrate what is understood as interviewing elites and the differences to expert interviews. Because of the differences in conceptualizing 'experts' and 'elites' as the target group, it may be not very productive to simply combine the two terms, as Bogner et al. (2018), for example, do.

Key Informant Interviewing

LeCompte and Preissle (1993) discuss a specific form of working with experts. They refer to 'key informant interviewing' and define their target group as:

> individuals who possess special knowledge, status, or communicative skills and who are willing to share that knowledge and skill with the researcher. ... They frequently are chosen because they have access – in time, space, or perspective – to observations denied to the ethnographer. ... They are often atypical individuals and should be chosen with care to ensure that representativeness among a group of key informants is achieved. (1993, p. 166)

Here we find similar aims for this kind of interview as in expert interviews, but the emphasis is more on interviewing key informants instead of the original target group that may be difficult to reach. Examples come from research with indigenous groups such as the Navajos in the United States. Thus, the comparability of the approach with the use of expert interviews is rather limited.

Planning and Preparing Expert Interviews

Box 10.6 is designed to help you to decide whether to use expert, elite or key informant interviews for your research. You may also apply these questions to studies with expert interviews you read.

Box 10.6 Research in the real world

Planning an expert interview

Planning an expert interview includes suggestions for preparing (1) the framework for listening in the expert interview (data protection, general guidelines on questions and on the length and type of the conversation) and (2) the conduct of the interview (introducing the subject, question areas, questions, etc.).

Steps involved in planning an expert interview	Six F's of designing interview research
Reflect in advance again	
1. Who will be relevant as a potential expert interviewee?	Finding
2. What is the research question behind the interview?	Focusing
Steps for preparing the framework for listening in the expert interview	
3. Reflect on what the interviewees should know in advance in order to be well prepared for the interview and to understand what the interview is about and what their role should be. Start from what the interviewee has perhaps already experienced about your study when making the appointment for the interview.	Framing
4. Phrase (in keywords) an appropriate introduction to the expert interview for the following aspects: the purpose of the expert interview, recording and data protection. (After agreement, turn on the recording device). Frame an explanation of what the interview will be about, e.g. a very personal view; and an explanation of how the conversation will proceed and how long it will probably take. (The actual interview starts at this point.)	Framing
5. Frame (in keywords) how to conclude the interview, including the question of whether anything important was not mentioned and gaining the interviewee's feedback.	Framing
Steps for preparing the conduct and content of expert interviews	
6. Have an overview of subjects of interest and forms of knowledge for the interview.	Foreseeing
7. What themes are of central interest?	Foregrounding
8. What area of the interviewees' professional or everyday life can provide information about the central topic(s)?	Foreseeing

(Continued)

Steps involved in planning an expert interview	Six F's of designing interview research
9. For every area, frame questions that might motivate the interviewee as clearly and unambiguously as possible to explain, for every topic under point 8, one or more cases related to the main themes (e.g. if you look back, what was your first experience or disagreement with ...? Could you tell me about this situation?).	Formulating
10. For every area, phrase questions about relationships, etc. that could stimulate the interviewees as clearly and unambiguously as possible to express their views on these relationships or concepts (e.g. what is ... for you? What do you associate with this term?).	Focusing
11. Note down some keywords for probing central aspects which you would like to return to if the interviewee does not spontaneously mention them.	Foreseeing

Being Interviewed: The Participants in Expert Interviews

Often, it may not be easy to identify the 'right' experts (or elites) when you are interested in processes in institutions, for example. Then it can be difficult to convince them to give an interview. Once the interviewee has agreed, the problem of confidentiality may come up – often delicate issues for an organization, also in competition with other players in the market, are mentioned. This may lead to answers being refused or to reservations about tape recording; it can also lead to complicated processes of approving the research by higher authorities.

This problem may be exacerbated by the fact that the interviewee may be one of the few or even the only one who could have been interviewed about this topic. This may raise issues of anonymity, data protection and privacy for interviewees who do not want to be identified in publications. At the same time, this exposed position may motivate experts to be identified in publications with their statements in the interview. A specific feature of this kind of interview for the participants is that they are not really the focus as individuals, with a specific subjectivity. Rather, they are interesting for the information they can give about an issue or a field. However, less than the facts they can provide, their interpretation of facts and processes is relevant. Some of the most interesting applications of this method refer to professional processes and overviews of a field, such as health care for homeless adolescents, for example. In such a case, the experts who are interviewed may also be relevant for finding the actual target group of the study, i.e. the homeless youth.

What is Different in Expert Interviews?

During the interview, the issue of time restrictions comes up – expert interviews often have to be calculated and run much more tightly than other forms of interviews. Finally, they demand a high level of expertise from the interviewer – for understanding the relevant, often rather complex processes the interview is about and for asking the right questions and probing in an appropriate way. Furthermore, the interview should be focused more on their relevant expertise and less on the interviewee's personal situation and biography. A consequence of this focus is that a rather limited approach to transcription is the case in expert interview research compared to other forms of interviewing. Meuser and Nagel (2009, p. 35) summarized the data management (see Chapter 16) for expert interviews:

> As a general rule interviews are being taped. Transcriptions of thematically relevant passages are a prerequisite of the analysis. A transcription of the whole recording – in contrast to working with biographical interviews – is not standard. The transcription is also less detailed; prosodic and paralinguistic elements are notated only to a certain extent.

Rather large parts of the interview are **paraphrased**, which means reduced to the central contents. Expert interviews are in most cases conducted as semi-structured interviews, and can be oriented around one of the forms discussed in Chapter 9. However, sometimes it can be helpful to orient expert interviews on ideas, as outlined in Chapter 11, and include elements of the episodic interview, in particular the invitation to recount situations for illustrating points and statements. Sensitive use of probing is very important in interviewing experts. Compared to other forms of qualitative interviews, the narrower focus in using the method can be a reason why it is often only applied as a complementary instrument. Time pressure and other technical problems that may come up can mean that it reaches its limits as a single method. For many research questions, the exclusive focus on the knowledge of a specific target group may be too narrow.

Steps, Aims and Criteria in Preparing and Doing Expert Interviews

Table 10.2 summarizes the steps involved in preparing and doing an expert interview, including the aims and actions for each step, as well as the criteria for judging whether these steps have been successfully planned and realized.

Table 10.2 Steps, aims and criteria in preparing and doing expert interviews

Six F's of designing interview research	Steps	Aims and actions	Criteria
Framing	1. Preparing the interview	• Prepare an interview guide based on a pre-analysis of the field under study	• Does the interview guide cover the area under study?
		• Run test interviews and interview training	• Did the interviewer(s) internalize the principle of the interview?
		• Prepare a documentation sheet for the context of the interview	• Does the documentation sheet cover the information relevant to the research question?

(Continued)

Table 10.2 (Continued)

Six F's of designing interview research	Steps	Aims and actions	Criteria
Framing	2. Introducing the interview principle	• Prepare a good introduction for the interviewee, and make sure it is clear	• Did the interviewee understand and accept the principle of the interview?
Formulating	3. The interviewee's concept of the issue and his/her biography in relation to the issue	• Prepare questions for subjective definitions of relevant concepts • Prepare questions covering relevant steps in the interviewee's professional history with the issue or the field under study • Pay attention to any point where a more in-depth inquiry is needed	• Do the questions encompass relevant aspects of the subjective meanings for the interviewee? • Did the interviewer enforce the expert knowledge-oriented principle of the interview and ask additional questions to bring more depth to the interview?
Foregrounding	4. The meaning of the issue for the interviewee's professional everyday life	• Try to cover relevant areas of the interviewee's professional everyday life	• Are questions heading towards process or state descriptions? • Are they open to the unexpected?
Focusing	5. Focusing the central parts of the issue under study	• Try to get to the detail of the central parts of the issue under study • Try to increase the depth and richness of the interviewee's responses by additional inquiries	• Has the interviewee gone into detail and depth? • Has the interviewer been sensitive to any extra depth on which to focus?
Foreseeing	6. More general topics referring to the issue under study	• Try to avoid personal reflections without any general statements in the interviewee's responses	• Has the interviewer managed to lead the interviewee's responses back to the level of expert statements?
Framing	7. Evaluation and small-talk	• Make room for some conversation • Make room for critique and additional aspects	• Were any additional aspects mentioned?
Foreseeing	8. Documentation	• Use the documentation sheet • Ensure a good recording and a detailed transcription	• Is all additional information (not on the recording) documented?

Six F's of designing interview research	Steps	Aims and actions	Criteria
Finding and Formulating	9. Analysing expert interviews	• Choose an appropriate method for coding and interpreting the answers	• Does the method take the quality of the data into account (e.g. the character of expert statements about groups and situations)?

What You Need to Ask Yourself

The questions in Box 10.7 are designed to guide you in the decision of whether to use expert interviews and which form might be best for your research. You may also apply these questions to studies with interviews you read.

Box 10.7   What you need to ask yourself

Expert and elite interviews

1. How far can your research topic be studied by asking people who are experts about it?
2. What is the main focus of your study; what should the main focus of interviewing your experts be?
3. Where and how can you access interview partners for your expert interviews?
4. How will you document your data – recording and transcription? If not, why not?
5. What is it important to document about the context of your interviews as part of the data?

What You Need to Succeed

This chapter should have provided you with a sound overview of what interviewing experts is about. It should help you to understand the specific challenges and differences compared to other forms of doing interviews.

Box 10.8   What you need to succeed

1. Do I understand what research with expert interviews is about?
2. Am I aware of the specific challenges of doing research with experts?
3. Do I see that I can use expert interviews in addition to other interviews with my target group or sometimes instead of them?

What you have learned

- Expert interviews are conceived for specific target groups.
- They are based on specific concepts of the knowledge that will be analysed with them.
- A very important step is planning for probing interviewees. Decide what you will ask if the interviewees' answers remain too general or if they miss the point that you intended.
- Sometimes expert interviews are used as stand-alone methods, but often in addition to other kinds of interviews.

Exercises

In the exercises, you are first invited to reflect on some of the main issues in this chapter. Then you are invited to apply the topics of this chapter to the development of a project of your own. Hence, the exercises are a combination of reflection and prospection.

Exercise 10.1

Reflecting on the Chapter: The Use of Expert Interviews in an Existing Study

1. Look through a journal for a qualitative study based on expert interviews (e.g. Flick et al., 2012). Try to identify how the method presented in this chapter was used in that study.
2. Consider the study's questions and then improve them by applying the methods presented in this chapter.

Exercise 10.2

Planning Your Project Using Expert Interviews

1. Think of your own study and develop an interview guide for your research question according to one of the interview forms presented here.

What's next

This book outlines various methods of interviewing experts and ways and problems of applying them:

Bogner, A., Littig, B., & Menz, W. (Eds.) (2009). *Interviewing Experts*. Basingstoke: Palgrave Macmillan.

This chapter presents a focused introduction to doing expert and elite interviews for data collection:

Bogner, A., Littig, B., & Menz, W. (2018). Collecting Data with Experts and Elites. In U. Flick (Ed.), *The SAGE Handbook of Qualitative Data Collection* (pp. 652–67). London: Sage.

This article illustrates the use of expert interviews in a multi-perspective study:

Walter, C., Fischer, F., Hanke, J.S., Dogan, G., Schmitto, J.D., Haverich, A., Reiss, N., Scmidt, T., Hoffmann, J.-D., & Feldmann, C. (2020). Infrastructural Needs and Expected Benefits of Telemonitoring in Left Ventricular Assist Device Therapy: Results of a Qualitative Study Using Expert Interviews and Focus Group Discussions with Patients. *The International Journal of Artificial Organs, 43*(6), 385–92. https://doi.org/10.1177/0391398819893702

The following chapter addresses the uses of expert and elite interviews in indigenous research:

Mji, G. (2019). Research Methodology that Drove the Study. In G. Mji (Ed.), *The Walk Without Limbs: Searching for Indigenous Health Knowledge in a Rural Context in South Africa* (pp. 109–34). Cape Town: AOSIS.

Doing Interview Research Navigator

How to understand interview research

- What doing interview research means
- Theories and epistemologies of interviewing
- When to choose interviews as a research method
- Methods and formats of interviewing

Designing interview research

- Planning and designing interview research
- How many interviewees: Sampling and saturation
- Accessing and recruiting participants

How to conduct interviews

- How to respect and protect: Ethics of interviewing
- Semi-structured interviews: Working with questions and answers
- Interviewing experts and elites
- Integrating narratives in interviews: Episodic interviews

Doing interviews in context

- How to work with life histories: Narrative interviews
- Working with focus groups as interviews
- Ask (in) the field: Ethnographic and mobile interviewing
- Doing online interviews

How to work with interview data

- Working with interview data
- Credibility and transparency: Quality and writing in interview research
- From interviewing to an inner view: Critiques and reflexivity

INTEGRATING NARRATIVES IN INTERVIEWS

EPISODIC INTERVIEWS

How this chapter will help you

You will:

- be introduced to the idea of using narratives as a part of an interview,
- see how to use this element in a systematic method in interviews rather than seeing narratives as something distinct from interviewing,
- appreciate that the method of the episodic interview is one alternative for doing interviews,
- learn the steps for planning and conducting episodic interviews, and
- understand the criteria for judging how well your planning and conducting have gone.

In Chapter 9, the focus was on using questions and an interview guide for collecting data with interviews. In the context of the semi-structured interview, narrative approaches do not play a big role. They are either discussed as a different type of interview, when Patton, for example, mentions 'narrative inquiry interviewing' (2015, p. 434), or in seeing narrative inquiry as quite distinct from interviewing.

Using narratives in interviewing is either based on specific types of interviews such as the narrative interview (see Chapter 12) focusing on the interviewees' life histories, which they are invited to recount in a comprehensive story; or the term 'narrative' research is seen as interchangeable with 'qualitative' research (as in Josselson, 2013, p. vii) or as an alternative to doing interview research (as in Patton, 2015). Mishler (1986, p. 235) has studied what happens when interviewees in semi-structured interviews spontaneously start to narrate, how these narratives are treated by interviewers, and how they are often suppressed rather than taken up.

Bamberg (2012, p. 77) has suggested a useful distinction between 'research on narratives' and 'research with narratives'. The first alternative refers to occasions when the narratives are analysed to understand how narratives work, are constructed and used. The second alternative refers to the use of narratives for understanding something else, like experiences, biographies, the representation of social problems, and the like.

What is missing in these definitions and in the major part of methodological discussions about doing interviews is a more systematic concept for integrating narratives and making use of them in more general approaches to semi-structured interviewing. Closing this gap was one of the aims in developing the episodic interview, which is the focus of this chapter.

Background to the Episodic Interview

The following example will serve to illustrate the central underlying assumption of the episodic interview. Most people who attended school will have an idea of what a teacher is and in particular what characterizes a teacher for them. They will also have an idea of what a 'good teacher' is, what characterizes (for them) a bad one and what distinguishes the two. If asked such a question, they could answer it by defining: 'For me, a good teacher is attentive, patient, understanding and interested in his or her students', for example. Their concepts of good or bad teachers are linked to concepts of 'school', of 'classes' and so on and part of their knowledge about school, teachers and so on. At the same time, most people remember their first day at school or the most significant parts of it. When asked, they will be able to recount that situation or even the first encounter with school and teachers, other students and so on. These memories have become a specific part of their knowledge. In psychology, Tulving (1972) has distinguished episodic from semantic memory, and Strube (1989) has applied this to knowledge and distinguished **semantic knowledge** and **episodic knowledge** as two parts of knowledge.

Episodic and semantic knowledge

According to this discussion, episodic knowledge comprises knowledge that is linked to concrete circumstances (time, space, people, events, situations), whereas semantic knowledge is more abstract and generalized, and decontextualized from specific situations and events. The two types of knowledge are complementary parts of 'world knowledge': 'Episodic knowledge is part of the world knowledge, whose other part – corresponding to semantic memory – is the general (i.e. not concrete, situatively anchored) knowledge, e.g. conceptual knowledge, rule knowledge, knowledge of schemes of events' (Strube, 1989, p. 13).

Semantic knowledge is based on concepts, assumptions and relations, which are abstracted and generalized from concrete events and situations. Episodic knowledge is organized closer to experiences and linked to concrete situations and circumstances. For the former, concepts and their relation to each other are the central units. For the latter, the course of the situation within its context is the main unit around which knowledge is organized. To access both forms of knowledge about a domain or an issue, I have designed a method to collect and analyse narrative-episodic knowledge using narratives, while semantic knowledge is made accessible by concrete pointed questions (Figure 11.1).

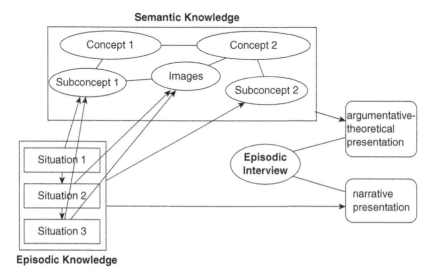

Figure 11.1   Forms of knowledge in the episodic interview

Triangulation of approaches in one method

These two forms of knowledge can be addressed in different ways: semantic knowledge, the concepts and links within it can be presented in a more argumentative and theoretical presentation (A good teacher is characterized by ...) which can best be addressed and stimulated by asking questions (What is a good teacher for you?). Episodic knowledge and the situations remembered can best be presented in a narrative format (When I think back to my first day in school, I remember the impressive building in which an unfriendly man was always insisting that we sat still on our bench ...). This can best be questioned with narrative stimuli (What is your first memory of attending school? Could you please recount the situation you recall for me?). If this distinction is taken seriously, we will combine two approaches (question/answers, narrative stimuli/narratives) in one method. Thus, the episodic interview includes a triangulation of two approaches in one method (Flick, 2018b).

In Chapter 9, Patton's suggestions for what kinds of questions can be asked and what kinds of issues can be addressed in interviews (experiences and behaviour questions; opinions and values questions; feeling questions; knowledge questions; sensory questions;

personal background and demographic situation questions) were discussed. They become relevant here again in several respects. The examples given by Patton show that interviewees are expected to respond to these kinds of questions by mentioning, reporting or describing opinions, feelings or knowledge. At the same time, Patton suggests distinguishing question types according to their timeframe (past, present, future – 2015, p. 128). We will see later how these timeframes for questions can be applied to episodic interviewing.

What is an episode?

An episode is defined in general as: 'an incident in the course of a series of events, in a person's life or experience, etc.; an incident, scene, etc., within a narrative, usually fully developed and either integrated within the main story or digressing from it' (www.dictionary.com/browse/episode). In narrative psychology, episodes are seen as a part of the meaning making of human experience through narratives, as Polkinghorne shows: 'Narrative meaning is a cognitive process that organizes human experiences into temporally meaningful episodes' (1988, p. 1). For our context of using episodes in interviews, I suggest the following definition: an episode is a situation, incident, period or occurrence which is relevant for understanding the meaning an issue has for the interviewee. An episode can be localized in different areas such as parts of everyday life, phases of a biography, stages of working life, etc. This corresponds to the so-called Thomas's theorem (when a person defines a situation as real, this situation is real in its consequences). The episodic interview is oriented on small-scale, situation-based narratives in the data collection. Small-scale narratives are short narratives referring to specific (past, current or future) situations: events in distinction to life history narratives, for example (see Chapter 12).

Constructing a Framework for Listening in Episodic Interviews

Preparing the interview

For giving the interviewer an orientation through the topical domains for which narratives and answers are required, the episodic interview is based on an interview guide. Different sources can be used for developing the interview: theoretical accounts of the area under study, other studies and their results, and the researcher's experiences of this area. In this step, it is important to develop a preliminary understanding of the area under study. This will help to address all relevant topics and domains and to formulate questions and invitations to recount situations. The interview guide should be open enough to allow the interviewee to select the episodes or situations he or she wants to recount, and also to decide which form of presentation he or she wants to give (for example, a narrative or a description). The point of reference should be the subjective relevance of the situation for the interviewee.

The guide should be formulated openly enough to accommodate any new aspects that may emerge or be introduced by the interviewees. The guide and the questions should be pre-tested in one or two test interviews. As in other kinds of interviews, a documentation sheet (see Chapter 16) should be prepared, in which context information about the interviewee and the interview situation should be documented in addition to the transcription of what was said and recorded.

Box 11.1 illustrates the parts of an interview guide for episodic interviews in a study with homeless adolescents with a chronic disease.

Box 11.1   Research in the real world

Living on the street being chronically ill: Parts of the interview guide

In the example of our study of homeless adolescents with a chronic disease, the interview guide comprised the following areas:

- the emergence of the disease
- everyday life with the disease on the street
- stress resulting from being ill
- the role of drugs and alcohol
- utilization of medical or social work support and experiences with it
- the role of homeless peers in dealing with the disease
- ideas about the future, expectations, fears and hopes
- life situation and transition to street life.

Introducing the idea of the episodic interview

The first part of the actual interview is to introduce the idea of the episodic interview to the interviewee. To make the interview work, it is important to explain the principle of the questions to the interviewees, and to familiarize them with this principle. The interview may be introduced by a sentence such as: 'In this interview I will ask you repeatedly to recount situations that are linked to the topic of "being ill" – your own but also illness or disease in general.'

The interviewees' concepts of the issue, and their biographies in relation to it

To introduce the topic, the interviewee is first asked for their subjective definition of the issue; in the example here, the interviewee's chronic disease(s) in questions such as: 'First of all, what do you link to the word [disease X, e.g. diabetes]?' Then the beginning of the confrontation with the issue under study is addressed, here the start of the disease:

'Could you please remember the beginnings of your illness: How did you find out that you were ill? Could you please tell me a situation which illustrates that for me.'

In questions like these, the main principle of the episodic interview is applied: to ask interviewees to remember a specific situation and to recount it. The interviewer does not define beforehand which situation the interviewees (should) remember or select in responding to this invitation. This decision of which situation is selected may be used in the later analysis to compare the interviewees' degrees of proximity to the issue under study, for example.

The way through interviewees' personal histories with the issue of the study is then continued by asking fore especially important or meaningful experiences with this issue: 'What was your most significant experience of your illness? Could you please tell me about that situation?' Again, the interviewees decide what the most significant experience was for them and what is selected is part of the analysis.

Another approach is to ask about specific situations and episodes: 'How did you experience the period after the doctor's diagnosis of your disease? Is there a situation you could recount about this?'

At this point or later in the interview, the transition to street life is mentioned, which can also refer to chains of situations: 'Now I would like to ask you to tell me what your family life was like; can you tell me one or more situations which would help me to understand this?' And: 'What made you turn to living on the street? Can you tell me about a situation which explains this for me?'

The issue's meaning and relevance for the interviewees' everyday lives

The next part of the interview is meant to clarify the role of the issue in the interviewees' everyday lives. In order to enter this realm, the interviewee is first asked to recount a day with reference to the issue: 'Please recount how your day went yesterday, and when your disease played a role in it.' In proceeding with this exploration, several areas of everyday life are mentioned in more detail for their link to the study's issue, for example: 'If you think of food, what role does your disease play in this context for you? Please tell me about a typical situation' and 'If you think of food, what role does health play in this context for you? Please recount a typical situation.' A more general view on the relation of the issue (here being chronically ill) and the interviewee's life situation can also be addressed: 'What role does your disease play for you these days? When exactly does it become an issue for you? Please tell me about a situation which illustrates this?'

Focusing on central aspects of the issue under study

The research started with a number of assumptions: for example, street life may include risks for the adolescents. These may also include health-related risks.

At the same time, the condition of being chronically ill might intensify these risks. Thus, the interview also focuses on risk perceptions and situations in which the interviewee sees and experiences risks, and how they are coping with these risks. For example: 'Do you avoid situations that you see as risky for your health? Please recount a situation in which you avoided a danger to your health' or 'Do you think that you sometimes risk your health by what you do? Is there a situation here you can tell me about?'

This could lead to a consideration of how the interviewees perceive health problems (symptoms, for example) and how they manage them: 'When you don't feel well, what are your major concerns? How do you think this problem [symptoms mentioned before by the interviewee] comes about? Could you tell me about a situation you experienced?' And more focused: 'In terms of drugs and alcohol, what do you use? Please give me a specific situation', and related to the health situation: 'When your illness becomes stressful, do you take alcohol or drugs to cope with it? Is your disease a reason for you to reduce your intake of alcohol and drugs? Do you recall such a situation you could recount for me?' These aspects refer to situations in which the interviewee needs to find a way to get along with symptoms and pain, for example, independently or by seeking professional help: 'What do you expect from your doctor with regard to your health? Please recount a typical situation.' However, such an interview also addresses more general aspects.

More generally relevant topics and prospects

A more general aspect would be the subjective concept of responsibility for one's own health ('In your opinion, who should be responsible for your health? Who is able to or should take responsibility?'). Another more general aspect is indulging in a fantasy about changes that are expected or feared: 'How do you expect your future life to develop – what plans do you have for yourself? Could you imagine a future situation in which you see yourself?' And, finally, more general concepts that are relevant in this context: 'We have talked quite a lot about your disease, now something different: What do you understand by "health"?'

Evaluation and small-talk

At the end of the interview, you should give room for the interviewee to evaluate it ('What was missing from the interview that could have given you an opportunity to mention your point of view?' or 'Was there anything bothering you during the interview?'). As in other interviews, you should also add a period of small-talk to allow the interviewee to talk about relevant topics outside the explicit interview framework ('What I forgot to mention ...'; 'What I actually wanted to say ...'; 'My friend had a funny experience, I don't know if this fits in your study, but ...'). The examples discussed so far are summarized in Box 11.2.

Box 11.2 Research in the real world

Example questions and narrative stimuli for an episodic interview with chronically ill homeless adolescents

In this list, the example questions are listed again, which does not mean that this is an interview guide, but rather illustrations for how to formulate questions leading to situation narratives:

In this interview, I will ask you repeatedly to recount situations that are linked to the topic of 'being ill' – your own illness, but also disease in general.

1. First of all, what do you link to the word [disease X e.g. diabetes]? *
2. Please recall the beginnings of your illness: How did you find out that you were ill, and could you please tell me a situation which would illustrate that for me?
3. What was your most significant experience of your illness? Could you please tell me about that situation?
4. How did you experience events following the doctor's diagnosis of your disease? Is there a situation you could tell me about this?
5. Now I would like to ask you to tell me what your family life was like. Can you tell me about one or more situations to help me to understand this?
6. What made you turn to living on the street? Can you tell me about a situation which explains this for me?
7. Please recount how your day went yesterday, and when your disease played a role in it.
8. If you think of food, what role does your disease play in this context for you? Please tell me about a typical situation.
9. What role does your disease play for you these days? When exactly does it become an issue for you? Please tell me about a situation which would illustrate this.
10. Do you avoid situations that you see as risky for your health? Please recount a situation in which you avoided a danger to your health. Or:
11. Do you think that you sometimes risk your health by what you do? Is there a situation here you can tell me about?
12. When you do not feel well, what are your major concerns? How do you think this problem [symptoms mentioned before by the interviewee] comes about? Could you tell me about a situation you have experienced?'
13. In terms of drugs and alcohol, what do you use?*
14. When your illness becomes stressful, do you take alcohol or drugs to cope with it? Is your disease for you a reason to cut down on alcohol and drugs? Do you remember such a situation you could recount for me?
15. What do you expect from your doctor with regard to your health? Please recount a typical situation.

16. In your opinion, who should be responsible for your health? Who is able to or should take responsibility?*

17. How do you expect your future life to develop – what plans do you have for yourself? Could you imagine a future situation in which you see yourself?

18. We have so far talked quite a lot about your disease; now something different: What do you understand by 'health'? *

19. What was missing from the interview that could have given you an opportunity to mention your point of view?

In this list of examples, we find some questions referring to semantic knowledge by addressing subjective definitions (1, 18) or general aspects (13, 16), which are marked with an asterisk (*). The other questions invite the interviewees to remember, select and recount specific situations and thus refer to their episodic knowledge.

If we relate these example questions and stimuli to Patton's suggestions for what kinds of questions can be asked and what kinds of issues may be addressed in interviews, we find the following links to the list in Box 11.2. We address knowledge (1, 18), experiences (2, 3, 4, 9), behaviours (6, 8, 13), opinions (10) and values (11, 14, 15, 16), feelings (4, 12, 17), sensory questions (5), personal background and demographic situation questions (5, 6). Patton (2015, p. 128) also suggests distinguishing between question types according to their timeframe, which can be applied to the list in Box 11.2 as well. We find questions referring to the past (2, 3, 4, 5, 6, 12), present (1, 7, 8, 9, 10, 11, 13, 18) and future (14, 15, 16, 17).

The distinctions of semantic and episodic knowledge and of questions addressing either one become relevant here again in several respects. The examples given by Patton show that interviewees are expected to respond to these kinds of questions by mentioning, reporting or describing opinions, feelings or knowledge. By adding situational references and narrative invitations, in the episodic interview these kinds of responses are linked to experiences and contexts and the interviewee will provide more details and more personally relevant aspects (see Box 11.3).

Box 11.3 Research in the real world

Being homeless and chronically ill: Examples of excerpts from the interviews

Some short examples from one of the interviews may illustrate the way interviewees responded to some of the questions. Responding to the first question (what do you link to the concept and the disease of 'obesity'?), an interviewee links her body to

(Continued)

her family background: 'my body cannot burn the nutrients I consume as well as other people's, and therefore this plumps out more quickly … That comes from my family … ninety per cent of our family is fat, thus you can't do anything about it.'

Thus, the disease remains something external for her. Responding to the fourth question (the period following the diagnosis), another of our respondents said that the diagnosis (neurodermatitis) took away the fear of the unknown. This made it possible to deal with the disease, which includes talking about it with other people who have it. The interviewee is more optimistic now that she knows the disease will not become serious: 'I have read through all what the others have experienced with all these ointments and have exchanged ideas with others quite a bit, that it is not so urgent in my case and whether it can become worse. And that was quite informative for me, because I know now, how to deal with it.'

Responding to the ninth question in Box 11.2 (role of the disease in current everyday life and when it becomes an issue), the interviewee recounts how the neurodermatitis becomes stressful because of its social consequences. The interviewee sees how he is viewed by the people around him because of the reddening of his skin and, at the same time, he is stigmatized as an outsider to keep away from: 'When I take a seat in the underground train, of course they all look like, "well he has some kind of disease. Let it be, let's sit somewhere else. … Mites or scabies or so, some contagious disease".'

In the life situation of homeless adolescents, he sees how the shared (skin) disease keeps the group together and sets the boundaries against a hostile environment: 'maybe a little solidarity because we have the same disease … is better for talking with someone than with someone in the underground, who has no idea about it'.

Types of Data in the Episodic Interview

These brief examples have illustrated that we are given accounts of specific situations (after the diagnosis) but also of states that are repeatedly experienced (like feeling rejected while in an underground train) in response to the invitation to describe a situation. These repeated episodes have been called '**repisodes**' (Neisser, 1981). When asking for concepts, we sometimes receive subjective definitions (for me, obesity is …), examples or stereotypes (as in the example of the family disposition to obesity). These various types of data are summarized in Figure 11.2. Taken together, they cover the range of experiences linked to the topic of a study using the episodic interview.

Planning and Preparing Episodic Interviews

There are two parts to plan in preparation of an episodic interview: first, the framework of the interview so that the interviewees know what they are expected and have agreed to do, and second, the conduct of the interview and the contents it should cover. This will help to reduce or avoid any reservation on the part of the interviewee, so that they can do the interview in an open and relaxed way. Box 11.4 presents instructions for preparing an episodic interview.

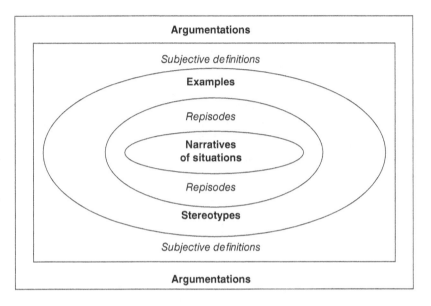

Figure 11.2   Types of data in the episodic interview

Box 11.4   Research in the real world

Planning for an episodic interview

Planning an interview includes suggestions for preparing (1) the framework for listening in the interview (data protection, general guidelines on questions and on the length and type of the conversation) and (2) the conduct of the interview (introducing the subject, question areas, questions, etc.).

Steps involved in planning an episodic interview	Six F's of designing interview research
Reflect in advance again	
1. Who will your potential interviewees be?	Finding
2. What is the research question underlying the interview?	Focusing
Steps for preparing the framework for listening in the episodic interview	

(Continued)

Steps involved in planning an episodic interview	Six F's of designing interview research
3. Reflect on what the interviewees should know in advance to be well prepared for the interview and to understand what it is about and what their role should be. Start from what the interviewee has perhaps already learned about your study when making the appointment for the interview.	Framing
4. Phrase (in keywords) an appropriate introduction to the interview for the following aspects: the purpose of the interview, recording and data protection. (After agreement, turn on the recording device). Frame an explanation of what the interview will be about, e.g. a very personal view; an explanation of how the conversation will proceed and how long it will probably take. (The actual interview starts at this point.)	Framing
5. Frame (in keywords) how to conclude the interview, including asking for any additional comments and for the interviewee's feedback.	Framing
Steps for preparing the conduct and content of episodic interviews	
6. Overview of subjects of interest for the interview.	Foreseeing
7. What themes are of central interest?	Foregrounding
8. What area of the interviewees' professional or everyday life, for example, can provide information about the central topic(s)?	Foreseeing
9. For every area, frame a narrative stimulus that might motivate the interviewee, as clearly and unambiguously as possible to tell, for every topic under point 8, one or more short stories related to the main themes (e.g. if you look back, what was your first experience or disagreement with ...? Could you tell me about this situation?).	Formulating
10. For every area, phrase questions about relationships, etc. that could encourage the interviewees, as clearly and unambiguously as possible, to express their views of these relationships or concepts (e.g. what is .... for you? What do you associate with this term?).	Focusing
11. Note down some keywords for probing central aspects which you would like to return to if the interviewee does not spontaneously mention them.	Foreseeing

Steps, Aims and Criteria in Preparing and Doing Episodic Interviews

Table 11.1 summarizes the steps involved in preparing and doing an episodic interview, including the aims and actions for each step, as well as the criteria for judging whether these steps have been successfully planned and realized.

Table 11.1 Steps, aims and criteria in preparing and doing episodic interviews

Six F's of designing interview research	Steps	Aims and actions	Criteria
Framing	1. Preparing the interview	• Prepare an interview guide based on a pre-analysis of the field under study • Run test interviews and interview training • Prepare a documentation sheet for the context of the interview	• Does the interview guide cover the area under study? • Did the interviewer(s) internalize the principle of the interview? • Does the documentation sheet cover the relevant information for the research question?
Framing	2. Introducing the interview principle	• Prepare a good introduction for the interviewee, and make sure it is clear	• Did the interviewee understand and accept the principle of the interview?
Formulating	3. The interviewee's concept of the issue and his/her biography in relation to the issue	• Prepare questions for subjective definitions of relevant concepts • Prepare questions covering relevant steps in the interviewee's personal history with the issue or the field under study • Pay attention to any point where a more in-depth inquiry is needed	• Do the questions encompass relevant aspects of the subjective meanings for the interviewee? • Are the questions oriented towards narratives of (relevant) situations? • Did the interviewer enforce the narrative principle of the interview and ask additional questions to bring more depth to the interview?
Foregrounding	4. The meaning of the issue for the interviewee's everyday life	• Try to cover relevant areas of the interviewee's everyday life	• Are questions heading towards situation narratives? • Are they open to the unexpected?
Focusing	5. Focusing the central parts of the issue under study	• Try to get into the detail of the central parts of the issue under study • Try to increase the depth and richness of the interviewee's responses by making additional inquiries	• Has the interviewee gone into detail and depth? • Has the interviewer been sensitive to any extra depth on which to focus?
Foreseeing	6. More general topics referring to the issue under study	• Try to avoid generalization in the replies without any personal or situational reference in the interviewee's responses	• Has the interviewer managed to lead the interviewee's responses back to the level of personal concerns?

(Continued)

Table 11.1 (Continued)

Six F's of designing interview research	Steps	Aims and actions	Criteria
Framing	7. Evaluation and small-talk	• Make room for some conversation • Make room for critique and additional aspects	• Were additional aspects mentioned?
Foreseeing	8. Documentation	• Use the documentation sheet • Ensure a good recording and a detailed transcription	• Is all additional information (not on the recording) documented?
Finding and Formulating	9. Analysing episodic interviews	• Choose an appropriate method for coding and interpreting the narratives and answers	• Does the method take the quality of the data into account (e.g. the narrative structure of accounts)?

What You Need to Ask Yourself

Episodic interviewing is more than just asking some questions. It is based on an interview guide, but it includes the systematic use of small-scale narratives. Thus, a combination of two approaches in one interview becomes possible. Narrative stimuli are part of the interview guide and narratives are integrated into the interview. The questions in Box 11.5 might help you in working with this method.

Box 11.5 What you need to ask yourself

Doing episodic interviews

1. How far can the issue of my research be studied by asking people questions about it?
2. Is the research topic linked to biographical experiences and to situations which can be recounted?
3. How should I arrange the sequence of narratives and questions in the interview?
4. How far is this method appropriate for my target group?
5. Do I know how to introduce the principle of episodic interviewing?

What You Need to Succeed

This chapter should have provided you with a solid introduction to what episodic interviewing comprising questions and short narratives entails. It should help you to understand and contextualize what episodic interviewing is before the following chapters cover alternative methods and interviewing in specific contexts in more detail. The following questions (see Box 11.6) should help you to review what to take home from this chapter for the next steps discussed in the book.

Box 11.6   What you need to succeed

Doing episodic interviewing

1. Do I understand what interview research with questions and small-scale narratives is about?
2. Do I know how to prepare the use of this specific method?
3. Can I construct a framework for listening in the episodic interview?

What you have learned

- Doing episodic interviews goes beyond asking people for answers.
- This kind of interviewing has been developed as an alternative to semi-structured and to narrative interviewing (see Chapter 12).
- The challenges involved in doing semi-structured interviewing are relevant here as well.
- The method produces several forms of knowledge.
- Episodic interviewing can and should be learned as well.

Exercises

In the exercises, you are first invited to reflect on some of the main issues in this chapter. Then you are invited to apply the topics of this chapter to the development of a project of your own. Hence, the exercises are a combination of reflection and prospection.

Exercise 11.1

Reflecting on the Chapter: The Use of Episodic Interviews in an Existing Study

1. Look through a journal for a qualitative study based on episodic interviews (e.g. Flick et al., 2010). Try to identify what forms of questions and narrative stimuli were used in it and how the authors designed their use of episodic interviewing.

Exercise 11.2

Planning Your Own Research with Episodic Interviews

1. Think of your own study and develop an interview guide with several kinds of questions and invitations to small-scale narratives for your research question.

What's next

In the following texts, the methodological background and applications of the episodic interview can be found:

Flick, U. (1994). Social Representations and the Social Construction of Everyday Knowledge: Theoretical and Methodological Queries. *Social Science Information*, 33, 179–97.

Flick, U. (1995). Social Representations. In R. Harré, J. Smith, & L. v. Langenhove (Eds.), *Rethinking Psychology* (pp. 70–96). London: Sage.

Flick, U. (2000). Episodic Interviewing. In M. Bauer & G. Gaskell (Eds.), *Qualitative Researching with Text, Image and Sound: A Practical Handbook* (pp. 75–92). London: Sage.

Flick, U. (2018). *Doing Triangulation and Mixed Methods* (Ch. 3, 'Methodological Triangulation in Qualitative Research'). London: Sage.

DOING INTERVIEWS IN CONTEXTS

In Part I of this book, the background to doing research interviews was outlined, before, in Part II, issues of planning and designing interview research were described.

In Part III, we turned to several specific methods of interviewing such as semi-structured, expert and episodic interviews. In that part, the basic structure of research interviewing was examined step by step for various extensions. In Chapter 9, the extension of semi-structured interviews by using tools was introduced, which could also be transferred to other forms of interviewing. In Chapter 10, the specific relation to experts was discussed as an extension to semi-structured interviews, although the expert interview has also been established as a method in its own right. In Chapter 11, the use of small-scale narratives in an interview was the issue, which is characteristic of the episodic interview. In all these methods, the basic setting – one interviewer, one interviewee and questions – is maintained but extended.

In Part IV, interviewing in different contexts is on the agenda. First, in Chapter 12, you will be introduced to a method in which the interview is embedded in the context of an overall narrative often covering the interviewee's life history. Questions do not play a major role here as they are only foreseen for the final part of the interview.

Second, we will address doing interviews in the context of a group, where members are interviewed at the same time in a focus group interview (Chapter 13). The third context is ethnographic fieldwork, in which ethnographic interviews are conducted or, more recently, mobile (walking or go-along) interviews, which are the issue of Chapter 14. The fourth context is the Internet, where contact with participants is transferred to media such as telephone, Skype, email or online interviews (see Chapter 15).

These developments and contextualizations come with new options and challenges for interviewing as a method and for specific methods of interviewing.

Doing Interview Research Navigator

How to understand interview research

- What doing interview research means
- Theories and epistemologies of interviewing
- When to choose interviews as a research method
- Methods and formats of interviewing

Designing interview research

- Planning and designing interview research
- How many interviewees: Sampling and saturation
- Accessing and recruiting participants

How to conduct interviews

- How to respect and protect: Ethics of interviewing
- Semi-structured interviews: Working with questions and answers
- Interviewing experts and elites
- Integrating narratives in interviews: Episodic interviews

Doing interviews in context

- How to work with life histories: Narrative interviews
- Working with focus groups as interviews
- Ask (in) the field: Ethnographic and mobile interviewing
- Doing online interviews

How to work with interview data

- Working with interview data
- Credibility and transparency: Quality and writing in interview research
- From interviewing to an inner view: Critiques and reflexivity

HOW TO WORK WITH LIFE HISTORIES

NARRATIVE INTERVIEWS

How this chapter will help you

You will:

- be introduced to the idea of using extended narratives as a context for doing interviews,
- learn how to use narratives in a systematic way as interviews, rather than to see narrative research as something distinct from interviewing,
- see the method of the narrative interview as one alternative for doing interviews,
- learn the steps of planning and conducting narrative interviews, and
- be aware of the criteria for judging how well the planning and conducting went.

In the preceding chapters, we focused on several ways of doing interviews mainly by asking several types of questions. After a more general chapter on semi-structured interviewing (Chapter 9), the special case of interviewing experts and elites was discussed in some detail (Chapter 10). In the preceding Chapter 11, the integration of small-scale narratives in semi-structured interviews was the topic, when the episodic interview was introduced. In this chapter, we take a different approach, which is linked to these preceding chapters in several ways. This chapter presents the narrative interview as an alternative to asking questions. While we still focus on doing interviews in pursuing a research question, here a longer and more comprehensive narrative is the context in which the interviewee provides information about the issue under study. We are still focusing on doing a specific type of interview and are not talking about narrative research as something alternative to or completely different from interviewing. Research questions are pursued and 'answered' in the context of a life history narrative. For this purpose, a specific method is presented in some detail. Narrative inquiry can be a broader programme for qualitative research, as shown by Clandinin and Conelly (2000), who have developed an approach to narrative inquiry which is based on a number of theoretical backgrounds and gives an introduction to using narratives in research. These authors (2000, p. 50) start with four dimensions to every inquiry: inward (the subjective experience) and outward (the social context), backward (the life history) and forward (one's future). However, we find little guidance in their book on how to collect or stimulate narrative data in interviews (see Chapter 11) or on narratives as data as a context for doing interviews, as we will discuss in this chapter.

Background to the Narrative Interview

Schütze (1977) developed the narrative interview as an alternative method to overcome the limitations of the classical semi-structured, question-based interview. The method was originally developed for doing research with experts (local politicians) about a specific topic (community policy decision-making), before it was transferred to a much wider field (biographical research). The narrative interview was originally developed in the context of a project on local power structures. Here the narratives stimulated by this method did not focus on the narrators' biographies but on their stories about this political decision-making process.

The method aims at using the more detailed, contextualized and personal style of talking in storytelling to enrich the interview data, which also drives the use of episodic interviewing (see Chapter 11). However, there are differences between episodic and narrative interviewing, although some authors mix the two (e.g. Mueller, 2019). Although several authors in the Anglo-Saxon literature use the term 'narrative interviewing', mostly in a different way from what Schütze intended, the specific methodology of the narrative interview will be the point of reference in this chapter. This will demonstrate the methodological character of narrative interviewing and allow us to extend the range of available methodological alternatives in doing interviews. The particular feature of a narrative interview is that a wide, open platform is created for the interviewees, who are expected to recount their life history and are given all the time they need for this purpose.

What is a narrative?

A narrative is characterized as follows: 'First the initial situation is outlined ("how everything started"), then the events relevant to the narrative are selected from the whole host of experiences and presented as a coherent progression of events ("how things developed"), and finally the situation at the end of the development is presented ("what became")' (Hermanns, 1995, p. 183).

Narratives here are understood as a specific kind of longer story, for example life histories, migration histories, including the situation before and after someone decided to emigrate or immigrate somewhere, or illness histories in the case of chronic or terminal disease. The focus is on extended processes, which develop over a lengthier period, rather than situations and episodes (as in the episodic interview), although both are part of such a process and the story it reveals. An important aspect of the narrative interview is its focus on **extempore** narratives and not carefully prepared stories. Thus, a situation should be created in which interviewees reflect on their life and present an ad hoc story about it.

Why narratives as interviews?

Several reasons have been discussed as to why narrative interviews are better than other forms of interviewing. The first is that people '"know" and are able to present a lot more of their lives than they have integrated in their theories of themselves and of their lives. This knowledge is available to informants at the level of narrative presentation but not at the level of theories' (Hermanns, 1995, p. 185). Thus, it is assumed that people can present more aspects of their situation and experiences in the format of a story than would come to their mind if they were asked to answer questions about these. A narrative takes on some independence and its own dynamics during its recounting: 'Narrators of unprepared extempore narratives of their own experiences are driven to talk also about events and action orientations, which they prefer to keep silent about in normal conversations and conventional interviews owing to their awareness of guilt or shame or their entanglements of interests' (Schütze, 1976, p. 225). Thus, narrative interviews allow a more immediate access to memories about an event or a process than other forms of interviewing. As a consequence, an analogous relationship between the narrative presentation and the narrated experience is assumed: 'In the retrospective narrative of experiences, events in the life history (whether actions or natural phenomena) are reported in principle in the way they were experienced by the narrator as actor' (Schütze, 1976, p. 197).

Some of the assumptions behind the method of narrative interviewing are based on findings from the research on how narratives and storytelling work in general.

Cognitive figures of extempore storytelling

Schütze (1984) has developed a theoretical model as a background for the narrative interview, which includes the following components. The narrative protagonist is the same as the actor, or if not, this is an indicator of the activity or passivity mode of the story: Is the narrative about something that the interviewee has actively pursued or passively endured? The narrative chain includes the whole process of what occurred segmented into single phases. Situations are particularly condensed crucial points, for example pinnacles, of the process. The thematic overall *Gestalt* is the central problem of the occurrences or their development, which typifies the story, and in comparison to other cases.

Constructing a Framework for Listening in Narrative Interviews

The narrative interview's basic principle of collecting data is described as follows: 'the informant is asked to present the history of an area of interest, in which the interviewee participated, in an extempore narrative. ... The interviewer's task is to make the informant tell the story of the area of interest in question as a consistent story of all relevant events from its beginning to its end' (Hermanns, 1995, p. 183). As using the term 'extempore narrative' emphasizes, the interviewees are not expected to prepare a story to present in the interview. Rather, a situation will be created in which the interviewee creates the story ad hoc and for the interviewer.

Preparing the interview

To make this ad hoc storytelling work, some precautions are necessary. As for other forms of research, for formulating a research question (see Chapter 5), and planning the sampling of participants and the access to interviewees for the study, the researchers should familiarize themselves with their area of study by reading the literature and existing research. But, in addition, a framework should be constructed which permits the interviewees to get themselves in the situation of telling the story of their lives to a stranger. This means that the interviewer must carefully reflect on what the interviewees should understand about this situation and what is expected of them. Thus, a carefully worded instruction about the interview should be prepared. Second, the initial question should be carefully reflected on, planned and formulated. This is of particular importance as the initial question is the only question that is asked before interviewees begin to tell their story. As the interviewer is expected to refrain from asking any other questions while the interviewees tell their story (see below), it is important to formulate the initial question in such a way that the interviewees know what they are expected to talk about, what process is relevant to the interview, and when their story should begin and end. Often, there is no single story that could be told about one's life, but the story of one's professional life, of one's life as a patient with a chronic disease, or of one's migration history. In most cases, the research will be interested in just one of these stories (and the part of life it addresses) so that the interviewee should be guided by the initial question to the area their story should be about.

Conducting a Narrative Interview

Introducing the idea of the narrative interview

Some researchers begin the interview with a strong focus on introducing the principal idea of the narrative interview and integrate their research interest into this introduction, as, for example, Küsters (2009) in her study on people starting to learn an instrument as adults:

> That my study is about people who have started as adults to learn an instrument you know already and above all it is about the life histories of these people. Therefore, I would like to begin by asking you to recount your life history, your whole life history until today. All that was important for you and as completely as possible. I will not interrupt you and if I have a question, I will write it down and ask you after you have finished your story. Well, now I only listen to you first. (2009, p. 50)

For some of the later interviews in her project, Küsters skipped 'your whole life history' and 'all that was important for you', as these parts had produced some irritation for some of the first interviewees (2009, p. 51). This is a good example of beginning a narrative interview as it provides sufficient information for the interviewees concerning what to expect and what is expected of them.

A second example comes from Rosenthal's wording for one or two interviewers doing the interview: 'Please tell me/us your family story and your personal life story; I/we am/are interested in your whole life. Anything that occurs to you. You have as much time as you like. We/I won't ask you any questions for now. We/I will just make some notes on the things that we would like to ask you more about later; if we haven't got enough time today, perhaps in a second interview' (2004, p. 51). Here again the opening of the interview is less about specific topics or a focus, but about the whole life story as the issue of the narration. The focus is more about the 'technical' details (no questions, note-taking, all is important, and, if necessary, a second interview for continuing or completing).

The initial question (for generating a narrative)

In many cases, the interview starts with an initial question focused on the topics of the story to be told in it. This is a typical example of a good **initial question for generating a narrative**:

> I want to ask you to tell me how the story of your life occurred. The best way to do this would be for you to start from your birth, with the little child that you once were, and then tell all the things that happened one after the other until today. You can take your time in doing this, and also give details, because for me everything is of interest that is important for you. (Hermanns, 1995, p. 182)

The following example is focused on a specific aspect (chronic disease): 'We are interested in the life stories of people with a chronic disease … , in your personal experience. Please tell me your life story, not just about your illness … , but about your whole life story. Anything' (Rosenthal, 2004, p. 51). The third example focuses on the experience of emigration: 'We are interested in the life history of people who have emigrated. We would like to ask you to recount your life story, thus not just to report about your emigration, but about all the experiences from the time before and the time after the emigration which come to your mind today' (Fischer-Rosenthal and Rosenthal, 1997, p. 142).

Main narration

If the initial question and the explanation of the interview principle 'work' and the interviewees have understood what is expected of them, a long biographical narration follows, which often runs for several hours. The interviewers now have three tasks: (1) to listen carefully and attentively; (2) to support the interviewee by showing their interest by paralinguistic expressions such as 'mhm', eye contact or asking 'And then what happened?' in order to encourage the interviewee to continue the narration; and (3) to refrain from any other intervention such as asking questions like 'what do you mean by that?' or 'Could you explain that?' or introducing new topics or referring the interviewee back to topics mentioned earlier. This means that the interviewer should refrain from everything that might interrupt the narration and must postpone all questions or introductions of new topics to after the end of the narration.

Coda

Typically, the end of the story is indicated by a '**coda**', such as: 'I think I've taken you through my whole life' (Riemann and Schütze, 1987, p. 353) or 'That's pretty well it by and large. I hope that has meant something to you' (Hermanns, 1995, p. 184). After this signal that the interviewees have finished their narration, the interviewer can become more involved again.

Narrative questioning

In the next stage – the questioning period – the story's fragments that have not been further spelled out are readdressed or the interviewer asks another **narrative-generative question** (Rosenthal, 2004) for those passages that had been unclear. For example, 'You told me before how it came about that you moved from X to Y. I did not quite understand how your disease progressed after that. Could you please tell me that part of the story in a little more detail?' Rosenthal (2004, p. 52) discusses five forms of narrative questions: (1) addressing a phase of the interviewee's life (e.g. Could you tell me more about the time when you were a child?); (2) addressing a single theme in the interviewee's life (Could you tell me more about your parents?); (3) addressing a specific situation already mentioned in the interview; (4) 'eliciting an argument already made before (*Can you remember a situation when somebody talked about this event (how your father died);*' or (5) a non-self-experienced event (e.g. Can you remember a situation when somebody talked about this event?).

In Küsters's (2009) example, four interviewees didn't refer to their instrument playing in their life narrative, so the researcher had to ask again: 'So how then did you come to play the instrument?' after the period of narrative questions (2009, p. 59).

Balancing phase

After these primarily narrative parts of the interview have finished, a part can be added in which more and more abstract questions are asked, which aim at description and argumentation. In this part of the interview, the participants are seen as 'experts of themselves' (Schütze, 1983), who are not only able to tell the story of their illness, for example, but are also able to present their views on causes, processes and consequences of their disease.

For this **balancing phase**, it is suggested first to ask 'how' questions, for example: 'How would you describe the symptoms of your disease in detail?' or 'How often did you have to consult a doctor at that time?', and then only afterwards complementing them with 'why' questions aiming at explanations, for example: 'Why could you not continue to work after your illness became known to your colleagues?' It is here also that issues that cannot be narrated find their place in the interview. This distinction is clarified by Hermanns (1995, p. 184), who uses the following example:

> My attitude towards nuclear plants cannot be narrated, but I could tell the story about how my present attitude came about. 'Well, I walked, it must have been 1972, across the site at Whyl [a nuclear power plant – UF], all those huts there and I thought, well that is great, what these people have got going here, but with their concern about nuclear energy they are kind of mad. I was strongly M/L (Marxist-Leninist, a political party – UF) at that time.

Collecting socio-demographic data

At the end of the interview, the necessary personal data such as the interviewee's year of birth, school or other degrees, and family situation are collected (e.g. based on a checklist). This should be planned for the end and not the beginning of the interview to avoid the interviewees assuming in their narratives that the interviewer has this information already or the interview is about such facts and dates.

That the narrative interview works (better than other interviews) as it produces richer data is seen as a result of the narrators' becoming entangled in certain constraints ('threefold narrative *zugzwangs*'). This entangling will start as soon as they get involved in the situation of the narrative interview and start the narrative.

The constraints are the **constraint of closing Gestalt**, the **constraint of condensing** and the **constraint of detailing**. The first constraint (**constraint of closing Gestalt**) makes narrators tell a story until its end once they have started it. The second constraint (**constraint of condensing**) makes narrators focus their story on what is necessary for understanding the process in the story as part of the presentation. The story is condensed not only because of limited time, but also so that the listener is able to understand and follow it. The constraint of detailing is the reason why the narrative provides the background details and relationships necessary for understanding the story. This constraint makes the narrator tell as many details as seem necessary to give the listener the chance to fully understand the story. Thus, details about personal motives, about features of other people involved, and so on, are provided.

The narrative interview is a method for collecting life histories, giving the interviews a wide space for recounting their stories, without being interrupted, which 'allows' them to reveal more about themselves and the issue than in other interviews. To make it work, the narrative and other parts should be clearly distinct. The interviewer is supposed to postpone any questions until after the narration has finished, and ask first more narrative questions, then any descriptive and explanatory questions.

Box 12.1   Research in the real world

Planning a narrative interview

Planning a narrative interview also includes suggestions for preparing (1) the framework for listening in the narrative interview (data protection, general guidelines on questions and on the length and type of the conversation) and (2) the conduct of the interview (entering the subject, initial question, narrative and other questions, etc.).

Steps involved in planning a narrative interview	Six F's of designing interview research
Reflect in advance again	
1. Who will your potential interviewees be?	Finding
2. What is the research question behind the interview?	Focusing
Steps for preparing the framework for listening in the narrative interview	
3. Reflect on what the interviewees should know in advance to be well prepared for the interview and to understand what it is about and what their role should be. Start from what the interviewee has perhaps already learned about your study when making the appointment for the interview.	Framing
4. Phrase (in keywords) an appropriate introduction to the interview for the following aspects: the purpose and the principle of the interview, recording and data protection. (After agreement, turn on the recording device). Frame an explanation of what the interview will be about, e.g. a very personal view; an explanation of how the conversation will proceed and how long it will probably take. (The actual interview starts at this point.)	Framing

Steps involved in planning a narrative interview	Six F's of designing interview research
5. Frame (in keywords) how to conclude the interview, including asking for any additional points and for the interviewee's feedback.	Framing
Steps for preparing the conduct and content of narrative interviews	
6. Overview of subjects of interest for the interview.	Foreseeing
7. What themes are of central interest?	Foreseeing
8. What period of the interviewee's life (beginning–end) and which biographical events can provide information about the central topic(s)?	Foregrounding
9. Phrase an initial question which will motivate and help the interviewees to tell a story of their life which is linked to the topics of the study (e.g. 'I would like to ask you to recount from the beginning how it came about that you … Begin with the day as you … and recount your story until …').	Formulating
10. For your initial question, check on (1) whether it is really a narrative stimulus, (2) whether it focuses on or at least relates to the topic of your study and (3) whether it is open enough to stimulate the interviewees to refer to the areas of their lives the topic might be relevant for.	Focusing
11. Phrase keywords for **narrative-generating questions** for central aspects you want to ask after the end of the main narrative, if the interviewee did not recount in enough detail referring to these aspects (e.g. 'You mentioned briefly … Could you please recount in more detail how this came about/went off?').	Foreseeing
12. Note down some keywords for probing central aspects you want to address after the narrative parts of the interview are finished, which you would like to return to if the interviewee does not spontaneously mention them.	Foreseeing

Types of Data in the Narrative Interview

The main type of data in this kind of interview is a long comprehensive narrative about the process under study and the interviewee's life history. In successful cases, this will have a narrative format throughout, though sometimes the interviewees switch to descriptions and explanations. The narrative interview is supposed to provide descriptions and explanations in the last part (balancing phase). Following the theory behind the methodology, it is the narrative parts of the data which provide the most valuable and valid information about the issue of the study and the interviewees' views.

Narrative Interviewing in Critical Research

Using narratives in interviewing has a kind of hybrid position in qualitative research, as this and the preceding chapter may have illustrated – as a part of interviews (see Chapter 11) and as a form of doing interviews as discussed here. At the same time, it has a hybrid position in what concerns critical approaches to interviewing. In Chapter 4, the approach of focused life-story interviews by Edwards et al. (2005) was briefly mentioned as a method in indigenous research. But we also find it in more critical approaches in feminist research of and with women of colour, as the case study in Box 12.2 illustrates.

Box 12.2   Research in the real world

Scholarly professional narratives about interviews with and by women of colour

In their article, 'When Researching the "Other" Intersects with the Self: Women of Color Intimate Research', Altheria Caldera, Sana Rizvi, Freyca Calderon-Berumen and Monica Lugo, an African-American scholar, a British Pakistani immigrant scholar and two Latina (Mexican) immigrant scholars working in the education departments of US and UK universities, discuss what happens when feminist researchers of colour interview women who share their identities, and the researchers reflect on their own experiences in 'scholarly personal narratives' (SPN – Caldera et al., 2020, p. 63). They reflect on language and identity issues in their relationships to interviewees and compare these reflections among the African-American, Latina and British Pakistani contexts. Issues of insider/outsider dichotomy (p. 78) or in or out/us or them representational dilemmas (p. 79) are discussed. In comparing their own experiences and examples found in the literature, they conclude:

> Our SPNs reveal that unique dynamics surface when women of color scholars conduct critical qualitative inquiry with participants who share many aspects of their cultural identity. We name this experience Women of Color Intimate Research (WOCIR). Four significant themes, extracted from our narratives, characterize WOCIR: 1. intimacy between researchers and participants, 2. intense emotional labor, 3. purposeful use of decolonizing language, and 4. complications related to ethical research guidelines. (2020, p. 81)

In the end, the authors emphasize that their reflections 'may also be valuable to anyone who endeavors to collaborate with marginalized individuals and populations for feminist critical qualitative inquiry' (2020, p. 83). These reflections are interesting in our context of narrative interviewing in this chapter, because the authors take a critical stance from a decolonizing perspective, but remain in the framework of working with interviews and narratives nevertheless.

Other examples of using narrative interviewing but without specifically spelling out how the interviews were done as narrative interviews, include Mizock, Harkins, Ray and Morant's (2011a) analysis of 'researcher race in narrative interviews on traumatic racism' in the United States. In indigenous research in the culture of Māori in New Zealand, we also find a number of studies which make use of narrative interviewing in a creative way (see the examples in Box 12.3).

Box 12.3   Research in the real world

Narrative interviews with Māori teenage mothers about contraception and violence

In two studies, a research team from Victoria and Otago Universities in Wellington, New Zealand, with colleagues from Canada, used narrative interviewing. Lawton et al. (2016) studied the access to contraception for indigenous Māori teenage mothers (14–19 years old), with Māori interviewers doing face-to-face narrative interviews with 22 Māori women (pre-birth cohort) four to five times over 20 months through pregnancy and the birth of their babies, and with 22 women (post-birth cohort) two to three times over nine months, and then with 41 of these 44 women at their babies' first birthdays in a longitudinal design (see Chapter 5). They found that the access 'worked well when there was a contraception plan that included navigation, free access, and provision of contraception' (2016, p. 52), so that the interviewees had no (navigation) problems in accessing appropriate services providing contraception (p. 57). Dhunna et al. (2018) used six of the narrative interviews from the pre-birth cohort of the above study by Lawton et al. (2016) to analyse the interviewees' experiences of intimate partner violence (IPV). They found how 'IPV manifests in the relationships of these six women. Their stories showed the various ways in which young Māori women resist violence, reclaim their Māori identities, and experience personal transformation during their motherhood journeys despite abuse' (pp. 1–2).

These examples illustrate the acceptance of using narratives for interviewing in these contexts, which in general are rather critical about interviewing and qualitative research and take a critical and decolonizing approach to methodologies. Chilisa (2020, p. 200) discusses how 'in qualitative research, the researcher can focus on the interview itself as a form of narrative or focus on stories that appear spontaneously in the course of the interview', referring to Kvale (1996). These examples show as well that the methodological concepts of doing narrative interviews or using narratives for or in interviews are not really spelled out. Thus, the methods presented in this and the preceding chapter may offer approaches for such a methodological elaboration of narrative interviews in these contexts.

Steps, Aims and Criteria in Preparing and Doing Narrative Interviews

Table 12.1 summarizes the steps involved in preparing narrative interviews and the criteria for evaluating their outcome.

Table 12.1   Steps, aims and criteria in preparing and doing narrative interviews

Six F's of designing interview research	Steps	Aims and actions	Criteria
Framing	1. Preparing the interview	• Prepare a draft for an initial question on a pre-analysis of the field under study • Run test interviews and interview training • Prepare a documentation sheet for the context of the interview (demographic data, etc.)	• Does the initial question cover the area under study? • Did the interviewer(s) internalize the principle of the interview? • Does the documentation sheet cover the relevant information for the research question?
Framing	2. Introducing the interview principle	• Prepare a good introduction for the interviewee, and make sure it is clear	• Did the interviewee understand and accept the principle of the interview?
Formulating	3. The initial question (for generating a narrative)	• Prepare an initial question which stimulates a narrative about the topic and periods of the interviewee's life history	• Does the question encompass relevant aspects of the subjective meanings for the interviewees and their biographies? • Is the question oriented towards a narrative? • Did the interviewer enforce the narrative principle of the interview to bring more depth to the interview?
Foregrounding	4. Narrative-generating questions	• Try to think about questions that cover relevant areas of the interviewee's biography, which might not be expressed in enough detail	• Are these questions narrative in character? • Do they add the missing aspects in the interview?
Focusing	5. More general topics referring to the issue under study for the final part of the interview	• Try to get into the detail of the central parts of the issue under study • Try to increase the depth and richness of the interviewee's responses with additional inquiries	• Has the interviewee gone into detail and depth? • Has the interviewer been sensitive to any extra depth on which to focus?

Six F's of designing interview research	Steps	Aims and actions	Criteria
Foreseeing	6. Socio-demographic data	• Develop a checklist for this purpose • Use the documentation sheet	• Is all information included that is necessary for contextualizing the interviewee's narrative?
Framing	7. Evaluation and small-talk	• Make room for some conversation • Make room for critique and additional aspects	• Were additional aspects mentioned?
Foreseeing	8. Documentation	• Ensure a good recording and a detailed transcription	• Is all additional information (not on the recording) documented?
Finding and Formulating	9. Analysing narrative interviews	• Choose an appropriate method for analysing and interpreting the narratives and answers	• Does the method take the quality of the data into account (e.g. the narrative structure of accounts)?

What You Need to Ask Yourself

The narrative interview is a kind of hybrid method. On the one hand, it is an interview, as the name and its use indicate; on the other, it is presented as an alternative to interviews, when its distinctive features are highlighted. In any case, it comes with specific and maybe more demanding challenges for the interviewer – sometimes also for the interviewee – compared to other forms of interviewing.

The questions in Box 12.4 are designed for you to check how far you understand the method's specific features and strengths and what they imply for doing an interview study with this method.

Box 12.4   What you need to ask yourself

Doing narrative interviews

1. How far can the issue of my research be studied by asking people to tell a story (of their lives)?
2. Who should my interview partners be – will they be able to tell their life history spontaneously?
3. Will it be possible to identify what I want to know for my research from such long narratives?

What You Need to Succeed

This chapter should have provided a solid introduction to narrative interviewing. It should help you to understand and contextualize this approach in the preceding and following chapters. The questions in Box 12.5 will help you to review what to take home from this chapter.

Box 12.5 What you need to succeed

Doing narrative interviews

1. Do I understand the main principle of the narrative interview – to stimulate the interviewee to recount a story and then to listen until it is finished without intervening with questions?
2. Do I see the challenges in making such a narrative approach work?
3. Do I see the advantages of interviewing with such an open format?

What you have learned

- Doing narrative interviews is more than just asking people questions. Narrative interviewing has been developed as an alternative method.
- This interview form gives interviewees as much leeway as possible to reveal their views and experiences. At the same time, they should be given a structure for what to talk about.
- Even if it is less visible than in other forms of interviewing, we are talking about a method here, too, which has features and interventions, which have to be applied in a systematic way to make the interview work.
- This method should be used where if the collected narratives are analysed in detail using a method that allows for their complexity and structure (see Chapter 16).

Exercises

In the following exercises, you are first invited to reflect on some of the main issues in this chapter. Then you are invited to apply the topics of this chapter to the development of a project of your own. Hence, the exercises are a combination of reflection and prospection.

Exercise 12.1

Reflecting on the Chapter: The Use of Narrative Interviews in an Existing Study

1. Look through a journal for a qualitative study based on narrative interviews (e.g. Riemann, 2003). Try to identify how this form of interview was used in the study.

Exercise 12.2

Planning Your Own Research with Narrative Interviews

1. Think of your own study and develop a first version of an initial generative narrative question for stimulating a life history narrative for your research question.

What's next

This book chapter can give you a fuller picture of the narrative interview for collecting qualitative data:

Jovchelovitch, S., & Bauer, M. (2000). Narrative Interviewing. In M.W. Bauer & G. Gaskell (Eds.), *Qualitative Researching with Text, Image and Sound* (pp. 58-74). London: Sage.

This handbook chapter outlines further details about the use of this method in biographical research:

Rosenthal, G. (2004). Biographical Research. In C. Seale, G. Gobo, J. Gubrium, & D. Silverman (Eds.), *Qualitative Research Practice* (pp. 48-65). London: Sage.

This open-access journal article gives some insights into the discussion and the research based on narrative interviews:

Riemann, G. (2003). A Joint Project Against the Backdrop of a Research Tradition: An Introduction to 'Doing Biographical Research' [36 paragraphs]. *Forum Qualitative Sozialforschung/Forum: Qualitative Social Research*, 4(3), Art. 18. http://nbn-resolving. de/urn:nbn:de:0114-fqs0303185

This study is an example of using narrative interviewing in the context of research by and with women of colour:

Caldera, A., Rizvi, S., Calderon-Berumen, F., & Lugo, M. (2020). When Researching the 'Other' Intersects with the Self: Women of Color Intimate Research. *Departures in Critical Qualitative Research*, 9(1), 63-88. doi:10.1525/dcqr.2020.9.1.63

In this article, examples of using narrative research in the context of research by and with Māori people are presented and discussed:

Dhunna, S., Lawton, B., & Cram, F. (2018). An Affront to Her Mana: Young Māori Mothers' Experiences of Intimate Partner Violence. *Journal of Interpersonal Violence*. https:// doi.org/10.1177/0886260518815712

Doing Interview Research Navigator

How to understand interview research
- What doing interview research means
- Theories and epistemologies of interviewing
- When to choose interviews as a research method
- Methods and formats of interviewing

Designing interview research
- Planning and designing interview research
- How many interviewees: Sampling and saturation
- Accessing and recruiting participants

How to conduct interviews
- How to respect and protect: Ethics of interviewing
- Semi-structured interviews: Working with questions and answers
- Interviewing experts and elites
- Integrating narratives in interviews: Episodic interviews

You are here in your project

Doing interviews in context
- How to work with life histories: Narrative interviews
- Working with focus groups as interviews
- Ask (in) the field: Ethnographic and mobile interviewing
- Doing online interviews

How to work with interview data
- Working with interview data
- Credibility and transparency: Quality and writing in interview research
- From interviewing to an inner view: Critiques and reflexivity

WORKING WITH FOCUS GROUPS AS INTERVIEWS

How this chapter will help you

You will:

- be introduced to the idea of using focus groups as interviews,
- learn how interviewing can be contextualized in focus groups,
- see how focus groups can be used to contextualize interviewing, and
- understand what is possible with online focus group interviews.

This chapter addresses a second way of doing interviews in context. Here it is not only the format – as was the case in the preceding chapter setting interviewing in a narrative context – but also the context in which participants are confronted with questions and expected to answer them. Group interviews and more recently focus groups have been used to do interviews for some time (going back to Merton et al., 1956) and will be discussed here for their potential as a method for doing interview research. However, this chapter does not aim at providing a comprehensive introduction to focus groups (see Barbour, 2018 instead).

Background to Focus Group Interviews

The methods of focus groups and of doing interviews have a special relation, which comprises five levels. First of all, we find authors rejecting interviews in favour of doing focus groups instead – thus a competitive relation. Second, focus groups can be used as a tool for developing an interview – for example, for deriving topic questions for the interview guide from a focus group discussion beforehand. Third, we find studies in which focus groups are run parallel to individual interviews. Fourth, we can use focus groups for feeding back results from single interviews to participants of these interviews or the groups. These are individual relations. And fifth, we can use groups for interviewing their members – either as an explicitly designed group interview or by asking people 'elaborate questions' (Puchta and Potter, 1999). This last example turns the relation around in some ways: here it is not the use of focus groups for asking questions, but the occurrence of questions during a focus group that is discussed. In all these variations, interviewing is embedded in the context of using focus groups.

Group interviews

One way to contextualize the interview situation is to interview people in a group. Beginning with Merton et al. (1956), group interviews have been conducted in a number of studies (Fontana and Frey, 2000; Merton, 1987). Patton, for example, defines the group interview as 'an interview with a small group of people on a specific topic. Groups are typically six to eight people who participate in the interview for one-half to two hours' (2015, p. 475).

Several procedures are differentiated, which are structured and moderated by an interviewer in varying ways. In general, the interviewer should be 'flexible, objective, empathic, persuasive, a good listener' (Fontana and Frey, 2000, p. 652). These authors see 'objectivity' mainly as the mediation between the different participants, so that everyone is heard. A major task for the interviewer is to prevent single participants or partial groups from dominating the interview and thus the whole group with their contributions. At the same time, interviewers should encourage hesitant members to get more involved in the interview and to share their views. Interviewers should aim at obtaining answers from each group member in order to cover the topic as far as possible. Finally, interviewers must balance their behaviour by (directively) steering the group, for example, with questions and (non-directively) moderating it.

Patton sees the focus group interview as a highly efficient qualitative data collection technique, which provides some quality controls on data collection: 'Participants tend to provide checks and balances on each other which weeds out false or extreme views. ... The extent to which there is a relatively consistent, shared view can be quickly assessed' (2015, p. 478). Among the weaknesses of the method, Patton discusses the limited number of questions that can be addressed and the problems of taking notes during the interview. Therefore, Patton suggests the employment of pairs of interviewers, one of whom is free to document the responses while the other manages the interview and the group. In contrast to other authors, Patton underlines that: 'The focus group interview is, first and foremost, an interview. It is not a problem-solving session. It is not a decision-making group. It is not primarily a discussion, although direct interactions among participants often occur. It is an *interview*' (2015, p. 475).

In summary, the main advantages of group interviews are that they are low cost and rich in data, that they stimulate the respondents and support them in remembering events, and that they can lead beyond the answers of the single interviewee.

Forms of groups

A brief look at the history of, and methodological discussion about, this procedure shows that there have been different ideas about what a group is. A common feature of the varieties of group discussions is to use as a data source the discussion on a specific topic in a **natural group** (i.e. existing in everyday life) or an **artificial group** (i.e. put together for the research purpose according to certain criteria). Sometimes there are even suggestions to use real groups, which means groups that are also concerned about the issue of the group discussion independently of the discussion and as a real group including the same members as in the research situation. One reason for this is that real groups start from a history of shared interactions in relation to the issue in focus and thus have already developed forms of common activities and underlying patterns of meaning.

Furthermore, there is a distinction between **homogeneous** and **heterogeneous groups**. In homogeneous groups, members are comparable in the essential dimensions related to the research question and have a similar background. In heterogeneous groups, members should be different in the characteristics that are relevant for the research question. This is intended to increase the dynamics of the discussion so that many different perspectives will be expressed and also that the reserve of individual participants will be broken down by the confrontation between these perspectives.

Constructing a Framework for Listening in Focus Group Interviews

Preparing the interview

Morgan (2012, p. 167) suggests asking oneself four questions when preparing a group discussion, which also apply to the actual interview situation when using focus groups for it:

- Who will the participants be?
- How will the group discussion be introduced to the participants?
- What questions will the participants be asked?
- How will the moderator interact with the group during the discussion?

Questions to consider in planning a focus group interview include the composition of the group (see above) and the size of the group (8–12 members are suggested) as well as the role of the researcher in the group. The role will be a mix of interviewer (asking questions) and moderator (between the members of the actual group) as in focus groups in general. For this reason and for the complexity of this combination, it is suggested to do focus group interviews with two researchers, one responsible for the questions and the other for moderating the group (Patton, 2015, p. 477).

When holding focus group interviews, an interview guide or a set of questions should be prepared. Krueger (1998, pp. 21–3) discusses several categories of questions that can be asked in focus group interviews. *Opening* questions or *introductory* questions are prepared to get a group going and make the participants familiar with each other and the situation. *Transition* questions are used for shifting the topic that is discussed in the group towards the more relevant aspects. *Key* questions help ensure that the major topics are mentioned. *Ending* questions and those for *putting the parts together* have a rounding up function in the interview. Krueger also suggests working with open-ended questions first, keeping them simple, avoiding why-questions and being cautious about giving examples. Practically, this means that you should prepare an interview guide with these kinds of questions, starting with more open questions and moving to more focused key questions: 'The interview guide for a focus group discussion generally consists of a set of very general open-ended questions about the topic or issue of interest. It does not include all the questions that may be asked during the group discussion' (Stewart et al., 2009, p. 600). Puchta and Potter (1999) discuss the role of elaborate questions in focus groups, which are helpful when using focus groups for interviewing.

Morgan discusses starter questions and basic principles for successfully promoting interaction in the discussion.

A starter question should be:

- something that is easy for each of the participants to answer
- something that makes participants want to hear what the other participants have to say
- something that creates the opportunity to express a diverse range of views. (2012, p. 169)

Stewart et al. (2009, p. 600) suggest that an interview guide for a focus group interview of around 90 minutes should comprise no more than 10–20 questions. Other issues to carefully plan for a focus group interview consider the room and its setting, where the interview will take place, rules for the situation (e.g. no mobile phones, please!) and an arrangement about mutual confidentiality (no participant should reveal anything learned about the other participants outside the group situation). Finally, the researchers should reflect in advance on how to deal with participants' cancellations in two respects – first, on the minimum number of participants necessary for the group session or whether to postpone the session when a certain number have cancelled. Second, are there specific participants who should definitely be at the interview session? In case of their cancelling, would it be better to postpone the session? These are problems familiar from using focus groups in general.

Introducing the idea of the focus group interview

As in interviews and focus groups in general, the first step with the participants should be to familiarize them with what will happen in the session and what will be expected of them. This should give room for clarifying the participants' questions, so that they know what they should be doing and feel safe and comfortable about it.

The following steps provide a rough outline of procedure:

- At the beginning, an explanation of the (formal) procedure is given. Here, the expectations for the participants are formulated. Expectations may be to answer questions, and be involved in the discussion that might evolve. For example: 'We would like you to answer the questions we ask the group, to openly discuss with each other the experiences you have had with our issues, and try to contribute to every issue we raise and question we ask.'
- Then follows a short introduction of the members to one another and a warm-up phase to prepare for exchanges within the group. Here, the interviewer should emphasize the common ground of the members in order to facilitate or to reinforce community, e.g. 'As former students of psychology, you should all know the problems, the …'.
- The actual interview starts with an opening question, revealing the a concrete problem the interview will be about. Note here some parallels to the focused interview (see Chapter 9, and Merton, 1987).
- In groups with members unfamiliar with each other in advance, an introductory question will be asked in the beginning and then the group develops in the following phases: of strangeness with, of orientation to, adaptation to and familiarity with the group, as well as conformity and, ultimately, the exchanges drying up.

Beginning a focus group interview might look like this (adapted from Stewart and Shamdasani, 1990):

Today we're going to talk about an issue that affects all of you. Before we get into our interview, let me make a few requests of you. First, you should know that we are recording the session so that I can refer back to what was said when I analyse it and when I write my report. If anyone is uncomfortable with being recorded please say so and, of course, you are free to leave. Do speak up and let's try to have just one person speak at a time. I will ask you a number of questions and I would like to have your answers and comments to each question and to hear from all of you. I will play traffic cop and try to ensure that everyone gets a turn. Finally, please say exactly what you think. Don't worry about what I think or what your neighbour thinks. We're here to exchange opinions and have fun while we do it. Why don't we begin by introducing ourselves?

Evaluation and small-talk

Other planning issues refer to the end of the interview, for which the following questions are a guide: How should the focus group interview be ended? How might the researcher provide a space for the participants to introduce aspects not covered in the main part of the interview and to maybe give feedback on the situation? How may we allow the group session to end smoothly?

Types of Data in Focus Group Interviews

The (successful) focus group interview will provide answers to the questions asked by the researchers. It will also give insights into how several people differ, comment and interact referring to an issue or a question. And it will provide insights into the interactional context of exchanges among the participants and of the answers that were given. Although this may be given less attention than in focus group discussions, we may analyse the interaction among the members of the group and with the researchers in group interviews as well. Participants may refer to others in the group by picking up their statements, by confirming them or by criticizing and rejecting what someone has said in answering a question. This can be seen as influencing or biasing the participants' answers in some ways, or as information about how the situation of data collection has stimulated specific kinds of answers and thus illuminated the role of the framework of listening the researcher has constructed.

Planning and Preparing Focus Group Interviews

To prepare a focus group interview, it is necessary to plan it in two parts, first, the framework of the interview so that the interviewees know what is expected of them and what they have agreed to do, and second, the conduct of the focus group interview and the contents it should cover. This will help to reduce or avoid any reservation on the interviewees' side so that they can do the interview in an open and relaxed way. Box 13.1 presents some instructions for preparing a focus group interview.

Box 13.1   Research in the real world

Planning for a focus group interview

Planning a focus group interview includes suggestions for preparing (1) the interview framework (data protection, general guidelines on questions and on the length and type of the conversation) and (2) the conduct of the interview (entering the subject, question areas, questions, etc.).

Steps involved in planning a focus group interview	Six F's of designing interview research
Reflect in advance again	
1. Who will your potential interviewees be?	Finding
2. What will the group composition be like?	Foreseeing
3. What is the research question for the focus group interview?	Focusing
Steps for preparing the framework for listening in a focus group interview	
1. Reflect on what the interviewees should know in advance to be well prepared for the interview and to understand what it is about and what their role is. Start from what the interviewee has perhaps already learned about your study when making the appointment for the focus group interview.	Framing
2. Phrase (in keywords) an appropriate introduction to the focus group interview for the following aspects: the purpose of the interview, recording, data protection and mutual confidentiality of the participants. (After agreement, turn on the recording device.)	Framing
3. Formulate an explanation of what the interview will be about, e.g. a very personal view; an explanation of how the conversation will proceed and how long it will probably take. (The actual focus group interview starts at this point.)	Formulating
4. Frame (in keywords) how to conclude the group and the interview, including the question of any additional thoughts and the interviewees' feedback.	Framing
Steps for preparing the conduct and content of focus group interviews	
5. Overview of subjects of interest for the interview.	Foreseeing
6. What themes are of central interest?	Foregrounding
7. What area of the interviewees' professional, everyday life, for example, can provide information about the central topic(s)?	Foreseeing
8. For every area, frame an opening stimulus that might motivate the interviewee, as clearly and unambiguously as possible, to respond, for every topic under points 9 and 10.	Formulating
9. For every area, phrase questions about relationships, etc. that might stimulate the interviewees, as clearly and unambiguously as possible, to express their views of the central issues of the interview (e.g. What is .... for you? What do you associate with this term?).	Focusing
10. Note down some keywords for probing central aspects which you would like to return to if the interviewees do not spontaneously mention them.	Foreseeing

Although generally focus groups are seen as being different from interviews, we find a number of examples using this format of data collection, of asking questions and receiving answers, as illustrated in Box 13.2

Box 13.2   Research in the real world

Using focus groups for analysing depoliticization

Sophie Duchesne (2017), a political scientist from the Centre Emile Durkheim at the National Centre of Scientific Research (CNRS) in Bordeaux in France, used focus groups for studying citizens' depoliticization in Europe. She 'ran the series of groups, about thirty collective interviews in three cities' (2017, p. 366), uses the term 'interviewees' for her participants ('purely lay citizens', p. 371) throughout the chapter and prefers the term 'collective interview' (p. 376) over 'focus groups'. The study was conducted with small groups of six to seven participants, whom the researchers 'asked a limited number of questions: five for three hours of discussion' (p. 377) and aimed at analysing attitudes (towards the European Union). This study is an example of how the use of focus groups for interviewing groups can also work with sensitive questions in political science.

Steps, Aims and Criteria in Preparing and Doing Focus Group Interviews

Table 13.1 summarizes the steps involved in preparing focus group interviews and the criteria for evaluating the outcomes of applying them.

Table 13.1   Steps, aims and criteria in preparing and doing focus group interviews

Six F's of designing interview research	Steps	Aims and actions	Criteria
Framing	1. Preparing the interview	• Prepare a draft of an interview guide for the group on a pre-analysis of the field under study • Run test interviews with a group and interview training • Prepare a documentation sheet for the context of the interview (demographic data of the group's members, etc.)	• Do the questions cover the area under study? • Did the interviewer(s) internalize the principle of the interview? • Does the documentation sheet cover the relevant information for the research question?

Six F's of designing interview research	Steps	Aims and actions	Criteria
Framing	2. Introducing the interview principle	• Prepare a good introduction to the group for the interviewees, and make sure it is clear to everyone	• Did the interviewees understand and accept the principle of the interview?
Formulating	3. The initial question	• Prepare an introductory question which stimulates answers about the topic	• Does the question encompass relevant aspects of the topic's subjective meanings for the interviewees? • Are the questions oriented towards discussion? • Did the interviewer enforce the aspect of exchange in the group to bring more depth to the interview?
Foregrounding	4. Key questions	• Try to think about key questions that cover relevant areas of the interview's topic	• Are these questions focused and clear? • Do they address the main aspects of the issue?
Focusing	5. Ending questions addressing the general topics referring to the issue under study for the final part of the interview	• Try to get into the detail of the central parts of the issue under study • Try to increase the depth and richness of the participants' responses by additional inquiries	• Have the participants gone into detail and depth? • Has the interviewer been sensitive to any extra depth on which to focus?
Foreseeing	6. Socio-demographic data	• Develop a checklist for this purpose • Use the documentation sheet	• Is all information included that is necessary for contextualizing the participants' statements ?
Framing	7. Evaluation and small-talk	• Make room for some conversation • Make room for critique and additional aspects	• Were additional aspects mentioned?
Foreseeing	8. Documentation	• Ensure a good recording and a detailed transcription	• Is all additional information (not on the recording) documented?
Finding and Formulating	9. Analysing focus group interviews	• Choose an appropriate method for analysing and interpreting the answers and discussions	• Does the method take the quality of the data into account (e.g. the interactive structure of accounts)?

Contextualizing Interviews by Focus Groups

As mentioned earlier in this chapter, the contextualization of questions and answers can occur in the use of focus groups for collecting answers. And it can help to contextualize the interview by running a focus group before it in order to identify topics and questions to ask in the actual interview. And, finally, focus groups can be used to feed back and evaluate the results coming from interviews, as in the example in Box 13.3 (taken from Flick, 2018a).

Box 13.3   Research in the real world

Using focus groups for feedback of interview results

In our study on health professionals' concepts of health and ageing (Flick et al., 2003), we first used episodic interviews (see Chapter 11) to collect data on these concepts, including the interviewees' ideas and experiences with prevention and health promotion. After analysing these data, we ran focus groups with general practitioners and nurses, with three goals. We wanted to give the participants feedback about our study's results. We also wanted to receive their comments on these results as a way of applying the concept of **member check** or **communicative validation** (see Chapter 17 for this). And we wanted to discuss with them the practical consequences of the findings for improving day-to-day routines in home care nursing and medicine. This improvement should be directed towards a stronger focus on health, health promotion and prevention.

To prevent the discussions in the groups from becoming too general and heterogeneous, we looked for a concrete sensitizing concept as an input, which opened up the overall issue. We used results referring to the barriers against a stronger focus on prevention in their own practice that the interviewees had mentioned in the interviews. We presented the results concerning the patients' and the professionals' readiness and resistance. First, we presented an overview of the barriers that had been mentioned. Then we asked the participants for a ranking of their importance. Next, we asked them to discuss the results in the wider context of health in their own practice. When the discussion started to calm down, we asked them to make suggestions on how to overcome the barriers mentioned before, and to discuss such suggestions. In the end, we had a list of comments and suggestions from each group, which we then compared and analysed as part of our study.

In this example, focus groups were used for a specific purpose. They were not used as a stand-alone method for data collection, but for feedback and member check of the first results of a study. The participants in the focus groups were the same as in the single interviews. However, not all the interviewees accepted our invitation to come and contribute again to our study. Using a stimulus – in this case, the presentation of a selection of results – was helpful to start and structure the discussion. In the end, when we compared the results, we had to use each group as a case, but ended up with comparable views and results.

Doing Focus Group Interviews Online

In a similar way as for individual interviews (see Chapter 15), the use of focus group interviews has been transferred to online interviewing and we find similar distinctions and discussions as in the context of individual online interviewing. Focus group interviews, similar to individual online interviews, can be done in a synchronous way – all participants and the researcher are online at the same time and the interaction of questions and answers occurs in an immediate way. Or the discussion is run in asynchronous communication – participants do not respond immediately or at the same time to a question asked but within a certain timeframe (see Chapter 15 for this distinction).

Why do online focus group interviews?

Reasons for doing focus group interviews online include: saving time and the economic and ecological costs of travelling, avoiding meeting people one does not really want to meet in the research situation, and the possibility of reaching people who are located far away and far from each other for a focus group. In addition to the loss of rapport between the participant and the researcher as in interviews, the loss of contact between the participants has to be taken into account here. At the same time, it can be helpful to have a discussion without too much of a group dynamic, when it is organized in an asynchronous way and statements are sent around to the other participants and everyone can take their time to respond.

How can the existing approaches of interviewing in groups be transferred to online focus group interviewing?

It is easier to transfer an approach of focus group research interested in statements and opinions than an approach that is mainly interested in provoking the participants into a developing group dynamic that makes the participants say things they would have avoided in an individual interview. If such a dynamic is a central aim of doing the focus group interview, the technical side of doing it online may disturb or destroy the dynamic if the (online) connection fails or is interrupted.

Practicalities of online focus group interviewing

Again, we find the distinction between **synchronous (or real-time)** and asynchronous (non-real-time) groups. The first type of online focus group requires that all participants are online at the same time and may take part in meetings using specific conferencing software. This means that all participants need to have this software on their computers (as in the case of Zoom or Skype – see Chapter 15) or that the researchers might have to provide it to participants who are supposed to load it onto their computers. Besides the technical problems this may cause, many people may hesitate to receive and install software on their computers for the purpose of taking part in a study.

Asynchronous focus groups do not require all participants to be online at the same time (and thus prevent the problems of coordinating this precondition). As in an email interview (see Chapter 15), people can take their time to respond to entries posted by the other participants (or to your questions or stimulus). Every participant's interventions will be addressed to a conference site and stored in a folder to which all participants have access. This type of focus group has its advantages in allowing people from different time zones to participate or when people vary in their speed of typing or responding, which might produce differences in the chance to articulate in the group.

In order to make online focus groups work, easy access for the participants should be set up. Mann and Stewart (2000, pp. 103–5) describe in some detail the software you can use for setting up synchronous focus groups ('conferencing software'). They also describe the alternatives of how to design websites, and whether these should facilitate access for those who are intended to participate and exclude others not intended to have access. Many more and updated suggestions can be found in Abrams and Gaiser (2017). Specialized focus group software, e.g. QualBoard, as programs one has to pay for; more general online meeting applications, e.g. Adobe Connect, Citrix GoToMeeting, Cisco Webex or Zoom, as free online meeting applications; and messaging apps like Google Hangouts or Skype, or social media like Facebook groups, can all be used.

When designing the venue of a focus group, concepts of naturalness and neutrality can be implemented in online settings. For example, it is important that participants can join the discussions from their computers at home or at their workplace and do not have to go to a special research site. As an opener, it is important to create a welcome message, which invites the participants, explains the procedures and what is expected of them, what the rules of communication are (e.g. 'please be polite to everyone …'), and so on (for an example, see Mann and Stewart, 2000, p. 108). The researcher should – as for any focus group interview – create a permissive environment.

For the recruitment of participants, we can basically use the same sources as for an online interview (see Chapter 15), such as snowballing (see Chapter 6) or scouring existing chatrooms or discussion groups for possible participants. Here again, the issue is that one cannot really be sure that the participants meet the criteria or that the representation they give of themselves is correct. This can become a problem if the researchers want to set up a homogeneous group of girls of a certain age, for example: 'Unless online focus group participation combines the textual dimensions of chat rooms or conferencing with the visual dimension of digital cameras and/or voice, the researcher will be unable to be sure that the focus group really is comprised of, for example, adolescent girls' (Mann and Stewart, 2000, p. 112).

The number of participants in real-time focus group interviews should be limited because too many participants might make the interaction in the group too fast and superficial. This problem can be managed more easily in asynchronous groups. Therefore, the number of participants does not have to be restricted in the latter case but should be limited in the former.

Compared to face-to-face focus groups, the issue of participant or group dynamics can be managed more easily in (especially asynchronous) online groups, yet it can also become a problem. Shy participants may hesitate to intervene when they are unsure of the procedure or the issue, but the researcher has more options to intervene and work on this problem than in normal focus groups. The greater anonymity in online focus groups that is produced by the use of usernames, nicknames and the like may facilitate topical disclosures by participants in the discussion more than in focus groups, in general.

Finally, it is important that the topic selected for the interview is relevant for the group and participants in the study, so that it is attractive for them to join the group and the discussion. Or, the other way around, it is important that you find groups for whom your topic is relevant in order to have fruitful discussions and produce interesting data.

Box 13.4   Research in the real world

Ways of using synchronous online focus groups

Bojana Lobe, who works in the Social Sciences at Ljubljana University in Slovenia, compares several ways of doing online focus groups in a synchronous way (Lobe, 2017). She uses her experience with a 'set of more than 50 synchronous focus groups conducted via online messaging tools; a set of 10 audio focus groups conducted via Skype; and a set of 15 video focus groups, conducted via the ZOOM conferencing tool' (2017, p. 227). She compares text-based, audio-only and audiovisual online groups for social context cues, organizational (design and recruitment), moderation and ethical issues (e.g. informed consent, anonymity – see Chapter 8) always with an eye to the differences to face-to-face focus groups (see also Lobe et al., 2020).

Focus Group Interviewing for Decolonizing Research

In the context of the discussion of indigenous methods and decolonizing qualitative research, focus group interviews seem to be quite accepted as a method. Chilisa (2020, p. 255) discusses 'indigenous focus group interviews' and stresses the need to insist that every member has equal 'opportunities to be heard' (p. 256). Sherman (2002) discusses the 'subjective experience of race and gender in qualitative research' and provides an example highlighting the tensions and problems here for his study called 'The Rock Ceiling: A Study of African American Women Managers' Experiences and Perceptions of Barriers Restricting Advancement in the Corporation', in which he, as a white, male doctoral student, wanted to do focus group interviews with African-American participants. He discusses the reactions of the research ethics committee and potential biases in conducting his study. The dilemmas this design produced, not only for him and this study but which were highlighted by the construction of the study, make the article (Sherman, 2002) an interesting read when reflecting on and planning a research. The example in Box 13.5 shows how such differences between researcher and participants might be taken into account in a more reflexive way.

Box 13.5   Research in the real world

Using focus groups for exploring vaccine acceptance among young gay and bisexual men and transgender women in Thailand

A research team from the Social Work Faculty at the University of Toronto, Canada and a foundation in Thailand (Newman et al., 2017) used focus groups to study young gay and bisexual men and transgender women in Thailand around vaccine acceptance in the context of HIV. In each subsample, they divided the groups by age (18–24 and 25–30 years) and gender identities; all in all, five focus groups with 37 participants were conducted. The researchers used a semi-structured topic guide, which was written in English, translated into Thai and back-translated into English to identify any inconsistencies and then finalized in Thai. The groups were led by a local Thai member of a community-based organization (which had also supported the access to the participants) and the Thai member in the research team. In the article, it becomes evident that the groups were run like semi-structured interviews, with questions and probes (see Chapter 9) complemented by an anonymous two-page, socio-demographic questionnaire (2017, p. 89). The use of the focus groups was embedded in a larger mixed methods study which also included a questionnaire, which was developed on the basis of the focus group findings. All in all, this is an example which illustrates the use of focus groups as a context for making an interview approach work in groups.

What You Need to Ask Yourself

Focus group interviews are again a kind of hybrid method. On the one hand, they can be used as an interview; on the other hand, they are presented and discussed as an alternative to interviews, when their distinctive features are highlighted. In any case, they also come with specific and maybe more demanding challenges for the interviewer – sometimes also for the interviewees – compared to other forms of (individual) interviewing.

The questions in Box 13.6 are designed for you to check how far you have understood the method's specific features and strengths, and what they mean for doing an interview study with this method.

Box 13.6   What you need to ask yourself

Doing focus group interviews

1. How far can my research topic be studied by asking people in a group?
2. Am I clear about the challenges of hearing all participants' voices in such a group?
3. What do I see as the advantages of doing interviews in groups instead of individually?

What You Need to Succeed

This chapter should have provided you with a solid grounding in what interviewing in groups is about. It should help you to understand and contextualize this approach in the preceding and following chapters. The questions in Box 13.7 aim to give you an overview of what to take home from this chapter for the other steps discussed in the book.

Box 13.7   What you need to succeed

Doing focus group interviews

1. Do I understand the main principle of doing focus group interviews – to stimulate the interviewees to answer questions while other participants are in the room?
2. Am I aware of the challenges in making such a group approach work?
3. Do I see the advantages of interviewing using this specific format?

What you have learned

- Focus groups are mostly used as a format for discussing issues among research participants, although they were originally developed as a format for interviewing groups.

(Continued)

- It is important to give all participants the same chance for their answers to questions to be heard.
- It is not always a way of saving time if you do your interviews in groups due to the logistic challenge of bringing the group together and of having everyone involved.

Exercises

In the following exercises, you are first invited to reflect on some of the main issues in this chapter. Then you are invited to apply the topics of this chapter to the development of a project of your own. Hence, the exercises are a combination of reflection and prospection.

Exercise 13.1

Reflecting on the Chapter: The Use of Focus Group Interviews in an Existing Study

1. Look through a journal for a qualitative study based on focus group interviews (e.g. Puchta and Potter, 1999). Try to identify how this format was used as an interview as part of the study.

Exercise 13.2

Planning Your Own Research with Focus Group Interviews

1. Think of your own study and develop a first version of an initial question to stimulate a group's members to respond to it for your research question.

What's next

Both these texts deal explicitly with group interviews as a method:

Fontana, A., & Frey, J.H. (2000). The Interview: From Structured Questions to Negotiated Text. In N. Denzin & Y.S. Lincoln (Eds.), *Handbook of Qualitative Research* (2nd ed., pp. 645–72). London: Sage.

Patton, M.Q. (2015). *Qualitative Evaluation and Research Methods* (4th ed.). London: Sage.

The following article emphasizes taking the interaction in focus groups into account, which is also important if they are used as an interview format:

Halkier, B. (2010). Focus Groups as Social Enactments: Integrating Interaction and Content in the Analysis of Focus Group Data. *Qualitative Research*, 10(1), 71–89.

This short book gives a concise introduction to working with focus groups:

Barbour, R. (2018). *Doing Focus Groups* (2nd ed.). London: Sage.

This chapter highlights cultural issues when doing focus group interviews with multicultural research teams and in specific communities:

Newman, P.A., Tepjan, S., & Rubincam, C. (2017) Exploring Sex, HIV and 'Sensitive' Space(s) Among Sexual and Gender Minority Young Adults in Thailand. In R. Barbour & D. Morgan (Eds.), *A New Era in Focus Group Research* (pp. 83–108). London: Palgrave Macmillan.

This article discusses doing focus groups in times of social distancing:

Lobe, B., Morgan, D., & Hoffman, K.A. (2020). Qualitative Data Collection in an Era of Social Distancing. *International Journal of Qualitative Methods*. https://doi. org/10.1177/1609406920937875

Doing Interview Research Navigator

How to understand interview research
- What doing interview research means
- Theories and epistemologies of interviewing
- When to choose interviews as a research method
- Methods and formats of interviewing

Designing interview research
- Planning and designing interview research
- How many interviewees: Sampling and saturation
- Accessing and recruiting participants

How to conduct interviews
- How to respect and protect: Ethics of interviewing
- Semi-structured interviews: Working with questions and answers
- Interviewing experts and elites
- Integrating narratives in interviews: Episodic interviews

You are here in your project

Doing interviews in context
- How to work with life histories: Narrative interviews
- Working with focus groups as interviews
- Ask (in) the field: Ethnographic and mobile interviewing
- Doing online interviews

How to work with interview data
- Working with interview data
- Credibility and transparency: Quality and writing in interview research
- From interviewing to an inner view: Critiques and reflexivity

ASK (IN) THE FIELD: ETHNOGRAPHIC AND MOBILE INTERVIEWING

┌─ How this chapter will help you ─

You will:

- be introduced to the concept of the ethnographic interview,
- see the advantages but also the challenges of this method,
- understand that ethnographic interviewing is a method,
- learn that it can be planned, and
- be shown the potentials and pitfalls of mobile interviewing.

Ethnography (or earlier: participant observation) has often been discussed as an alternative to doing interviews and many of the critiques of interviewing are formulated against the backdrop of ethnography (see Chapters 1 and 18). At the same time, it is not questioned that ethnography includes talking to people in the field in one way or another. Ethnography has often used talking in formalized or less formalized ways and rather similar to doing interviews. In ethnographic field research, doing interviews can be included in four ways. One is to see ethnography as a comprehensive research strategy, which can include several methods. In our study on adolescents' homelessness and health, we took an ethnographic approach starting with observation and participation, but then included two forms of interviewing – episodic interviews (see Chapter 11) with the adolescents and expert interviews (see Chapter 10) with health care professionals.

Both kinds of interviews were conducted via appointments, in specific settings and not *en passant* in the field. The second way is to do interviews in the field more informally: getting in touch with participants and conducting the interview on the spot – without creating a specific interview setting. The third way is to apply a particular method in the field based on what Spradley (1979) has developed as the ethnographic interview. This will be discussed here in the first part of the chapter. The fourth way is to use walking or go-along interviews as a specific form of mobile methods in the field, which will be discussed in the second part of the chapter.

The Ethnographic Interview

The term 'ethnographic interview' has been used in different ways over the years. Spradley has made some suggestions for conducting this type of interview:

> It is best to think of ethnographic interviews as a series of friendly conversations into which the researcher slowly introduces new elements to assist informants to respond as informants. Exclusive use of these new ethnographic elements, or introducing them too quickly, will make interviews become like a formal interrogation. Rapport will evaporate, and informants may discontinue their co-operation. (1979, pp. 58–9)

Although the ethnographic interview is understood as an interview, Munz (2017) and Gobo (2008) emphasize a number of differences to other forms of interviewing. The main difference is that an ethnographic interview often results from participant observation and builds on an existing relationship between researcher and interviewee, which would have to be established in other forms of interviewing. An ethnographic interview is not generally explicitly arranged but occurs spontaneously, and it will be shorter and more focused in its topics compared to other forms of interviewing. Finally, ethnographic interviewing is not necessarily limited to a one-spot encounter, but the researcher and participant can meet repeatedly and continue their conversation on several occasions throughout the ongoing ethnography. The local and temporal framework is less clearly delimited than in other interview situations, where time and place are arranged exclusively for the interview. Barker (2012) discusses two features of ethnographic interviewing in distinction to other forms of interviewing. The first is 'embeddedness' in two respects. The ethnographic interview is situated in the social world that is studied – also in the respect that it is conducted in that world rather than a separate room such as an office. And it is embedded 'within a field of knowledge about the social, cultural and material world of the interviewee' (2012, p. 55). The second feature Barker (2012) mentions is 'openness'. The dialogue will occur without an interview guide or any kinds of formalized questions. However, according to Spradley (1979, pp. 59–60), ethnographic interviews include the following elements that distinguish them from being just 'friendly conversations':

- a specific request to hold the interview (resulting from the research question);

- ethnographic explanations in which the interviewers explain the project (why an interview at all) or that they will take notes of certain statements (and why they note certain kinds of statements) – these are expressed in everyday language (with the aim that informants talk about the issues in their everyday language, too); and interview explanations (making clear why this specific form of talking is chosen, with the aim that the informant gets involved), along with explanations for certain (types of) questions, explicitly introducing the way of asking;
- ethnographic questions, that is descriptive questions, structural questions (answering them should show how informants organize their knowledge about the issue) and contrast questions (which should provide information about the meaning dimensions used by informants to differentiate objects and events in their world).

Spradley further distinguishes several kinds of ethnographic questions. Descriptive questions include *grand tour questions*, which can have various formats. *Typical* grand tour questions address routines and how things usually proceed, e.g. Could you describe a typical day on the street? *Specific* grand tour questions focus on the most recent day, for instance, e.g. Could you describe what happened yesterday when you came to this place? *Guided* grand tour questions ask to be shown around and given a tour of an area, e.g. Could you show me around where you meet your peers on the street? *Task-related* grand tour questions ask the interviewee to perform a simple task, e.g. Could you draw a map of where you hang out and move during the day and explain that to me? *Mini tour questions* are much more focused on a topic or practice, e.g. Could you describe what you eat on such a day? *Example questions* address instances of situations or activities, e.g. Can you give me an example of a conflict with the other kids here? More focused on the participants' personal views and interpretations are *experience questions* (e.g. What were your most significant experiences here?), whereas *native language questions* (e.g. How would you refer to the other kids here?) aim at identifying the vocabulary used in a field. *Structural* questions go one step further than descriptive questions: for example, *verification* questions are aimed at finding out about a part of a domain the researcher has identified (e.g. Are there different kinds of drugs for you? Or, is nicotine a kind of drug for you?). *Contrast* questions aim at clarifying the concepts used by the interviewee and their structural dimensions. Spradley's suggestions for types of questions to be used in the ethnographic interview are the starting point for the study described in Box 14.1.

Box 14.1 Research in the real world

Native and non-native language in ethnographic interviews

While working in education at Durham University in the UK, Shu-Hsin Chen from Taiwan did a study with ethnographic 'interviews in English and Chinese with native and nonnative speakers/teachers of English in Taiwan. In the course of the study,

(Continued)

the significance of language choice as a factor in power relationships in the inter-viewing became evident' (Chen, 2011, p. 120). In her article, she compared native and non-native language speakers carrying out interviews. She found: 'that my English was not as fluent as that of my foreign interviewees seemed to put me at an advantageous position because I could, in a seemingly natural way, probe for more information from my foreign participants who spoke English as a native language' (p. 131), and she illustrates this with extracts from her interviews. This finding is similar to other experiences of how fruitful it can be to approach interviews as 'learning from strangers' (Weiss, 1994), or where the interviewer is perceived by the inter-viewees as someone to help by answering their questions and by providing as much additional information as they might need to understand what the interviewee is talking about and because they might lack the interviewee's knowledge and expe-rience in the field (see Adamson, 2006, for a similar discussion of ethnographic interviewing and the issue of language use).

Spradley's suggestions for various types of questions may at some points be a bit outdated (e.g. the various types of questions aiming at verification in the interview). At the same time, they show that the ethnographic interview is understood as an interview and thus as a method, which goes beyond conversations in the field. They can be instructive for planning an interview similar to other forms of interviews, although the ethnographic interview is more integrated within a process in the field and in relation to the interviewee. With this method, the general problem of making and maintaining interview situations arises because of the open framework. The characteristics that Spradley mentions for designing and explicitly defining inter-view situations apply also to other contexts in which interviews are used. In these, some of the clarifications may be made outside the actual interview situation. Nonetheless, the explicit clarifications outlined by Spradley are helpful for produc-ing a reliable working agreement for the interview, which guarantees that the interviewee really joins in. The method is mainly used in combination with field research and observational strategies.

The discussion around the ethnographic interview often stresses its distinctions from other forms of interviewing: 'Much of the writing about ethnographic inter-views continues to reinforce the long-held assumption that authentic and fulsome meaning is best found through unstructured, unmediated face-to-face, voice-to-voice interviews that take place within what ... is implicitly assumed to be the interviewee's "natural" setting' (Barker, 2012, p. 65). However, some overviews of using ethnographic interviews emphasize its character as a specific type of inter-view rather than as something completely different. Following Kvale (1996), Heyl (2001) emphasizes the interview as being a co-construction created by the inter-viewer and the interviewee. Heyl links the field of ethnographic interviewing with current works concerning how to shape interviews in general but does not develop a specific approach to ethnographic interviewing. Gobo (2008) addresses the ethnographic interview too, but mainly discusses the limitations of doing interviews in general. However, he suggests a number of probing questions (see Chapter 9) in the context of ethnographic interviewing, such as: reformulating a question the interviewee has not understood, comments documenting the interviewer's interest, repeating and summarizing the answers and asking for clarification. Ethnographic interviews can also be used in the context of teaching reflexive social work skills (see Box 14.2).

Box 14.2 Research in the real world

Using ethnographic interviewing in teaching for promoting students' intercultural skills

Yochay Nadan is a senior lecturer at the Paul Baerwald School of Social Work and Social Welfare, the Hebrew University of Jerusalem. He has 'developed a pedagogical practice for training social workers to work in a diverse, multi-cultural reality. Students conduct an ethnographic interview with a person from a different, unfamiliar group, creating an encounter with the other. They then analyze the interview and complete a written reflective assignment' (2019, p. 396). The author pursues the idea that interviewing skills can be helpful for learning how to talk with clients in social work, in particular in intercultural contexts.

> Adopting the ethnographic interview as a method in multicultural social work education holds great potential for developing a more reflective, critical, and context-informed perspective among practitioners. Using the ethnographic interview as an experiential learning assignment can assist students and professionals to listen to and explore the clients' stories in their own words. (2019, p. 399)

A similar approach is pursued by Ekaterina Arshavskaya (2018) at the language department of Utah State University in the US, who let her students use ethnographic interviewing in an intercultural context for developing their intercultural skills in language education. The author did a mixed methods study on this (Arshavskaya, 2018).

All in all, these authors highlight that the ethnographic interview goes beyond an occasional friendly conversation during participant observation by using questions, types of questions and probing, which should all be prepared in advance. The challenge is how to document what the participant says. If possible, the interviews should be recorded and transcribed (see Chapter 16). In general, the ethnographic interview is a specific kind of semi-structured interview (see Chapter 9), which can also be based on the episodic interview (see Chapter 11). It can also be used for interviewing experts (see Chapter 10) in the field, but it is less compatible with the principles of the narrative interview, as described in Chapter 12. In the end, the literature on ethnographic interviewing, starting from Spradley (1979), can offer some suggestions as to how to design descriptive (and maybe structural and confrontational) questions, drawing on the context of other forms of interviewing.

Constructing a Framework for Listening in Ethnographic Interviews

Preparing the interview

Here as well, interviewers should reflect in advance on what they want to ask, how they would probe if answers are not exhaustive, whom to ask what, where to find interviewees and so on (see Box 14.3).

Box 14.3   Research in the real world

Planning an ethnographic interview

Planning an ethnographic interview also includes suggestions for preparing (1) the framework for listening in the interview (data protection in the interview, general guidelines on questions and on the length and type of the conversation) and (2) the conduct of the interview (introducing the subject, initial questions, descriptive and structural ethnographic and other questions, etc.).

Steps involved in planning an ethnographic interview	Six F's of designing interview research
Reflect in advance again	
1. Who will your potential interviewees in the field be?	Finding
2. What is the research question behind the interview?	Focusing
Steps for preparing the framework for listening in an ethnographic interview	
3. Reflect on what the interviewees should know in advance to be well prepared for the interview and to understand what it is about and what their role should be. Start from what the interviewee has perhaps already learned about your study when making the appointment for the interview.	Framing

Steps involved in planning an ethnographic interview	Six F's of designing interview research
4. Phrase (in keywords) an appropriate introduction to the interview for the following aspects: the purpose and the principle of the interview, recording and data protection. (After agreement, turn on the recording device straight away.) Frame an explanation of what the interview will be about, e.g. a very personal view; an explanation of how the conversation will proceed and how long it will probably take. (The actual interview starts at this point.)	Framing
5. Frame (in keywords) how to conclude the interview, including a request for any additional points and the interviewee's feedback.	Framing
Steps for preparing the conduct and content of ethnographic interviews	
6. Overview of subjects of interest for the interview.	Foreseeing
7. Which topics are of central interest?	Foregrounding
8. Which part of the field and which events and experiences can provide information about the central topic(s) in the specific interviewee's case?	Foreseeing
9. Phrase an initial question which will motivate and help the interviewee to turn into interview 'mode' and to address the topics of the study (e.g. 'I would like to ask you some questions about … Could you please take your time in answering them for me?')	Formulating
10. For every area, descriptive and maybe structural questions should be prepared in advance, which can be used if appropriate.	Focusing
11. Note down some keywords for probing central aspects which you would like to return to if the interviewee does not spontaneously mention them.	Foreseeing

Extend the Setting: Mobile Interviewing

The idea behind the ethnographic interview of taking interviewing into the field has been extended in the context of mobile methods. Here we find several terms in the literature. 'Mobile methods' (Sheller and Urry, 2006) is the broader term referring to a variety of methods that are applied in a mobility paradigm. Jones et al. see in mobilizing interviews 'a means to take the interviewing process out of the "safe" confines of the interview room and allow the environment and the act of walking itself to move the collection of interview data in productive and sometimes entirely unexpected directions' (2008, p. 8). 'Go-alongs' are a specific person-centred (concentrating on a specific participant) and interactive (between participant and researcher) form of ethnography which focuses on specific places (relevant for the participant). The approach is systematic in the selection of the participants and the focus of the research activities (Kusenbach, 2018, p. 349). They combine mobile methods (walking), observation, conversations, descriptions and explanations from the participant (talking).

In particular, the concept of *mobile interviews* means that the participants are asked to take the researcher for a walk through an area they live in or where they move regularly and show the researcher those places, buildings, streets and institutions that are relevant for them. At the same time, they should talk about these routes and elements, what they mean to them, and so on. We used this approach in a project about immigrants' experiences of long-term unemployment (Flick et al., 2019). By sharing space, time and experience with the study participants, we wanted to see how their everyday lives are rooted in the use of space and places. So, we asked participants to display on a map those places in their neighbourhood and/or Berlin as a whole that were relevant to them and to describe their everyday activities. Then, we asked them to show us around from place to place by either walking or using public transport. Participants were invited to describe in detail what the respective places meant to them, which activities they associated with them, and to further tell us whatever seemed important, for example their aspirations and past experiences. Following Kusenbach (2018, pp. 350–1) and Evans and Jones (2011), the go-alongs covered 'trails' in which the routes and times of outings were entirely determined by participants, as well as 'tours' in which researchers took more control of the itinerary. The go-alongs lasted five hours on average. The researcher accompanied the participant and documented the process. Where necessary, a native-speaking research student supported the researcher by translating. Some of the conversations with the participants were recorded and transcribed, while others were documented in field notes. After the go-along, the researcher repeated the tours, this time supported by a colleague who had not taken part in the original go-along. Being asked about the tour and the participants' reactions and attitudes toward certain places not only helped to complement field notes but also allowed for triangulation of the participant's original choice of places for the go-along by juxtaposing it with an outside perspective, relating the participants' choice and comments to the overall urban environment. This example shows some of the potential and challenges of using mobile interviewing. The example in Box 14.4 integrates photovoice in the use of mobile interviewing.

Box 14.4 Research in the real world

Photovoice in mobile interviews

Girang et al. (2020) from the Department of Psychology, Ateneo De Manila University, Quezon City, Philippines, integrated photovoice in mobile interviewing in a study on university students' experiences of stress alleviation through the everyday use of campus spaces. They interviewed 16 students from groups such as 'undergraduate first-year students, university dormers, financial aid scholars, fourth-year students, and student-athletes' (2020, p. 4). The researchers found 'three over-arching spatial experiences of stress alleviation ... : being away from stressful places, being present but mentally away from a place, or being engaged within communal spaces' (2020, p. 1).

Challenges

Mobile methods come with a number of challenges on a practical level. What mode of mobility? If the area is restricted to a particular neighbourhood, then walking can be used – that's why the method is also called 'walking interview' (King and Woodroffe, 2017). If the 'area' covers several parts of a big city, public transportation or driving to these parts may be necessary and then the question is when the data collection begins. If going-along is not only referring to the places the interviewee might present to the researcher, who looks and takes notes, but is also used as a method of interviewing, the question comes up of how to motivate the participants to talk about the places and the meaning they have for them and in particular in the context of the research issue. 'Depending on researchers' goals and preferences, go-alongs can resemble open field observations or semi-structured interviews' (Kusenbach, 2018, p. 354), but that may depend on the participants' readiness to talk about the places, and so on in some kind of public situation – where people pass by, for example. Finally, recording the information is an issue here, too. First, there is the question of how to document what the participants say during walking by using a voice recorder or taking notes, for example, without making the shared stroll too artificial (given the presence of members of the public again). Second, there are considerations around how to document which places the go-along passed by and how the participants (maybe non-verbally) reacted and how to document the process of walking. When in the end only the participants' statements are available for analysis and the walking was just a specific way to elicit them, the effort of go-along might have been in vain. Not only that, but when the research topic is something like drug traffic king, for example, go-alongs may pose a physical danger to the researcher and the interviewee and should not be used. Carpiano (2009) discusses the problems linked to go-alongs used to analyse the relationship between place and health in two relatively deprived areas of Milwaukee, USA.

One of the main advantages of using walking interviews is that they take interviewing into the context of the participants' everyday lives or – seen the other way around – they draw the context and everyday life into the interview and what is mentioned in it. There are a number of technical solutions to the challenges experienced by researchers in trying to find a way to combine walking, talking and documenting what was said and what becomes evident beyond the words. To document where the walking took the participants in the interview, the use of GPS technology is suggested. This is no surprise as a lot of research with walking interviews is done in fields such as geography. Another tool for documenting is the use of head cameras with microphones. Asking participants to draw a map of the walk (or to draw the route onto a map) and to comment on the process and result may provide further insights.

Radley et al. (2010) used photography as a means of documenting where a walking interview with homeless people took them. The researchers asked the participants to walk through their everyday life areas and photograph what was important for them and then to comment on these places, streets, buildings, institutions and so on. There is an overlap here with photo elicitation (see Chapter 9). Walking interviews again are closer to semi-structured (see Chapter 9) and episodic (see Chapter 11) than to narrative interviews (see Chapter 12) and can be employed for interviewing experts, too (see Chapter 10). In Box 14.5, you will find an extract from a walking interview done to explore a local spot (a park) for its meaning for the people using it.

Box 14.5   Research in the real world

Extract from an ethnographic go-along interview

The following extract was collected by Kate Moles, who is a lecturer in sociology at Cardiff University, and conducts research with a focus on mobilities (notably walking and swimming), heritage, the past, memory and the family. The interviews were conducted with visitors to Phoenix Park in Dublin, as part of an ethnography of the place. Included is one extended interview extract with a man in his sixties called V, sitting in the sun on a bench in Phoenix Park. KM is the researcher.

KM: Could I talk to you for a little while?

V: Why? What d'ya want?

KM: I'm trying to find out about stories about Phoenix Park, and I just wanted to talk to you about the park, you can tell me to go away the second you want!

V: No, no no no. Go ahead, what do you want to know?

KM: Are you from Dublin originally?

V: I am yeah.

KM: how long have you been coming to the park?

V: oooooh, the last fifteen year maybe.

KM: And what do you think keeps making you come here?

V: I love coming up here, it's near me, the fresh air, it's a nice place to come for a walk. You know?

KM: Uh huh. And do you come up here and feel any sense of the history of the place?

V: Ah yea well, when we were all young we played football up here. You know so it holds them sort of memories you know.

KM: Yea, what about anything else? Have you seen the park change over the past 15 years?

V: No, not really. Just every so often they resurface the roads and just there's no no really big change. As far as I'm concerned there's no really big change you know what I mean.

KM: Do you hope it stays like this in the future?

V: Yes, I think it's great. Yea, to be able to come up and sit down. Not just winter but summer as well. You can relax. It's nice yea.

KM: Do you think it's important to Irish people?

V: Very important. Most important to Dublin people.

KM: You reckon?

V: Oooh yea. I mean a lot of us were reared up here you know. I mean you mother and father brought you up here when you were kids and you played around and then when you were twelve or thirteen you come up yourself and played football. Ah it was good. I like coming up here now you know and I'm a grandfather, a great-grandfather now and I still come up read me paper go for a bit of a walk. Hehehehe.

Moles (2018)

Shadowing

Walking interviews have some parallels to **shadowing**, which is a technique used in organizational research. Here, the researcher basically follows individuals through their (sometimes whole) days in the organization. This method is often discussed as a specific way of carrying out participant observation (although the researcher does not participate, but stays in the shadow of the participant) and as an alternative to interviewing. However, McDonald elucidates the role of questions in this process:

> Throughout the shadowing period the researcher asks questions which will prompt a running commentary from the person being shadowed. Some of the questions will be for clarification, such as what was being said on the other end of a phone call, or what a departmental joke means. Other questions will be intended to reveal purpose, such as why a particular line of argument was pursued in a meeting, or what the current operational priorities are. (2005, p. 456)

This suggests seeing shadowing and, in a similar way, walking interviews as an extension of doing interviews and, more generally, as a specific way of doing interviews.

Steps, Aims and Criteria in Preparing and Doing Ethnographic and Mobile Interviews

Table 14.1 summarizes the steps in preparing ethnographic and mobile interviews together with the criteria for evaluating the outcomes of applying them.

Table 14.1   Steps, aims and criteria in preparing and doing ethnographic and mobile interviews

Six F's of designing interview research	Steps	Aims and actions	Criteria
Framing	1. Preparing the interview	• Prepare a draft for an initial question on a pre-analysis of the field under study • Run test interviews and interview training • Prepare a documentation sheet for the context of the interview (demographic data, etc.)	• Do the initial questions cover the area under study? • Did the interviewer(s) internalize the principle of the interview? • Does the documentation sheet cover the relevant information for the research question?
Framing	2. Introducing the interview principle	• Prepare a good introduction for the interviewee, and ensure it is clear	• Did the interviewee understand and accept the principle of the interview?
Formulating	3. Descriptive questions	• Prepare grand tour and mini tour questions which stimulate descriptions of the field about the topic and periods of the interviewee's life history	• Do the questions encompass relevant aspects of the subjective meanings for the interviewees and of the field? • Are the questions oriented towards description?
Foregrounding	4. Structural questions	• Try to think about questions that cover relevant areas of the field which might not be expressed in enough detail	• Are these questions structural in character? • Do they add the missing aspects in the interview?
Focusing	5. More general topics referring to the issue under study for the final part of the interview	• Try to get into the detail of the central parts of the issue under study • Try to increase the depth and richness of the interviewee's responses by making additional inquiries	• Has the interviewee gone into detail and depth? • Has the interviewer been sensitive to any extra depth on which to focus?

Six F's of designing interview research	Steps	Aims and actions	Criteria
Foreseeing	6. Socio-demographic data	• Develop a checklist for this purpose • Use the documentation sheet	• Is all information included that is necessary for contextualizing the interviewee's narrative?
Framing	7. Evaluation and small-talk	• Make room for some conversation • Make room for critique and additional aspects	• Were additional aspects mentioned?
Foreseeing	8. Documentation	• Ensure a good recording and a detailed transcription	• Is all additional information (not on the recording) documented?
Finding and Formulating	9. Analysing ethnographic interviews	• Choose an appropriate method for analysing and interpreting the descriptions and answers	• Does the method take the quality of the data into account (e.g. the descriptive structure of accounts)?

Box 14.6   What you need to ask yourself

Doing ethnographic and mobile interviews

1.   How far can the issue of my research be studied by asking people in the field during observation or while walking with them through an area, for example?
2.   Am I aware of the challenges of documenting what can be learned from using these methods, which go beyond other forms of interviewing, but also of the challenge of the interviewing part of the method?
3.   What do I see as the advantages of doing interviews while walking or during ethnography in the field instead of in a more classic setting of interviewing?

What You Need to Ask Yourself

Ethnographic and walking interviews are a kind of multimodal method. They entail going out into the field, walking with the participants, and include a lot of observation and being active. At the same time, they are interviews, as the name and their use show; they go beyond interviewing and are presented as an alternative to interviews when their distinctive features (mobile methods, ethnography) are emphasized. In any case, the method comes with specific and maybe more demanding challenges for the interviewer – sometimes for the interviewee also – compared to other forms of interviewing.

What You Need to Succeed

This chapter has provided an introduction to interviewing in the field and mobile interviewing. It should help you to understand and contextualize these approaches in the preceding and following chapters. The questions in Box 14.7 will help you to review your take-home points from this chapter.

Box 14.7   What you need to succeed

Doing ethnographic and mobile interviews

1.   Do I understand the main principle of ethnographic interviews – to turn encounters with participants into interviewing them and to invite them to answer questions while other participants are around?
2.   Do I see the challenges of making interviewing work in the field or while walking with the interviewees?
3.   Do I see the advantages of interviewing using such specific formats?

What you have learned

- Ethnographic interviewing was originally developed for turning friendly conversations during ethnographic fieldwork into more formalized interviews, although a defined setting (a separate room, free from interruptions) and high-quality recordings were not always available.
- Mobile interviews allow the participants to take the interviewer into their life world and allow the interviewer to study place, space and surroundings.
- These methods will make information available on more levels than other interviews, but it may be difficult to capture the complexity of this information beyond noting what the interviewee has said.

Exercises

In the following exercises, you are first invited to reflect on some of the main issues in this chapter. Then you are invited to apply the topics to the development of a project of your own. Hence, the exercises are a combination of reflection and prospection.

Exercise 14.1

Reflecting on the Chapter: The Use of Walking Interviews in an Existing Study

1. Look through a journal for a qualitative study based on walking interviews (e.g. Flick et al., 2019). Try to identify how this format was used as an interview in the study.

Exercise 14.2

Planning Your Own Research with Mobile Interviews

1. Think of your own study and develop a set of questions for stimulating participants to walk you through a part of their life world which is instructive for your research and to talk about the issues relevant to answering your research question.

What's next

This article gives an up-to-date description of ethnographic interviewing:

Barker, J. (2012). The Ethnographic Interview in an Age of Globalization. In R. Fardon, O. Harris, & T.H. Marchand (Eds.), *The SAGE Handbook of Social Anthropology* (Vol. 2, pp. 54–68). London: Sage.

The following article illustrates the use of walking interviews:

Flick, U., Hirseland, A., & Hans, B. (2019). Walking and Talking Integration: Triangulation of Data from Interviews and Go-Alongs for Exploring Immigrant Welfare Recipients' Sense(s) of Belonging. *Qualitative Inquiry*, 25(8), 799–810. https://doi.org/10.1177/1077800418809515

In this third article, the concept of shadowing is outlined in some detail:

McDonald, S. (2005). Studying Actions in Context: A Qualitative Shadowing Method for Organisational Research. *Qualitative Research*, 5(4), 455–73.

The fourth article addresses issues of language choice in ethnographic and other interviews:

Chen, S.-H. (2011). Power Relations between the Researcher and the Researched: An Analysis of Native and Nonnative Ethnographic Interviews. *Field Methods*, 23(2), 119–35. doi:10.1177/1525822X10387575

Doing Interview Research Navigator

How to understand interview research

- What doing interview research means
- Theories and epistemologies of interviewing
- When to choose interviews as a research method
- Methods and formats of interviewing

Designing interview research

- Planning and designing interview research
- How many interviewees: Sampling and saturation
- Accessing and recruiting participants

How to conduct interviews

- How to respect and protect: Ethics of interviewing
- Semi-structured interviews: Working with questions and answers
- Interviewing experts and elites
- Integrating narratives in interviews: Episodic interviews

Doing interviews in context

- How to work with life histories: Narrative interviews
- Working with focus groups as interviews
- Ask (in) the field: Ethnographic and mobile interviewing
- Doing online interviews

How to work with interview data

- Working with interview data
- Credibility and transparency: Quality and writing in interview research
- From interviewing to an inner view: Critiques and reflexivity

DOING ONLINE
INTERVIEWS

How this chapter will help you

You will:

- be introduced to the potential and problems of doing interviews online,
- learn about email interviewing,
- understand the limits but also the advantages of telephone, Skype and Zoom interviews, and
- see that interviewees should have the chance to select the type of online interviewing if a choice is possible.

Background to Online Interviewing

Why conduct interviews online?

In Chapter 13, we have already addressed the transfer of focus group interviews to online research. In this chapter, we will focus on doing individual interviewing online in several ways. Doing qualitative interviews online has been discussed and practised since the early 1990s (Baym, 1995; Markham, 1998). In particular, telephone interviews attracted much attention quite early on, but also email interviews. Skype, Zoom and Webex have been added to the variety of alternatives more recently. Online focus group interviews have been used for the same period and profit from the software environments just mentioned. For each case, we can distinguish three issues in the methodological discussions:

1. Why would we use interviews in a virtual or mediated setting? How can this use be justified?
2. How can existing interviewing approaches be transferred to the new formats such as telephone, Skype and Zoom conversations or email exchange? Which methods are easy to transfer and work well? Which ones are difficult to transfer or don't function so well online?
3. What are the practicalities of doing telephone, Skype, Zoom or email and online interviews?

Constructing a Framework for Listening in Online Interviews

Discussions of the above issues have often been driven by the idea that it is a matter of choice whether to do interviews face-to-face or via technologies and media. However, as the situation around Covid-19 has shown, under specific circumstances telephone and online interviewing can become the only ways to talk to participants.

In many articles and overviews (e.g. Meho, 2006, p. 1284), three principal ways of Internet-based interviews are distinguished: online synchronous interviews, online asynchronous interviews and virtual focus groups. Telephone interviews are only partly covered in this distinction as they do not necessarily use the Internet but are always done synchronously. Skype is based on the Internet and always synchronously applied. Email interviews can be done both synchronously and asynchronously, but much of the earlier discussion about them is based on their asynchronous use.

Mann and Stewart (2000, p. 129), following Baym (1995), see five important questions to consider for computer-mediated interaction in interviews. They are:

1. What is the purpose of the interaction/interview? This will influence potential participants' interest in whether or not to become involved in the study.
2. What is the temporal structure of the research? Are synchronous or asynchronous methods to be used, and will there be a series of interactions in the research or not?
3. What are the possibilities and limitations of the software, which will influence the interaction?
4. What are the characteristics of the interviewer and the participants? What about their experience of and attitude towards using technology? What about their knowledge of the topics, writing skills, insights, etc.? Is one-to-one interaction or researcher–group interaction planned? Has there been any interaction between researcher and participant before? How is the structure of the group addressed by the research (by hierarchy, gender, age, ethnicity, social status, etc.)?
5. What is the external context of the research – the inter/national culture and/or communities of meaning that are involved? How do communicative practices outside of the research influence the research itself?

With transferring interviews to a mediated context (telephone, online or Skype, for example), the researcher constructs a specific framework for listening to the participants. Much of this is determined by what kind of interview is transferred to digital use, but the digital context can lead to both new possibilities and specific limitations of this framework.

Doing Qualitative Telephone Interviews

Telephones have been around as a medium to use for doing research much longer than email or Skype. Although not everyone can be assumed to have a telephone, landline and mobile phones are widespread, and not only in privileged societies and groups. Therefore, telephone surveys have often been used in quantitative, market, polling and voting research. However, in qualitative research, interviewing on the telephone was often seen as the second best way or the 'next best thing to being there' (Tausig and Freeman, 1988). In most textbooks on qualitative research and interviewing, such as Rubin and Rubin (2005), telephone interviewing is discussed rather seldom, briefly and mostly in a sceptical way in comparison to or as a substitute for face-to-face interviewing. Shuy (2001), for example, sticks very much to structured and survey interviewing in his chapter in the first edition of the *Handbook of Interview Research* (Gubrium and Holstein, 2001). Its second edition (Gubrium et al., 2012) covers this issue in a chapter on survey interviews.

Novick (2008) did a systematic analysis of the literature to answer the question of whether there is 'a bias against telephone interviews in qualitative research'. She comes to the result that the 'neglect of, or bias against, telephone interviewing in the qualitative research literature contrasts strikingly with the growing interest in qualitative electronic interviewing' (2008, p. 396).

Why use qualitative telephone interviews?

Several studies using this methodology and articles reflecting on it have been published (e.g. Irvine, 2011). Situations such as the lockdown due to Covid-19 have produced a new demand for this technology as well, which sometimes goes beyond individual researchers' preferences because face-to-face interviews are not possible in contexts of social distancing. The more general arguments in favour of using telephone interviews are, for example, reduced costs as no travelling to interviewees is necessary, or that distant interviewees can be reached more easily, for example. Block and Erskine (2012, p. 431) report that the cost reductions with telephone interviews compared to face-to-face interviews have been calculated in the range of 45 to 75%. There are also the known time savings in telephone surveys compared to other forms of surveys, which again is estimated to be around 50%. In the case of qualitative interviewing, the discussion stresses the loss of – visual, non-verbal, contextual – data when only the telephone conversation is recorded and available. As Sturges and Hanrahan (2004) report, other reasons for using telephone interviews are that sensitive topics can be talked about more easily in the rather anonymous situation on the telephone, hard-to-reach respondent groups can be accessed, who otherwise might not be studied, and there is the issue of interviewer safety when studying dangerous settings, for example.

How can the existing approaches of qualitative interviewing be transferred to telephone interviewing?

As has been mentioned here before, and by many authors, most of the methodological discussion around telephone interviewing is related to survey and structured interviews. In more qualitative-oriented research, the main method used in telephone interviews tends to be semi-structured interviewing. Interview guides can be adapted to use in a conversation without seeing the other participant. Thus, for the interviewer it is crucial to develop a sensibility as to whether a question was clearly understood by the interviewee. We find several examples of using expert interviews via telephone (e.g. Stephens, 2007), which work in the rather pragmatic use of expert interviews in general.

More complex forms of interviewing are more difficult to transfer to telephone interviews. Photo elicitation (see Chapter 9) and using objects as tools in interviews obviously cannot be used via telephone. Approaches such as the narrative interview, according to Schütze (1977) and Rosenthal (2004; see Chapter 12), are also problematic to transfer to telephone communication. That the interviewee begins and continues a (long) narrative and the interviewer mainly confines themselves to listening may be a bit artificial, when the interviewers are not even seen or able to support the interviewees through eye contact and by expressing their interest and attention non-verbally. Accordingly, this method is seldom used in telephone interviewing.

Box 15.1 Research in the real world

Parents' narratives of children with justice system careers

In a more general conceptualization of narrative interviewing, Amanda Holt from Criminal Psychology at the Institute of Criminal Justice Studies at the University of Portsmouth, UK, has in fact used the telephone for research (Holt, 2010). She interviewed 20 parents of children who developed a criminal and youth justice system involvement career. Holt explains her reasons for using the telephone: 'It was only when I struggled to access suitable participants for interview in my local community that I began to consider the use of the telephone for narrative interviews as a more practical option for more geographically dispersed participants' (2010, p. 114). Her rather narrow approach to the narrative interview becomes visible in the way she started the interview: 'The interviews themselves began with me explaining that I only wanted to know "what happened, regarding their and their child's involvement in the youth justice system".' Holt describes the narrative process: 'I explained that I only wanted to know what they wanted to tell me. Then the participants talked. Once they told their stories, I asked the participants what their experiences were of being interviewed in this way' (2010, p. 114). As there are few discussions about using narrative interviewing via the telephone beyond this rather pragmatic approach, it seems it would be difficult to maintain the aims of narrative interviewing as going beyond merely answering questions, as in other forms of interviewing, when it comes to using the telephone. In Holt's example, it is the interviewees' option to limit what they talk about which makes the narrative interview setting work, rather than the idea that interviewees will talk about more and more sensitive issues compared to other interviews once they get going in their narrative - as the methodological discussion on face-to-face narrative interviews emphasizes.

The combination of narrative and question–answer sequences in the episodic interview (see Chapter 11) is more easily transferable to telephone interviews without abandoning the methodological features of the method. Here, narratives are more focused on situations and embedded in the interviewers' questions, so that a conversation can be maintained throughout the interview.

Practicalities of doing qualitative telephone interviews

The use of telephone interviewing is embedded in a general process of doing qualitative research but there are specific aspects to consider. Irvine (2010, p. 2) emphasizes that sampling and recruitment should never start with 'cold calling' the potential interviewees (as is prevalent in market research), meaning that they receive a call out of the blue and the interview starts right away. She suggests that potential participants should be contacted first by email, a flyer or a personal letter. After establishing an agreement to participate via one of these ways and clarifying informed consent, a future date is agreed for the actual interview. Telephone interviews are seen as more relaxed than face-to-face interviews, but it is important to maintain concentration and focus on the interview on both sides. The interviewees should be given breaks, so that they do not start to drift off or move around during the interview. The interviewer should prepare a space for doing the interview which is free from distractions (no computer, no email checking, etc. during the interview). And, finally, the ease of telephone interviewing should not lead to planning and doing too many interviews on the same day (Irvine, 2010, pp. 2–3). On a technical level, the interviewer should take care that the recording of the conversation is good and complete. A good landline for traditional telephones and a good network connection for mobile phones should be (made) available. There are several apps for recording telephone interviews done with mobiles or smartphones and there are Dictaphones with a phone adapter for recording telephone conversations in traditional landline calls.

In the literature, we find quite a number of reflections on the quality and quantity of the data that can be obtained in qualitative telephone interviews. The missing contextual data are one complaint as well as the limited rapport that can be achieved in the interview situation, though other comments emphasize that this means, at the same time, that the interviewee is freer to talk without seeing the interviewer's non-verbal reactions. It is also seen as being easier for interviewees to talk about embarrassing or compromising issues when the other person (the interviewer) is not physically or visually 'present'. Empirical studies comparing telephone and face-to-face interviews often refer to quantitative contexts. The few examples referring to qualitative research (Irvine, 2011; Kassianos, 2014) show that many of the assumed drawbacks in telephone interviews are more assumptions than empirically evident. Non-verbal data missing in telephone interviews can be misinterpreted in face-to-face interviews (Sturges and Hanrahan, 2004), not only by the researchers but also by the interviewee, and thus can influence the quality of the verbal data. The general assumption that telephone interviews are shorter in dealing with the same issues than face-to-face interviews could not be confirmed in these studies. Telephone interviews can be applied as an alternative to face-to-face interviews, which means researchers will decide between the two (as in the study by Irvine, 2008). They can also be applied in combination – with some participants being interviewed face-to-face, and some via telephone for practical reasons (because they are overseas as in the case of Stephens, 2007). Or they can be used a in a sequence – in a longitudinal study, which consists of three interviews with every participant, for example, the first two are face-to-face and the third is on the telephone (see the case study in Box 15.2).

Box 15.2   Research in the real world

Refugees' perception of the Covid-19 crisis

In an ongoing study about refugees' integration in professional work (and in society) in Germany at the Freie Universität Berlin and the Institute of Employment Research in Nuremberg (see Seidelsohn et al., 2020), the Covid-19 pandemic raised a new situation and topic. About 60 refugees had been interviewed using episodic interviews (see Chapter 11), which referred to their trajectory to Germany and their experiences in finding regular work and making social connections in Germany. About 30 of them were interviewed again about a year later about how their general and professional situation had developed. Both interviews were done face-to-face. When the Covid-19 crisis started, about 25 of the participants were interviewed again, this time in telephone interviews, which referred to the further developments of the job situation, the perception and impact of the pandemic and their experiences and fears in this context (see Falkenhain et al., 2020). The turn to telephone interviews had pragmatic reasons – face-to-face interviews could not be done for health reasons, interviewees came from all over Germany, travel was not possible and the university in general did not permit travelling and face-to-face interviews. The interviews were mostly done with smartphones and recorded with the apps available for them. As the interviews built on the preceding interviews and rapport, they could be realized quite easily and on a comparable level of talking about the issues to the face-to-face interviews. A main problem was how to contact some of the interviewees as their telephone or mobile numbers no longer worked, which had already been an issue between the first two rounds of (face-to-face) interviews. The telephone interviews not only provided insights into the current situation of lockdown and pandemic from the participants' perspective but also into further developments in the integration processes, their progress and failures (see Falkenhain et al., 2020).

Irvine's (2010) reflections on the method are based on her own study on mental health and work, in which she interviewed people with mental health issues over the telephone. Both examples show that telephone interviews can also be applied to populations who are, in general, difficult to interview.

Doing Email Interviews

The use of email interviews goes back to the early days of doing interviews online. It was never the dominant way of doing interviews in a digital format, but it continues to attract attention.

Why use email interviews?

There have always been a number of pragmatic reasons mentioned for using email interviewing, which are similar to those in the context of telephone interviewing. Costs are a major factor compared to face-to-face interviews. Here, the savings in travel costs are emphasized but also the transcription costs, as the answers already come in written form. The latter is also seen as an advantage of email interviews compared to telephone or Skype interviews (Meho, 2006, p. 1285). Another advantage is that email interviews can be applied with hard-to-reach groups in the literal sense of the word – people who are too far away or whom the interviewer is not able to travel to. Ison (2009) describes how email interviews allow for the interviewing of people who have a verbal communication impairment and for whom, in studies relying on face-to-face interviews, caregivers or relatives would have to be interviewed as proxies. Thus, using email interviews can become a means of empowerment for such a target group, allow-ing them to answer for themselves.

Finally, the relatively anonymous situation of using email for interviewing can be seen in two ways. First, the interviewers lack a part of the information about their interviewees as there is no personal contact and they do not see their participants. This means interviewers have to rely on the information the participants send them about their gender, age, location, and so on. This may raise questions about the reliability of such demographic information and lead to problems of contextualizing the state-ments in the later interview, as Markham (2004, p. 360) illustrates for an example where she misread the gender of someone she interviewed for some time before she found out the interviewee's correct gender. In contrast to face-to-face interviews, in email interviews the supposed interviewee may have delegated the task of answering to someone else or run the draft responses past someone else for approval before send-ing them to you. This may contradict one of the major aims of interviewing – to elicit the spontaneous and subjective views of the interviewee – without giving the inter-viewer the chance to become aware of this.

However, this kind of anonymity may also be a chance to interview people who shy away from meeting interviewers in person – and in unfamiliar places (e.g. researchers' offices) or where they do not want to let in strangers (their flats or institutions, for example). This anonymity may also be helpful for some people who do not want to get in touch through monitors (as in Skype interviews), which display them as a person to the interviewer and the context such as their office or room at the same time.

And, finally, this specific kind of exchange in email interviews may be helpful for reaching people who cannot travel (e.g. in case of disabilities) to interview meetings or at times when personal meetings are not possible (such as when social distancing during the Covid-19 pandemic).

In methodological discussions, online interviewing to specific Internet-savvy popu-lations is sometimes seen as limiting such interviews to young and more privileged target groups. However, using email and chat has become widespread among many diverse social groups more recently, so that familiarity and access should no longer be a general problem.

How can the existing approaches of interviewing be transferred to email?

Email interviewing is mostly developed from semi-structured interviewing, which means an interview guide, a set of questions and probes are used for reconstructing participants' views and experiences from them. Several of the methods discussed in Chapters 4, 9, 10 and 11 can be taken as starting points for developing questions and the structure of the interview guide, for example by combining various types of (open, focused, more structured) questions. Expert and elite interviews (see Chapter 10) are also a good starting point for developing an email interview and, vice versa, email interviews can facilitate the interviewing of elites and experts. It seems more difficult to transfer approaches like the narrative interview which should lead to the inter-viewee recounting a process or a life history in a comprehensive and uninterrupted story. Ideas such as *zugzwangs* (see Chapter 12) which develop during the narration and make the interviewees tell more than they intended to, would be difficult to make work in a situation where the interviewees write, maybe read and rewrite or edit their accounts. Nevertheless, email interviews are used for narrative research. James (2007, 2016) used them to construct online narratives (see Box 15.3)

Box 15.3   Research in the real world

Construction of identity through online narratives

Nalita James from the Centre for Labour Market Studies, University of Leices-ter, UK, has done a study (James, 2007) with email interviews with 20 academics (12 female, 8 male) to understand how they construct their identities. James intended to construct online narratives, although her interviews are based on a set of 11 questions she sent to her participants. Among them she asked the following:

1.   How have your experiences shaped your professional identity?
2.   What images would you use to describe your professional identity?
3.   In what way has your professional identity been shaped by formative experiences?
4.   In what way is your professional identity shaped across communities of practice? (2007, p. 967)

In the appendix to her article (2007, p. 976), she presents the guidance notes she sent to her participants, informing them that she would send 11 questions but one at a time and asking for a response in three working days, and to place the answers above the questions, for example. She also informed participants that she would send supplementary questions following the answers and about the planned completion of the email dialogue within 10 weeks. The guidelines also informed interviewees about confidentiality and anonymity. From the study, a num-ber of methodological articles resulted (e.g. James, 2016) and the data and results she presented in them show that her interviews via email 'worked'. How far it is possible to describe the answers she received as narratives – and more generally how far this can be seen as an example of transferring narrative research to email research – needs to be further discussed.

When email interviews are done in an asynchronous way, the interviewer and inter-viewee do not have to arrange a common time for doing their interview, which also may allow the interviewer to run several interviews in parallel.

Practicalities of Doing Email Interviews

Email interviews replace the face-to-face contact with the interviewee with a written exchange based on sending questions by email and waiting for the answers. This means first that the interviewers' personal impressions of their interviewees, the non-verbal parts of an interview as well as the nuances of how something is said, are not part of the data. The data basically consist of written text, which is detailed to a greater or lesser degree and comprehensible to both participants – the interviewee and the researcher.

Ways of doing email interviewing

We find three basic ways of doing email interviewing. The first is to create a list of questions and inform the potential interviewees about the number of questions. Once they have agreed to participate in the study, the whole set of questions is sent to them and the researcher waits for the responses. The advantage is that the interviewer can more easily manage interviewing several participants in parallel. One disadvantage is that the interviewer may wait a long time for responses and sometimes they will fail to arrive. Another disadvantage is that this kind of interview is more like a survey with not much exchange or probing in the interview process. This kind of email interviewing is also discussed as asynchronous interviewing as there is no need for the participant and interviewer to 'meet' at the same time.

The second way of doing email interview is much closer to face-to-face interview procedures. Here the exchange begins with the interviewer sending the first question and waiting for the interviewee's response before deciding to probe and deepen or extend the way this first question was answered or to move on to the next question. As both are involved in a question–answer exchange at the same time, this approach is also called synchronous email interviewing. The questions are part of an interview guide which can be adapted, extended or reduced according to the ongoing interview and to the interviewee's answers. This form of interviewing can also run for a longer time, as Meho notes: 'online, asynchronous, in-depth interviewing, which is usually conducted via e-mail, is, *unlike e-mail surveys,* semi-structured in nature and involves multiple e-mail exchanges between the interviewer and interviewee over an extended period of time' (2006, p. 1284).

The third way is a mixture of the first two alternatives. Here, a smaller number of questions are sent at the same time, for instance those covering a specific part of the interview's topics. After the interviewee's responses, the next part of the interview questions is sent – or probes referring to the first part. This third way can be applied in a synchronous way – the interviewer waits for the responses and then sends the next questions – or asynchronously. Then no one is forced to respond immediately, but there is still more dialogue than in the first alternative.

The research process in email interviewing

The interview is embedded in a process of several steps:

1. Sampling is often based on 'individual solicitations, snowballing, or invitations through listservs, message boards, discussion groups, or personal research Web sites' (Meho, 2006, p. 1288).
2. Informed consent also has to be obtained. Sometimes it is suggested to ask for it by sending a form by mail to be returned by the interviewee in a printed and signed version.
3. Confidentiality issues are discussed for both sides – that not only does the interviewer have to guarantee it for the interviewee's responses but the interviewee is also asked not to circulate the questions to other potential participants of the study (Kazmer and Xie, 2008, p. 266).
4. Questions to be used in the interview should be formulated in a clear and self-explanatory way. It is suggested to double-check this in pre-test interviews.
5. Probing is a special challenge, as it means asking for clarification or extension in follow-up questions in further emails, which may not be answered by the interviewee. Serving up such follow-up questions can be when interviewees disappear or pull out of a study.
6. Kazmer and Xie (2008, p. 262) discuss a number of such points in the process – such as the call for participation, the clarification of informed consent, the presentation of the questions or too many questions in the process or probing.
7. Transcripts are a specific issue discussed around email interviews. On the one hand, email interviews are 'self-transcribing' (e.g. Kazmer and Xie, 2008, p. 262) and are free of any context or background noise, which may reduce their quality in face-to-face interviews. On the other hand, the emails contain questions and answers, which have to be formatted by transferring them to a document in a word-processing program, adding line numbers and bringing questions and answers into a sequence which shows the question an answer refers to or the answer a follow-up question refers to.
8. It is important to take care that the email exchange is documented by saving the emails in a way that is safe in case the email program crashes and so on.
9. It is also suggested to document the process of getting in touch with interviewees, of obtaining their consent and of anything that happens in the exchange before and after the questions.

Gibson (2010) provides a helpful toolkit for using email interviews. The nine steps in the research process outlined above show that transferring interviewing from face-to-face settings to email exchange involves more than just asking questions in a different environment.

These steps are important process elements in constructing a specific setting and situation in which the interviewer as constructing listener creates a space in which the interviewees can explore and present their knowledge, experiences and views concerning the issue of the study.

Fritz and Vandermause (2018, p. 1645) discuss a number of lessons they learned from doing studies with email interviews. These include that we should refrain from running too many email interviews at the same time to avoid over-challenging the researcher. A second suggestion is to ensure you construct the emails sent to participants really well, to clarify expectations and instructions, and to avoid over-challenging the participants on their part. It is also important to be aware of 'participant's timing, language, and use of emoticons' when constructing and sending the email and planning the process. Plan the documentation and storage of the emails in a 'folder labelling system' as a means of improving the data quality and use in the project. Transcripts should include all information about the email, context and conditions as data and not only the list of answers.

Preparing the interview

Here too, interviewers should reflect in advance, what they want to ask, how they would probe if answers are not exhaustive, whom to ask what, where to find interviewees and so on (see Box 15.4).

Box 15.4   Research in the real world

Planning an episodic email interview

Planning an episodic email interview also includes suggestions for preparing (1) the interview framework (data protection, general guidelines on questions and on the length and type of the conversation) and (2) how to conduct the interview (entering the subject, initial question, narrative and other questions, etc.)

Steps involved in planning an episodic email interview	Six F's of designing interview research
Reflect in advance again	
1. Who will the potential interviewees be?	Finding
2. What is the research question behind the interview?	Focusing
Steps for preparing the framework for listening in an email interview	
1. Reflect on what the interviewees should know in advance to be well prepared for the interview and to understand what it is about and what their role is. Start from what the interviewee has perhaps already learned about your study when making the appointment for the interview.	Framing
2. Phrase an appropriate introduction to the interview for the following aspects: the purpose and the principle of the interview via email, recording statements by saving the emails, and data protection. Frame an explanation of what the interview will be about, e.g. a very personal view; an explanation of how the conversation will proceed and how long it will probably take. (The actual interview starts at this point.)	Framing

Steps involved in planning an episodic email interview	Six F's of designing interview research
3. Plan the interview as an exchange with the interviewee. Do not send the whole set of questions and wait for the answers, but send the questions piecemeal per email and ask for an immediate response.	Framing
4. Send a probe if something was answered rather briefly or a new aspect results from the response.	Foregrounding
5. Send the next question once an aspect has been answered exhaustively and continue with probes, etc.	Foregrounding
6. As in other interviews, bring questions planned for later forward which fit the current answers.	Foregrounding
7. Frame (in keywords) how to conclude the interview, including asking for any additional points and the interviewee's feedback.	Foreseeing
Steps for preparing the conduct and content of email interviews	
8. Overview of subjects of interest for the interview.	Foreseeing
9. What themes are of central interest?	Foregrounding
10. What area of the interviewees' professional, everyday life, for example, can provide information about the central topic(s)?	Foreseeing
11. For every area, frame a narrative stimulus that might motivate the interviewee, as clearly and unambiguously as possible, to tell, for every topic under point 10, one or more small-scale stories related to the main themes (e.g. If you look back, what was your first experience or disagreement with …? Could you tell me about this situation?).	Formulating
12. For every area, phrase questions about relationships, etc. that might stimulate the interviewees, as clearly and unambiguously as possible, to express their views of these relationships or concepts (e.g. What is … for you? What do you associate with this term?).	Focusing
13. Note down some keywords for probing central aspects which you would like to return to if the interviewee does not spontaneously mention them.	Foreseeing

The instructions in Box 15.4 were applied to the study summarized in Box 15.5.

Box 15.5   Research in the real world

Everyday life with children under Covid-19 and the conditions of lockdown

From April to July 2020, an online research seminar was held at the Freie Universität Berlin in the master's programme in Educational Science. Thirty students worked in

(Continued)

small groups to develop their research questions referring to the subjective perceptions and experiences of various actors, mostly students, with school or kindergarten
children staying at home in lockdown with their parents. The groups addressed
research questions such as student single parents' experiences, home-schooling
from the perspective of parents and teachers, the communication between teachers
and parents during home-schooling and the potential for conflict between children
and parents working in their home-office. As face-to-face interviews were not possible due to lockdown, episodic email interviews were developed and applied to
answer these research questions. The students sampled and accessed interviewees.
The interview guides comprised 7 to 10 questions and each group conducted around
6 to 8 interviews per email, which were then made up into full transcripts (line numbers, sequence of questions and answers) and complemented by demographic data.
The students then wrote research reports about their studies. For example, on the
individual level, the students could show that school children struggled with a loss
of motivation for learning, which wasn't really compensated for by parental support in home-schooling. On a more general level, it became evident that the social
inequality among school children was intensified during and by home-schooling due
to the lack of (good) technical equipment for participating in online teaching and the
challenge to parents in coordinating home-schooling and work when they had jobs
in non-academic professions .

Doing Qualitative Skype Interviews

Interviews using email are reduced to the (written) text as a means of communication
and as data available for analysis. They lack non-verbal contexts and direct communication with the interviewee, which also gives the latter greater anonymity. The data
the researchers receive have a limited focus as non-verbal contexts are not part of it.
However, data consist of the text in the emails and need not be transcribed; geographically remote and difficult-to-reach people can be interviewed this way. Telephone
interviews are also good for reaching people who are far away, difficult to reach
and/or prefer more anonymity than they receive in face-to-face interviews. These
interviews provide the verbal statements without the image of the participants and
much of the context. They have to be recorded and transcribed and rely on (good)
landline or mobile connections for which the researchers have to pay sometimes. The
following approach is based on computer connections, brings in the visual component of interviews again, but also needs recording and transcription. Skype (and
Facetime in a comparable way) has attracted more attention recently, as it is digital,
visual, computer-based and free. It requires that both interviewer and interviewee
have or download and install the Skype software on their computers.

Why use Skype interviews?

The arguments for using Skype for interviews (and those against it) are similar to those put forward for email and telephone interviewing – saving time and money, not needing to travel and reaching people otherwise difficult to reach, but with no personal meeting. What makes it interesting to use Skype is the visual component. Researchers can see their interviewees and have an impression of their non-verbal communication, such as how they move when saying something. The methodological discussion mostly focuses on the limits and losses when interviews are done on Skype rather than physically face-to-face. However, Jenner and Myers (2019) compared both ways of interviewing and their 'findings suggest that synchronous video interviewing deserves equal consideration and may in fact surpass in-person interviews in some instances. Our study demonstrates that, rather than being inferior to in-person interviews, Skype interviews can yield a quality of data that is equal to or exceeds in-person interviews' (2019, p. 176) and they did not find a 'loss of rapport or reduction in intimacy' in Skype interviews. In particular, people who have trouble travelling due to impaired mobility might prefer Skype. And those who prefer being in their own surroundings and at a distance from the interviewer, might benefit from being interviewed via Skype.

How can the existing approaches of interviewing be transferred to Skype?

For Skype (and Facetime), again semi-structured interviews with an exchange of questions and answers rather than narrative interviews should be suggested and are mostly used. Beyond all the maybe unfamiliar context of video talking, technical issues may cause interruptions and breakdowns of (digital and verbal) communication (see Seitz, 2016 and below), which may make a lifetime narrative collapse. Therefore, semi-structured interviews may be easier to maintain if such technical problems arise. If narrations are intended as part of the data, small-scale narratives such as those in episodic interviewing may be more compatible with the potential technological challenges. Although telephone interviews in principle can be run as a telephone conference with several participants at the same time and thus allow group interviews and focus groups, the technical issues (not least the invisibility of the other participants) may obstruct a flow of discussion or answering questions. In Skype and Facetime settings, the visual element supports turn-taking management much more than in telephone interviewing. However, technical problems with sound quality, connection stability and interruptions may become more relevant the more participants are involved.

Practicalities of doing Skype interviews

A number of very helpful research notes inform on the practical issues related to using Skype for interviewing (e.g. Cater, 2011; Deakin and Wakefield, 2014; Hanna, 2012; Seitz, 2016; Weller, 2015). On the one hand, Skype is available for free and runs on most platforms (Windows, Mac, Linux, smartphones). On the other hand, there are a number of prerequisites not only for the researcher but also for the interviewee: the software has to be downloaded and installed on their computers; a stable, fast and broadband Internet connection has to be available; computers need to have a camera and a microphone to use Skype, or even better would be a good headset (USB connected would be best); both should have a quiet room for the interview (not a kitchen or other room where everyday activities are run and produce noise); the rooms should be checked for what will be visible on the screen (and should not for privacy reasons ...); and disturbances resulting from children, pets or partners coming into the room or the focus of the camera should be avoided. The quality of the interaction depends on the quality of the input and output devices. On a technical level, the use of headsets is very helpful, but this may obstruct or make the image of the speaker artificial, which will lessen again the advantages of video-based communication that Skype allows.

Seitz suggests carefully preparing both sides of the communication:

> ... in order to have a successful qualitative Skype interview, an interview preparation checklist for the researcher and participant should be created and discussed ahead of time. The Skype interview checklist should include tasks for both researchers and participants, including: confirming a stable internet connection, finding a quiet room without distractions, slowing down and clarifying talk, being open to repeating answers and questions, and paying close attention to facial expressions. Emailing several times before Skyping might also strengthen rapport. (2016, p. 233)

This shows how demanding Skype interviewing can be. It is also recommended that the researcher test out their Skype communication before the (first) interview (2016, p. 231). When the technical side of the communication is working, its impact on the rapport and flow of both verbal and non-verbal communication can be reduced at least. Skype also allows for audio only, so that those interviewees who are uneasy about being filmed may turn off their cameras and 'only talk'. Skype interviews have to be recorded; there are devices available and instructions can be found on YouTube for how to manage that step. Transcription will be similar to a face-to-face interview, but here the transcription may suffer from any technical problems that occur in using Skype. Despite the reservations found in some publications about Skype interviews, Deakin and Wakefield suggest the following, in presenting their own experiences using Skype for interviewing: 'The online interview should be treated as a viable option to the researcher rather than as an alternative or secondary choice when face-to-face interviews cannot be achieved' (2014, p. 604).

Using Zoom, Webex and Microsoft Teams for Doing Interviews

In the era of online teaching, the home-office and virtual meetings in the context of the Covid pandemic, digital platforms such as Zoom, Webex or Microsoft Teams have become a part of the everyday lives of many people. These platforms can be used for doing interviews (and focus groups) online as well. Some of them have to be downloaded and installed on every participant's computer (or smartphone or tablet) to be used, while others are less demanding in this respect. For example, Webex needs to be installed on the host's computer (in our case the interviewer), whereas the other participants (in our case the interviewee/s) receive an invitation to their email address, which allows them to join the meeting after typing in a password. Zoom, for example, is based on the idea that all participants should download the software onto their devices to join a meeting. Zoom has been criticized for difficulties in removing the software from one's device again. It can be used from a browser and a website but with limited performance. There is advice from several institutions on the ethical and practical use of Zoom in interviews, for instance from Brynmawr University (www. brynmawr.edu/grants/irb) or the London School of Economics (https://info.lse.ac.uk/ staff/divisions/dts/services/infosec/Using-Zoom-for-Research-Interviews). Practical information for using Zoom can also be found at: https://thelai.com/using-zoom-for-qualitative-research. Zoom and other such platforms enable the meeting to be recorded (there is a button on the screen for this). But you should be careful that you use the 'record to this computer' option if you are recording and not 'record to the cloud' which saves the recording to Zoom's servers in the US. It is sometimes suggested that everyone who is not speaking turn off their cameras and microphones (muting) to improve the connection. Zoom in particular has been reported in the media for 'bombing', which means that meetings can be hacked by people not supposed to be part of them, but that might happen with the other platforms as well. The example in Box 15.6 illustrates participants' experiences with being interviewed on Zoom.

Box 15.6   Research in the real world

Zoom interviews – experiences and perceptions of participants

A group of Australian and Canadian researchers in nursing (Archibald et al., 2019) analysed the researchers and participants' perceptions and experiences in a study using Zoom for doing qualitative interviews with 16 female nurses (45-54 years, living in major cities, regional and remote areas in Australia). The researchers found a number of advantages which were mentioned. Rapport with the researcher was seen as easier by two thirds of the interviewees. Time and cost-effectiveness as well as user-friendliness and simplicity of the tool were also positives. Disadvantages, mentioned by the majority of the participants, included difficulties in connecting, as well as call quality and reliability.

Lobe et al. (2020, p. 3) provide a very helpful comparison of several platforms (Webex, Zoom, Skype) for doing individual and focus group interviews online.

Steps, Aims and Criteria in Preparing and Doing Online Interviews

Table 15.1 summarizes the steps of preparing and doing an online interview, including the aims and actions for each step, as well as the criteria for judging whether these steps have been successfully planned and realized.

Table 15.1 Steps, aims and criteria in preparing and doing online interviews

Six F's of designing interview research	Steps	Aims and actions	Criteria
Framing	1. Preparing the interview	• Prepare a draft for an initial question on a pre-analysis of the field under study • Run test interviews and interview training • Prepare a documentation (sheet) for the context of the interview (demographic data, etc.)	• Does the initial question cover the area under study? • Did the interviewer(s) internalize the principle of the interview? • Does the documentation sheet cover the relevant information for the research question?
Framing	2. Introducing the interview principle	• Prepare a good introduction for the interviewee, and make sure it is clear	• Did the interviewee understand and accept the principle of the interview?
Formulating	3. The initial question	• Prepare an initial question which stimulates the interviewee to reflect on the topic and its role in the interviewee's life	• Does the question encompass relevant aspects of the subjective meanings for the interviewees and their situation? • Did the interviewer enforce the principle of the interview to bring more depth into the interview?
Foregrounding	4. Probing	• Try to think about questions that cover relevant areas of the interviewee's case which might not be expressed in enough detail	• Are these questions revealing in character? • Do they provide the missing aspects in the interview?

Six F's of designing interview research	Steps	Aims and actions	Criteria
Focusing	5. More general topics referring to the issue under study	• Try to get into the detail of the central parts of the issue under study • Try to increase the depth and richness of the interviewee's responses by making additional inquiries	• Has the interviewee gone into detail and depth? • Has the interviewer been sensitive to any extra depth on which to focus?
Foreseeing	6. Socio-demographic data	• Develop a checklist for this purpose • Use the documentation sheet	• Is all information included that is necessary for contextualizing the interviewee's answers?
Framing	7. Evaluation and small-talk	• Make room for some conversation • Make room for critique and additional aspects	• Were any additional aspects mentioned?
Foreseeing	8. Documentation	• Ensure a good recording and a detailed transcription	• Is all additional information (not on the recording) documented?
Finding and Formulating	9. Analysing online interviews	• Choose an appropriate method for analysing and interpreting the responses	• Does the method take the quality of the data into account (e.g. the format of emailing)?

How to Select the Appropriate Form of Interviewing

In selecting the form of interviewing – face-to-face, telephone, Skype, or email interviewing – the researcher constructs a framework for listening to what the interviewee has to say. Online interviewing can be a cheaper, easier to organize, pragmatic way of doing interviews. It could be one of several ways of interviewing, of which the respondent may select the most adequate. It may also be the only choice in times such as the coronavirus lockdown. It might be the most appropriate method for the participant, for the interviewer or for the topic. If interviewing in general is a fragile situation, which can be influenced by various factors, the technical aspects that come into play when Skype, telephone or email are the medium of 'talking' may make things even more complicated. It is expected that online interviewing will become more prominent in the future and that the interviewer will be a constructing listener on two levels – in terms of the actual interview and the technical format it is embedded in. It is important to take into account that not every form of interviewing can be transferred to an online format in the same way, and we should be careful not to abandon the available variety of interviews for the practical advantages of interviewing online. Extending the technical side of communication to integrating the element of video will not necessarily suit or support all participants. That which can be said about recording and transcribing face-to-face interviewing applies to online interviewing, too: video should be used for (or added to) the recording if it suits the participants, is necessary for answering the research question, if the transcription of the data also covers visual elements, as well as the analysis. If not, this addition extends the amount of data referring to the single participant, which can produce reservation on their part and extra risks of data abuse.

Online Interviews in Indigenous Research

The use of interviews in an online format is not broadly discussed in the discourse about decolonizing and indigenous research. Heather Goodall, a history professor, Heidi Norman, a political scientist, and Belinda Russon, a Chief Officer at National Indigenous Adult Education and Training (Goodall et al., 2019), from Sydney, Australia, used digital tools, among them online interviewing, to evaluate a programme of indigenous adult education. They gave the interviewees, former students in this education programme, a maximum of control about their data: 'No pressure was to be exerted on any potential interviewees to take part, and they could withdraw at any time or modify any content in their interviews. A copy of the audio and transcript of each interview has been returned to the interviewees, who are invited to edit the transcript and to identify which parts, if any, of the audio file are to be preserved' (Goodall et al., 2019, pp. 59–60). Interviews were complemented by archive data. The Internet is also used for making the interviews available on a website.

As in the general discussion of decolonizing qualitative research (e.g. Chilisa, 2020; Smith, 2012), storytelling as a way of preserving indigenous knowledge (see Chapters 1 and 12) is taken as a point of reference in online research in this context (see the examples in Box 15.7).

Box 15.7   Research in the real world

Digital storytelling in indigenous research

A Canadian transdisciplinary team of indigenous and non-indigenous researchers from several universities working in epidemiology (Sherilee Harper, Victoria Edge) and geography (Ashlee Cunsolo Willox) collaborated with two indigenous institutions (My Word Storytelling Digital Lab and Rigolet Inuit Community Gov.) in Labrador (Cunsolo Willox et al., 2013). They developed a digital narrative method for working with a remote community in studying the links between 'climate change and physical, mental, emotional, and spiritual health and well-being' (p. 129). One aim was to overcome the limits of interview-based storytelling in this way by linking storytelling and digital media in research, so that this combination could complement other methods such as interviews and focus groups.

In a second example, four researchers from the School of Nursing at the University of Auckland, New Zealand, used **digital storytelling** research methods to support the reassertion and retention of indigenous end-of-life care customs in Māori groups in New Zealand (Moeke-Maxwell et al., 2020). The authors did 61 face-to-face interviews with 103 people in total, as they did the interviews with several family members at the same time. These interviews were complemented as: 'Sixteen participants took part in one of three digital story-telling workshops and consented to their videos being used on social media', so 'that these stories could assist New Zealand's palliative care community to become more culturally aware and competent' (2020, p. 102).

What You Need to Ask Yourself

This chapter has discussed various ways of using online contexts as well as the telephone for interviewing. It will have shown that there may be good reasons for doing online interviews but that not all formats of interviewing can be transferred to digital contexts in the same way (see Box 15.8).

Box 15.8　What you need to ask yourself

Doing interview research online

1. How far can your research topic be studied by interviewing people online about it?
2. What is the main focus of your study; and what should the main focus of your interview be?
3. What kind of interview would you do offline, and is this method ready to be transferred online?
4. Who should your interview partners be and are they all online and not only in exceptional cases?

What You Need to Succeed

This chapter has provided a sound grounding in interviewing in online and similar contexts. It should help you to understand what elements of the earlier and the following chapters' content can be transferred to these new contexts. The questions in Box 15.9 will help you to review your take-home points for doing your interview research.

Box 15.9   What you need to succeed

Doing interview research online

1.   Do I understand what online interview research is about?
2.   Am I aware of the development of interviewing as a method of doing research in digital contexts?
3.   Do I have a good idea of what online interviewing is used for in social research?
4.   Do I see the challenges linked to doing online interviews?
5.   Do I see the advantages of these interviews in building on relations without face-to-face contact?

What you have learned

- Doing interviews online is more than just asking people in a more pragmatic way. Interviewing online is different from traditional interviewing.
- Not all formats of interviewing can be transferred smoothly to an online context.
- Not all potential participants can be reached online for interviewing.
- Telephone and Skype interviewing can be easier to organize than email and online interviews in the strict sense.
- The ways of doing interviews discussed in this chapter can also be combined with face-to-face interviews.

Exercises

In the following exercises, you are again invited to reflect on some of the main issues in this chapter. Then you are invited to apply the topics of this chapter to the development of a project of your own. Hence, the exercises are a combination of reflection and prospection.

Exercise 15.1

Reflecting on the Chapter: The Use of Online Interviews in an Existing Study

1.   Look through a journal for a qualitative study based on online interviews (e.g. Fritz and Vandermause, 2018). Try to identify which form of interview was used in it or could be seen as an orientation in relation to the study.
2.   Consider the study's questions and then reflect on how the interviewing was transferred to online contexts and whether this was adequate.

Exercise 15.2

Planning Your Own Research with Interviews

1. Think of your own study and how you would transfer the interview to an online context for answering your research question.

─────── **What's next** ──

In this article, telephone interviewing is discussed:

Block, E.S., & Erskine, L. (2012). Interviewing by Telephone: Specific Considerations, Opportunities, and Challenges. *International Journal of Qualitative Methods*, 428–45. https://doi.org/10.1177/160940691201100409

This article is still a very good overview of the challenges and advantages of doing email interviews:

Meho, L.I. (2006). E-mail Interviewing in Qualitative Research: A Methodological Discussion. *Journal of the American Society for Information Science and Technology*, 57(10), 1284–95.

This article discusses the use of Skype for doing qualitative interviews:

Deakin, H., & Wakefield, K. (2014). Skype Interviewing: Reflections of Two PhD Researchers. *Qualitative Research*, 14(5), 603–16. doi:10.1177/1468794113488126

This chapter summarizes the method concisely and gives some practical advice:

O'Connor, H., & Madge, C. (2017). Online Interviewing. In N.G. Fielding, R. Lee, & G. Blank (Eds.), *The SAGE Handbook of Online Research Methods* (2nd ed., pp. 416–34). London: Sage.

The following chapter gives an overview of how to do focus group interviews online:

Abrams, K., & Gaiser, T. (2017). Online Focus Groups. In N.G. Fielding, R. Lee, & G. Blank (Eds.), *The SAGE Handbook of Online Research Methods* (2nd ed., pp. 435–49). London: Sage.

This article describes the use of Zoom for doing interviews:

Archibald, M.M., Ambagtsheer, R.C., Casey, M.G., & Lawless, M. (2019). Using Zoom Videoconferencing for Qualitative Data Collection: Perceptions and Experiences of Researchers and Participants. *International Journal of Qualitative Methods*. https://doi.org/10.1177/1609406919874596

(Continued)

This article provides a very helpful overview of using various platforms for doing online interviews with individuals and groups:

Lobe, B., Morgan, D., & Hoffman, K.A. (2020). Qualitative Data Collection in an Era of Social Distancing. *International Journal of Qualitative Methods*. https://doi.org/10.1177/1609406920937875

This study is an example of the use of digital storytelling in indigenous research:

Cunsolo Willox, A., Harper, S.L., & Edge, V.L. (2013). Storytelling in a Digital Age: Digital Storytelling as an Emerging Narrative Method for Preserving and Promoting Indigenous Oral Wisdom. *Qualitative Research*, 13(2), 127–47. https://doi.org/10.1177/1468794112446105

HOW TO WORK WITH
INTERVIEW DATA

In this final part of the book, we will address the steps on the agenda after doing the actual interviews, which is the main topic of the book. The three remaining chapters will be about five issues.

In Chapter 16, the focus is on turning the interviews into data, how to manage the data and prepare them for the analysis. The **secondary analysis** of existing interview data will be treated briefly before a number of alternatives for analysing interview data such as coding and interpretation will be discussed.

Chapter 17 first turns to the quality of interview research – how to maintain and assess it in an interview study. Second, we will address how to communicate an interview study – how it was planned and conducted, which methods were applied and how, what the results of the study are and how to reflect on what was done, what went well and what did not.

In the final chapter, Chapter 18, we will return to the critical discussions about interviewing as a method and to how the contents of this book relate to such critiques. Without rejecting them completely, we will try to find a solution for how to continue with doing interview research by taking these critiques into account. The answer presented here is a combination of methodical reflection and the researchers' personal and relational reflexivity.

Doing Interview Research Navigator

How to understand interview research
- What doing interview research means
- Theories and epistemologies of interviewing
- When to choose interviews as a research method
- Methods and formats of interviewing

Designing interview research
- Planning and designing interview research
- How many interviewees: Sampling and saturation
- Accessing and recruiting participants

How to conduct interviews
- How to respect and protect: Ethics of interviewing
- Semi-structured interviews: Working with questions and answers
- Interviewing experts and elites
- Integrating narratives in interviews: Episodic interviews

Doing interviews in context
- How to work with life histories: Narrative interviews
- Working with focus groups as interviews
- Ask (in) the field: Ethnographic and mobile interviewing
- Doing online interviews

You are here in your project

How to work with interview data
- Working with interview data
- Credibility and transparency: Quality and writing in interview research
- From interviewing to an inner view: Critiques and reflexivity

WORKING WITH INTERVIEW DATA

How this chapter will help you

You will:

- see that interviews are not data already but have to be turned into data,
- learn about recording, transcribing and administrating interview data,
- gain an idea about the secondary analysis of existing interview data,
- understand the need for managing data for the analysis, and
- learn the basics of methodological alternatives for analysing interviews.

Constructing a Framework for Listening to Interviews as Data

Following our discussion in Chapter 3, it may be helpful to clarify again what the purpose of a research interview and its analysis in qualitative research is not and what that means for the analytic framework that is constructed. As an interview in research is not a therapeutic interview, the analysis should not aim at producing personal profiles of the interviewees or characterizations of their personalities. So psycho-diagnostic analysis and categorizations should be avoided. A research interview is also not an investigative interview as in journalism or in court. Thus, the aim of the analysis should not be to convict the interviewee of something. The researchers should not confuse themselves with detectives, police investigators or investigative journalists aiming at naming and shaming the interviewee. In general, researchers should keep in mind that the participant was interviewed as an exemplary or sample case for analysing a specific topic, but not as a person in their own right. Even if a life-history narrative interview was conducted, it is not the interviewed persons but the process or developments they experienced that are in focus. The aim is to compare views and statements of several interviewees for a better understanding of a phenomenon from several angles or perspectives and to identify commonalities and differences in these perspectives on the phenomenon. Generalizing results, for example in a typology or in patterns relating to a phenomenon and reaching beyond the individual interviewees, should be the aim.

Constructing a framework for listening to the interviews as expressions of individual perspectives on a phenomenon and building a platform for a comparative analysis, which does justice to the single participants' views and expression, should be the outcomes of the analysis.

How to Turn Interviews into Data

What do we take home from doing an interview? From listening to an interviewee, we will receive statements, descriptions, narratives, answers, comments, questions, definitions, explanations and other forms of verbal utterances. In face-to-face, video, Skype, Webex or Zoom interviews, we will see non-verbal expressions such as gestures, looks, emotions and the like. Parts of both the verbal and the non-verbal responses will be relevant for our research, while others will be less important for our analysis. This already shows that the verbal and non-verbal raw materials we take home from an interview are not necessarily data we use in the further process. Before any analysis is done with them, the materials will be **turned into data** – by documenting them (e.g. by recording), by making them up (e.g. by transcribing), by selecting them (e.g. by focusing on specific parts of a narrative or on particular statements of an interviewee) and by giving them a meaning (for understanding the interview and the interviewee or for answering our research question). This turning of interviews into data is a selective process in two respects: (1) Not everything that could be documented or transcribed will be covered due to limits in capacity (a microphone or a video camera have a focus and a range, for example). (2) By selecting a way of documenting and the makeup of what occurs in an interview, researchers have a focus on what is relevant and what should be in the foreground of recording or transcribing.

In order to become data to be analysed, interviews have to be:

1. elaborated on for the actual analysis, for example by transcription;
2. checked for consistency (e.g. by clarifying unclear parts);
3. looked at for what can be found out from analysing them, by defining a research question for the analysis;
4. processed by applying the methods of analysis, for example coding procedures;

5. interpreted for the meaning of the findings they offer;
6. focused on the major findings and conclusions they allow, for example by developing a typology;
7. evaluated for their quality and that of the analysis (see Chapter 17); and
8. turned into a presentation of the knowledge that was developed from them (see Chapter 17).

Steps 1–6 are elaborated on in this chapter.

Recording

Although there are some exceptions, doing interviews and analysing them is based on recording in one way or another. The exceptions are discussed, for example, by Rutakumwa et al. (2020), who compare the use of recording and transcribing interviews with taking notes during the interview and turning these into an interview script. A second exception is ethnographic and mobile interviews when, in some cases, recording is not possible for technical or practical reasons. And sometimes the recording device does not work, but the interview is so relevant for the study that the researcher decides to use notes or memory protocols from the interview for the analysis. Beyond these exceptions, it is quite common to do an acoustic or audiovisual recording. In most cases, using a tape (which might be a bit outdated) or mp3 recorder may be sufficient for capturing the essential (verbal) contents of an interview. Using a smartphone for recording can be practical, but you have to take care with data protection, to transfer the recording to a safer environment on a computer and to erase the recording on the smartphone afterwards (see Chapter 8 on this). Beyond technical challenges – can I be sure that the recording device works and the recording is easy to understand afterwards? – you should limit the recording to what you will really use later. This refers to the decision between video and audio recording – if the visual elements will not be used later, it would be better to limit the recording to audio only. You should also avoid the recording being too obvious in the interview situation – ideally, the interviewees after agreeing to the recording forget about the recorder's presence. In Skype and other formats of doing interviews online, the software supports recording. In email interviews, recordings (and transcribing afterwards) are not necessary as the dialogue between interviewer and interviewee occurs in a written format already. For telephone interviews, a number of recording apps are available.

Interview protocols

To document interviews in mobile and digital contexts, often **interview protocols** are the main way of documentation. However, it is strongly suggested that you use interview protocols or documentation sheets in addition to the recording in any form of interviewing. What you should include as information depends on the design of your study. For example, when several interviewers are involved you should note who did the actual interview. If interviews are conducted at changing locations (which might have influenced the interviews), this should also be documented. In addition, the research questions determine what you should concretely note on these sheets. Box 16.1 presents an example of such a sheet.

Box 16.1   Research in the real world

Example of a documentation sheet

Information about the Interview and the Interviewee

Date of the interview: ....
Place of the interview: ....
Duration of the interview: ....
Interviewer: ....
Indicator for the interviewee: ....
Gender of the interviewee: ....
Age of the interviewee: ....
Occupation of the interviewee*: ....
Working in this occupation since*: ....
Professional field*: ....
Where raised (countryside/city)*: ....
Number of children*: ....
Age of the children*: ....
Gender(s) of the children*: ....
Special occurrences in the interview:

....
....
....
....
....

* This information is required only when relevant for your specific project; or replaced by alternative information appropriate to your study.

Transcribing

Transcribing is a crucial step in turning interviews into data. Here again, you should reflect in advance on which details might be relevant for your analysis. Most rules for transcription have been set up by linguists for doing linguistic analysis and thus may be too detailed (and too time-consuming) for interview research and analysis, for example in education, psychology and sociology. The role of transcription is to provide the interview conversation in a comparable way so that the analysts can be sure that if two interviewees have mentioned something in the same particular way, this will be documented in both interview transcripts in the same way. This means that differences between interviewees come from the differences in how they said something and not from the different ways their interviews were transcribed. Box 16.2 includes a set of rules for transcribing interviews, which are not too detailed but secure a comparability of transcripts.

Box 16.2　Research in the real world

Rules for transcription

Layout

Font	Times New Roman 12
Margin	Left 2, right 5 cm
Line numbers	Turn on this function in your word processor
Line spacing	1.5
Page numbers	On top, right
Interviewer:	I: Interviewer
Interviewee:	IP: Interviewee

Transcription

Spelling	Conventional
Punctuation	Conventional
Breaks　Short break	*; if longer than 1 sec: *no of seconds*
Incomprehensible	((incomp))
Uncertain transcription	(abc)
Loud	With commentary
Low	With commentary
Emphasis	With commentary
Break off word	Abc-
Break off sentence	Abc-
Simultaneous talk	# abc #
Paralinguistic utterance	With commentary (e.g. sighs ...)
Commentary	With commentary
Verbal quote	Conventional
Abbreviations	Conventional
Anonymization	Names marked by:

If you use these suggestions for transcribing your interviews, transcripts should look like the one in Box 16.3.

Box 16.3 Research in the real world

Example from a transcript

1 I: Yeah the first question is, what is this for you, health? ((telephone rings)) Do 2
2   you want to pick it up first?
3 IP: No.
4 I: No? Okay.
5 IP: Health is relative, I think. Someone can be healthy, too, who is old
6   and has a handicap and can feel healthy nevertheless. Well, in earlier
7   times, before I came to work in the community, I always said,
8   'someone is healthy if he lives in a very well ordered household, where
9   everything is correct and super exact, and I would like to say, absolutely
10   clean'. But I learnt better, when I started to work in the community.
11   I was a nurse in the NAME OF THE HOSPITAL-1 before that, in
12   intensive care and arrived here with ...

I = Interviewer; IP = Interviewee.

Transcribing interviews can be time-consuming and exhausting, but you will learn a lot about your interviews and interviewing during the transcription process. McLellan et al. (2003) address transcription and other steps of data preparation after the interview in some detail. Some facilitating software (f4transkript) and devices (USB foot pedals) as well as a number of helpful suggestions can be found at the website of audiotranskription (www.audiotranskription.de/english).

Secondary Analysis of Interview Data

In the preceding chapter (see Chapter 15), we discussed a number of strategies for doing interviews in times of crisis, such as a pandemic, on the one hand, and where the interviewees are far away and difficult to reach. Online, telephone, Skype and email interviews have become serious methodological alternatives and substitutes under these circumstances. Before we turn to techniques of analysing interviews in general, a second strategy to substitute doing one's own interviews (face-to-face or online) will be briefly mentioned here which has become more widely accepted. 'Secondary analysis' means that you analyse data, e.g. interviews, you did not collect for your own research project. Instead, you use existing data sets that were produced for other purposes. Hakim's (1982, p. 1) definition of secondary analysis as 'any further analysis of an existing dataset which presents interpretations, conclusions or knowledge additional to, or different from, those presented in the first report on the inquiry as a whole and its main results' has been a benchmark in the literature on this field (see Corti, 2018). Although most **secondary data** research occurs in quantitative research, the interest in reanalysing existing interviews is growing (see Hughes et al., 2020). Basically, three sources for (interview) data in a secondary analysis can be distinguished: (1) Researchers take interviews from an earlier study they did for a different purpose and reanalyse them with a new focus. (2) They ask other researchers for their data to use them in the new study, which does not necessarily mean that these data are publicly or officially available. (3) Researchers use interview data from one of the archives for qualitative data (such as the UK Data Service – www.ukdataservice.ac.uk – or the Australian Data Service – https://ada.edu.au) after seeking permission. In funded research, one obligation in many contexts now is to make qualitative data also available for other researchers by integrating them in such an archive. At the same time, funding sometimes foresees the use of existing data rather than producing new data.

There has been a long debate about whether such a 'secondary' analysis of existing data by other researchers can be compared with primary research, in which researchers analyse data they collected themselves. Moore (2007, p. 1) argues that 'reuse may be more productively understood as a process of recontextualising data, and that attending to the reflexive production of data in the contemporary research project may offer more hopeful possibilities for reuse'. Accordingly, secondary analysis can be seen as another way of doing research, which has to be planned as in the usual ways of doing primary research, but comes with some extra challenges linked to the steps of the research process. First, it is important to reverse-check one's current research question for whether it fits (1) the use of existing data and (2) the research question of the study for which these were originally collected. 'Fit' does not mean the two research questions have to be identical but compatible enough to make the secondary use a promising approach. Second, the step of sampling becomes relevant in three respects: (1) researchers should reflect on which existing data set to select for their own study and (2) which of the interviews in that data set to sample for their new study; and (3) they should check how far the sample criteria of the original study match their own research question. Third, ethical issues should be reflected upon (is the informed consent available and does it foresee or permit a secondary analysis?). Fourth, the data collection: do the interviews, the questions and answers, for example, cover the aspects relevant for the new study, and does the conduct of the interviews meet the new researchers' criteria as though they had run the interviews themselves? Fifth, does the documentation of the interviews – from the recording to the transcription and the context information about the interview and interviewees – provide the information needed for the current analysis? And in which form are the original data available – the recordings of the interviews, their transcripts, summaries or only their analysis, and if so, do the categories used match the new project and analysis? Depending on the source from which the original data are taken (one's own, other researchers', or archival data), the above questions can be answered more easily and comprehensively or with difficulty. If the answers to these questions are satisfying, the (re-)analysis of the existing data can proceed in a very similar way to the original data collected in interviews for a study (see also Corti, 2018, 2022).

Data Management and Administration

This step includes organizing your interviews, transcripts, data and analyses in a way that will allow you to keep track of them for using and comparing them. Beyond this internal organization of your work, an external side of it becomes relevant as well. In writing about your research (see Chapter 17), it will be necessary to have an indexing system, which allows you to see which quotes come from the same interviewee. Once your interviews, are stored in an archive, it will be necessary for other users of your interviews, in a secondary analysis, to have an orientation through the material.

Indexing data

It will be helpful to have a storage system for your transcripts. This is known as **indexing data**. For example, in a study with several interviewees, it would be wise to store each transcript with an indicator, for example IP-1 for the first, IP-2 for the second interviewee, and so on. If you do repeated interviews with the same intervicwees, I suggest using IP-1-1 for the first interview of interviewee number 1, IP-1-2 for the second interview with this person, IP-2-1 and IP-2-2 for the next interviewee, and so on. I would suggest using these indicators both for labelling the files in which you store the transcripts and in the header of the transcripts (indicated on every page). You should develop a system of indicators or nicknames, which allows you to keep track of the interview throughout the chain from recording and the interview protocol to the **memo** and to the quotes and analyses (and back if necessary). Software packages such as Atlas.ti or MAXQDA are popular tools for analysing the data (see below) but they are even more helpful for administrating the elements of this chain. It is also helpful to set up a table of the sample of interviewees available for analysis, which includes the indicators and some of the most important information about the interviewees (e.g. age, profession, gender, local context, if these are relevant for your study, or whatever information is most important for it).

Memos

Memos are short (sometimes longer) notes reflecting the whole process of a research study, starting from developing the research question to field contacts (with interviewees), the actual interviews and first thoughts about analysing them. In grounded theory research, these memos become part of the analysis and are integrated in the writing about the results and the project and, in this specific kind of research, in the theory that is developed.

Use of software at various stages of doing the interview research

In an interview study, software can be helpful at various stages: in data collection and fieldwork; transcription of interviews; writing of a research diary; collecting virtual data in online interviews and focus groups; processing collected data coding (attaching keywords or tags to segments of text to permit later retrieval); storage (keeping text in an organized database); archiving, search and retrieval (locating relevant segments of text and making them available for inspection); data 'linking' (connecting relevant data segments to each other, forming categories, clusters or networks of information); memo writing (writing reflective commentaries on some aspect of the data, as a basis for deeper analysis); and content analysis (counting frequencies, sequence, or locations of words and phrases). Software continues to be utilized in finalizing and presenting the analysis; data display (placing selected or reduced data in a condensed organized format, such as a matrix or network, for inspection); the drawing of conclusions and their verification – aiding the analyst to interpret displayed data and to test or confirm findings; theory building (developing systematic, conceptually coherent explanations of findings and testing hypotheses); graphic mapping (creating diagrams that depict findings or theories); report writing (interim and final reports; see also Miles and Huberman, 1994, p. 44; Weitzman, 2000, p. 806); finally, in the management of the project; in collaboration and communication with other researchers by email or social networks or using cloud applications ('apps'); in dissemination of findings; and in publication and peer reviews.

Computer-assisted qualitative analysis of interviews

The most important program packages are Atlas.ti (https://atlasti.com) and MAXQDA (www.maxqda.com). Although these packages are promoted as software for analysing qualitative data, many researchers use them mainly for data management. They support (1) text retrieval, which allows researchers to search, summarize, list, and so on, certain word sequences. (2) Text-based management for administering, searching, sorting and ordering text passages becomes easier with them. (3) In the analysis, they support coding and retrieval for splitting the text into segments, to which codes are assigned, and for retrieving or listing all segments of the text, marked with each code. (4) The software packages offer tools for marking, ordering, sorting, and linking texts and codes are supported and both (text and code) are presented and administered together. Some more analytic tools complement these administrative functions.

Sampling in the material

As already mentioned in Chapter 6, sampling becomes relevant again in this step. Not everything that has been said, maybe not every interview, is relevant for the analysis in the same way. Thus in the analysis, the researchers will select material which is more relevant and more illuminating from the interview(s). This sampling can refer to specific topics in the interview, to particular statements or narratives. It can also refer to interviews that illustrate variation in the material and later in the findings. Thus, the sampling may be about comparing the interviews or the interviewees for certain topics.

When to start to analyse

In general, I would suggest starting your analysis immediately after the first few interviews, (1) to listen to the recordings, (2) to transcribe and read the transcripts, (3) to write an initial summary or short description (see below) or a memo about each interview and (4) to ask questions of the material (see below as well). These steps can give an orientation as to what the interview might contribute to answering your research question and also on what to consider for the following interviews and for the more systematic analysis of the material.

How to Analyse Interview Data

We find several methodological alternatives for analysing interview data (see Flick, 2014b, for an overview of approaches to qualitative data analysis). In this brief chapter, we cannot go into the detail of single methods of analysis (see Flick, 2018a, for more information), but will outline some basic strategies you can apply to analysing your interviews. The analysis of interviews can have various aims. The first such aim may be to describe a phenomenon. The phenomenon could be, for example, the subjective experiences of a specific individual or group (e.g. the way people continue to live after starting to study at a university). Such a study could focus on the case (individual or group) and its special features and the links between them. Or the analysis could focus on comparing several cases (individuals or groups) and on what they have in common, or on the differences between them. The second aim may be to identify the conditions on which such differences are based. This means looking for explanations for such differences, for instance circumstances which make it more likely that the coping with a specific transition is more successful than in other cases. The third aim may be to develop a theory of the phenomenon under study from the analysis of empirical material, such as a theory of educational trajectories. In addition, we can distinguish the analysis of interviews for their content (1) from that of formal aspects (2) and from approaches that combine both (3). For example, we can look at what participants report about their transition experiences and compare the contents of such reports to statements made by other participants (1). Or we can look at formal aspects of talking about these experiences, when the language becomes unclear, pauses become longer, and the like (2). Or we can (3) look for formal aspects and content in interviews and link this to a discourse about transitions to higher education.

Qualitative analysis of interviews – a working definition

Thus, we can define the qualitative analysis of interviews as follows:

Qualitative analysis of interviews is the interpretation and classification of linguistic (or visual) material with the following aims: to make statements about implicit and explicit dimensions and structures of meaning making in the material and what is represented in it. Qualitative analysis of interviews combines summarizing analysis of the material (overviews, condensation, summaries) with detailed analysis (development of categories or hermeneutic interpretations). Often the final aim is to arrive at statements that can be generalized in one way or the other by comparing various cases.

The most prominent methods for analysing interviews are grounded theory coding, **thematic coding**, thematic analysis, qualitative content analysis and interpretive analysis of narratives. In all these methods, coding plays a more or less (in narrative analysis) important role.

Coding

There are various understandings of the term '**coding**'. They have in common that they describe the relation of materials to categories used in the analysis. In qualitative content analysis (see below), coding is a central feature: 'The method is also systematic in that it requires coding (i.e. assigning segments of the material to the categories of the coding frame) to be carried out twice (double-coding), at least for parts of the material' (Schreier, 2014, p. 171). However, in qualitative content analysis, in contrast to other approaches, an emphasis is on developing codes and categories mainly from the theory rather than from the material. Here, the focus is on developing a coding frame, which is a well-defined system of categories. The material, for example the interviews, is not the starting point for developing codes and categories.

In grounded theory research (see Flick, 2018c), for example, coding has been defined as 'naming segments of data with a label that simultaneously categorizes, summarizes, and accounts for each piece of data' (Charmaz, 2014, p. 111). Here, coding means to develop codes and categories from the material that is analysed, for example interviews.

In general, coding is a process of labelling and categorizing data as a first step in the analysis. In several methods, there are several steps of coding – for example, **initial** and **focused coding** in recent grounded theory research or open and selective coding in earlier versions. Coding first is mainly oriented on developing concepts, which can be used for labelling, sorting and comparing excerpts of the data (e.g. several statements), and later for allocating further excerpts to the developing coding system.

Grounded Theory Coding

In grounded theory research, coding is understood and processed starting from the empirical material, such as a transcript, and aiming for developing codes and links between them. The suggestions for coding – and more generally for analysing empirical materials – are also widely used as a general method beyond the developing of theories from the empirical material, e.g. interviews. However, two things should be kept in mind: first, this approach to analysing materials and to coding in particular was originally created for a specific purpose – to develop a theory from empirical material. This is not always the aim of researchers analysing interviews. Second, the approach was not developed specifically for analysing (single) interviews but for all sorts of (ethnographic) data (observation, or documents), among which interviews could play a role but not with a focus on the single interviewee. Nevertheless, the suggestions for coding in grounded theory analysis can be instructive for analysing interviews, too.

A helpful suggestion which was made rather early in the development of the method is to use several forms of coding in the process. In the process of analysis, as Strauss and Corbin (1990) characterize it, a number of 'procedures' for working with text can be differentiated. They are termed **'open coding'**, **'axial coding'** and **'selective coding'**.

Open coding

The first step of the coding process aims at developing codes from the material by identifying concepts (Strauss and Corbin, 1990, p. 74) and at developing a deeper understanding of the material. Strauss and Corbin summarize open coding as follows:

> Concepts are the basic building blocks of theory. Open coding in grounded theory method is the analytic process by which concepts are identified and developed in terms of their properties and dimensions. The basic analytic procedures by which this is accomplished are: the asking of questions about the data; and the making of comparisons for similarities and differences between each incident, event and other instances of phenomena. Similar events and incidents are labelled and grouped to form categories. (1990, p. 74)

Possible sources for labelling codes are concepts taken from interviewees' expressions (***in vivo* codes**) or concepts borrowed from the social science literature (*constructed* codes). Of the two types of codes, the first are preferred because they are closer to the studied material. The categories found in this way are then further developed.

Among other techniques, two are most helpful here. For open coding (and the other coding strategies), it is suggested first that the researchers regularly address the text with a number of so-called basic questions:

- What? What is the issue here? What phenomenon is mentioned?
- Who? What persons/actors are involved? What roles do they play? How do they interact?
- How? Which aspects of the phenomenon are mentioned (or not mentioned)?
- When? How long? Where? Time, course and location.
- How much? How strong? Aspects of intensity.
- Why? What reasons are given or can be reconstructed?
- What for? With what intention, to which purpose?
- By which? Means, tactics and strategies for reaching the goal.

The second technique included in coding is the *constant comparison* of phenomena, cases, concepts, and so on. This means that the researchers should continuously look for comparison in the material they analyse – within the same interview, for example (e.g. what did the interviewee say in a different part of the interview?), or between several interviews (e.g. how did several interviewees respond to the same question?). Starting from the data, the process of coding leads to the development of theories through a process of abstraction. Concepts or codes are attached to the empirical material. They are first formulated as closely as possible to the text, and later more and more abstractly. Categorizing in this procedure refers to the summary of such concepts into *generic concepts* and to the elaboration of the relations between concepts and generic concepts or categories and superior concepts.

Axial coding

After the first step aimed at identifying a number of substantive categories, the next step is to refine and differentiate the categories resulting from open coding. As a second step, Strauss and Corbin suggest doing more formal coding for identifying and classifying links between substantive categories. In axial coding, the relations between categories are elaborated on. Concepts may be classified in four ways: (1) as a *phenomenon* for this category; (2) as the *context* or *conditions* for other categories; (3) as a *consequence*; and finally (4) as *strategies*. It is important to note that the coding paradigm only names possible relations between phenomena and concepts: the purpose of coding is to facilitate the discovery or establishment of structures of relations between phenomena, between concepts and between categories. In order to formulate such relations, Strauss and Corbin (1998, p. 127) suggest a coding paradigm model, which is presented in Figure 16.1.

This model helps to clarify the relations between a phenomenon, its causes and consequences, its context, and the strategies of those who are involved. This model is

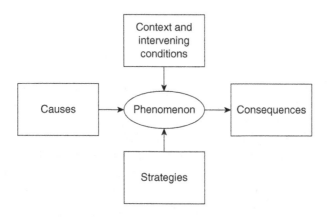

Figure 16.1 Coding paradigm model

based on two axes: one goes from causes to phenomena and to consequences, the other one links context, intervening conditions, and action and interactional strategies of participants to the phenomenon.

Selective coding

The third step, selective coding, elaborates on the development and integration of the model and focuses on potential core concepts or core variables. In this step, you look for further examples and evidence of relevant categories. This should lead to formulating the *story of the case*. Strauss and Corbin understand the issue or the central phenomenon of the study as a case and not a person or a single interview. One should bear in mind here that the aim of this formulation is to give a short descriptive overview of the story and the case, and it should therefore comprise only a few sentences. The analysis goes beyond this descriptive level when the *story line* is elaborated on – a concept is attached to the central phenomenon of the story and related to the other categories. The core category again is developed in its features and dimensions and linked to (all, if possible) other categories by using the parts and relations of the coding paradigm. The analysis and the development of the theory aim at discovering patterns in the data as well as the conditions under which these apply. Grouping the data according to the coding paradigm allocates specificity to the theory and enables the researcher to say, 'Under these conditions (listing them) this happens; whereas under these conditions, this is what occurs' (1990, p. 131).

For a more general approach to coding interviews, several elements of this procedure are helpful: first, to develop codes and categories from the material (open coding); second, to look for links and structures between codes (axial coding); and third, to aim at a condensation of the analysis by looking for core categories or story lines in the material beyond the single interview. Strauss and Corbin's approach, however, does not pay much attention to the individual case of the interviewee; rather, it immediately sees the complete set of interviews as a case.

Initial and focused coding

Charmaz (2014; see also Thornberg and Charmaz, 2014) has developed an updated version of grounded theory coding. It starts from **line-by-line coding**, which is called **initial coding**. This step includes asking questions such as 'What process(es) is at issue here? How can I define it?' 'How does this process develop?' 'How does the research participant(s) act and profess to think and feel while involved in this process?' (Thornberg and Charmaz, 2014, p. 156). Charmaz illustrates this with the example in Box 16.4. The codes Charmaz developed can be found in the left-hand column and an excerpt from the interview is in the right-hand column of the box.

Box 16.4   Research in the real world

Example of initial line-by-line coding

Shifting symptoms, having inconsistent days	If you have lupus, I mean one day it's my liver; one day it's my joints; one day it's my head, and
Interpreting images of self given by others	it's like people really think you're a hypochondriac if you keep complaining about
Avoiding disclosure	different ailments ... It's like you don't want to say anything because people are going to start
Predicting rejection	thinking, you know, 'God, don't go near her, all
Keeping others unaware	she is – is complaining about this.' And I think
Seeing symptoms as connected	that's why I never say anything because I feel like everything I have is related one way or
Having others unaware	another to the lupus but most of the people don't
Anticipating disbelief	know I have lupus, and even those that do are not
Controlling others' views	going to believe that ten different ailments are the
Avoiding stigma	same thing. And I don't want anybody saying,
Assessing potential losses and risks of disclosing	you know, [that] they don't want to come around me because I complain.

Source: Charmaz (2003, p. 96)

After line-by-line coding at the beginning (see Box 16.4), Charmaz continues by exploring some of the resulting codes more deeply (focused coding). In the example given in Box 16.4, these were the two codes 'avoiding disclosure' and 'assessing potential losses and risks of disclosing' (highlighted in bold). In this step, codes are assessed for their relevance and for becoming conceptual categories in the continuing process or analysis, and the relationships between them are assessed. As a third step, Charmaz suggests *theoretical coding*, explicitly referring to using concepts from the literature and existing theories as well as analytic logics from pre-existing theories. The example in Box 16.5 refers to a study critiquing the ethical and racial bias of grounded theory research in health.

Box 16.5   Research in the real world

Postcolonial critiques of grounded theory research

Draucker et al. (2014) have analysed 44 grounded theory (GT) studies, published in the journal *Qualitative Health Research* from 2008 to 2013, for how far the research reported in these studies has contributed to addressing racial/ethnic disparities.

(Continued)

They found that this diversity was absent in 33 of the studies, played a complementary role in one study and a primary role in five studies. From these findings, they develop suggestions that grounded theory research could contribute more to health disparities research, 'if techniques were developed to better analyze the influence of race/ethnicity on health-related phenomena' (p. 1). However this critique may be justified, the question is whether this is a problem of the method *per se* or of the research that is done with the method.

Thematic Coding

Thematic coding was originally developed for analysing episodic interviews (see Chapter 11) and, unlike grounded theory coding, tends to maintain the reference to interviewees, for example, as a (particular) case when using the coding procedure. Here, the analysis starts with case studies for which a thematic structure is developed. It refers to what characterizes, across several substantive areas, how the interviewee deals with health, for example.

Short description

To prepare the analysis, first a short description of each case is developed, which can continually be checked and modified throughout the further interpretation of the case, if necessary. This description will include a statement which is typical for the interview, a short characterization of the interviewee with respect to the research question (e.g. age, profession, number of children, if relevant for your issue of research) and the major topics mentioned in the interview with respect to the issue under study. This short description is firstly a heuristic tool for the following analysis. The example in Box 16.6 comes from a study on transitional processes in the educational careers of people with substantial disabilities (Gangnus, 2020).

Box 16.6   Research in the real world

Example of a short description of a case

It occurred to ME to do everything on my own

The female interviewee is 54 years old and grew up very sheltered. At the age of nine, she received her diagnosis of an early loss of sight. Due to the slow progression of the illness, she was still able to attend a regular school for a long time. At 19 she moved out of her parents' home to be independent early on. Soon she started training at a bank. However, it was difficult to organize her workplace in a disability-friendly way. She submitted a proposal for supporting her own integration into the workplace by herself. The interviewee still has to struggle with big challenges at work and since 2014 has used accessible software. She is very proactive and has pursued further education for e-learning and marketing coaching. She also founded an advocacy group for visually impaired people in the bank and actively supports other people affected. In particular, her own family and medical personnel are very supportive, in addition to being buoyed by her own resilience.

In thematic coding, you will then go more into the depth of the material by focusing on a single case (for example, looking at a particular interview as a whole). This single-case analysis has several aims: it preserves the meaningful relations that the respective person deals with in the topic of the study, which is why a case study is done for all interviews; and it develops a system of categories for analysis of the single case.

In the further elaboration of this system of categories (similar to grounded theory coding), first apply open coding and then selective coding. With selective coding, here you will aim less at developing a grounded core category across all cases than at first generating thematic domains and categories for the particular case.

Following the first case analysis, you will cross-check the categories you have developed with the thematic domains that are linked to the single cases. A thematic structure results from this cross-check, which underlies the analysis of further cases in order to increase their comparability.

The exemplary excerpts in Box 16.7 of such a thematic structure come from the same master's thesis as used in Box 16.6 (Gangnus, 2020).

Box 16.7   Research in the real world

Excerpt of a thematic structure in thematic coding

1.   Growing up

  1.1   **Parents show initiative**
  1.2   **Long-term attendance at regular school**
  1.3   **Early moving out of home**

2.   Receiving diagnosis

  2.1   **Becoming aware of restriction**

3.   Phase of professional orientation
4.   Entering professional life

(Continued)

5. Professional challenges

    5.1 **Problems with recognizing writing**
    5.2. **Problems with screens/accessibility**
    5.3 **Use of software**
    5.4 **Colleagues' lack of understanding**

6. Experiences of stigmatization

    6.1 **Colleagues at work**
    6.2 **Organizations**

7. Challenges of transition

    7.1 **No sick notes**
    7.2 **No answers/lack of support**
    7.3 **Rehabilitation**

8. Feeling of being left alone

    8.1. **No reaction to enquiries**
    8.2. **Supervisors' ignorance**
    8.3. **Physicians**

The structure developed from the first cases will be applied and continually assessed for all further cases in the analysis. If new or contradictory aspects emerge, the structure should be modified and used to analyse all cases that are part of the interpretation. For a fine interpretation of the thematic domains, single passages of text (e.g. narratives of situations) are analysed in greater detail. The coding paradigm suggested by Strauss and Corbin (see above) is taken as a starting point. The result of this process, complemented by a step of selective coding, is a case-oriented display of the way it specifically deals with the research issue, including oft-repeated topics (e.g. support or challenges) that can be found in viewpoints across different domains (e.g. work, leisure, household).

The thematic structure developed will also serve for comparing cases and groups (that is, for elaborating on correspondences and differences between the various groups in the study). Thus, you analyse and assess the social distribution of perspectives on the issue under study.

Fine interpretation of thematic areas

For a fine interpretation of the thematic domains, single passages of the text (e.g. narratives of situations) are analysed in greater detail. The coding paradigm suggested by Strauss and Corbin (1990, pp. 27–8) is taken as a starting point for deriving a number of key questions: (1) Conditions: Why? What has led to the situation? Background? Course? (2) Interaction among the actors: Who acted? What happened? (3) Strategies and tactics: What ways of handling situations, for example avoidance, adaptation? And (4) Consequences: What changed? Results? In advancing the analysis, selective coding of material to the parts of the thematic structure is applied. The thematic structure thus developed may also serve for comparing cases and groups (i.e. for elaborating on correspondences and differences between the various groups in the study).

Qualitative Content Analysis

One of the practical questions in working with codes and categories in analysing qualitative interviews is where the codes come from. The answer it that either they are developed in an inductive way from the material, or in a *deductive* way from the literature or the researcher's prior knowledge. The second alternative is the driving force behind qualitative content analysis. According to Schreier (2014, p. 170), 'qualitative content analysis is a method for systematically describing the meaning of qualitative data. ... This is done by assigning successive parts of the material to the categories of a coding frame.'

The process of qualitative content analysis

Schreier (2014, p. 174) outlines the process of qualitative content analysis in the following steps: After (1) deciding on a research question for the analysis, (2) material is selected and (3) a coding frame built which results from structuring (which means developing its main categories) and generating (which means creating the subcategories for each main category). Both can be applied in a concept- or data-driven way: categories result either from the existing literature or from the research interest behind the study. Then the material is (4) segmented into units (e.g. sentences, or answers, or topics) and (5) a trial coding is applied. Its results are used for (6) evaluating and modifying the coding frame. The final version is (7) applied in the main analysis of the material, before, at the end, the researcher (8) interprets the findings. In qualitative content analysis, building a coding frame is central. Developing categories from the interviews that are analysed – as in grounded theory or thematic coding (see above) – should only be used in exceptional cases, as Schreier holds, similar to other theorists of qualitative content analysis. The coding frame and the use of theory-based categories are features that are supposed to make qualitative content analysis more systematic than other methods of qualitative data analysis. With the possibility of adding categories developed from the material, this method has some degree of flexibility.

However, the major aim of qualitative content analysis, according to Schreier (2014) or Mayring (2000), is to work with rather large data sets comprising many interviews, which have to be reduced in the analysis. Before the coding frame is applied, the categories are defined by giving them a name, describing what this name means, and giving positive examples and decision rules for applying it. If necessary, the coding frame is adapted by revising and expanding it.

With this emphasis on the use of a coding frame, the three features that characterize the method, according to Schreier, can be put into practice: qualitative content analysis reduces data; it is systematic; and it is flexible (2014, p. 170). Mayring (e.g. 2000) suggests some concrete procedures for how to analyse interview material with qualitative content analysis (see also Flick, 2018a, Ch. 26).

Summarizing content analysis

In the stage of **summarizing content analysis**, the material is paraphrased so that less relevant passages and paraphrases with the same meanings (this is the first reduction) are bundled and summarized in similar paraphrases (the second reduction) and can be skipped. For example, in an interview with an unemployed teacher, the statement 'and actually, quite the reverse, I was, well, very, very keen on finally teaching for the first time' (Mayring, 1983, p. 59) was paraphrased as 'quite the reverse, very keen on practice' and generalized as 'rather looking forward to practice'. The statement 'therefore, I couldn't wait for it, to go to a seminar school, until I could finally teach there for the first time' was paraphrased as 'couldn't wait to finally teach' and generalized as 'looking forward to practice'. Owing to the similarity of the two generalizations, the second one is then skipped and reduced with other statements to 'practice not experienced as shock but as big fun' (1983, p. 59).

Explicative content analysis

The next step aims at clarifying vague, ambiguous or contradictory passages by involving contextual material in the analysis. This is known as **explicative content analysis**. Definitions taken from dictionaries are used or formulated. 'Narrow context analysis' picks up additional statements from the text in order to explicate the passages to be analysed, whereas 'wide context analysis' seeks information outside the text (about the author, the generative situations, from theories). On this basis, an 'explicating paraphrase' is formulated and tested.

For example, in an interview, a teacher expressed her difficulties in teaching by stating that – unlike successful colleagues – she was no 'entertainer type' (Mayring, 1983, p. 109). In order to find out what she wished to express by using this concept, definitions of 'entertainer' were assembled from two dictionaries. The features of a teacher who fits this description were then sought from statements made by the teacher in the interview. Further passages were consulted. Based on the descriptions of such colleagues included in these passages, an 'explicating paraphrase can be formulated: an entertainer type is somebody who plays the part of an extroverted, spirited, sparkling, and self-assured human being' (1983, p. 74). This explication was assessed again by applying it to the direct context in which the concept was used.

Structuring content analysis

When you come to be **structuring content analysis**, you look for types or formal structures in the material. You can look for and find four kinds of structure. You may find specific topics or domains, which characterize the texts (content structure) – for example, xenophobic statements in interviews are always linked to issues of violence and crime. Or you may find an internal structure on a formal level, which characterizes the material – for example, every text begins with an example and then an explanation of the example that follows. Scaling structure means that you find varying degrees of a feature in the material – for example, texts which express xenophobia in a stronger way than other texts in the material. Finally, you may find a typifying structure – for example, that interviews with female participants are systematically different from those with male participants in how the main questions are answered.

In this approach, you will basically use the research question and the interview guide to develop a coding frame consisting of a set of categories, to which you will allocate statements from the interview. Qualitative content analysis is helpful if you have a large data set of many interviews and need to reduce the material. It is also helpful if you are mainly interested in reducing the ambiguity of statements and doing a rather quick categorization of statements to answer your research question. The particular statements, views or experiences of the single interviewee do not play a major role in the analysis. Exploration and discovery of new insights are also not the central focus of such an analysis. Coding mainly means allocating material to existing categories.

Planning the Analysis of an Interview

Analysing interviews is a major step in doing an interview study but it is also a central issue in designing interview research. In analysing an interview, the researchers continue their work as a constructing listener to what the interviewees have to say. The framework the researchers construct for the analysis will be decisive for what is taken up in the analysis and how. In this context, the *six F's of designing interview research* become relevant as well, from finding and foreseeing to formulating, from framing to foregrounding and focusing (see Box 16.8).

Box 16.8 Research in the real world

Planning the analysis of an interview

Planning the analysis of an interview also includes suggestions for preparing (1) the analytical framework (making up the data, protection of data and privacy, general guidelines on how to analyse, on the comparative perspective, the role of the single

(Continued)

case, etc.) and (2) the analytical approach to the interview material (focusing on specific topics, processes, statements, etc.).

Steps involved in planning the analysis of an interview	Six F's of designing interview research
Reflect in advance again	
1. Which of the interviewees will be most relevant for the analysis?	Finding
2. What is the research question behind analysing the interview?	Focusing
Steps for preparing the framework of listening for the interview analysis	
3. Reflect on which interviewees should be compared, might be fruitful for constructing a typology or patterns, etc.	Framing
4. Clarify what the analysis will mainly be about and what role the single interviewees will have in it.	Foreseeing
5. Frame (in keywords) the aims of analysing the interview, including what would be an end point for analysing it.	Framing
Steps for preparing the interview analysis	
6. Overview of subjects of interest for the interview analysis.	Foreseeing
7. What themes are of central interest?	Foregrounding
8. What area or period of the interviewees' life and which biographical events can provide information about the central topic(s)?	Foreseeing
9. Identify areas, topics and content for summarizing the interviews, for example in short descriptions of the interview.	Formulating
10. For every area, identify statements that might illustrate the interviewee as clearly and unambiguously as possible. Note, also, what context information about the interviewees should be included in the short descriptions and the later analysis.	Focusing
11. Note down some keywords for central issues that should be covered in the analysis and areas that should be addressed.	Foregrounding
12. Note down some keywords for looking for connections between aspects that should be linked in the analysis.	Finding
13. Think about where the categories should mainly come from – the material, the questions in the interview guide, or the literature?	Foreseeing

Interpretation and Discovery

The steps discussed so far are, first, about the make-up and elaboration of the interview data. Second, they are about ordering, classifying and structuring the data by using codes and coding systems. Sometimes, in qualitative content analysis, for example, the aim is also to identify frequencies of statements or to reduce the variety of statements to paraphrases. But in all the methods mentioned above, these steps do not answer the question of meanings – what is the meaning of coding a statement in a category (whether the code and category come from the material or from the literature) to answer the study's research question? This meaning can be identified in a process of interpretations. Interpretation is the core activity of qualitative data analysis for understanding or explaining what is in the data – whether explicitly mentioned or implicitly alluded to and to be elaborated on. Coding is a preparatory step for accessing the data and making them ready for interpretation. Interpretation means to understand the internal logic of an excerpt of the data or to put it into context: for example, what has an interview statement about patients' needs got to do with the fact that it comes from a male physician and not from a female nurse? As Willig holds:

> Interpretation is the challenge at the heart of qualitative research. Without interpretation, we cannot make sense of our data. As qualitative researchers, we aim to find out more about people's experiences, their thoughts, feelings and social practices. To achieve this aim, we need to ask questions about their meaning and significance; we need to make connections between different components and aspects of the data in order to increase our understanding. In other words, we need to make the data meaningful through a process of interpretation. (2014b, p. 136)

Interpretation links statements and answers back to the personal situation of the interviewees, to the circumstances in their life situation and social group and to the phenomenon that is being studied. Interpretation is also the approach for discovering new insights in a field, in a process or about the situation of the interviewee(s) and about the phenomenon under study. The following questions from Charmaz et al. (2019, pp. 8–9) will act as guidelines in analysing excerpts of the data – with the aim of coding or with the aim of interpretation:

- What is happening here?
- How do we know what is happening?
- What knowledge can we gain from the excerpt about individuals and their social world?
- How does the excerpt reveal people's situations and social locations?
- How does the excerpt illuminate major concepts?

These guiding questions mean interpretations should be referred to material in the interview, which could be quoted and thus go beyond speculation or assumptions.

Reflecting the interactional context

For focus groups, Halkier (2010) has emphasized that we should take the interaction context into account, not just the content: When a statement relevant for the analysis is made, we should consider to whom in the group this statement refers, and to which statement, and what was said before, and so on. This idea can be transferred to analysing interviews: We should take into account who said something, which of the interviewer's questions it referred to, how exactly it was said, in which interactional context it came up, and so on. Practically, this means that we should look at the context of statements, have an eye on the interaction between interviewer and interviewee, take into account whether something was said spontaneously in a different context or was stimulated by a question referring to the topic. This means that the qualitative analysis of interviews should be more than analysing the contents and also include the analysis of the conversation and the conversational context of statements. Part of the analysis should be that statements are not only 'picked' from the transcript and treated as context-free. Referring statements back to their conversational context is an important step in analysing interviews.

Analysing narrative interviews

To analyse narrative interviews (see Chapter 12), it is suggested that you first identify all passages of the text where the interviewee gives a narrative presentation and that you focus on them, before including other formats (e.g. descriptions or explanations). Rosenthal and Fischer-Rosenthal (2004) accordingly suggest six steps for analysing narrative interviews:

1. Analysis of biographical data (data of events)
2. Text and thematic field analysis (sequential analysis of textual segments from the self-presentation in the interview)
3. Reconstruction of the case history (life as lived)
4. Detailed analysis of individual textual locations
5. Contrasting the life story as narrated with life as lived
6. Formation of types.

The questions Lucius-Hoene and Deppermann (2002, p. 321; see also 2000) have developed as a heuristic for analysing a narrative text are helpful for analysing other kinds of interviews as well:

- What is presented?
- How is it presented?
- For what purpose is this presented – and not something else?
- For what purpose is this presented now – and not at a different time?
- For what purpose is this presented in this way – and not in a different way?

What is common to these methods for analysing narrative data is that they take the overall form of the narrative as a starting point for the interpretation of statements, which are seen in the context of the process of the narrative. Furthermore, they include a formal analysis of the material: which passages of the text are narrative passages, and what other forms of text can be found?

The one and only interpretation, or a multitude of possible interpretations?

Interpretations of the same interview can vary according to the theoretical background but also to the methodological approach applied to the material, as Box 16.9 may illustrate.

Box 16.9   Research in the real world

Ways of analysing an interview

In their book, Wertz et al. (2011) take one interview and analyse it by five different methods – among them grounded theory, discourse analysis and narrative research (see Chapter 12). The book also provides some detailed comparisons of what the various methods produced as differences in analysing the text and what was similar. It also becomes evident that not only does the procedure of how the text is analysed vary, but also the aspects put in the foreground vary across the five approaches. Thus, we find 'Constructing a grounded theory of loss and regaining a valued self' (Charmaz, 2011) as the approach and result of the grounded theory approach, while the discourse analysis of the same material focuses on 'Enhancing oneself, diminishing others' (McMullen, 2011). Hence, this book provides an interesting insight into the differences and commonalities between various empirical approaches to the same transcript.

Comparison and Generalization

As already said at the beginning of this chapter, the aim of analysing research interviews is not to diagnose the interviewees or to describe their current situation and need for intervention as in a therapeutic interview. At the same time, qualitative interviews are not conducted to obtain results that can be generalized to society, to adolescents or vulnerable people per se (as in a survey). But when analysing interviews, we do aim at some kind of generalization beyond the single interviewee. The way to achieve this is through comparison. Statements are compared with other statements from the same interview to develop a pattern of, for example, coping with specific challenges. And they are compared with statements by other interviewees to identify commonalities and differences and thus to develop a typology, for example. In the end, findings mostly refer to the issue under study and not to the single case that was interviewed. Thus, comparison and generalization (in a limited and focused way) are part of a qualitative analysis of research interviews.

Postcolonial Approaches to Analysing Interview Data

The methodological discussion of a postcolonial and indigenous qualitative research focuses less on the analysis of data and more on how to collect them. In Chilisa's (2020) textbook, this step is often listed in sentences referring to 'data collection and analysis'. Often, references are made to standard procedures of data analysis such as thematic analysis and to general textbooks of social research such as Neuman (2000) and critiques of them. We find suggestions mainly on a practical level referring to how to include communities in the data analysis: 'Community members involved regarding their interpretation of the findings within the local social and cultural context' (Chilisa, 2020, p. 274). Here suggestions by Hill et al. (1997) concerning consensual qualitative research are a starting point (see Box 16.10).

Box 16.10 Research in the real world

Analysing interviews in indigenous research

Terry L. Cross, Kathleen Earle, Holly Echo-Hawk Solie and Kathryn Mannes of the National Indian Child Welfare Association in Portland, US, did a study based on focus groups and key informant interviews with providers and parents that examined the efficacy of five American Indian children's mental health projects funded by the Center for Mental Health Services (CMHS) (Cross et al., 2000). The data were collected and analysed referring to the 'medicine wheel' and its four quadrants (2000, pp. 22–4): 'the context includes culture, community, family, peers, work, school, and social history. The mind includes cognitive processes such as thoughts, memories, knowledge, and emotional processes such as feelings, defenses and self-esteem. The body includes all physical aspects, such as genetic inheritance, gender and condition, as well as sleep, nutrition and substance use. The spirit area includes both positive and negative learned teachings and practices, as well as positive and negative metaphysical or innate forces. This gives an orientation on which aspects to include in the analysis but less on specific steps and practices' (2000, pp. 20–1). For our context, the suggestions for an extensive analysis of interview data in the context of indigenous research are very interesting, but do not include any specific methods or procedures for how to analyse the data.

Working with several languages in analysing interviews

Suh et al. (2009), working in nursing at Seoul National University in Korea, have discussed how to take the use of other languages into account in the analysis of interview data, where the team mainly consists of English-language researchers.

They suggest three strategies: (1) to translate the interviews before the analysis (2009, p. 197); (2) a contextual comparison during the analysis, which means the 'translation should occur with constant contextual comparisons between meanings in two languages during the categorization of the codes' (p. 198); and (3) 'translating the research findings into English after the study is completed' (p. 198).

Steps, Aims and Criteria in Preparing and Doing the Analysis of an Interview

Table 16.1 summarizes the steps in preparing narrative interviews and the criteria for evaluating their outcome.

Table 16.1 Steps, aims and criteria in preparing and doing the analysis of an interview

Six F's of designing interview research	Steps	Aims and actions	Criteria
Framing	1. Preparing the analysis	• Prepare a documentation sheet for the context of the interview (demographic data, etc.) • Transfer the interviews into a data set • Reflect on the research questions for the analysis • Start analysing the first interviews and check back how it works	• Does the documentation sheet cover the relevant information for the research question? • How does the documentation work for analysing the first interview? • Does the research question cover the area under study? • Is the data set of interviews adequately constructed for the analysis?
Foreseeing	2. Define the methodological principle for analysing the interviews	• Prepare a good focus for beginning the analysis of the interview and ensure it is clear to work with	• Do you have a clear idea of how to begin and where to go to in the analysis?
Formulating	3. Write short descriptions of the interviews	• Collect the relevant information from the interviews	• Do the descriptions give an overview of the case(s)? • Is all the information included that is necessary for contextualizing the interviewee's narrative or answers?

(Continued)

Table 16.1 (Continued)

Six F's of designing interview research	Steps	Aims and actions	Criteria
Foregrounding	4. The initial open coding	• Start analysing parts of the material for developing codes	• Does the approach encompass relevant aspects of the subjective meanings for the interviewees and their biographies? • Are the first coding approaches open?
Focusing	5. Axial coding	• Try to think about questions for how to link codes • Try to get into the detail of the central parts of the issue under study • Try to increase the depth and richness of coding the interviewee's responses by linking the codes	• Are these questions adequate? • Do they add missing aspects in the analysis of the interview? • Has the analysis of the interview gone into detail and depth?
Foreseeing	6. Develop categories for selective coding or a thematic structure of the case	• Focus on the research question and the case again • Use the documentation sheet	• Does a story line or central category become visible?
Framing	7. Develop a coding frame if you do a content analysis	• Set up a list of categories from the literature	• Does this take the interviewees' cases into account?
Foregrounding	8. Analyse the interactional context of the statements you code	• Give room for analysing the conversation in the interview	• Does additional information become visible?
Finding and Formulating	9. Do an interpretation of the coding and develop patterns or a typology by comparing the interviews	• Choose an appropriate method for interpreting the narratives and answers	• Does the method take the quality of the data into account (e.g. the narrative structure of accounts)?

What You Need to Ask Yourself

In this chapter, we discussed various ways of analysing qualitative data. To use a particular one, you should consult the literature peculiar to that method. The chapter should have shown that there are different aims and understandings of qualitative data analysis, so that you have to decide at some point which one you will subscribe to. A guideline would be how far the analytic method fits your interview format, data and, of course, your research question.

Box 16.11   What you need to ask yourself

Doing interview analysis

1.   Did you turn your interviews into data in an adequate way?
2.   How far can the outcome of your interviews be analysed with the specific method of analysis you have in mind?
3.   Is the analytic approach too limited or too differentiated for the level of complexity of your data?

What You Need to Succeed

This chapter has provided an introduction to turning interviews into data and to how to analyse them. It should help you to understand and contextualize what of the earlier chapters' content (e.g. the sampling, the framework of listening and ways of asking) should be taken into account. The questions in Box 16.12 will help you to to review your key take-home points from this chapter around interview research.

Box 16.12   What you need to succeed

Doing interview analysis

1.   Do I understand what turning interviews into data is about?
2.   Do I know what 'coding' means and that there are different forms of coding?
3.   Do I see that coding leads to results that have to be interpreted?

What you have learned

- Analysing interviews includes turning interviews into data.
- Coding is a way of analysing data.
- Interpretation turns such analysis into insights and answers to research questions.
- Analysing data is part of constructing a framework for listening to what interviewees have to say.
- It is also an issue of designing interview research.

Exercises

In the following exercises, you are again invited to reflect on some of the main issues in this chapter. Then you are invited to apply the topics of this chapter to the development of a project of your own. Hence, the exercises are a combination of reflection and prospection.

Exercise 16.1

Reflecting on the Chapter: The Analysis of Interviews in an Existing Study

1. Look through a journal for a qualitative study based on interviews (e.g. Neill, 2010). Try to identify which form of interview and which kind of analysis was used in it.

Exercise 16.2

Planning Your Own Research with Interviews

1. Think of your own study and how you would analyse the interviews you are planning, or have already conducted, to answer your research question.

What's next

This chapter gives you a comparative and more detailed overview of analytic methods in qualitative research:

Flick, U. (2014). Mapping the Field. In U. Flick (Ed.), *The SAGE Handbook of Qualitative Data Analysis* (pp. 3–18). London: Sage.

Gibbs's short book outlines a general account of analysing data and provides a comparative view on the available software in this context:

Gibbs, G. (2018). *Analysing Qualitative Data* (2nd ed.). London: Sage.

This book gives a short, comparative overview of the various ways of doing grounded theory analysis:

Flick, U. (2018). *Doing Grounded Theory*. London: Sage.

This article summarizes Mayring's approach to qualitative content analysis:

Mayring, P. (2000). Qualitative Content Analysis [28 paragraphs]. *Forum Qualitative Sozialforschung / Forum: Qualitative Social Research*, 1(2): Art. 20. http://nbn-resolving.de/urn:nbn:de:0114-fqs0002204 (last accessed 13 August 2013).

In this book chapter, Schreier's version of qualitative content analysis is summarized:

Schreier, M. (2014). Qualitative Content Analysis. In U. Flick (Ed.), *The SAGE Handbook of Qualitative Data Analysis* (pp. 170-83). London: Sage.

In this chapter, some applications and the methodological background to thematic coding can be found:

Flick, U. (1995). Social Representations. In R. Harré, J. Smith, & L. v. Langenhove (Eds.), *Rethinking Psychology* (pp. 70-96). London: Sage.

This article reflects on the issues of translation in interviews which were done in a different language:

Suh, E.E., Kagan, S., & Strumpf, N. (2009). Cultural Competence in Qualitative Interview Methods with Asian Immigrants. *Journal of Transcultural Nursing*, 20(2), 194-201. https://doi.org/10.1177/1043659608330059

Doing Interview Research Navigator

How to understand interview research

- What doing interview research means
- Theories and epistemologies of interviewing
- When to choose interviews as a research method
- Methods and formats of interviewing

Designing interview research

- Planning and designing interview research
- How many interviewees: Sampling and saturation
- Accessing and recruiting participants

How to conduct interviews

- How to respect and protect: Ethics of interviewing
- Semi-structured interviews: Working with questions and answers
- Interviewing experts and elites
- Integrating narratives in interviews: Episodic interviews

Doing interviews in context

- How to work with life histories: Narrative interviews
- Working with focus groups as interviews
- Ask (in) the field: Ethnographic and mobile interviewing
- Doing online interviews

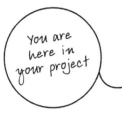

You are here in your project

How to work with interview data

- Working with interview data
- Credibility and transparency: Quality and writing in interview research
- From interviewing to an inner view: Critiques and reflexivity

CREDIBILITY AND TRANSPARENCY

QUALITY AND WRITING IN INTERVIEW RESEARCH

You will:

- understand that the question of quality of interviewing can be seen as a methodological problem,
- see that it is also related to the outcome – what new knowledge we learn from an interview,
- appreciate that quality refers to the whole process of doing interview research,
- know that it has to do with constructing a framework for listening,
- understand that a good design for the study, including the selection of the best method for a study, is central to interview research quality, and
- see that credibility and transparency become visible in writing up interview research.

Approaches to Quality in Qualitative Research

The question of how the quality of qualitative research can be assessed has been discussed ever since this kind of research was rediscovered in the 1960s. Different from quantitative research, this discussion has not led to a generally accepted set of criteria. The discussion has proliferated in various fields (such as health or evaluation) and for various approaches in qualitative research. However, we can distinguish several threads of discussion. (1) Some authors pursue a rather narrowly focused but at the same time generalist concept: narrowly focused because the wider question of quality is reduced to formulating criteria (e.g. for the validity of interview statements); generalist because – often, at least – the hope is in the background that the criteria are the same as or at least similar to quantitative research and that they will fulfil the same function here as there. (2) Other authors prefer a more widely framed but at the same time specific concept: widely framed because the question of quality is not reduced to meeting methodological criteria; specific because it is assumed that for qualitative research other paths for assessing quality than in quantitative research and maybe specific paths for particular approaches should be taken. In our current context, the focus will be on (1) the quality of qualitative interview research and (2) the embeddedness of this method in a specific understanding of the qualitative research process. (3) We will extend the discussion to focus on presenting and writing about qualitative interview research.

Quality in Doing Qualitative Interview Research

As noted above, there has been a long and extended discussion about how to define and assess the quality of qualitative research (see Flick, 2018e, as an overview), which did not (yet) lead to satisfying answers or even a set of accepted criteria. Among the criteria which have remained a point of reference, Lincoln and Guba's (1985) list of credibility, **trustworthiness**, dependability, transferability and confirmability as criteria for qualitative research, is preeminent, in particular their concept of credibility. This is demonstrated by the discussion on quality in grounded theory research (e.g. in Charmaz and Thornberg, 2020) in which credibility is still mentioned as a major criterion.

Credibility

In this and other contexts, credibility is considered to be the main criterion to fulfil, which will be discussed briefly here and then in more detail in a later section in this chapter. Lincoln and Guba (1985) outline five components of the credibility of qualitative research:

- increasing the likelihood that credible results will be produced by a 'prolonged engagement' and 'persistent observation' in the field and the triangulation of different methods, researchers and data;
- **'peer debriefing'**: regular meetings with other people who are not involved in the research in order to disclose one's own blind spots and to discuss working hypotheses and results with them;
- the analysis of negative cases in the sense of **analytic induction**;
- appropriateness of the terms of reference of interpretations and their assessment;
- 'member checks' in the sense of communicative validation of data and interpretations with members of the fields under study.

These features of credibility are relevant for assessing interview research. The first sounds a bit tailored to participant observation. For interviewing, it emphasizes that interviewers should not just apply an overly pragmatic approach of collecting statements but should also view interviewing as being embedded in a process, which starts a good while before the actual interview and emphasizes that context and not just content should be taken into account. Peer debriefing and member checks will be addressed later in this chapter. The adequacy of interpretation and the reflection on negative cases (which contradict the results of a study in general, or do not fit a pattern or typology) is a case of reflexivity (see Chapter 18). However, credibility is also a prominent point of reference, when the use of criteria is critically discussed in qualitative research, as it is difficult to define how much credibility is given in a concrete study or what **benchmarks** of (enough or not enough) credibility are like. In quantitative research, such benchmarks are an important feature of quality criteria (see Flick, 2018e, 2020, for such discussions). The consequence is to take the above features as strategies for increasing credibility rather than a criterion.

Quality as a methodological issue (only)?

Weiss (1994, p. 147) discussed this topic as 'issues of validity: Do respondents tell the truth, the whole truth, and nothing but the truth?' This metaphorical formulation reminds one more of a police or court investigation, but it sheds light on the problem: Can we trust the information provided in an interview? Can the respondents and we trust their memories when answering our questions? How far is this problem a general one and how far does it depend on the concrete interview situation or the interviewer's skills and mistakes?

What's new?

Going back to the early grounded theory research works of Glaser and Strauss and more recently to Charmaz (2014), the quality of qualitative interview research has much to do with the outcomes of a study. Charmaz and Thornberg (2020) discuss the originality and usefulness of the findings in addition to their credibility (2020, p. 11). Such criteria extend the quality and criteria discussion known from quantitative research from a methodological focus on the data collection to a wider focus on the process of doing interview research. We find a number of suggestions for such a process focus on quality.

Quality of Interviewing in the Process

Briggs (1986, pp. 94–111), for example, has suggested a four-step model of methodological sophistication for doing interviews. The first phase refers to *learning* to ask – by 'knowing the communicative norms of the society'. The second phase is to *frame an appropriate methodology*, which means to select an adequate method for interviewing, to design its application including a detailed but not too intrusive (e.g. audio instead of video) recording. Phase three refers to *reflexivity* (see Chapter 18) in the interviewing process, which may include listening to interview recordings with colleagues, consultants, peers to identify problems in the communication and gaps in the data. Phase four is about *analysing the interviews* as 'cooperative products of interactions between two or more persons who assume different roles and who frequently come from contrasting social, cultural, and/or linguistic backgrounds' (p. 102). This means that analysis should not only focus on single statements or utterances by the interviewee, which can be used in coding, but also on the structure of the interview and the communication in it. Briggs suggests having an eye on meta-communicative features – how far did the interviewer manage to establish an adequate rapport also on the level of communication and wording? And how far are statements contextualized in the way they were made and in what was said before or what the exact question was that the interviewer asked – which is not necessarily the one in the interview guide?

Quality Before and After the Interview

Rubin and Rubin (2005, pp. 61–70) have suggested a number of goals to reach in good interviews (or in other words: criteria for interviewing) with a focus on the research process. (1) Interviews should be *fresh and real*, which includes the point that interviewers 'as much as possible, rely on **first-hand knowledge**' (p. 61). Interviewers should try to find people as interviewees who are in the situation under study and not only interviewees who can talk about people in that situation. (2) Interviews should be *balanced and thorough*, which means without major information gaps (p. 62), and include a range of perspectives on the issue under study. (3) Interviews should be *accurate and credible* (p. 64). You can increase accuracy by recording and detailed transcription of interviews (instead of taking notes), and by transcribing immediately after the interview. 'Credibility is achieved in part by showing that you have talked with people who are informed about your research concerns' (p. 65). Interviews will be more instructive when interviewees talk about their own experiences and not just about what they know through hearsay. If necessary and ethically acceptable, interviewers should confront and challenge people with their questions. Beyond the interview situation, credibility has a lot to do with transparency (what happened in the interview, how did the interviewer deal with contradictions and vagueness, how was probing applied in the interview?) in the report about the research (see below). (4) Interviews and what they produce as insights should be *rich and detailed* (p. 69). This means that questions and answers should be as clear, focused and precise as possible, and where the answers (or stories) remain vague and general, the interviewer should probe and insist on details and more complex descriptions being provided by the interviewee.

Rubin and Rubin's suggestions show that the quality of interviews and of the data and insights they produce depends on: (1) the preparation of the interviewer and the questions; (2) the interaction and probing in the interview as well as the documentation of the interview situation; and (3) the transparency in the presentation of the research and the interview situation. Quality depends on three forms of interaction: that of the interviewers with their issues (how well did they understand their issue and pre-process the interview situation?), with the interviewee (the art of asking questions and of probing) and with the readers (transparency of the report about findings and about the way they were produced in the contact with the interviewee).

Practical Aspects of Advancing Quality in Qualitative Interviews

Some aspects linked to the topic of reflexivity will be addressed in the next chapter. But there are some more practical aspects, which can be helpful for advancing quality in interviewing.

Evaluation of questions in the interview guide

We have focused on the development of interview guides and forms of questions to ask in interviews in Chapters 9–15 in some detail. If you want to check your instruments before conducting your interviews, a list of questions for reflecting on the way you constructed your interview guide and how you formulated your questions can be helpful. Ulrich (1999) suggests asking oneself, for example: Why are you asking this specific question (theoretical relevance; link to the research question)? Why did you formulate the question in this way (is it clear, unambiguous)? Why did you position this question here, and how are types of question spread across the guide? What are relations between various questions?

Here the focus is on question wording, intentions behind questions and the structure of the interview guide, also with the idea in the background that questions will influence what interviewees answer to the next and following questions. Furthermore, the idea of using a variety of question types can be taken up by checking an interview guide with Ulrich's (1999) suggestions just mentioned. But formulating the questions is just one important part in preparing to do an interview successfully.

Creating a specific setting for the interview situation as a second part of the preparation can be as important as the actual questions.

Stage directions for interviewing

For this purpose, Hermanns (2004) has made some helpful suggestions for preparing and conducting the interview itself. He sees the interview interaction as an evolving drama. The interviewer's task is to facilitate the development of this drama. The author also suggests interviewers should avoid being too anxious about using a recording device during the interview: he emphasizes that most interviewees have no problem with the recording of an interview and that it is often the interviewers who project their own uneasiness of being recorded onto the interviewee.

Hermanns has formulated a set of 'stage directions' for interviewing (2004, pp. 212–13). Here you will find suggestions on such matters as: how to explain to the interviewees what you expect from them during the interview; how to create a good atmosphere in the interview; and how to give room to allow your interviewees to open up. A very important point in his suggestions is that you should try to discover the life world of the interviewee during the interview and not theoretical concepts, which are on the agenda of the data analysis. You should also be aware that research questions are not the same as interview questions. In the interview situation, you should try to use everyday language instead of scientific concepts in the questions. Discovering theoretical concepts and using scientific concepts is something for the data analysis process; using concrete everyday wording is what, in contrast, should happen in your questions and the interview.

Assessing the quality of the interview situation

Whereas the above suggestions address the planning of the interview and the interview situation, Brinkmann and Kvale (2015) have suggested a number of criteria for evaluating the actual interview. They can be used for assessing the quality of what happens in and what comes out of the interview, and include:

- The extent of spontaneous, rich, specific and relevant answers from the interviewee
- The shortest of the interviewer's questions and the longest of the subjects' answers
- The degree to which the interviewer follows up and clarifies the meanings of the relevant aspects of the answers
- To a large extent, the interview being interpreted throughout the interview
- The interviewer attempting to verify his or her interpretations of the subjects' answers in the course of the interview
- The interview being 'self-reported', a self-reliant story that hardly requires additional explanation. (2015, p. 192)

These criteria can be used for asking how far the interviewer succeeded in construct-ing a framework for listening to the interviewee; which means having clear and self-explanatory statements rather than vague ones needing clarification and suffering from too much presence of the interviewer's own utterances in the interview.

Transcription quality

Interview (and focus group) analysis is based on transcriptions (see Chapter 16) in most cases. In general, the aim is to produce verbatim documents of 'what transpired' (Poland, 2001, p. 631) in the data collection situation. But, as already discussed in Chapter 16, the relation between recording and transcription is not a one-to-one transfer, and nor is the relation between the interview situation and the transcript. In both relations, aspects can be lost, such as non-verbal behaviour in the recording, or highlighted as a non-verbal but recorded behaviour in the transcription, such as sighs or emphasis on words, and so on.

Poland identifies a number of challenges in meeting the goal of documenting 'what transpired'. In comparing audio recordings with the transcriptions, he found a num-ber of deviances or repairs of what was said in what was written down. The author also describes errors resulting from moving back and forth in the recording to understand better what was said and then having a problem in finding the exact spot in the recording again (2001, p. 633). Mishearing words for similarly sounding words is another source of mistakes ('an evaluation model' was turned into 'and violation of the model' – 2001, p. 632). What is in the context of how something is said is some-times difficult to note down and also the act of recording already has implications for the quality of data (see also Jenks, 2018, on issues of recording and transcription). These implications are intensified because in most studies the data analysis is only applied to the transcript and the original recording is shelved and stored.

Member checks and credibility

For Lincoln and Guba, member checks are 'the most crucial technique for establishing credibility' (1985, p. 314). This technique has been discussed by using different labels, sometimes with different intentions. Labels are communicative or respondent validation, member validation, consensual validation, member reflection, participant feedback, and so on, but refer to the same basic idea. The common feature is that consensus of partici-pants is taken as a criterion or as an indicator for assessing research products – from data to results. Bloor (1997) notes three basic forms of member validation:

> The validation of the researcher's taxonomies by the attempted prediction
> of members' descriptions in the field ... ; the validation of the researcher's
> analysis by the demonstrated ability of the researcher to 'pass' as a member
> ... ; the validation of the researcher's analysis by asking collectivity members

to judge the adequacy of the researcher's analysis, taking results back to the field and asking 'if the members recognize, understand and accept one's description' (Douglas, 1976, p. 131). (Bloor, 1997, p. 41)

On a practical level, researchers can send the participants (1) the transcript for commenting and maybe correcting, or (2) summaries of the statements in the transcript, or (3) case summaries of their own interview or its analysis for comment, or (4) the draft report on the research, or (5) the practical implications drawn from the data and the analysis. In principle, the idea is that participants' consent to one or the other documents listed above will add to the study's credibility and transparency.

However, there are a number of questions linked to this idea in practice. Sending a transcript may be confusing for participants not used to reading their own talk or to what transcripts with the additional notations (of sighs, for example) look like. Uncommented sending of a transcript may cause irritation, or even crises, if the topic is sensitive or providing a new view on how badly one's life has developed, for example. If the material provided for review goes beyond the interviewee's own interview, it may be sufficient that the researcher summarizes what other participants said (as in a focus group interview) and what the trends in statements of several participants were. Here also data protection issues may come up such as information about the other participants. If the report to comment upon includes a strong interpretation of what was said, it may over-challenge the participants emotionally to give their feedback. Other issues arise when some of the participants agree with the results or the material they were sent and others do not. The question then is how many participants have to be commenting positively on the material, and how many can reject it or be critical, and the researchers can still continue to use the materials and their interpretation. What happens with cases in which the comments were negative? Does that mean these interviewees have be taken out of the sample and data set, and so on?

In general, it should be reflected on whether it is a good idea to confront the participants with their statements, transcripts or other material alone or whether such a confrontation should be embedded in a second meeting with the researcher. In Chapter 13, I presented an example in which the results of an interview analysis were presented to the (same) participants in focus group discussions, with the aim of member checking but also of developing the practical implications from these results together with the members (see Box 13.3 in Chapter 13).

Peer debriefing

One alternative and/or addition is the use of peer debriefing for improving the quality of interview research and for collecting a different view on one's own proceedings. In funded research and in publications, peer reviews play a more and more important role, but these reviews are mostly anonymous and are judgements rather than commentaries and dialogues. Peer debriefing means to seek open discussions with other researchers or experts about one's own research and how it develops or progresses. Lincoln and Guba (1985) suggest peer debriefing for the development of research designs, for discussing working hypotheses and for discussing results. Here again, peer debriefing is a way to collect second opinions, different views and diversity in the perspectives on the material and the research process. Peer debriefing as well can be based on sending materials such as reports, lists of implications, excerpts of interpretations, drafts of instruments such as the interview guide and the like. An alternative is to arrange meetings with peers for presenting, discussing and commenting on the materials. Again, this is a step in advancing the credibility – Lincoln and Guba (1985) had listed this step in their concept – and transparency of the research.

Validity Concepts in Indigenous Research

Chilisa (2020) refers to the concept of cultural validity Kirkhart (2013) has developed in the context of evaluation. This concept includes nine dimensions for improving the multicultural validity of evaluation (2013, p. 11): *history* (of place, people and programme and knowledge of cultural traditions), *location, power, voice* (whose perspectives are amplified, whose silenced), *time, relationship, return* (benefit for those being studied), *plasticity* (which Chilisa, 2020, p. 140, defines as 'the ability to be molded, to receive new information, recognize and change response to new experience') and *reflexivity*. Chilisa discusses a postcolonial indigenous framework of validity, in which she takes up Guba and Lincoln's concept of credibility and emphasizes aspects like fairness, ontological and educative authenticity and the role of specific communities as arbiters of quality (2020, pp. 219–20). These authors contextualize validity in the framework of culture and community much more than in strictly methodological terms, when they emphasize the role of integrating participants in the evaluation processes and in the assessment of research.

Trustworthiness

This is another prominent criterion in qualitative research discussed by and since Lincoln and Guba (1985). More recently, Cloutier and Ravasi (2021) discuss using tables to enhance trustworthiness in qualitative research in the context of organizational research as tables help not only increase transparency about data collection, analysis, and findings, but also—and no less importantly—organize and analyze data effectively' (2021, p. 113). In management research, Pratt et al. (2020) argue to uncouple transparency from replication (see below) and discuss a wider framework for trustworthiness of qualitative research. Birt et al. (2016) discuss whether member checking can be seen as a tool to enhance trustworthiness: 'The trustworthiness of results is the bedrock of high quality qualitative research. Member checking, also known as participant or respondent validation, is a technique for exploring the credibility of results' (2016, p. 1802). In the context of evaluation research, Abraham et al. (2021) write about developing trustworthiness and preserving the richness of qualitative data in large data sets. These examples from several areas of research illustrate that trustworthiness, just as credibility, has become a kind of overarching criterion for assessing the quality of interviewing and qualitative research in general (see also Flick, 2018e, for a broader discussion).

Credibility and Transparency

The ways of advancing credibility in qualitative interview research will be successful if they are also seen as a way of making research transparent. The credibility of research is also an issue of transparency and writing. In this context, transparency becomes relevant in several ways for enhancing the quality of qualitative research. Research transparency is 'defined as the obligation to make data, analysis, methods, and interpretive choices underlying their claims visible in a way that allows others to evaluate them' (Moravcsik, 2019, p. 2). Transparency in general means making the research process, its steps and the decisions that influenced how data and results were produced, understandable in the broadest sense to readers. It also means to document how the research question was developed in the first step and how it perhaps was changed in the course of the project. As well, it should be documented why the particular persons, groups, cases, situations, and so on, were selected as empirical material – what the rationale of the sampling was and how the researchers made it work. Following what was said before, the documentation and the report on the project and the research should provide insights into why specific methods were selected, perhaps which alternatives were discussed and why they were rejected. Information about claims to quality in the project, how the criteria were established, who was involved in defining them and, finally, how they were realized, is another issue of documentation.

Transparency starts from a detailed documentation of the research process, its steps and the decisions taken in it. This documentation should find its way into the report about the research and about how results were produced. In the best examples, it should not only make transparent what was done and why, but also allow the reader to obtain an idea of how different the results would have been if the researchers had taken a different decision at some specific point. Then it comes close to the function that Lüders sees for the report about the research – that it 'is the only basis for answering the question of the quality of the investigation' (1995, p. 325).

Reichertz (1992) goes one step beyond a text-centred treatment of credibility. He makes it clear that this form of persuasion concerning credibility is produced not only in the text but also in the interaction of author, text and reader: 'It is not the way of accounting claimed for in the writing which is relevant for the reader, but the attitude of accounting which is shown in the text, which of course always has to use semiotic means, and these are means which are sensitive to cheating' (1992, p. 346).

Transparency and the transparency crisis

Transparency, as outlined above, has been a feature in the discussion about the quality of qualitative research with interviews and beyond for quite some time. More recently, however, it has become rather a hot topic. After the so-called **replication crisis** in psychological (experimental) research has shown that quite some classical studies could not be replicated to reach the same or at least similar results (see Stroebe and Strack, 2014), a general discussion about research transparency began. This discussion also affected qualitative research, although here transparency and quality of research had not been associated with replication. As Moravcsik (2019, p. 2) holds, a transparency revolution is under way across the social sciences as publishers and funders, for example, press researchers 'to make their data, analysis, and methods public'. Three dimensions of research transparency are discussed: data transparency is the claim to make the data available, so that other researchers can reanalyse them. Analytic transparency refers to analytic and interpretive procedures in a study, so that other researchers can reconstruct the data analysis. Production transparency makes the method choices and the research design in a study public. Skukauskaite (2012), for example, discusses how to make the transcription and the theoretical background to the way the researchers carried it out transparent.

In any discussion about such claims, it becomes evident that such an understanding of research transparency is not compatible with qualitative research. Such data transparency reveals so much about an interviewee that data protection is violated. Analytic transparency understood in the way outlined above would not only need to make data and procedures available, but would need to discuss the epistemology and theory behind the analysis and interpretation.

There are several trends linked to transparency claims. One is to mix up transparency and replication (see above), while the other is to see data archiving as a solution to the claim for data and analytic transparency. Some authors see **CAQDAS** as the solution to how to make qualitative research transparent (O'Kane et al., 2021), but that will only support production transparency.

At the same time, the word limits of journal articles have been reduced now by several editors and publishers, which makes transparency even more complicated for qualitative researchers. As a way to make transparency possible, Moravcsik (2019, p. 8) discusses **'active citation'**, which means articles come with an appendix to which there will be a link in the published article. Such an appendix would include several 'entries' (i.e. files) to make the material available and transparent. Every entry includes:

1. 'a verbatim excerpt from the textual source (if ethical, legal, or logistical limitations require it, a description may be substituted);
2. an annotation explaining how the author interprets the source to support the corresponding claim in the main text;
3. a complete citation; and
4. optionally, a link to or scan of the full source' (2019, p. 8).

Thus, to do qualitative research in a way that meets high standards and expectations is one thing. To address the issue of quality in the research process – by meeting standards, by using strategies, and so on – is a second. But this will only become visible as quality in qualitative research, if the researchers manage to communicate their aims and claims, their strategies and standards and how they worked with them, to the readers of their research.

These issues and discussions may not (yet) apply to all studies with qualitative interviews, but this short overview demonstrates why transparency is not only a general claim for qualitative research but also one that might endanger some of the central features of qualitative research. At the same time, looking at publications of qualitative studies shows that they do not always meet the basic standards of transparency in the presentations and write-ups about the research.

Making Interview Research Transparent – Writing Research

In this way, writing about research is maybe the most important part of qualitative research if we want to assess the goodness of research and if we want to allow readers to assess it, thus making transparent what we did in our study. Writing then becomes not only a technical problem, but also an issue of reflexivity – but in a different sense from what has been discussed so vehemently as the crisis of representation (Denzin and Lincoln, 2000). Writing about research and the procedures used in it (see Flick, 2018a, Ch. 30) becomes an important instrument for conveying what was done in the project, how it was done and how well it was done.

Making research visible through writing about it

It has long been discussed that only writing about it makes research visible at all:

> Research experiences have to be transformed into texts and to be understood
> on the basis of texts. A research process has findings only when and as far
> as these can be found in a report, no matter whether and which experiences
> were made by those who were involved in the research. (Wolff, 1987, p. 333)

In this context, writing plays a role in qualitative research in four ways:

- for presenting the findings of a project;
- for making findings relevant in contexts of implementation;
- as a starting point for evaluating the proceedings which led to them and thus the results themselves;
- as a point of departure for reflexive considerations about the overall status of the research altogether.

In Box 17.1 a study is presented which looked at the combination of transparency and **replicability** for interviews with participants from management elites.

Box 17.1   Research in the real world

Transparency in elite interviews in management research

Herman Aguinis from the School of Business, George Washington University, US, and Angelo M. Solarino from Leeds University Business School, UK, did a study about the role of transparency and its link to replicability in management research (Aguinis and Solarino, 2019). They first set up 12 transparency criteria – among them: kind of qualitative method, research setting, sampling procedures, documenting interactions with participants, data coding and first-order codes, data analysis and second- and higher-order codes and data disclosure (see 2019, pp. 1295–6). They provided definitions for these criteria and why each is necessary for replicability and they distinguish three types of replication: 'Exact replication' means that a 'study is replicated with the same population and the same procedures' (p. 1297), whereas empirical replication refers to a different population but the same methods, and conceptual replication refers to the same population and different methods. For their study, they analysed 52 articles published in the *Journal of Strategic Management*, in which the authors had done elite interviews (see Chapter 10) with elite informants (members of top management teams). The articles did not have to mention transparency explicitly, but Aguinis and Solarino discuss how this issue is addressed in them. They found: 'None of the 52 studies we examined [was] sufficiently transparent to allow for exact replication' (p. 1305), whereas some of the criteria relevant for conceptual replication was met by more of the studies and is seen as the more adequate version for qualitative studies with (elite or other forms of) interviewing.

The study discussed in Box 17.1 highlights the concept of transparency as a demand for qualitative research but at the same time its limitation as a criterion for qualitative research when it is linked to replicability in the way it was conceptualized in natural sciences and psychology (where it does not work all the time either). In Box 17.2, the planning for making an interview study transparent is outlined.

An interesting aspect in this discussion is the trend to make qualitative data available in archives and also for reanalysing them by other researchers (see Chapter 16). This is not necessarily linked to the idea of replicability, but the research becomes more transparent (also discussed as 'open science') because of these new forms of availability – once the ethical issues linked to such extended accessibility of interviews are considered (see Chapter 8).

Box 17.2   Research in the real world

Planning to make an interview study transparent

Planning to make an interview study transparent includes suggestions for preparing to make transparent (1) the interview framework (data protection, general guidelines on questions and on the length and type of the conversation) and (2) the conduct of the interview (introducing the subject, initial question, narrative and other questions, etc.).

Steps involved in planning to make an interview study transparent	Six F's of designing interview research
Reflect in advance again	
1. Who were seen to be relevant as potential interviewees?	Finding
2. What is the research question behind the interview?	Focusing
Steps for making the framework for listening in an interview transparent	
3. Reflect on and report what the interviewees knew in advance to be well prepared for the interview and to understand what it was about and what their role should be. Reporting this should start from what the interviewees perhaps already had learned about your study when making the appointment for the interview.	Framing
4. Show what the introduction to the interview was like regarding the following aspects: the purpose and the principle of the interview, ways of recording statements, and data protection. How did you explain what the interview was to be about, e.g. a very personal view; an explanation of how the conversation would proceed and how long it would probably take?	Framing
5. Elucidate how you had planned the interview as an exchange with the interviewee: What kinds of questions were used, and how were they presented (or sent) to the interviewee?	Framing
6. Demonstrate how probing was planned, whether something was answered very briefly or a new aspect resulted from the response.	Foregrounding
7. Clarify how the turns to the next question happened once an aspect had been answered exhaustively and how you continued with probes, etc.	Foregrounding
8. How were questions brought forward which fitted the current answers in the interview?	Foregrounding
9. Explain how the conclusion of the interview was planned, including asking for any additional points and for the interviewee's feedback.	Foreseeing
Steps for making the conduct and content of interviews transparent	
10. Give an overview of subjects of interest for the interview.	Foreseeing
11. What were the themes of central interest?	Foregrounding

Steps involved in planning to make an interview study transparent	Six F's of designing interview research
12. What area of the interviewee's professional, everyday life, for example, was expected to provide information about the central topic(s)?	Foreseeing
13. For each area, how were questions or narrative stimuli framed to motivate the interviewee, as clearly and unambiguously as possible, to talk (answer the questions, tell a story, etc.) comprehensively, for every topic under point 12.?	Formulating
14. For every area, how were questions about relationships, etc. phrased that would stimulate the interviewees, as clearly and unambiguously as possible, to express their views on these relationships or concepts?	Focusing
15. What keywords were used for probing central aspects to return to if the interviewees did not spontaneously mention them?	Foreseeing

Writing about qualitative research is also writing about the field, how research was in the field, how the researchers found access to the field and the people in it. For writing about interviewing, the three basic forms of presenting research that Van Maanen (1988) distinguishes (or tales of the field as he calls them) are a good guide. Four conventions characterize *realist tales*. First, the author is absent from the text: observations, statements and outcomes are reported as facts or documented by using quotations from statements in interviews. Here, interpretations are not presented in subjective formulations. Second, in the presentation, emphasis is placed on the typical forms of what is studied. Therefore, many details are analysed and presented. Third, the viewpoints of the members of a field or of interviewees are emphasized in the presentation: How do they experience their own life in its course? What is health for the interviewees? Further, presentations may seek to give the impression of 'interpretive omnipotence' (1988, p. 51). The interpretation does not stop at subjective viewpoints, but goes beyond them with various and far-reaching interpretations. The authors demonstrate that they are able to provide a grounded interpretation and to transfer the subject's statements to a general level using experience-distant concepts (Geertz, 1974) taken from the social science literature for expressing relations.

Confessional tales is the second form Van Maanen discusses. These are characterized by a personalized authorship and authority. Here, the authors demonstrate the role that they played in what was observed, in their interpretations, and also in the formulations that are used. The authors' viewpoints are treated as an issue in the presentation as well as problems, crises, mistakes, and so on (Van Maanen, 1988, p. 79) in the field. Nevertheless, the researchers' own findings are presented as grounded in the issue that was studied. Naturalness in the presentation is one means of creating the impression of 'a fieldworker and a culture finding each other and, despite some initial spats and misunderstandings, in the end making a match' (1988, p. 79). The resulting text is a mixture of descriptions of the studied object and the experiences made in studying it. An example of this form of presentation is the description of entering the field as a learning process, or descriptions of failing to successfully enter the field (see Wolff, 2004).

Impressionist tales are written in the form of dramatic recall of how events have occurred: 'The idea is to draw an audience into an unfamiliar story world and to allow it, as far as possible, to see, hear, and feel as the fieldworker saw, heard, and felt. Such tales seek to imaginatively place the audience in the fieldwork situation' (Van Maanen, 1988, p. 103).

Conventions of writing reports about qualitative research have changed, as Van Maanen documents for his own styles of writing: today fewer realist and more impressionist or confessional tales are published. This change has occurred in two respects: more works are not only written in these styles, but also accepted for publication. There is a shift from realist tales to confessions and also an increasing awareness that there exists neither the perfect theory nor the perfect report about it. Thus, the dimension of partial failure and the limits of one's own knowledge should be taken into account as elements of the findings which are worthy of presentation. For our context of how to write about interviewing, a combination of these three styles of writing might be apt: a presentation of findings (realist tale) embedded in an account of how the process into the field and to the findings went (confessional tales) and of what was specific, puzzling, new or surprising in the field where the study was done (impressionist tales).

Box 17.3 Research in the real world

Writing about an interview study

In the book about our interview study of homelessness and health of adolescents (Flick and Röhnsch, 2008), we use a combination of three formats of writing and informing the readers about our empirical experiences. First, we present a chapter called 'A little on-site visit' in which we described the meeting points of the adolescents' everyday lives and where we met them and did the interviews. Second, we have several chapters in which we present the results of our interviews in relation to specific topics (e.g. 'Homeless adolescents' health concepts' or 'Chronic diseases – how homeless adolescents deal with them' or 'Illness on the street – experts' views'), and take a comparative perspective on what all or some of the participants mentioned in the interviews. Complementary to this more realist tale (in Van Maanen's terminology), we take a more impressionist perspective when we present four more extended (but not too long) case studies of single interviewees, in which their statements and our analyses across several areas of the interviews are presented in an interlinked way. This is all embedded in a kind of confessional tale of how we analysed the research and literature, developed research questions and instruments, found access to the adolescents and experts and what our impressions in the field were like.

What should you include in writing about your interview study?

In writing about your study, you should basically address all the steps of your project. This means you should present the steps we have covered in the chapters of this book. Readers should be enabled by your report to know what your concept of interviewing is, that is, what your theoretical and epistemological orientation to interviewing is like. Different from the discussion in this book, you need not address the variety of theories or epistemologies, but you should inform the reader which theory or which epistemology you took as an orientation. The same applies to the contents of the other chapters and the contents of your report about the other steps. Readers should know from your report, which kind of interview – which method and format – you selected and why you chose this one. To contextualize your results, you should inform the readers how you designed your study, how the sampling was done and how it was realized in the ways you sought and found access. It will also be helpful and necessary to address the ethical challenges relevant to your project and how you managed them, before you discuss the methodological principles and features of the method of interviewing you used and how you applied and adapted it to your research question and field. Finally, you should make transparent how you analysed your data (which method, what characterizes it and how you worked with it) and what were the quality issues in your study.

Writing up results of interview research

In Chapter 6, we discussed the issue of sampling mainly for selecting interviewees, but also mentioned that sampling is an issue in writing up the study. In most cases, you will have a big number of interesting quotes from your interviews that you used to analyse the interviews and for what they say about your research issue. You will need to use enough quotes in your report on the research as evidence for your results and analysis. At the same time, limitations of space in the text and of how much readers can perceive without being 'lost' in the material, demand that you select a limited number of – the best, most illustrative, most convincing – quotes from the interview. The challenge of writing about your research lies in finding the best connections between your text about your interviews, interviewees and findings, and quotations providing evidence for this text. This challenge has three levels: (1) you should not provide too few quotations from your material, thus avoiding the impression of a lack of evidence; (2) nor should you overload the text with quotes, thus avoiding the flow of your text and argumentations or narrative becoming overshadowed by the interruption of quotes; and (3) the major challenge is how to really integrate the quotes in the text in a contextualized way.

This again has three aspects: (1) quotes should be linked with the interpretation referring to them (and why they were selected); (2) quotes should be presented in a way that allows for understanding of the context in which they occurred, e.g. by mentioning the interviewer's question; and (3) the context should be referred to in the text. And, finally, a challenge in reporting results from interview studies is to find a balance between quotes from single interviews and demonstrating how this went into a comparative analysis. Working with a typology or patterns in the data is often a missing link between referring to single interviewees and the general conclusions drawn from an analysis.

Steps, Aims and Criteria in Preparing and Doing the Writing up of Interview Studies

Table 17.1 summarizes the steps of preparing and doing the writing up of interview studies, including the aims and actions for each step as well as the criteria for judging whether these steps have been successfully planned and realized.

Table 17.1 Steps, aims and criteria in preparing and doing the writing up of interview studies

Six F's of designing interview research	Steps	Aims and actions	Criteria
Framing	1. Preparing the interview	• Show how a draft was prepared for (initial, narrative, etc.) questions based on a pre-analysis of the field under study • Show how test interviews and interview training were run • Give information on the documentation (sheet) for the context of the interview (demographic data, etc.)	• Can you show how the initial question covered the area under study? • Can you demonstrate that the interviewer(s) internalized the principle of the interview? • Can you show how the documentation sheet covered the relevant information for the research question?
Framing	2. Introducing the interview principle	• Illustrate how you prepared the introduction for the interviewee, and ensured it was clear	• Can you show that the interviewees understood and accepted the principle of the interview?
Formulating	3. The initial question	• What were the initial, narrative or opening questions to stimulate the interviewees to reflect on the topic and its role in their lives?	• Did you show that the questions encompassed relevant aspects of the subjective meanings for the interviewees and their situation? • Can you illustrate how the interviewer enforced the principle of the interview to bring more depth to the interview?

Six F's of designing interview research	Steps	Aims and actions	Criteria
Foregrounding	4. Probing	• How did you prepare and apply questions to cover relevant areas of the interviewees' cases which they might not have expressed in enough detail?	• Can you show how these questions are revealing in character? • Did they add the missing aspects to the interview?
Focusing	5. More general topics referring to the issue under study	• How did you plan to get into the detail of the central parts of the issue under study? • Show how you extended the depth and richness of the interviewees' responses by making additional enquiries	• Show how the interviewee went into detail and depth • Show how the interviewer was sensitive to any extra depth on which to focus
Foreseeing	6. Socio-demographic data	• Demonstrate how you developed and used a checklist for this purpose • Illustrate the documentation sheet you used	• Demonstrate that all information is included that is necessary for contextualizing the interviewee's narrative or answers
Framing	7. Evaluation and small-talk	• How did you make room for some conversation? • How did you make room for critique and additional aspects?	• Illustrate how additional aspects were mentioned
Foreseeing	8. Documentation	• What did you do to ensure a good recording and a detailed transcription?	• Can you say whether all additional information (not on the recording) is documented?
Finding and Formulating	9. Analysing online interviews	• How did you choose an appropriate method for analysing and interpreting the responses?	• Illustrate how the method takes the quality of the data into account (e.g. the format of emailing)

Making Qualitative Research Relevant

In times when qualitative interview research has to defend its place against several developments – such as the approach of mixed methods – the challenge of how to prove the relevance of qualitative research findings becomes even more significant. In this context, it is important how you present your research findings, so that they are also convincing for readers outside the qualitative research community. Sandelowski and Leeman (2012) make this point quite clearly in their article 'Writing Usable Qualitative Health Research Findings'. They present a number of suggestions, for example: 'The key strategy for enhancing the accessibility and usability of qualitative health research findings is to write in the language of the readers to whom they are directed' (2012, p. 1407). They also suggest translating findings into thematic sentences, so that not only is the mention of an issue in interviews the basis of a presentation, but so too is the formulation of statements about relations between issues and how they vary across participants.

To make findings relevant, the authors further suggest translating them into the languages of intervention and of implementation, so that the practical consequences of findings become more evident. These are suggestions coming from the context of qualitative health research, but they are helpful in other areas as well, where qualitative results are intended to be used for changing existing practices or for designing new ones.

What You Need to Ask Yourself

The questions in Box 17.4 are designed to help you to decide how to advance the credibility and transparency of your interview research. You may also apply these questions to studies using interviews you read.

Box 17.4   What you need to ask yourself

Credibility and transparency of interview research

1. How did you advance the credibility of your study?
2. How far can you communicate your study in a credible way?
3. How do you use member checks and peer debriefing in your study?
4. How do you find a balance in using quotes from the material in the presentation of your findings?
5. What is it important to document about the context of your interviews as part of the presentation?
6. Which parts should your report include to make your research transparent and credible?

What You Need to Succeed

This chapter should have given you a sound introduction to how to write about your interview research and how to deal with any issues of quality interviewing. The questions in Box 17.5 will help you to see what to take away from this chapter as we reach the final steps in our journey through interview research.

Box 17.5   What you need to succeed

Credibility and transparency of interview research

1. Did I understand the concept of credibility of interview research?
2. Do I see the role of transparency in interview research?
3. Am I aware of the challenges of writing about my research and how this is important for making my research credible and transparent?

What you have learned

- Credibility and transparency are issues of quality of interview research and of writing about it.
- Both are quality criteria but not in the way this term is used in quantitative research.
- Quality of interview research is not only a methodological problem (how was the interview conducted?) but also an issue of contents (what is new?).
- Quality of interview research depends on the whole process of doing interview research.
- It has to do with constructing a framework for listening to the interviewee and an adequate design of the interview and the study.
- Member checks and peer debriefing are important approaches in advancing quality.
- Writing about interview research should include results and procedures so that the reader may contextualize the findings in the process.

Exercises

The exercises again first invite you to reflect on some of the main issues in this chapter. Then you are invited to apply the topics of this chapter to the development of a project of your own. Hence, the exercises are a combination of reflection and prospection.

Exercise 17.1

Reflecting on the Chapter: The Quality of an Existing Study Using Interviews

1. Look through a journal for several qualitative studies based on interviews. Try to identify how the authors presented their decisions in their projects with an eye on quality.

(Continued)

2.   Reflect on how far the authors made these decisions and the process transparent in their writing about the studies and interviewing. Do you think they succeeded in this?

Exercise 17.2

Planning Your Project Using Interviews

1.   Think of your own study and reflect on how you would present it to make it credible and transparent.

What's next

This book gives a more extended, but brief overview of the criteria and strategies in managing the quality of qualitative research:

Flick, U. (2018). *Managing Quality in Qualitative Research* (2nd ed.). London: Sage.

In this text, the authors seek to develop specific criteria for qualitative research:

Lincoln, Y.S., & Guba, E.G. (1985). *Naturalistic Inquiry*. London: Sage.

This overview presents some debates around the concept of transparency in qualitative research:

Moravcsik, A. (2019). Transparency in Qualitative Research. In P. Atkinson, S. Delamont, A. Cernat, J.W. Sakshaug, & R.A. Williams (Eds.), *SAGE Research Methods Foundations*. London: Sage.

In this article, the concept of trustworthiness from administration research is linked to the other concepts discussed in this chapter:

Pratt, M.G., Kaplan, S., & Whittington, R. (2020). Editorial Essay – The Tumult over Transparency: Decoupling Transparency from Replication in Establishing Trustworthy Qualitative Research. *Administrative Science Quarterly*, 65(1), 1–19. https://doi.org/10.1177/0001839219887663

This text goes further into the details of the practical problems of writing in qualitative research:

Becker, H.S. (1986). *Writing for Social Scientists*. Chicago: University of Chicago Press.

This book elaborates on the styles of writing about qualitative research:

Van Maanen, J. (1988). *Tales of the Field: On Writing Ethnography*. Chicago: University of Chicago Press.

These authors give advice on how to make qualitative research findings relevant, beginning with the style of writing when presenting them:

Sandelowski, M., & Leeman, J. (2012). Writing Usable Qualitative Health Research Findings. *Qualitative Health Research*, 22(10), 1404–13.

This article presents an empirical study about the concept of transferability in qualitative management research:

Aguinis H., & Solarino, A.M. (2019). Transparency and Replicability in Qualitative Research: The Case of Interviews with Elite Informants. *Strategic Management Journal*, 40, 1291–315. https://doi.org/10.1002/smj.3015

Doing Interview Research Navigator

How to understand interview research

- What doing interview research means
- Theories and epistemologies of interviewing
- When to choose interviews as a research method
- Methods and formats of interviewing

Designing interview research

- Planning and designing interview research
- How many interviewees: Sampling and saturation
- Accessing and recruiting participants

How to conduct interviews

- How to respect and protect: Ethics of interviewing
- Semi-structured interviews: Working with questions and answers
- Interviewing experts and elites
- Integrating narratives in interviews: Episodic interviews

Doing interviews in context

- How to work with life histories: Narrative interviews
- Working with focus groups as interviews
- Ask (in) the field: Ethnographic and mobile interviewing
- Doing online interviews

How to work with interview data

- Working with interview data
- Credibility and transparency: Quality and writing in interview research
- From interviewing to an inner view: Critiques and reflexivity

You are here in your project

FROM INTERVIEWING TO AN INNER VIEW

CRITIQUES AND REFLEXIVITY

──How this chapter will help you──

You will:

- be introduced to the points raised in critical debates about interview research,
- see what the authors suggest as remedies to their critiques,
- be reminded how this book has kept these critiques in mind and what it suggests to counter them, and
- see that reflexivity is a matter of decisions and research practice.

Critiques of Interviewing

As mentioned already in Chapter 2, doing interviews has been criticized from a number of angles. The authors engaged in these critiques come mostly from other areas of doing qualitative research, such as **ethnomethodology** (Silverman, 2017), ethnography (Atkinson and Silverman, 1997; Hammersley, 2003, 2017; Whitaker and Atkinson, 2019), and discourse and conversation analysis (Potter and Hepburn, 2012; Rapley, 2012). To such critiques, three responses are possible in general:

1. To take the theoretical and methodological background of the critiques (and authors) into account. These types of research are interested in analysing social processes and practices in the doing – which means they work with transcripts of interactions (conversation analysis) or field notes or recordings of practices and interactions (ethnography). Although these approaches are sophisticated and fruitful in their research, they lack an important dimension of what they study, as it is not really possible to refer directly to past events or issues outside the situations that are analysed, except by talking to participants about them in interviews that are formalized to a greater or less extent (see Chapter 14). Reconstructing these 'outsides of situations' is in ethnography and conversation analysis only possible by referring to them indirectly or by talking to people. That does not mean that the critiques coming from these angles are not relevant for improving interviewing as a research practice. Potter and Hepburn (2012), Hammersley (2017) and Rapley (2012) make suggestions in this respect.

2. To stop doing interviews as these critiques look convincing. But given what was said for response one, the consequence should rather be to reflect on when to use interviewing (see Chapter 3) or when to use one of the other forms of research that are the starting points for the critiques. This decision should be based less on the fundamental preferences or dislikes of a researcher and more on the issue under study and the research question that is pursued.

3. The third solution is the way taken in this book: to have these critiques in mind – that it is not possible to access the inner views of participants by interviewing them or to look into their minds and to access meanings and experiences as they 'really are' – and to design the doing of research interviews carefully and in a reflexive way throughout the process. This also builds on the fact that 'the interview – like any other research method – reflexively constructs the phenomena it seeks to describe. The interview invites – sometimes implicitly, often explicitly – the production of biographical accounts' (Whitaker and Atkinson, 2019, p. 621; see also Hammersley, 2021).

Critiques and exemplary responses

Potter and Hepburn (2012) have formulated their critique in eight challenges to doing interview research, which fall into two sets.

Critiques about how interview research is reported

The first set of challenges refers to the ways the interview study is reported (see Chapter 17) and the authors suggest four ways of meeting them. The authors suggest (1) 'improving the transparency of the interview setup', which means to address why and for what purposes the participants were selected and recruited and how they were accessed (see Chapters 5, 6 and 7) and what they were told that the interview is about and what it will be used for (see Chapters 2 and 8).

Potter and Hepburn (2) suggest to display more fully the active role of the inter-viewer. Approaches to meet this challenge are to reflect on how the interviewer constructs a framework for listening (see Chapter 2) in selecting the method (see Chapter 4 and below), how the concrete use of this method is planned (see the tables in Chapters 9–15) and how the interview situation and the research process are designed (using the idea of the six F's, see Chapter 5 and the subsequent chapters).

In addition, Potter and Hepburn (3) suggest 'using representational forms that show the interactional production of interviews'. The suggestion to extend the focus of the analysis from single statements to be coded to the interactions between interviewer/ question and interviewee/answer which produced them as a starting point in the analysis (see Chapter 16), goes in this direction. Furthermore, it is suggested that you take the variety of how specific topics were introduced in questions in various interviews into account (see Chapter 16).

Their fourth suggestion – 'tying analytic observations to specific interview elements' – is an argument for a detailed transcription of the interview and a compre-hensive documentation of the context of statements and the like (see Chapter 16 on transcription and turning interviews into data). The authors warn against repairing the specific way an interviewee has expressed something in an interview into conventional orthography or only to summarize statements, and so on.

Critiques about how interviews are analysed

Potter and Hepburn's second set of challenges refers to the analysis of the interview. The authors suggest interview researchers pay more attention to the following issues: (5) 'how interviews are flooded with social science categories, assumptions, and research agendas' (2012, p. 556). We have addressed this challenge in Chapter 16, where we sug-gested, with Hermanns (2004), that the interviewers in the interview situation should focus on the interviewees' life worlds rather than the theoretical concepts they want to discover or assess. Potter and Hepburn's sixth point – 'the varying footing of interviewer and interviewee' – means taking into account that the participants in the interview situ-ation bring different backgrounds to the conversation and that the interviewee may refer to some other people or situations when answering the interviewer's questions.

In the same direction, their seventh and eighth points caution that 'the orienta-tions to stake and interest on the part of the interviewer and interviewee' and 'the way cognitive, individualist assumptions about human actors are presupposed' be taken into account (Potter and Hepburn, 2012, p. 556). Again, we have suggested in the analysis of data and in the interview itself that we should not focus too much on the person of the interviewees and on their interests or aim at a personal, psychological or diagnostic profile of the single interviewee. Doing research interviews – and interview research – is about a topic for which interviewees are carefully selected. Their state-ments and narratives are carefully analysed and compared and this comparison should be orientated around the analysis rather than inner views or individual experiences, and whether the reports about these can be 'trusted'. To address the points Potter and Hepburn raise, and similarly those Silverman (2017) makes, a thoughtful planning and documentation of interviews is important (see Parts II, III and Chapter 16 in this book) as well as seeking feedback from participants in member checks or from other researchers in peer debriefing (see Chapter 17).

In Silverman's (2017) critique of interviewing, we see a three-level argument, which could actually be conflated into just the one. It starts by (1) building on Atkinson and Silverman (1997), as a general critique, which is (2) strongly linked to his observation (or opinion?) that interviews are used too often in qualitative research and (3) basically underpinned by bad examples of interviews and their analysis. While the third point may be correct – certainly, the examples he uses to illustrate his critique are not really convincing as interview research – it is a bit too simplistic for attacking interviewing in general, which means that levels 3 and 1 of his critique are conflated. That interviewing is too prominent may not be a problem if interviewing in general were correctly applied, which conflates levels 2 and 3 in his analysis. However, Silverman also offers some advice on what to do in this situation, building on Potter and Hepburn's (2012) above suggestions. Silverman (2017, p. 154) advises to 'ignore what you know about your interviewees' and to look at 'how interviewees (and interviewers) construct or perform identities and subjectivities' (Rapley, 2012, p. 551). Silverman also suggests to 'avoid line-by-line interpretations of what has been said ... find some outcomes in the talk and work backwards' (2017, p. 154). A third suggestion is to look for 'when speakers appeal to some warrant for what they have just said', but this is (a) a rather specific focus on the interview conversation which may or may not be relevant for the research question and (b) contradicts somewhat the second suggestion (to avoid line-by-line interpretation). Referring to Holstein and Gubrium (2016), Silverman further suggests asking 'how' and 'what' questions about the course of the interview and finally (following a suggestion by Potter) looking at what is ordinary and what is exceptional.

Again, after reading these suggestions, the critiques of Silverman do less to justify not doing interviews and more to doing them (and then their analysis) in a better way in the tension between openness and structuration, planning and flexibility and finally in a reflexive way. The preceding chapters aim at suggesting solutions for how to do interviews in such a way.

Interviews as a journey to interviewees' inner views

These critiques have implicitly and explicitly one point in common: they are sceptical about the idea that we can access the inner world of interviewees' minds, opinions, experiences and meanings, and 'read others' minds', as Silverman (2017, p. 146) mentions. As an example, he uses McCracken's (1988) idea that his method – the long interview – is able to 'take us into the mental world of the individual ... [and] into the life-world of the individual' (McCracken, 1988, p. 9; see also Chapter 1 for his argument). This idea, that interviews take the researcher on a journey into the interviewees' inner views and reveal them as they are, is methodologically naïve and the scepticism towards this idea is more than justified. However, this understanding of interviewing is more the particular view of particular authors and though it may be taken up by some researchers, it cannot be seen as the understanding behind interview research in general, as many examples in this book demonstrate.

Reflexivity

In this context of critiquing and improving interviews, reflexivity has become a rather prominent issue in interviewing (see Roulston, 2010a), in qualitative research in general and also in the discussion of research quality. May and Perry (2014, p. 111) see 'two different yet interrelated dimensions of reflexive practice: endogenous and referential reflexivity' as being relevant, which they define as follows:

> Endogenous reflexivity refers to the ways in which the actions and understandings of researchers contribute to the modes in which research practices are constituted. ... Referential reflexivity is not just a reflection of everyday life, but must begin with that experience. The movement from endogenous to referential reflexivity may be characterized as one from reflexivity *within* actions to reflexivity *upon* actions, enabling connections to be made between individuals and the social conditions of which they are a part. (2014, pp. 111–12)

For our context of doing interview research, reflexivity means that we carefully construct our research and reflect on how it works, how it can be improved and what we can do to achieve such an aim in the various steps of the process of doing interviews. As should have become evident in the course of this book – even if reflexivity as a term was not always used – such a careful construction of interview research begins in the following steps long before the first interview is conducted.

Learning to interview

Interviewing can be learned, by reading about interviews and, if available, reading interview transcripts as well, and by practising interviewing in general and the concrete interview that is planned. In teaching, interview training has proved helpful, in which interviewers practise the use of the interview guide and the interaction with interviewees in role-plays, which are commented on by a group of other potential interviewers.

Failure and learning from mistakes

A particularly helpful resource for improving interviews and interviewers' skills are interviews which did not work well, in which mistakes occurred or which even failed: 'In cases where interviews seem to have "failed" – I use this term with reservations since "failed" interviews provide fruitful grounds for asking methodological questions, which are rarely the kinds of questions initially posed – students might ask themselves how they might evaluate the "quality" of the interviews that they have conducted and the study as a whole' (Roulston, 2010b, p. 200). Mistakes do not necessarily mean that the wrong questions were asked at the wrong time. This can also refer to the way the framework for listening was constructed – did interviewees know what they were to expect and what was expected of them in the interview situation? Was the method chosen adequate? Did it fit with the interviewees and the research?

Transparency of interviewing by making data and other material available

The discussion about archiving interview data and materials from the study and about making them available for reanalysis by other researchers (see Chapters 16 and 17) can also contribute to advancing reflexivity in doing interviews in general. But this will only be the case if the production of the interviews (from research questions to sampling, data collection and management) is reflected upon, rather than just taking the interviews as data and (re-) using them.

Taking deviant cases into account

As mentioned a couple of times before, the aim of analysing interviews mostly is not to make statements about a single case, but to develop types, patterns, group comparisons and the like, referring always to the research question and the topic of the study. A critical issue of reflexivity in this context is how to deal with deviant (sometimes also called 'negative') cases – the one or more cases that do not fit in our typology, our patterns or the groups we identify for comparison. This is an issue for the analysis itself – maybe we have to adjust and readjust the typology or the patterns so that all cases fit – or it fits to all cases. But it is also an issue to include in our write-up and in our efforts to make the study transparent – how did the researchers deal with these specific cases? And it is an issue for reflexivity – thinking carefully about why this phenomenon of **deviant cases** came up during the analysis and for these specific cases in particular. In this sense, the treatment of negative cases becomes an issue for credibility if we follow Lincoln and Guba (1985).

Selecting the appropriate method of interviewing

Throughout this book, it has been emphasized that doing interviews is not just interviewing. In Parts III and IV, we presented a variety of forms of doing interview research, each appropriate depending on what is being studied and who interviewed, and in Part V a variety of ways of how to analyse interview data. To answer the question of the appropriateness of a method of interviewing, the questions in Box 18.1 can be used in two ways – for planning and selecting ways of doing interviews beforehand, and afterwards for checking how the interviews went, what went wrong, or which mistakes occurred. This check should be done after the first interview and then repeatedly so that the procedures can be adapted for subsequent interviews if necessary.

Box 18.1 Research in the real world

Selecting a method for doing interview research

1. Research question

Can the interview type and its application address the essential aspects of the research question?

2. Interview type

Has the method been applied according to the methodological elements and target?

Has jumping between interview types been avoided, except when it is grounded in the research question or theoretically?

3. Interviewer

Are the interviewers able to apply the interview type?

What are the consequences of their own fears and uncertainties in the situation?

4. Interviewee

Is the interview type appropriate to the target group?

How can one take into account the fears, uncertainties and expectations of (potential) interviewees?

5. Scope allowed the interviewee

Can the interviewees present their views within the framework of the questions?

Can they assert their views against the framework of the questions?

6. Interaction

Have the interviewers conducted the interview according to the correct procedure?

Have they left sufficient scope for the interviewee?

Did they fulfil their role? (Why not?)

Were the interviewee's role, the interviewer's role, and the situation clearly defined for the interviewee?

Could the interviewee fulfil his or her role? (Why not?)

Analyse any inconsistencies in order to validate the interview between the first and second interview if possible.

(Continued)

> ### 7. Aim of the interpretation
>
> Are you interested in finding and analysing limited and clear answers, or complex, multiple patterns, contexts, etc.?
>
> ### 8. Claim for generalization
>
> On what level should statements be made:
>
> - For the single case (the interviewed individual and his or her biography, an institution and its impact, etc.)?
> - With reference to groups (about a profession, a type of institution, etc.)?
> - General statements?

Constructing a framework for listening

Part of this reflexive practice of doing interviews is to carefully construct a framework for listening – in which the researcher has the chance to listen to what the interviewees have to say, want to say and how they want to say it, and the interviewee can do so without mistrusting the situation and so on. This construction of a framework includes the steps before the actual interview – selecting and accessing the interviewees, allowing them a really informed consent – and after the interview – careful documentation and analysis of the interview. This analysis should focus on the content of what was said, but also the conversational context – what was the question the interviewer asked (and not only the one in the interview guide that should have been asked) – and the relational and situational context in which the conversation was embedded.

Six F's of designing interview research

Constructing such a framework is also an issue of designing the interview and the research as a whole. Designing interview research includes *finding* – interviewees, statements, connections between them, quotes for making transparent what was found – and *focusing* in identifying the relevant topics throughout the research process. It also includes *framing* – the interview situation, the sample, the analysis and reflexivity in the research – and *foreseeing* – what and who should be included in the interviews, what should be asked and how it should be probed. Also included are *foregrounding* – that the interviewees' views and statements are the focus and which aspects in the analysis should be emphasized – and *formulating* – how to ask the questions, how to word the probing, how to emphasize and summarize the findings of the study, so that the reader will see what has emerged, what is relevant within it and what can be done with it in a practical, political or other way the research wants to contribute to.

Doing Interviews – Not a Case of Mind-reading but Varieties of Talking about an Issue in Context

Interviews do not allow interviewers to read interviewees' minds or lead us to their inner views in a direct, unfettered way. Interviews also do not take us into the interviewee's life world. Interviews allow researchers to understand how interviewees talk about their experiences and life worlds and what various interviewees' ways of talking about both have in common and how they differ. Therefore, the steps of sampling and accessing a variety of interviewees for including a variety of expressions of experiences and life worlds are important in constructing the framework for listening in an interview study. As the discussions about decolonizing and indigenous interviewing have pointed out, it is essential to take the interviewees' and the community's specific contexts into account when doing interviews. The methods presented and discussed in this book may support research in a variety of such contexts and with diversity in mind – also inside Western societies and with a focus on specific groups such as the LGBTQ+ community or communities of colour.

What You Need to Ask Yourself

This chapter has a double function: it is supposed to raise your awareness about issues that are critically discussed for doing interview research. At the same time, it should not make you turn away from interviewing per se, but help to advance your sensitivity and reflexivity in doing your interview research. At the same time, it has roughly summarized how this book intends to help avoid these criticisms and how to take them into account in planning and doing interview research, and where to find answers in the book to the critical questions raised about interviewing. The questions in Box 18.2 are designed to help you reflect on interviewing and on your interview research.

Box 18.2 What you need to ask yourself

Doing interview research in a reflexive way

1. How far have you understood what the critiques on interviewing are about?

(Continued)

---

2. Do you understand that interviews do not lead into the inner worlds of interviewees, but show how a variety of interviewees talk about issues and experiences?

3. Do you see that constructing this variety of interviewees through a differentiating way in sampling and accessing interviewees is an important step in this context?

4. Do you understand that these critiques are more relevant as starting points for reflecting on and improving interview research than for rejecting it as a whole?

5. Do you understand that reflexivity is not just a general, vague attitude but has concrete relevance in several practical steps and decisions before, during and after doing interviews?

What You Need to Succeed

To move on with your interview project, the questions in Box 18.3 may give you a few final guidelines at the end of your journey through interview research and your interview project.

Box 18.3 What you need to succeed

Doing interview research in a reflexive way

1. Do I understand what the limits of interview research are and how to deal with critiques of interviewing?

2. Am I aware that interviewing can be criticized and reflected on from within, with a focus on improving it without rejecting it, and from outside with a healthy scepticism?

3. Do I still see good reason to proceed with my project of doing interview research?

4. Do I see what I can acquire from doing interviews – varieties of statements rather than the inner views of single interviewees?

What you have learned

- Interviewing is criticized from several sides.
- This can be used for improving interview practices.
- Interviews are not always the best way of doing (qualitative) research.
- They address research issues other methods don't reach.

- Reflexivity is something that can be put to work in designing interview practices in a reflective way.
- Interviews are not about reading another person's mind but listening to a variety of people talk about an issue for seeing the diverse experiences of this issue.

Exercises

In the exercises, you are first invited to reflect on some of the issues in this chapter. Then you are invited to apply the topics of this chapter to the development of a project of your own. Hence, the exercises are a combination of reflection and prospection.

Exercise 18.1

Reflecting on the Chapter: The Use of Interviews in an Existing Study

1. Look through a journal for a qualitative study based on interviews (e.g. Garcia et al., 2012). Try to identify which of the critiques of interviewing would apply to it and how this could have been prevented.

Exercise 18.2

Planning Your Own Research with Interviews

1. Think of your own study and of how to avoid the points in the critiques in this chapter in your own research.

What's next

This handbook chapter summarizes the critical points and makes suggestions on how to address them:

Potter, J., & Hepburn, A. (2012). Eight challenges for interview researchers. In J.F. Gubrium, J.A. Holstein, A.B. Marvasti, & K.D. McKinney (Eds.), *The SAGE Handbook of Interview Research: The Complexity of the Craft* (pp. 555–70). Thousand Oaks, CA: Sage.

These two articles give reasonable overviews of the debate and outline ways of how to move on:

Hammersley, M. (2017). Interview Data: A Qualified Defence against the Radical Critique. *Qualitative Research*, 17(2), 173–86. doi:10.1177/1468794116671988

Hammersley, M. (2021). The 'Radical Critique of Interviews': A Response to Recent Comments. *International Journal of Social Research Methodology*, 24(3), 393–5. doi: 10.1080/13645579.2020.1841881

GLOSSARY

Active citation A format for publishing additional materials with an article to increase the transparency of the published study.

Active listening Signalling the attention by 'mh', looking at the speaker without intervening with one's own contribution.

Analytic induction A strategy to use negative or deviant cases for assessing and elaborating findings, models or theories developed.

Anonymization Taking all information about people, dates, locations, institutions out of a research document, such as a transcript.

Artificial group A group that is set up for focus group interviews but does not exist outside the research.

Artificially bound group A group in sampling which shares a feature (e.g. a profession) but does not exist as a group in which members know each other or communicate.

Asynchronous communication A form of communication in which the partners do not interact at the same time but with a certain delay, as in email communication for example.

Axial coding A way of coding that treats a category as an axis around which the analyst delineates relationships and specifies the dimensions of this category. Axial coding brings data back together again in a structure after they were fractured in open coding.

Balancing phase The last step in a narrative interview, in which regular questions can be asked and answered.

Benchmark A cut-off point for distinguishing good/bad or successful/unsuccessful research.

Biographical research Studies focusing on life histories or that take a life history perspective.

CAQDAS Acronym for 'Computer Assisted Qualitative Data Analysis Software', such as MAXQDA or Atlas.ti.

Chicago School of Sociology A very influential group of researchers and approaches in the history of qualitative research at the University of Chicago who provided the methodological backgrounds of currently influential approaches like grounded theory. For example, research focused on how the community of (e.g. Polish) immigrants in Chicago was socially organized, how members maintained their cultural identity or adapted to a new one (of being American).

Coda A signal of the narrator that a story is finished (in the narrative interview).

Codes of ethics Sets of rules of good practice in research (or interventions) set up by professional associations or by institutions as an orientation for their members.

Coding Development of concepts in the context of grounded theory, for example, to label pieces of data and allocate other pieces of data to them (and the label).

Communicative validation Assessment of results (or of data) by asking the participants for their consensus.

Complete collection A form of sampling that includes all elements of a population defined in advance.

Constraint of closing Gestalt In narratives, the narrator is implicitly driven to tell a story until its end.

Constraint of condensing In narratives, the narrator is implicitly driven to condense as many details as necessary for making the story understandable for the listener.

Constraint of detailing In narratives, the narrator is implicitly driven to provide as many details as necessary to make the story understood by the listener.

Constructionism/constructivism Epistemologies in which social reality is seen as the result of constructive processes (activities of the members of processes in their minds). For example, living with an illness can be influenced by the way an individual sees their illness, what meaning they ascribe to it, and how this both the illness is seen by other members of their social world. On each of these levels, both the illness and living with it are socially constructed.

Convenience sampling The sampling is less based on a systematic sampling plan and more on who is ready and able to participate in the study.

Conversation analysis Study of language (use) for formal aspects (e.g. how a conversation starts or ends, or how turns from one to the other speaker are organized).

Credibility A criterion for evaluating qualitative research based on prolonged engagement in the field.

Data protection Conduct or means that guarantee the anonymity of research participants and ensure that data do not end up in or are passed into the hands of unauthorized persons or institutions.

Decolonizing methods A research approach challenging Eurocentric/Western research methods that undermine the local knowledge and experiences of marginalized populations and groups.

Designing qualitative interviews This includes research questions, sampling, the interview guide and planning the analysis.

Deviant cases Cases not fitting a typology or pattern resulting from a study.

Digital storytelling A short form of digital narratives for everyday people to share their experiences and stories.

Elite interview A way of using interviews to study representatives of the top of any hierarchical system, for example, in enterprises, political parties, administrations, sports, sciences, and the like.

Email interview Questions are sent per email and answers returned per email as well, in an immediate exchange or with longer delays in between.

Episodic interview A specific form of interview which combines question–answer sequences with narratives (of episodes).

Episodic knowledge Knowledge based on memories of situations and their concrete circumstances.

Epistemology Theories of knowledge and perception in science.

Ethics committees Committees in universities and sometimes also in professional associations which assess research proposals (for dissertations or funding) for their ethical soundness. If necessary, these committees pursue violations of ethical standards.

Ethnographic interviewing An approach to turn friendly conversations during ethnographic fieldwork into a more formalized exchange with several formats of questions.

Ethnography A research strategy combining different methods, but based on participation, observation and writing about a field under study. For example, for studying how homeless adolescents deal with health issues, a participant observation in their community is combined with interviewing the adolescents. The overall picture from this participation, observation and interviewing is presented in a written text about the field. The writing style gives the representation of the field a specific form.

Ethnomethodology A theoretical approach interested in analysing the methods people use in their everyday life to make communication and routines work.

Experience-distant A concept that is taken from (social) science and not from the life world of participants of a study for labelling social phenomena or subjective experiences. For example, the conceptual term 'trajectory' used to describe the biographical processes (e.g. loss of a job) linked to the progress of a chronic illness.

Experience-near A concepts taken from mundane language or the language of interviewees.

Expert interview A form of interview that is defined by the specific target group – people in certain professional positions, which enables them to inform on professional processes or a specific group of patients, for example.

Expert knowledge Knowledge coming from professional experience in an area or about a specific clientele.

Explicative content analysis A step in qualitative content analysis aiming at clarifying unclear statements.

Extempore A Latin expression for 'spontaneous, unprepared', e.g. a narrative.

Facetime A platform for video telephony.

First-degree construction Lay explanations of a phenomenon which can be used to develop a scientific explanation (second-degree construction). For example, people's lay theories of their specific disease can become a first step for developing a more general concept of everyday knowledge of the disease.

First-hand knowledge The knowledge of someone who was part of a situation and who did not only hear about it from others.

Focus group A research method used in market and other forms of research in which a group is invited to discuss the issue of a study for research purposes. It is used for interviewing as well.

Focused coding After initial coding, researchers focus on the most frequent and/or significant codes among their initial codes and test these codes against large batches of data.

Focused interview A specific interview form which was developed systematically for analysing the effects of propaganda by asking a number of different types of questions. Its concept can still be very informative for developing semi-standardized interviews.

Follow-up question A question for clarifying an answer to the question before, if it has remained unclear.

Gatekeeper People who can be helpful or a barrier if you want to gain access to a field or a population.

Generalization Transfer of research results to situations and populations that were not part of the research situation.

Go-along method Methods used while walking with the participants you want to interview.

Grounded theory A theory developed from analysing empirical material or from studying a field or process.

Grounded theory research Research that aims at developing a theory from material and its analysis.

Hard-to-reach group People who seldom take part in research or utilize social and other services.

Heterogeneous group Members of a group who are different in one or several dimensions.

Homogeneous group Members of a group who are similar on several dimensions.

Indexing data Labelling cases in a data set, e.g. IP1 for the first interviewee.

Indigenous research Systematic inquiry involving people from indigenous communities as investigators or partners to extend knowledge that is significant for them.

Informed consent Participants' agreement, willingly provided, to cooperate with research that has been explained to them and that they are able to understand. This is a requirement for ethically sound research.

Initial coding The first step of engaging with and defining data. Initial coding forms the link between collecting data and developing a theory for understanding the data.

Initial question (for **generating a narrative**) A question designed for stimulating interviewees to tell a story or their life history.

Intensive interviewing The method of interviewing in grounded theory research.

Interpretation Clarifying the meaning of something.

Interview guide A set of questions developed for a semi-structured interview, for example.

Interview protocol Here information beyond the answers or narratives in the recording are noted, such as the particularities of the interview situation or setting.

Interview questions The questions the interviewee is actually asked to answer; not to be conflated with the research questions of the study.

Interview training Role-play to simulate an interview in a group of observers and analysing it afterwards for the interviewer's non-verbal behaviour, use of questions, relation to the interviewee and mistakes in general.

Investigative journalism A specific form of journalism aiming at uncovering a scandal, for example.

In vivo code Coding based on concepts that are taken from an interviewee's statements.

Line-by-line coding Coding along the text for understanding how the meaning of a text is built up and for being sure that nothing is left out of the analysis.

Longitudinal study A design in which the researchers come back repeatedly to the field and the same participants after some time to do interviews several times again in order to analyse development and changes.

Member check Assessment of results (or of data) by asking the participants for their consensus.

Memo A document written in the research process to note ideas, questions, relations, results, etc. In grounded theory research, memos are building blocks for developing a theory.

Mixed methods An approach combining qualitative and quantitative methods on a rather pragmatic level.

Mobile method Interviews are done while walking with the interviewee through a significant field.

Narrative A story told in a sequence of words, actions or images, and more generally the organization of the information within that story.

Narrative-generating question After the main narrative in a narrative interview has ended, such a question is asked to stimulate further narrations.

Narrative interview A specific form of interview based on one extensive narrative. Instead of asking questions, the interviewer asks participants to tell the story of their life (or their illness, for example) as a whole, without interrupting them with questions.

Natural group A group used for focus groups which also exists outside the research.

Naturalistic research A form of field research trying to understand the field under study from within and with its own categories by using methods such as participant observation and ethnography. Categories for analysing data are developed from the material and not derived from existing theories.

Naturally bound group Groups in sampling that share one or more features (e.g. a university degree) and live in a community.

Non-directive counselling A style of conversation in which the counsellor just listens to the client without intervening with new topics, which has informed the style of interaction in interviews.

Online interviewing Interviews that are conducted via the Internet or by using Skype, for example.

Open coding The first step in grounded theory coding aiming at developing codes from the material.

Open question A question that does not predetermine what and how the interviewee will answer.

Paraphrase A formulation of the core of information in a specific sentence or statement without taking the specific formulations into account.

Participant observation A specific form of observation based on the researcher becoming a member of the field under study in order to do the observation.

Peer debriefing A criterion of validity for which colleagues' comments about the results of a study are obtained.

Photo elicitation The interviewee is presented with some photos or asked to take some photos and is then asked about their content and meaning.

Photovoice A method by which people can identify, represent and enhance their community through making photographs for the research technique.

Postmodernism A social theory which criticizes modernism and its concept of facts and science, and takes the way science and facts are produced more into account.

Probe Asking again in a deeper way during an interview.

Process knowledge A form of knowledge about how processes or institutions work, which is held by experts.

Pseudonymization Names of people, institutions and the like are replaced by made-up names, which cannot lead to identifying an interviewee or who is mentioned in the interview.

Purposive sampling Participants are not selected in a formal process (randomly) but directly for their specific characteristics.

Rapport The relation between an interviewee and an interviewer, for example.

Recruitment This means winning over people to take part in a study.

Reflexivity A concept of research which refers to acknowledging the input of the researchers in actively co-constructing the situation they want to study. It also alludes to the use to which such insights can be put in making sense of or interpreting data. For example, presenting oneself as an interviewer in an open-minded and empathic way can have a positive and intensifying impact on the interviewees' way of dealing with their experiences. Researchers' irritations after reading a transcript can be a starting point for asking specific questions about the text.

Repisode This means 'repeated episodes', which occur regularly (e.g. Christmas Eve) and not only once (e.g. someone's 65th birthday).

Replicability The degree to which the results of a study can be reproduced.

Replication crisis Contrary to claims, several classic studies in social psychology could not be repeated in terms of leading to the same results, which led to an undermining of the criterion of replication, which was central for quantitative research and often an argument against qualitative research, where it had never been seen as a reasonable criterion. This crisis of replication led to new claims of data transparency in both areas.

Research design A systematic plan for a research project including who to integrate in the research (sampling), who or what to compare for which dimensions, etc.

Research question The question the whole study is supposed to answer, which is not the same as interview questions the participants are asked in the interview.

Responsive interviewing A specific style of interviewing, which can inform interviewing in general.

Retrospective design A design in which research looks back on processes developing or events happening in the past.

Sampling A selection of cases or materials for study from a larger population or variety of possibilities.

Secondary analysis The use of existing data sets that were produced for other purposes.

Secondary data Data that have not been produced for the current study but are available from other studies or from qualitative data archives.

Second-degree construction Scientific explanations or conceptualizations based on lay concepts in the life world, which are held by the members. For example, lay theories concerning a specific illness can be taken as a starting point for analysing the social representations of this illness.

Selective coding Coding looking for additional material for codes that have been developed before.

Semantic knowledge Knowledge organized around concepts, their meaning and relation to each other.

Semi-structured interview A set of questions formulated in advance, which can be asked in a variable sequence and perhaps slightly reformulated in an interview in order to allow interviewees to present their views on certain issues.

Shadowing A researcher follows single participants through their everyday life in an institution, for example.

Skype A format for doing video calls.

Snowball sampling The researcher asks participants for suggestions of who else to contact for participation.

Stand-alone method The method is the only one used for data collection in a study.

Structured interview The interview consists of set of questions which is asked exactly in the sequence in the interview guide.

Structured question A question with a limited number of possible answers the interviewee can select from.

Structuring content analysis The analysis is about coding statements to a set of categories with a structure (e.g. from less to more important).

Subjective theory Lay people's knowledge about certain issues. This knowledge can be organized similarly to scientific theories (e.g. subjective theories of health or illness).

Summarizing content analysis The analysis is about reducing material by paraphrasing similar statements.

Synchronous (or real-time) group The (online) focus group is organized in a way that all participants are online at the same time.

Systematic review A way of reviewing the literature in a field that follows specific rules, is replicable and transparent in its approach and provides a comprehensive overview of the research in the field.

Thematic coding An approach involving analysis of data in a comparative way for certain topics after case studies (e.g. of interviews) have been done.

Theoretical sampling The sampling procedure in grounded theory research, where cases, groups, or materials are sampled according to their relevance for the theory that is developed and against the background of what is already the state of knowledge after collecting and analysing a certain number of cases.

Theoretical saturation The point in grounded theory research at which more data about a theoretical category do not produce any further theoretical insights.

Therapeutic interview The therapist asks the client in an interview about the development of a problem for designing the adequate therapy for this client.

Thomas's theorem The theorem says that when a person defines a situation as real, this situation is real in its consequences. This is a basic concept from symbolic interactionism.

Transparency The degree to which a reader of a research study is enabled to understand how the research went on in concrete terms.

Triangulation The combination of different methods, theories, data and/or researchers in the study of one issue.

Trustworthiness A criterion for assessing the quality of qualitative research.

Turn into data Interviews, for example, are not used immediately for analysis, but have to be transcribed, anonymized and the like to become data for analysis.

Verstehen (understanding) The German word for 'to understand'. It describes an approach to understanding a phenomenon more comprehensively than reducing it to one explanation (e.g. a cause–effect relation). For instance, to understand how people live with their chronic illness, a detailed description of their everyday life may be necessary, rather than identifying a specific variable (e.g. social support) for explaining the degree of success in their coping behaviour.

Vignette A short fictive story presented to interviewees so that they can be asked about elements in the story.

Webex Originally a video platform for digital meetings, which can also be used for doing interviews.

Zoom Originally a video platform for digital meetings, which can also be used for doing interviews.

***Zugzwang* (in a narrative)** A term taken from the context of playing chess. It means that sometimes you are forced to take a second move once you have made a certain first move. For example, once you have started a narrative, a certain implicit force may drive you to continue this narrative to its end or to provide enough details so that your listeners may understand the situation, process and point in your story.

REFERENCES

Abraham, T.H., Finley, E.P., Drummond, K.L., Haro, E.K., Hamilton, A.B., Townsend, J.C., Littman, A.J., & Hudson, T. (2021). A Method for Developing Trustworthiness and Preserving Richness of Qualitative Data During Team-based Analysis of Large Data Sets. *American Journal of Evaluation*, 42(1), 139–56.

Abrams, K., & Gaiser, T. (2017). Online Focus Groups. In N. Fielding, R. Lee, & G. Blank (Eds.), *The SAGE Handbook of Online Research Methods* (pp. 435–49). London: Sage.

Abrams, L.S. (2010). Sampling 'Hard to Reach' Populations in Qualitative Research: The Case of Incarcerated Youth. *Qualitative Social Work*, 9(4), 536–50. https://doi.org/10.1177/1473325010367821

Adamson, J. (2006). The Semi-structured Interview in Educational Research: Issues and Considerations in Native-to-Non-Native Speaker Discourse. *Bulletin of Shinshu Honan Junior College*, 23, 1–22.

Adamson, J. (2022). Designing Qualitative Research for Studies in Asia: Decentering Research Practices for Local Norms of Relevance. In U. Flick (Ed.), *The SAGE Handbook of Qualitative Research Design*. London: Sage.

Agar, M.H. (1980). *The Professional Stranger*. New York: Academic Press.

Aguinis, H., & Solarino, A.M. (2019). Transparency and Replicability in Qualitative Research: The Case of Interviews with Elite Informants. *Strategic Management Journal*, 40, 1291–315. https://doi.org/10.1002/smj.3015

Allmark, P. (2002). The Ethics of Research with Children. *Nurse Researcher*, 10(2), 7–19.

Allmark, P., Boote, J., Chambers, E., Clarke, A., McDonnell, A., Thompson, A., & Tod, A.M. (2009). Ethical Issues in the Use of In-depth Interviews: Literature Review and Discussion. *Research Ethics*, 5(2), 48–54.

Alvesson, M. (2003). Beyond Neopositivists, Romantics, and Localists: A Reflexive Approach to Interviews in Organizational Research. *The Academy of Management Review*, 28(1), 3–33.

Archibald, M.M., Ambagtsheer, R.C., Casey, M.G., & Lawless, M. (2019). Using Zoom Videoconferencing for Qualitative Data Collection: Perceptions and Experiences of Researchers and Participants. *International Journal of Qualitative Methods*. https://doi.org/10.1177/1609406919874596

Aroztegui Massera, C. (2006). *The Calabozo: Virtual Reconstruction of a Prison Cell Based on Personal Accounts*. Unpublished Doctoral Dissertation, Texas A&M University, College Station.

Arshavskaya, E. (2018). Promoting Intercultural Competence in Diverse US Classrooms through Ethnographic Interviews. *Teaching Education*, 29(2), 194–210. doi:10.1080/10476210.2017.1373277

Atkinson, P., & Coffey, A. (2001). Revisiting the Relationship between Participant Observation and Interviewing. In J.F. Gubrium & J.A. Holstein (Eds.), *Handbook of Interview Research* (pp. 801–14). London: Sage.

Atkinson, P., & Silverman, D. (1997). Kundera's Immortality: The Interview Society and the Invention of the Self. *Qualitative Inquiry*, 3(3), 304–25. http://dx.doi. org/10.1177/107780049700300304

Ayres, L. (2008). Active Listening. In L.M. Given (Ed.), *The SAGE Encyclopedia of Qualitative Research Methods* (p. 8). Thousand Oaks, CA: Sage.

Back, L. (2013). *The Art of Listening*. New York: Bloomsbury.

Baker, S.E., & Edwards, R. (Eds.) (2012). *How Many Qualitative Interviews is Enough?* Discussion Paper, National Centre of Research Methods. http://eprints.ncrm.ac.uk/2273

Bamberg, M. (2012). Narrative Analysis. In H. Cooper (Editor-in-chief), *APA Handbook of Research Methods in Psychology* (pp. 77–94). Washington, DC: APA Press.

Barbour, R. (2018). *Doing Focus Groups* (2nd ed.). London: Sage.

Barker, J. (2012). The Ethnographic Interview in an Age of Globalization. In R. Fardon, O. Harris, & T.H. Marchand (Eds.), *The SAGE Handbook of Social Anthropology* (Vol. 2, pp. 54–68). London: Sage.

Baym, N.K. (1995). The Emergence of Community in Computer-Mediated Communication. In S. Jones (Ed.), *Cybersociety: Computer-Mediated Communication and Community*. London: Sage. pp. 138–63.

Becker, H.S. (1965). Review. *American Sociological Review*, 30(4), 602–3.

Becker, H.S., & Geer, B. (1957). Participant Observation and Interviewing: A Comparison. *Human Organization*, 16, 28–32.

Becker, H.S., & Geer, B. (1960). Participant Observation: Analysis of Qualitative Data. In R.N. Adams & J.J. Preiss (Eds.), *Human Organization Research* (pp. 267–89). Homewood, IL: Dorsey Press.

Bell, S.T., Fisher, D.M., Brown, S.G., & Mann, K.E. (2018). An Approach for Conducting Actionable Research with Extreme Teams. *Journal of Management*, 44(7), 2740–65. https://doi.org/10.1177/0149206316653805

Bengry, A. (2018). Accessing the Research Field. In U. Flick (Ed.), *The SAGE Handbook of Qualitative Data Collection* (pp. 99–117). London: Sage.

Birt, L., Scott, S., Cavers, D., Campbell, C., & Walter, F. (2016). Member Checking: A Tool to Enhance Trustworthiness or Merely a Nod to Validation? *Qualitative Health Research*, 26(13), 1802–11. https://doi.org/10.1177/1049732316654870

Blaikie, N., & Priest, J. (2019). *Designing Social Research: The Logic of Anticipation*. New York: Wiley.

Block, E.S., & Erskine, L. (2012). Interviewing by Telephone: Specific Considerations, Opportunities, and Challenges. *International Journal of Qualitative Methods*, 428–445. https://doi.org/10.1177/160940691201100409

Bloor, M. (1997). Techniques of Validation in Qualitative Research: A Critical Commentary. In G. Miller & R. Dingwall (Eds.), *Context and Method in Qualitative Research* (pp. 37–50). London: Sage.

Bloor, M., & Wood, F. (2006). Vignettes. In M. Bloor & F. Wood (Eds.), *Keywords in Qualitative Methods* (pp. 184–5). London: Sage.

Blumer, H. (1969). *Symbolic Interactionism: Perspective and Method*. Berkeley and Los Angeles: University of California Press.

Bogner, A., & Menz, W. (2009). The Theory-generating Expert Interview: Epistemological Interest, Forms of Knowledge, Interaction. In A. Bogner,

B. Littig, & W. Menz (Eds.), *Interviewing Experts* (pp. 43–80). Basingstoke: Palgrave Macmillan.

Bogner, A., Littig, B., & Menz, W. (Eds.) (2009). *Interviewing Experts*. Basingstoke: Palgrave Macmillan.

Bogner, A., Littig, B., & Menz, W. (2014). *Interviews mit Experten. Qualitative Sozialforschung*. Wiesbaden: Springer.

Bogner, A., Littig, B., & Menz, W. (2018). Collecting Data with Experts and Elites. In U. Flick (Ed.), *The SAGE Handbook of Qualitative Data Collection* (pp. 652–67). London: Sage.

Bondy, C. (2013). How Did I Get Here? The Social Process of Accessing Field Sites. *Qualitative Research*, 13(5), 578–90.

Bortz, J., & Döring, N. (2006). *Forschungsmethoden und Evaluation für Human- und Sozialwissenschaftler* (3rd ed.). Berlin: Springer.

Brannen, J. (2012). How Many Qualitative Interviews is Enough? In S.E. Baker & R. Edwards (Eds.), *How Many Qualitative Interviews is Enough?* (p. 16). Discussion Paper, National Centre of Research Methods. http://eprints.ncrm.ac.uk/2273

Brickmann Bhutta, C.B. (2012). Not by the Book: Facebook as a Sampling Frame. *Sociological Methods & Research*, 41(1), 57–88. https://doi.org/10.1177/0049124112440795

Briggs, C. (1986). *Learning How to Ask: A Sociolinguistic Appraisal of the Role of the Interview in Social Science Research*. Cambridge: Cambridge University Press.

Brinkmann, S. (2013). *Qualitative Interviewing*. Oxford: Oxford University Press.

Brinkmann, S., & Kvale, S. (2015). *InterViews – Learning the Craft of Qualitative Research Interviewing*. London: Sage.

Brinkmann, S., & Kvale, S. (2018). *Doing Interviews* (2nd ed.). London: Sage.

Burgess, E.W. (1928). What Case Records Should Contain to be Useful for Sociological Investigation. *Social Forces*, 6(4), 526–8.

Butler, C. (2018). *Developing the Capacity to Recognise the Capabilities of Pupils with PMLD, to Promote Learning Opportunities and to Reduce Isolation*. Harpur Trust. https://core.ac.uk/download/pdf/161941324.pdf

Caelli, K., Ray, L., & Mill, J. (2003). 'Clear as Mud': Toward Greater Clarity in Generic Qualitative Research. *International Journal of Qualitative Methods*, 2(2), 1–13.

Caldera, A., Rizvi, S., Calderon-Berumen, F., & Lugo, M. (2020). When Researching the 'Other' Intersects with the Self: Women of Color Intimate Research. *Departures in Critical Qualitative Research*, 9(1), 63–88. doi:10.1525/dcqr.2020.9.1.63

Carpiano, R.M. (2009). Come Take a Walk with Me: The 'Go-Along' Interview as a Novel Method for Studying the Implications of Place for Health and Well-being. *Health & Place*, 15(1), 263–72.

Cassell, J. (1988). The Relationship of Observer to Observed when Studying up. In R.G. Burgess (Ed.), *Studies in Qualitative Methodology* (pp. 89–108). Greenwich, CT: JAI Press.

Cater, J.K. (2011). SKYPE – A Cost-effective Method for Qualitative Research. *Rehabilitation Counselors and Educators Journal*, 4(2), 3–4.

Charmaz, K. (2003). Grounded Theory. In J.A. Smith (Ed.), *Qualitative Psychology: A Practical Guide to Research Methods* (pp. 81–110). London. Sage.

Charmaz, K. (2011). A Constructivist Grounded Theory Analysis of Losing and Regaining a Valued Self. In F.J. Wertz, K. Charmaz, L.M. McMullen, R. Josselson, R. Anderson, & E. McSpadden, *Five Ways of Doing Qualitative Analysis* (pp. 165–204). New York: Guilford.

Charmaz, K. (2014). *Constructing Grounded Theory: A Practical Guide through Qualitative Analysis* (2nd ed.). London: Sage.

Charmaz, K., & Thornberg, R. (2020). The Pursuit of Quality in Grounded Theory. *Qualitative Research in Psychology*. doi:10.1080/14780887.2020.1780357

Charmaz, K., Harris, R.S., & Irivine, L. (2019). *The Social Self and Everyday Life – Understanding the World through Symbolic Interactionism*. Oxford: Wiley.

Chen, S.-H. (2011). Power Relations Between the Researcher and the Researched: An Analysis of Native and Nonnative Ethnographic Interviews. *Field Methods*, 23(2), 119–135. doi:10.1177/1525822X10387575

Chilisa, B. (2009). Indigenous African-centered Ethics: Contesting and Complementing Dominant Models. In D.M. Mertens & P.E. Ginsberg (Eds.), *The Handbook of Social Research Ethics* (pp. 407–25). London: Sage.

Chilisa, B. (2020). *Indigenous Research Methodologies* (2nd ed.). London: Sage.

Chilisa, B., & Phatshwane, K. (2022). Qualitative Research within a Post-colonial Indigenous Paradigm. In U. Flick (Ed.), *The SAGE Handbook of Qualitative Research Design*. London: Sage.

Christensen, P., & Prout, A. (2002). Working with Ethical Symmetry in Social Research with Children. *Childhood*, 9(4), 477–97.

Clandinin, D.J., & Conelly, F.M. (2000). *Narrative Inquiry: Experience and Story in Qualitative Research*. San Francisco: Jossey-Bass.

Clark, T. (2008). 'We're Over-researched Here!': Exploring Accounts of Research Fatigue within Qualitative Research Engagements. *Sociology*, 42(5), 953–70. https://doi.org/10.1177/0038038508094573

Clark, T. (2011). Gaining and Maintaining Access: Exploring the Mechanisms that Support and Challenge the Relationship between Gatekeepers and Researchers. *Qualitative Social Work*, 10(4), 485–502.

Cloutier, C., & Ravasi, D. (2021). Using Tables to Enhance Trustworthiness in Qualitative Research. *Strategic Organization*, 19(1), 113–33.

Coltart, C., & Henwood, K. (2012). On Paternal Subjectivity: A Qualitative Longitudinal and Psychosocial Case Analysis of Men's Classed Positions and Transitions to First-time Fatherhood. *Qualitative Research*, 12(1), 35–52.

Copes, H., Tchoula, W., Brookman, F., & Ragland, J. (2018). Photo-elicitation Interviews with Vulnerable Populations: Practical and Ethical Considerations. *Deviant Behavior*, 39(4), 475–94. doi: 10.1080/01639625.2017.1407109

Corbin, J., & Morse, J.M. (2003). The Unstructured Interactive Interview: Issues of Reciprocity and Risks when Dealing with Sensitive Topics. *Qualitative Inquiry*, 9(3), 335–54. https://doi.org/10.1177/1077800403009003001

Corti, L. (2018). Data Collection in Secondary Analysis. In U. Flick (Ed.), *The SAGE Handbook of Qualitative Data Collection* (pp. 164–82). London: Sage.

Corti, L. (2022). Data Collection in Secondary Analysis. In U. Flick (Ed.), *The SAGE Handbook of Qualitative Data Design*. London: Sage.

Cram, F. (2022). Designing Indigenous Qualitative Research for Policy Implementation. In U. Flick (Ed.), *The SAGE Handbook of Qualitative Research Design*. London: Sage.

Creswell, J.W. (2003). *Research Design: Qualitative, Quantitative, and Mixed Methods Approaches*. Thousand Oaks, CA: Sage.

Creswell, J.W., & Poth, C.N. (2017). *Qualitative Inquiry and Research Design* (4th ed.). Thousand Oaks, CA: Sage.

Crilly, N., Blackwell, A.F., & Clarkson, P.J. (2006). Graphic Elicitation: Using Research Diagrams as Interview Stimuli. *Qualitative Research*, 6(3), 341–66. https://doi.org/10.1177/1468794106065007

Cross, T., Earl, K., Echo-Hawk Solie, H., & Mannes, K. (2000). *Cultural Strength and Challenges in Implementing a System of Care Model in American Indian Communities* (Systems of Care: Promising Practices in Children's Mental Health, Vol. 1). Washington, DC: American Institutes for Research, Center for Effective Collaboration and Practice.

Cunsolo Willox, A., Harper, S.L., & Edge, V.L. (2013). Storytelling in a Digital Age: Digital Storytelling as an Emerging Narrative Method for Preserving and Promoting Indigenous Oral Wisdom. *Qualitative Research*, 13(2), 127–47. https://doi.org/10.1177/1468794112446105

Deakin, H., & Wakefield, K. (2014). Skype Interviewing: Reflections of two PhD Researchers. *Qualitative Research*, 14(5), 603–16. doi:10.1177/1468794113488126

Deeke, A. (1995). Experteninterviews – ein methodologisches und forschungspraktisches Problem. Einleitende Bemerkungen und Fragen zum Workshop. In C. Brinkmann, A. Deeke, & B. Völkel (Eds.), *Experteninterviews in der Arbeitsmarktforschung. Diskussionsbeiträge zu methodischen Fragen und praktischen Erfahrungen. Beiträge zur Arbeitsmarkt- und Berufsforschung* 191 (pp. 7–22). Nürnberg: Bundesanstalt für Arbeit.

Denzin, N., & Lincoln, Y.S. (Eds.) (2000). *Handbook of Qualitative Research* (2nd ed.). London: Sage.

Department of Health (2001). *Research Governance Framework for Health and Social Care*. London: Department of Health.

DeVault, M.L. (1990). Talking and Listening from Women's Standpoint: Feminist Strategies for Interviewing and Analysis. *Social Problems*, 37(1), 96–116. https://doi.org/10.2307/800797

DFG (German Research Foundation) (2018). Data Protection Information for the Initialisation and Development Phase of the National Research Data Infrastructure (NFDI). www.dfg.de/download/pdf/foerderung/programme/nfdi/nfdi_data_protection.pdf (last accessed 23 April 2019).

Dhunna, S., Lawton, B., & Cram, F. (2018). An Affront to Her Mana: Young Māori Mothers' Experiences of Intimate Partner Violence. *Journal of Interpersonal Violence*. https://doi.org/10.1177/0886260518815712

Dimond, R. (2014). Negotiating Blame and Responsibility in the Context of a 'De novo' Mutation. *New Genetics and Society*, 33(2), 149–66. doi:10.1080/14636778.2014.910450

Dimond, R. (2015). Dataset. In J. Lewis, (Ed.), *Analysing Semi-structured Interviews: Understanding Family Experience of Rare Disease and Genetic Risk*. London: Sage.

Döringer, S. (2020). 'The Problem-centred Expert Interview'. Combining Qualitative Interviewing Approaches for Investigating Implicit Expert Knowledge. *International Journal of Social Research Methodology*. doi:10.1080/13645579.2020.1766777

Dot.magazine (2017). Germany: Land of Data Protection and Security – But Why? *Dot.magazine*, February. www.dotmagazine.online/topics/unnamed (last accessed 23 April 2019).

Douglas, J.D. (1976). *Investigative Social Research*. Beverly Hills, CA: Sage.

Draucker, C.B., Al-Khattab, H., Hines, D.D., et al. (2014). Racial and Ethnic Diversity in Grounded Theory Research. *The Qualitative Report*, 19(17), Article 34.

Drawson, A.S., Toombs, E., & Mushquash, C.J. (2017). Indigenous Research Methods: A Systematic Review. *The International Indigenous Policy Journal*, 8(2). doi:10.18584/iipj.2017.8.2.5

Duchesne, S. (2017). Using Focus Groups to Study the Process of (de)Politicization. In R. Barbour & D. Morgan (Eds.), *A New Era in Focus Group Research* (pp. 365–88). London: Palgrave Macmillan.

Duncan, R., Drew, S., Hodgson, J., & Sawyer, S. (2009). Is My Mum Going to Hear This? Methodological and Ethical Challenges in Qualitative Health Research with Young People. *Social Science and Medicine*, 69, 1691–9.

Edwards, R. (1998). A Critical Examination of the Use of Interpreters in the Qualitative Research Process. *Journal of Ethnic and Migration Studies*, 24(1), 197–208.

Edwards, R., & Temple, B. (2002). Interpreters/Translators and Cross-language Research: Reflexivity and Border Crossings. *International Journal of Qualitative Methods*, 1(2), Article 1. www.ualberta.ca/~iiqm/backissues/1_2Final/pdf/temple.pdf

Edwards, S., McManus, V., & McCreanor, T. (2005). Collaborative Research within Maori on Sensitive Issues: The Application of Tikanga and Kaupapa in Research on Maori Sudden Infant Death Syndrome. *Social Policy Journal of New Zealand*, 25, 88–104.

Ensign, J. (2003). Ethical Issues in Qualitative Health Research with Homeless Youths. *Journal of Advanced Nursing*, 43(1), 43–50.

ESRC (2019). Gateway to Research: Principles for ethical research. https://esrc.ukri.org/funding/guidance-for-applicants/research-ethics/our-core-principles

EU (2018). Ethics and Data Protection. 14 November. http://ec.europa.eu/research/participants/data/ref/h2020/grants_manual/hi/ethics/h2020_hi_ethics-data-protection_en.pdf (last accessed 21 April 2019).

Evans, J., & Jones, P. (2011). The Walking Interview: Methodology, Mobility and Place. *Applied Geography*, 31(2), 849–58.

Falkenhain, M., Flick, U., Hirseland, A., Naji, S., Schilling, A., Seidelsohn, K., & Verlage, T. (2020). Setback in Labour Market Integration due to the Covid-19 Crisis? An Explorative Insight on Forced Migrants' Vulnerability in Germany. *European Societies*, 23, sup1, S448–S463.https://doi.org/10.1080/14616696.2020.1828976

Fielding, N.G. (2018). Combining Digital and Physical Data. In U. Flick (Ed.), *The SAGE Handbook of Qualitative Data Collection* (pp. 584–98). London: Sage.

Fischer-Rosenthal, W., & Rosenthal, G. (1997). Narrationsanalyse biographischer Selbstpräsentation. In R. Hitzler & A. Honer (Eds.), *Sozialwissenschaftliche Hermeneutik* (pp. 133–64). Opladen: Leske + Budrich.

Flick, U. (1992). Knowledge in the Definition of Social Situations: Actualization of Subjective Theories about Trust in Counselling. In M. v. Cranach, W. Doise, & G. Mugny (Eds.), *Social Representations and the Social Bases of Knowledge* (pp. 64–8). Bern: Huber.

Flick, U. (1994). Social Representations and the Social Construction of Everyday Knowledge: Theoretical and Methodological Queries. *Social Science Information*, 33, 179–97.

Flick, U. (1995). Social Representations. In R. Harré, J. Smith, & L. v. Langenhove (Eds.), *Rethinking Psychology* (pp. 70–96). London: Sage.

Flick, U. (1997). *The Episodic Interview: Small Scale Narratives as Approach to Relevant Experiences*. Discussion Paper. London: LSE Methodology Institute. www.lse.ac.uk/methodology/pdf/qualpapers/flick-episodic.pdf

Flick, U. (Ed.) (1998). *Psychology of the Social: Representations in Knowledge and Language*. Cambridge: Cambridge University Press.

Flick, U. (2000). Episodic Interviewing. In M. Bauer & G. Gaskell (Eds.), *Qualitative Researching with Text, Image and Sound: A Practical Handbook* (pp. 75–92). London: Sage.

Flick, U. (2012). In S.E. Baker & R. Edwards (Eds.), *How Many Qualitative Interviews is Enough?* Discussion Paper, National Centre of Research Methods. http://eprints.ncrm.ac.uk/2273

Flick, U. (Ed.) (2014a). Challenges for Qualitative Inquiry as a Global Endeavor (Special Issue). *Qualitative Inquiry*, 20.

Flick, U. (Ed.) (2014b). *The SAGE Handbook of Qualitative Data Analysis*. London: Sage.

Flick, U. (2014c). Mapping the Field. In U. Flick (Ed.), *The SAGE Handbook of Qualitative Data Analysis* (pp. 3–18). London: Sage.

Flick, U. (2018a). *An Introduction to Qualitative Research* (6th ed.). London: Sage.

Flick, U. (2018b). *Doing Triangulation and Mixed Methods Research*. London: Sage.

Flick, U. (2018c). *Doing Grounded Theory*. London: Sage.

Flick, U. (2018d). *Designing Qualitative Research* (2nd ed.). London: Sage.

Flick, U. (2018e). *Managing Quality in Qualitative Research* (2nd ed.). London: Sage.

Flick, U. (Ed.) (2018f). *The SAGE Handbook of Qualitative Data Collection*. London: Sage.

Flick, U. (2020). *Introducing Research Methodology* (3rd ed.). London: Sage.

Flick, U., & Röhnsch, G. (2007). Idealization and Neglect – Health Concepts of Homeless Adolescents. *Journal of Health Psychology*, 12(5), 737–50.

Flick, U., & Röhnsch, R. (2008). *Gesundheit auf der Straße*. Weinheim: Juventa.

Flick, U., Fischer, C., Neuber, A., Walter, U., & Schwartz, F.W. (2003). Health in the Context of Being Old: Representations Held by Health Professionals. *Journal of Health Psychology*, 8(5), 539–56.

Flick, U., Garms-Homolová, V., & Röhnsch, G. (2010). 'When They Sleep, They Sleep' – Daytime Activities and Sleep Disorders in Nursing Homes. *Journal of Health Psychology*, 15(5), 755–64.

Flick, U., Garms-Homolová, V., & Röhnsch, G. (2012). 'And Mostly They Have a Need for Sleeping Pills': Physicians' Views on Treatment of Sleep Disorders with Drugs in Nursing Homes. *Journal of Aging Studies*, 26(4), 484–94.

Flick, U., Hans, B., Hirseland, A., Rasche, S., & Röhnsch, G. (2017). Migration, Unemployment, and Lifeworld: Challenges for a New Critical Qualitative Inquiry in Migration. *Qualitative Inquiry*, 23(1), 77–88.

Flick, U., Hirseland, A., & Hans, B. (2019). Walking and Talking Integration: Triangulation of Data from Interviews and Go-alongs for Exploring Immigrant Welfare Recipients' Sense(s) of Belonging. *Qualitative Inquiry*, 25(8), 799–810. https://doi.org/10.1177/1077800418809515

Flick, U., Hoose, B., & Sitta, P. (1998). Gesundheit und Krankheit gleich Saúde & Doenca? – Gesundheitsvorstellungen bei Frauen in Deutschland und Portugal. In U. Flick, U. (Ed), *Wann fühlen wir uns gesund? – Subjektive Vorstellungen von Gesundheit und Krankheit* (pp. 141–159). Weinheim: Juventa.

Flynn, L.R., & Goldsmith, R.E. (2013). *Case Studies for Ethics in Academic Research in the Social Sciences*. Thousand Oaks, CA: Sage.

Fontana, A., & Frey, J.H. (2000). The Interview: From Structured Questions to Negotiated Text. In N. Denzin & Y.S. Lincoln (Eds), *Handbook of Qualitative Research* (2nd ed., pp. 645–72). London: Sage.

Fritz, R.L., & Vandermause, R. (2018). Data Collection via In-depth Email Interviewing: Lessons From the Field. *Qualitative Health Research*, 28(10), 1640–9. https://doi.org/10.1177/1049732316689067

Fujii, L.A. (2018). *Interviewing in Social Science Research: A Relational Approach*. New York: Routledge.

Gaiser, T.J., & Schreiner, A.E. (2009). *A Guide to Conducting Online Research*. London: Sage.

Gangnus, A. (2020). *LebensQuerschnitt – Transitionsprozesse im Bildungsverlauf von Menschen mit schweren Lebensbehinderungen*. Unpublished Master's Thesis, Freie Universität Berlin.

García, A., & Fine, G. (2018). Fair Warnings: The Ethics of Ethnography with Children. In R. Iphofen & M. Tolich (Eds.), *The Sage Handbook of Qualitative Research Ethics* (pp. 367–81). London: Sage.

Garcia, C.M., Eisenberg, M.E., Frerich, E.A., Lechner, K.E., & Lust, K. (2012). Conducting Go-Along Interviews to Understand Context and Promote Health. *Qualitative Health Research*, 22(10), 1395–403.

Geertz, C. (1974). 'From the Native's Point of View': On the Nature of Anthropological Understanding. *Bulletin of the American Academy of Arts and Sciences*, 28(1), 26–45. doi:10.2307/3822971

Gibson, L. (2010). Using Email Interviews to Research Popular Music and the Life Course. *'Realities' Toolkit*, ESRC National Centre for Research Methods. www.socialsciences.manchester.ac.uk/realities/resources/toolkits/email-interviews/index.html

Girang, B.C., Chu, D.P., Endrinal, M.I., & Canoy, N. (2020). Spatializing Psychological Well-being: A Photovoice Approach on the Experience of Stress Alleviation among University Students. *Qualitative Research in Psychology*. doi:10.1080/14780887. 2020.1716424

Glaser, B.G., & Strauss, A.L. (1967). *The Discovery of Grounded Theory: Strategies for Qualitative Research*. Chicago: Aldine.

Gobo, G. (2008). *Doing Ethnography*. London: Sage.

Gobo, G. (2011). Glocalizing Methodology? The Encounter between Local Methodologies. *International Journal of Social Research Methodology*, 14(6), 417–37. doi:10.1080/13645579.2011.611379

Gobo, G. (2018). Qualitative Research across Boundaries: Indigenization, Glocalization or Creolization? In C. Cassell, A.L. Cunliffe, & G. Grandy (Eds.), *The Sage Handbook of Qualitative Business and Management Research Methods* (pp. 495–514). London: Sage.

Goodall, H., Norman, H., & Russon, B. (2019). 'Around the Meeting Tree': Methodological Reflections on Using Digital Tools for Research into Indigenous Adult Education in the Networking Tranby Project. *Archives and Manuscripts*, 47(1), 53–71. doi:10.1080/01576895.2018.1551144

Graham, J., Grewal, I., & Lewis, J. (2007). *Ethics in Social Research: The Views of Research Participants*. Government Social Research.

Gubrium, J.F., & Holstein, J.A. (Eds.) (2001). *The SAGE Handbook of Interview Research*. Thousand Oaks, CA: Sage.

Gubrium, J.F., Holstein, J.A., Marvasti, A.B., & McKinney, K.D. (Eds.) (2012). *The SAGE Handbook of Interview Research: The Complexity of the Craft* (2nd ed.). Thousand Oaks, CA: Sage.

Guest, G., Bunce, A., & Johnson, L. (2006). How Many Interviews Are Enough? An Experiment with Data Saturation and Variability. *Field Methods*, 18(1), 59–82.

Hakim, C. (1982). *Secondary Analysis in Social Research: A Guide to Data Sources and Method Examples*. London: George Allen & Uwin.

Halkier, B. (2010). Focus Groups as Social Enactments: Integrating Interaction and Content in the Analysis of Focus Group Data. *Qualitative Research*, 10(1), 71–89.

Hammersley, M. (2003). Recent Radical Criticism of Interview Studies: Any Implications for the Sociology of Education? *British Journal of Sociology of Education*, 24(1), 119–26. doi:10.1080/01425690301906

Hammersley, M. (2015). On Ethical Principles for Social Research. *International Journal of Social Research Methodology*, 18(4), 433–49. doi:10.1080/13645579.2014.924169

Hammersley, M. (2017). Interview Data: A Qualified Defence against the Radical Critique. *Qualitative Research*, 17(2), 173–86. doi:10.1177/1468794116671988

Hammersley, M. (2021). The 'Radical Critique of Interviews': A Response to Recent Comments. *International Journal of Social Research Methodology*, 24(3), 393–5. doi:10.1080/13645579.2020.1841881

Hanna, P. (2012). Using Internet Technologies (such as Skype) as a Research Medium: A Research Note. *Qualitative Research*, 12(2), 239–42.

Harding, S. (1998). *Is Science Multicultural? Postcolonialisms, Feminisms, and Epistemologies*. Bloomington: Indiana University Press.

Harper, D. (2002). Talking about Pictures: A Case of Photo Elicitation. *Visual Studies*, 17(1), 13–26.

Harrington, W. (1997). *Intimate Journalism: The Art and Craft of Reporting Everyday Life*. Thousand Oaks, CA: Sage.

Harvey, W.S. (2011). Strategies for Conducting Elite Interviews. *Qualitative Research*, 11(4), 431–41.

Hermanns, H. (1995). Narratives Interview. In U. Flick, E. v. Kardorff, H. Keupp, L. v. Rosenstiel, & S. Wolff (Eds.), *Handbuch Qualitative Sozialforschung* (2nd ed., pp. 182–5). Munich: Psychologie Verlags Union.

Hermanns, H. (2004). Interviewing as an Activity. In U. Flick, E. v. Kardorff, & I. Steinke (Eds.), *A Companion to Qualitative Research* (pp. 209–13). London: Sage.

Heyl, B. (2001). Ethnographic Interviewing. In P. Atkinson, A. Coffey, S. Delamont, J. Lofland, & L. Lofland (Eds.), *Handbook of Ethnography* (pp. 369–83). London: Sage.

Hildenbrand, B. (1995). Fallrekonstruktive Forschung. In U. Flick, E. v. Kardorff, H. Keupp, L. v. Rosenstiel, & S. Wolff (Eds.), *Handbuch Qualitative Sozialforschung* (2nd ed., pp. 256–60). Munich: Psychologie Verlags Union.

Hildenbrand, B., & Jahn, W. (1988). Gemeinsames Erzählen und Prozesse der Wirklichkeitskonstruktion in familiengeschichtlichen Gesprächen. *Zeitschrift für Soziologie*, 17, 203–17.

Hill, C.E., Thompson, B.J., & Williams, E.N. (1997). A Guide to Conducting Consensual Qualitative Research. *The Counseling Psychologist*, 25(4), 517–72.

Hochschild, A.R. (1983). *The Managed Heart*. Berkeley: University of California Press.

Hodgetts, D., Radley, A., Chamberlain, C., & Hodgetts, A. (2007). Health Inequalities and Homelessness: Considering Material, Spatial and Relational Dimensions. *Journal of Health Psychology*, 12(5), 709–25.

Holstein, J.A., & Gubrium, J.F. (1995). *The Active Interview*. Thousand Oaks, CA: Sage.

Holstein, J.A., & Gubrium, J.F. (1997). The Active Interview. In D. Silverman (Ed.), *Qualitative Research* (pp. 113–29). London: Sage.

Holstein, J.A., & Gubrium, J.F. (2003). Inside Interviewing: New Lenses, New Concerns. In J.A. Holstein & J.F Gubrium (Eds.), *Inside Interviewing* (pp. 2–30). Thousand Oaks, CA: Sage

Holstein, J.A., & Gubrium, J.F. (2016). Narrative Practice and the Active Interview. In D. Silverman (Ed.), *Qualitative Data Analysis* (pp. 67–82). London: Sage.

Holt, A. (2010). Using the Telephone for Narrative Interviewing: A Research Note. *Qualitative Research*, 10, 113–21.

Homan, R. (1991). *The Ethics of Social Research*. London: Longman.

Hopf, C. (1978). Die Pseudo-Exploration: Überlegungen zur Technik qualitativer Interviews in der Sozialforschung. *Zeitschrift für Soziologie*, 7, 97–115.

Hopf, C. (2004). Research Ethics and Qualitative Research: An Overview. In U. Flick, E. v. Kardorff, & I. Steinke (Eds.), *A Companion to Qualitative Research* (pp. 334–9). London: Sage.

Hsiung, P.-C. (2012). The Globalization of Qualitative Research: Challenging Anglo-American Domination and Local Hegemonic Discourse [27 paragraphs]. *Forum Qualitative Sozialforschung/Forum: Qualitative Social Research*, 13(1), Article 21. http://nbn-resolving.de/urn:nbn:de:0114-fqs1201216

Hughes, K., Hughes, J., & Tarrant A. (2020). Re-approaching Interview Data through Qualitative Secondary Analysis: Interviews with Internet Gamblers. *International Journal of Social Research Methodology*, 23(5), 565–79. doi:10.1080/13645579.2020.1766759

Hughes, R. (1998). Considering Vignette Technique and its Application to a Study of Drug Injecting and HIV Risk and Safer Behaviour. *Sociology of Health & Illness*, 20(3), 381–400.

Hutchinson, S.A., Wilson, M.E., & Wilson, H.S. (1994). Benefits of Participating in Research Interviews. *Journal of Nursing Scholarship*, 26, 161–4.

Iacono, V.L., Symonds, P., & Brown, D.H.K. (2016). Skype as a Tool for Qualitative Research Interviews. *Sociological Research Online*, 21(2), 1–15. https://doi.org/10.5153/sro.3952

Inhetveen, K. (2012). Translation Challenges: Qualitative Interviewing in a Multi-lingual Field. *Qualitative Sociology Review*, 8(2), 28–45. www.qualitativesociologyreview.org.

Irvinc, A. (2008). *Managing Mental Health and Employment*. Department for Work and Pensions Research Report, 537, Corporate Document Services, Leeds.

Irvine, A. (2010). *Using Phone Interviews*. Realities Toolkit #14. www.socialsciences.manchester.ac.uk/morgan-centre/research/resources/toolkits/toolkit-14

Irvine, A. (2011). Duration, Dominance and Depth in Telephone and Face-to-Face Interviews: A Comparative Exploration. *International Journal of Qualitative Methods*, 10(3), 202–20. https://doi.org/10.1177/160940691101000302

Ison, N.L. (2009). Having their Say: Email Interviews for Research Data Collection with People Who Have Verbal Communication Impairment. *International Journal of Social Research Methodology*, 12(2), 161–72.

James, N. (2007). The Use of Email Interviewing as a Qualitative Method of Inquiry in Educational Research. *British Educational Research Journal*, 33(6), 963–76.

James, N. (2016). Using Email Interviews in Qualitative Educational Research: Creating Space to Think and Time to Talk. *International Journal of Qualitative Studies in Education*, 29(2), 150–63. doi:10.1080/09518398.2015.1017848

James, N., & Busher, H. (2006). Credibility, Authenticity and Voice: Dilemmas in Online Interviewing. *Qualitative Research*, 6(3), 403–20.

Jeffries, C., & Maeder, D.W. (2005). Using Vignettes to Build and Assess Teacher Understanding of Instructional Strategies. *The Professional Educator*, 27(1&2), 17–28.

Jenkins, N., Bloor, M., Fischer, J., et al. (2010). Putting it in Context: The Use of Vignettes in Qualitative Interviewing. *Qualitative Research*, 10(2), 175–98.

Jenkins, N., Keyes, S., & Strange, L. (2016). Creating Vignettes of Early Onset Dementia: An Exercise in Public Sociology. *Sociology*, 50(1), 77–92. https://doi.org/10.1177/0038038514560262

Jenks, C. (2018). Recording and Transcription of Qualitative Data. In U. Flick (Ed.), *The SAGE Handbook of Qualitative Data Collection* (pp. 118–30). London: Sage.

Jenner, B.M., & Myers, K.C. (2019). Intimacy, Rapport, and Exceptional Disclosure: A Comparison of In-person and Mediated Interview Contexts. *International Journal of Social Research Methodology*, 22(2), 165–77.

Jerolmack, C., & Khan, S. (2014). Talk is Cheap: Ethnography and the Attitudinal Fallacy. *Sociological Methods & Research*, 43(2), 178–209. doi:10.1177/0049124114523396

Jones, P., Bunce, G., Evans, J., Gibbs, H., & Ricketts Hein, J. (2008). Exploring Space and Place with Walking Interviews. *Journal of Research Practice*, 4(2), 1–9.

Josselson, R. (2013). *Interviewing for Qualitative Inquiry: A Relational Approach.* New York: The Guilford Press.

Jovchelovitch, S., & Bauer, M. (2000). Narrative Interviewing. In M.W. Bauer & G. Gaskell (Eds.), *Qualitative Researching with Text, Image and Sound* (pp. 58–74). London: Sage.

Kassianos, A.P. (2014). The Use of Telephone Interviews in Qualitative Psychology Research: A Reflective Methodological Exercise. *QMiP Bulletin Issue 18* (pp. 23–26). The British Psychological Society.

Kazmer, M., & Xie, B. (2008). Qualitative Interviewing in Internet Studies: Playing with the Media, Playing with the Method. *Information, Communication & Society*, 11(2), 257–78.

Khanolainen, D., & Semenova, E. (2020). School Bullying through Graphic Vignettes: Developing a New Arts-based Method to Study a Sensitive Topic. *International Journal of Qualitative Methods.* https://doi.org/10.1177/1609406920922765

King, A.C., & Woodroffe, J. (2017). Walking Interviews. In P. Liamputtong (Ed.), *Handbook of Research Methods in Health Social Sciences.* Cham: Springer.

King, N., & Horrocks, C. (2010). *Interviews in Qualitative Research.* London: Sage.

Kinney, P. (2018). Walking Interview Ethics. In R. Iphofen, & M. Tolich (Eds.), *The Sage Handbook of Qualitative Research Ethics* (pp. 174–87). London: Sage.

Kirkhart, K.E. (2013). *Repositioning Validity.* CREA Inaugural Conference. Chicago: Syracuse University.

Kleinman, A. (1988). *The Illness Narratives: Suffering, Healing and the Human Condition.* New York: Basic Books.

Kluge, U. (2011). Sprach- und Kulturmittler im interkulturellen psychotherapeutischen Setting. In W. Machleidt, & A. Heinz (Eds.), *Praxis der interkulturellen Psychiatrie und Psychotherapie. Migration und psychische Gesundheit* (pp. 145–54). München: Urban & Fischer.

Koro-Ljungberg, M., & Bussing, R. (2013). Methodological Modifications in a Longitudinal Qualitative Research Design. *Field Methods*, 25(4), 423–40. https://doi.org/10.1177/1525822X12472877

Kovach, M. (2009). *Indigenous Methodologies: Characteristics, Conversations and Contexts.* Toronto: University of Toronto Press.

Kristensen, G.K., & Ravn, M.N. (2015). The Voices Heard and the Voices Silenced: Recruitment Processes in Qualitative Interview Studies. *Qualitative Research*, 15(6), 722–37. https://doi.org/10.1177/1468794114567496

Krueger, R.A. (1998). *Focus Group Kit: Developing Questions for Focus Groups* (Vols 1–3). Thousand Oaks, CA: Sage.

Kusenbach, M. (2018). Go-Alongs. In U. Flick (Ed.), *The SAGE Handbook of Qualitative Data Collection* (pp. 344–61). London: Sage.

Küsters, Y. (2009). *Narrative Interviews.* Wiesbaden: VS-Verlag.

Kvale, S. (1996). *InterViews.* London: Sage.

Lau, T., & Wolff, S. (1983). Der Einstieg in das Untersuchungsfeld als soziologischer Lernprozeß. *Kölner Zeitschrift für Soziologie und Sozialpsychologie*, 35, 417–37.

Lawton, B., Makowharemahihi, M., Cram, F., Robson, B., & Ngata, T. (2016). E Hine: Access to Contraception for Indigenous Māori Teenage Mothers. *Journal of Primary Health Care*, 8, 52–9.

LeCompte, M.D., & Preissle, J. (1993). *Ethnography and Qualitative Design in Educational Research* (2nd ed.). San Diego: Academic Press.

Lee, R.M. (2004). Recording Technologies and the Interview in Sociology, 1920–2000. *Sociology*, 38(5), 869–89.

Lewis, J., & McNaughton Nichols, C. (2014). Design Issues. In J. Ritchie, J. Lewis, C. McNaughton Nichols, & R. Ormston (Eds.), *Qualitative Research Practice* (pp. 47–74). London: Sage.

Libakova, N.M., & Sertakova, E.A. (2015). The Method of Expert Interview as an Effective Research Procedure of Studying the Indigenous Peoples of the North. *Journal of Siberian Federal University. Humanities & Social Sciences*, 8, 114–29.

Lincoln, Y.S., & Gonzalez, G. (2008). The Search for Emerging Decolonizing Methodologies in Qualitative Research: Further Strategies for Liberatory and Democratic Inquiry. *Qualitative Inquiry*, 14(5), 784–805.

Lincoln, Y.S., & Guba, E.G. (1985). *Naturalistic Inquiry*. London: Sage.

Littig, B. (2009). Interviewing Experts or Interviewing Elites: What Makes the Difference? In A. Bogner, B. Littig, & W. Menz (Eds.), *Interviewing Experts* (pp. 98–113). Basingstoke: Palgrave Macmillan.

Littig, B., & Pöchhacker, F. (2014). Socio-translational Collaboration in Qualitative Inquiry: The Case of Expert Interviews. *Qualitative Inquiry*, 20(9), 1085–95.

Lobe, B. (2017). Best Practices for Synchronous Online Focus Groups. In R. Barbour & D. Morgan (Eds.), *A New Era in Focus Group Research* (pp. 227–50). London: Palgrave Macmillan.

Lobe, B., Morgan, D., & Hoffman, K.A. (2020). Qualitative Data Collection in an Era of Social Distancing. *International Journal of Qualitative Methods*. https://doi.org/10.1177/1609406920937875t

Lucius-Hoene, G., & Deppermann, A. (2000). Narrative Identity Empiricized: A Dialogical and Positioning Approach to Autobiographical Research Interviews. *Narrative Inquiry*, 10, 199–222. doi:10.1075/ni.10.1.15luc

Lucius-Hoene, G., & Deppermann, A. (2002). *Rekonstruktion narrativer Identität*. Wiesbaden: VS-Verlag.

Lüders, C. (1995). Von der Teilnehmenden Beobachtung zur ethnographischen Beschreibung - Ein Literaturbericht. In E. König & P. Zedler (Eds.), *Bilanz qualitativer Forschung* (Vol. 1., pp. 311–42). Weinheim: Deutscher Studienverlag.

Lüders, C. (2004a). Field Observation and Ethnography. In U. Flick, E. v. Kardorff, & I. Steinke (Eds.), *A Companion to Qualitative Research* (pp. 222–30). London: Sage.

Lüders, C. (2004b). The Challenges of Qualitative Research. In U. Flick, E. v. Kardorff, & I. Steinke (Eds.), *A Companion to Qualitative Research* (pp. 359–64). London: Sage.

Lyotard, C.F. (1984). *The Postmodern Condition*. Manchester: Manchester University Press.

Mann, C.S.F., & Stewart, F. (2000). *Internet Communication and Qualitative Research: A Handbook for Researching Online*. London: Sage.

Manokaran, R., Pausé, C., Roßmöller, M., & Vilhjálmsdóttir, T.M. (2020). 'Nothing About Us Without Us': Fat People Speak. *Qualitative Research in Psychology*. doi:10.1080/14780887.2020.1780355

Markham, A. (1998). *Life Online: Researching Real World Experience in Virtual Space*. Walnut Creek, CA: Altamira.

Markham, A.N. (2004). The Internet as Research Context. In C. Seale, G. Gobo, J. Gubrium, & D. Silverman (Eds.), *Qualitative Research Practice* (pp. 358–74). London: Sage.

Marshall, C., & Rossman, G.B. (2016). *Designing Qualitative Research* (6th ed.). Thousand Oaks, CA: Sage.

Mason, M. (2010). Sample Size and Saturation in PhD Studies Using Qualitative Interviews [63 paragraphs]. *Forum Qualitative Sozialforschung / Forum: Qualitative Social Research*, 11(3), Article 8. http://nbn-resolving.de/urn:nbn:de:0114-fqs100387

Massey, A., & Kirk, R. (2015). Bridging Indigenous and Western Sciences: Research Methodologies for Traditional, Complementary, and Alternative Medicine Systems. *SAGE Open*. https://doi.org/10.1177/2158244015597726

Maxwell, J.A. (2012). *Qualitative Research Design: An Interactive Approach* (3rd ed.). Thousand Oaks, CA: Sage.

May, T., & Perry, B. (2014). Reflexivity and the Practice of Qualitative Research. In U. Flick (Ed.), *The SAGE Handbook of Qualitative Data Analysis* (pp. 109–22). London: Sage.

Mayring, P. (1983) *Qualitative Inhaltsanalyse: Grundlagen und Techniken*. Weinheim: Deutscher Studien Verlag.

Mayring, P. (2000). Qualitative Content Analysis [28 paragraphs]. *Forum Qualitative Sozialforschung / Forum: Qualitative Social Research*, 1(2), Article 20. http://nbn-resolving.de/urn:nbn:de:0114-fqs0002204

McCracken, G. (1988). *The Long Interview*. Thousand Oaks, CA: Sage.

McDonald, S. (2005). Studying Actions in Context: A Qualitative Shadowing Method for Organisational Research. *Qualitative Research*, 5(4), 455–73.

McLellan, E., MacQueen, K.M., & Neidig, J.L. (2003). Beyond the Qualitative Interview: Data Preparation and Transcription. *Field Methods*, 15(1), 63–84. https://doi.org/10.1177/1525822X02239573

McMullen, L. (2011). A Discursive Analysis of Teresa's Protocol: Enhancing Oneself, Diminishing Others. In F.J. Wertz, K. Charmaz, L.M. McMullen, R.R. Anderson, & E. McSpadden, *Five Ways of Doing Qualitative Analysis* (pp. 205–23). New York: The Guilford Press.

McNaughton, C. (2008). *Transitions Through Homelessness – Lives on the Edge*. Basingstoke: Palgrave Macmillan.

McNaughton, D., Hamlin, D., McCarthy, J., Head-Reeves, D., & Schreiner, M. (2008). Learning to Listen: Teaching an Active Listening Strategy to Preservice Education Professionals. *Topics in Early Childhood Special Education*, 27, 223–31. doi:10.1177/0271121407311241

Meho, L.I. (2006). E-mail Interviewing in Qualitative Research: A Methodological Discussion. *Journal of the American Society for Information Science and Technology*, 57(10), 1284–95.

Mertens, D. (2014). Ethical Use of Qualitative Data and Findings. In *The SAGE Handbook of Qualitative Data Analysis* (pp. 510–23). London: Sage.

Merton, R.K. (1987). The Focused Interview and Focus Groups: Continuities and Discontinuities. *Public Opinion Quarterly*, 51(4), 550–6.

Merton, R.K., & Kendall, P.L. (1946). The Focused Interview. *American Journal of Sociology*, 51(6), 541–57.

Merton, R.K., Fiske, M., & Kendall, P.L. (1956). *The Focused Interview*. Glencoe, IL: Free Press.

Meuser, M., & Nagel, U. (2002). ExpertInneninterviews – vielfach erprobt, wenig bedacht. Ein Beitrag zur qualitativen Methodendiskussion. In A. Bogner, B. Littig, & W. Menz (Eds.), *Das Experteninterview* (pp. 71–95). Opladen: Leske & Budrich.

Meuser, M., & Nagel, U. (2009). The Expert Interview and Changes in Knowledge Production, in A. Bogner, B. Littig & W. Menz (Eds.), *Interviewing Experts* (pp. 17–42). Basingstoke: Palgrave Macmillan.

Migala, S., & Flick, U. (2020). Making It Relevant: Qualitative Inquiry in the Public Sphere Focusing End-of-Life Care and Migration. *Qualitative Inquiry*, 26(2), 187–99.

Mikecz, R. (2012). Interviewing Elites: Addressing Methodological Issues. *Qualitative Inquiry*, 18(6), 482–93.

Miles, M.B., & Huberman, A.M. (1994). *Qualitative Data Analysis: A Sourcebook of New Methods* (2nd ed.). Newbury Park, CA: Sage.

Mills, C.W. (1959). *The Sociological Imagination*. Oxford: Oxford University Press.

Mishler, E.G. (1986). The Analysis of Interview-Narratives. In T.R. Sarbin (Ed.), *Narrative Psychology* (pp. 233–55). New York: Praeger.

Mizock, L., Harkins, D., Ray, S., & Morant, R. (2011a). Researcher Race in Narrative Interviews on Traumatic Racism. *Journal of Aggression, Maltreatment & Trauma*, 20(1), 40–57. doi:10.1080/10926771.2011. 537597

Mizock, L., Harkins, D., Ray, S., & Morant, R. (2011b). Researcher Interjecting in Qualitative Race Research [39 paragraphs]. *Forum Qualitative Sozialforschung / Forum: Qualitative Social Research*, 12(2), Article 13. http://nbn-resolving.de/ urn:nbn:de:0114-fqs1102134

Mji, G. (2019). Research Methodology that Drove the Study. In G. Mji (Ed.), *The Walk Without Limbs: Searching for Indigenous Health Knowledge in a Rural Context in South Africa* (pp. 109–34). Cape Town: AOSIS.

Moeke-Maxwell, T., Mason, K., Williams, L., & Gott, M. (2020). Digital Story-telling Research Methods: Supporting the Reclamation and Retention of Indigenous End of Life Care Customs in Aotearoa New Zealand. *Progress in Palliative Care*, 28, 101–6.

Moewaka Barnes, H., & McCreanor, T. (2022). Decolonising Qualitative Research Design. In U. Flick (Ed.), *The SAGE Handbook of Qualitative Research Design*. London: Sage.

Moles, K. (2018). Dataset. In J. Lewis (Ed.), *Ethnographic Interviews: Walking as Method*. London: Sage.

Moore, N. (2007). (Re-)using Qualitative Data. *Sociological Research Online*, 12(3).

Moravcsik, A. (2019). Transparency in Qualitative Research. In P. Atkinson, S. Delamont, A. Cernat, J.W. Sakshaug, & R.A. Williams (Eds.), *SAGE Research Methods Foundations*. London: Sage.

Morgan, D. (2012). Focus Groups and Social Interaction. In J.F. Gubrium, J.A. Holstein, A.B. Marvasti, & K.D. McKinney (Eds.), *The SAGE Handbook of Interview Research: The Complexity of the Craft* (pp. 161–76). Thousand Oaks, CA: Sage.

Morse, J.M. (1998). Designing Funded Qualitative Research. In N. Denzin & Y.S. Lincoln (Eds.), *Strategies of Qualitative Research* (pp. 56–85). London: Sage.

Morse, J. (2007). Sampling in Grounded Theory. In T. Bryant & K. Charmaz (Eds.), *The SAGE Handbook of Grounded Theory* (pp. 229–44). London: Sage.

Mueller, R.A. (2019). Episodic Narrative Interview: Capturing Stories of Experience with a Methods Fusion. *International Journal of Qualitative Methods.* doi:10.1177/1609406919866044

Munz, E. (2017). Ethnographic Interview. In M. Allen (Ed.), *The SAGE Encyclopedia of Communication Research Methods* (pp. 455–7). Thousand Oaks, CA: Sage.

Murphy, E., & Dingwall, R. (2001). The Ethics of Ethnography. In P. Atkinson, A. Coffey, S. Delamont, J. Lofland, & L. Lofland (Eds.), *Handbook of Ethnography* (pp. 339–51). London: Sage.

Nadan, Y. (2019). Teaching Note – The Ethnographic Interview as a Method in Multicultural Social Work Education. *Journal of Social Work Education*, 55(2), 396–402. doi:10.1080/10437797.2018.1544521

Neale, B. (2019). *What is Qualitative Longitudinal Research?* London: Bloomsbury.

Neill, S.J. (2010). Containing Acute Childhood Illness within Family Life: A Substantive Grounded Theory. *Journal of Child Health Care*, 14(4), 327–44. doi:10.1177/1367493510380078

Neisser, U. (1981). John Dean's Memory: A Case Study. *Cognition*, 9(1), 1–22.

Neuman, W.L. (2000). *Social Research Methods – Qualitative and Quantitative Approaches* (4th ed.). Boston: Allyn & Bacon.

Newman, P.A., Tepjan, S., & Rubincam, C. (2017). Exploring Sex, HIV and 'Sensitive' Space(s) Among Sexual and Gender Minority Young Adults in Thailand. In R. Barbour & D. Morgan (Eds.), *A New Era in Focus Group Research* (pp. 83–108). London: Palgrave Macmillan.

Nikunen, M., Korvajärvi, P., & Koivunen, T. (2019). Separated by Common Methods? Researchers and Journalists Doing Expertise. *Qualitative Research*, 19(5), 489–505. doi:10.1177/1468794118782896

NordForsk (2017). *Ethical Review, Data Protection and Biomedical Research in the Nordic Countries: A Legal Perspective.* Policy Paper 1/2017. http://sareco.fi/erpspdbrnc_single.pdf (last accessed 23 April 2019).

Northway, R. (2002). Commentary. *Nurse Researcher*, 10, 4–7.

Novick, G. (2008). Is there a Bias against Telephone Interviews in Qualitative Research? *Research in Nursing and Health*, 31, 391–8.

O'Connor, H., & Madge, C. (2017). Online Interviewing. In N.G. Fielding, R. Lee, & G. Blank (Eds.), *The SAGE Handbook of Online Research Methods* (2nd ed., pp. 416–34). London: Sage.

O'Dell, L., Crafter, S., de Abreu, G. et al. (2012). The Problem of Interpretation in Vignette Methodology in Research with Young People. *Qualitative Research*, 12(6), 702–14.

O'Kane, P., Smith, A., & Lerman, M.P. (2021). Building Transparency and Trustworthiness in Inductive Research through Computer-aided Qualitative Data Analysis Software. *Organizational Research Methods*, 24(1), 104–39.

O'Reilly, M., & Parker, N. (2013). 'Unsatisfactory Saturation': A Critical Exploration of the Notion of Saturated Sample Sizes in Qualitative Research. *Qualitative Research*, 13(2), 190–7.

Oakley, A. (1981). Interviewing Women: A Contradiction in Terms. In H. Roberts (Ed.), *Doing Feminist Research* (pp. 30–61). London: Routledge and Kegan Paul.

Patton, M.Q. (2015). *Qualitative Evaluation and Research Methods* (4th ed.). London: Sage.

Pawlowski, C.S., Andersen, H.B., Troelsen, J., & Schipperijn, J. (2016). Children's Physical Activity Behavior During School Recess: A Pilot Study Using GPS, Accelerometer, Participant Observation, and Go-Along Interview. *PLoS ONE*, 11(2), e0148786. doi:10.1371/journal.pone. 0148786

Platt, J. (2012). The History of the Interview. In J.F. Gubrium, J.A., Holstein, A.B. Marvasti, & K.D. McKinney (Eds.), *The SAGE Handbook of Interview Research: The Complexity of the Craft* (pp. 9–26). Thousand Oaks, CA: Sage.

Poland, B.P. (2001). Transcription Quality. In J.F. Gubrium & J.A. Holstein (Eds.), *Handbook of Interview Research: Context and Method* (pp. 629–50). Thousand Oaks, CA: Sage.

Poland, F., & Birt, L. (2018). Protecting and Empowering Research with the Vulnerable Older Person. In R. Iphofen & M. Tolich (Eds.), *The Sage Handbook of Qualitative Research Ethics* (pp. 382–95). London: Sage.

Polkinghorne, D. (1988). *Narrative Knowing and the Human Sciences*. New York: SUNY.

Porst, R. (2014). *Fragebogen: Ein Arbeitsbuch*. Wiesbaden: VS-Verlag.

Potter, J., & Hepburn, A. (2012). Eight Challenges for Interview Researchers. In J.F. Gubrium, J.A. Holstein, A.B. Marvasti, & K.D. McKinney (Eds.), *The SAGE Handbook of Interview Research: The Complexity of the Craft* (pp. 555–70). Thousand Oaks, CA: Sage.

Pratt, M.G., Kaplan, S., & Whittington, R. (2020). Editorial Essay: The Tumult over Transparency: Decoupling Transparency from Replication in Establishing Trustworthy Qualitative Research. *Administrative Science Quarterly*, 65(1), 1–19. https://doi.org/10.1177/0001839219887663

Puchta, C., & Potter, J. (1999). Asking Elaborate Questions: Focus Groups and the Management of Spontaneity. *Journal of Sociolinguistics*, 3(3), 314–35.

Pyer, M., & Campbell, J. (2013). The 'Other Participant' in the Room: The Effect of Significant Adults in Research with Children. *Research Ethics*, 9(4), 153–65. doi:10.1177/1747016112464721

Radley, A., Chamberlain, K., Hodgetts, D., Stolte, O., & Groot, S. (2010). From Means to Occasion: Walking in the Life of Homeless People. *Visual Studies*, 25(1), 36–45. doi:10.1080/14725861003606845

Ragin, C.C. (1992). 'Casing' and the Process of Social Inquiry. In C.C. Ragin & H.S. Becker (Eds.), *What is a Case? Exploring the Foundations of Social Inquiry* (pp. 217–26). Cambridge: Cambridge University Press.

Ragin, C.C. (1994). *Constructing Social Research*. Thousand Oaks, CA: Pine Forge Press.

Ragin, C.C., & Becker, H.S. (Eds.) (1992). *What is a Case? Exploring the Foundations of Social Inquiry*. Cambridge: Cambridge University Press.

Rapley, T. (2012). The (Extra)ordinary Practices of Qualitative Interviewing. In J.F. Gubrium, J.A. Holstein, A.B. Marvasti, & K.D. McKinney (Eds.), *The SAGE Handbook of Interview Research: The Complexity of the Craft* (pp. 541–54). Thousand Oaks, CA: Sage.

Rapley, T. (2014). Sampling Strategies. In U. Flick (Ed.), *The SAGE Handbook of Qualitative Data Analysis* (pp. 49–63). London: Sage.

Read, B.L. (2018). Serial Interviews: When and Why to Talk to Someone More Than Once. *International Journal of Qualitative Methods*, December. doi:10.1177/1609406918783452

Reeves, C.L. (2010). A Difficult Negotiation: Fieldwork Relations with Gatekeepers. *Qualitative Research*, 10(3), 315–31. doi:10.1177/1468794109360150

Reichertz, J. (1992). Beschreiben oder Zeigen: Über das Verfassen ethnographischer Bericht. *Soziale Welt*, 43, 331–50.

Resch, K., & Enzenhofer, E. (2018). Collecting Data in Other Languages – Strategies for Cross-language Research in Multilingual Societies. In U. Flick (Ed.), *The SAGE Handbook of Qualitative Data Collection* (pp. 131–46). London: Sage.

Richards, D. (1996). Elite Interviewing: Approaches and Pitfalls. *Politics*, 16(3), 199–204.

Riemann, G. (2003). A Joint Project Against the Backdrop of a Research Tradition: An Introduction to 'Doing Biographical Research' [36 paragraphs]. *Forum Qualitative Sozialforschung / Forum: Qualitative Social Research*, 4(3), Article 18. http://nbn-resolving.de/urn:nbn:de:0114-fqs0303185

Riemann, G., & Schütze, F. (1987). Trajectory as a Basic Theoretical Concept for Analyzing Suffering and Disorderly Social Processes. In D. Maines (Ed.), *Social Organization and Social Process: Essays in Honor of Anselm Strauss* (pp. 333–57). New York: Aldine de Gruyter.

Riese, J. (2019). What is 'Access' in the Context of Qualitative Research? *Qualitative Research*, 19(6), 669–84. doi:10.1177/1468794118787713

Ritchie, J., Lewis, J., McNaughton Nichols, C., & Ormston, R. (Eds.) (2014). *Qualitative Research Practice*. London: Sage.

Robinson, O.C. (2014). Sampling in Interview-based Qualitative Research: A Theoretical and Practical Guide. *Qualitative Research in Psychology*, 11(1), 25–41.

Rogers, C.R. (1945). Chapter V: Counseling. *Review of Educational Research*, 15(2), 155–63. doi:10.3102/00346543015002155

Röhnsch, G., & Flick, U. (2015). Barrieren der Inanspruchnahme suchtspezifischer Hilfen aus Sicht von MigrantInnen aus der früheren Sowjetunion. Heterogene Sozialisationshintergründe in der Suchttherapie. *Zeitschrift für Soziologie der Erziehung und Sozialisation (ZSE)*, 35(1), 69–85.

Rosenthal, G. (2004). Biographical Research. In C. Seale, G. Gobo, J. Gubrium, & D. Silverman (Eds.), *Qualitative Research Practice* (pp. 48–65). London: Sage.

Rosenthal, G., & Fischer-Rosenthal, W. (2004). The Analysis of Biographical-Narrative Interviews. In U. Flick, E. v. Kardorff, & I. Steinke (Eds.), *A Companion to Qualitative Research* (pp. 259–65). London: Sage.

Roulston, K. (2010a). *Reflective Interviewing: A Guide to Theory and Practice*. London and Thousand Oaks, CA: Sage.

Roulston, K. (2010b). Considering Quality in Qualitative Interviews. *Qualitative Research*, 10, 199–228.

Roulston, K. (2011a). Working through Challenges in Doing Interview Research. *International Journal of Qualitative Methods*, 10(4), 348–366. doi:10.1177/160940691101000404

Roulston, K. (2011b). Interview 'Problems' as Topics for Analysis. *Applied Linguistics*, 32(1), 77–94.

Rubin, H.J., & Rubin, I.S. (2005). *Qualitative Interviewing – the Art of Hearing Data* (2nd ed.). London: Sage.

Rugkåsa, J., & Canvin, K. (2011). Researching Mental Health in Minority Ethnic Communities: Reflections on Recruitment. *Qualitative Health Research*, 21(1), 132–43. https://doi.org/10.1177/1049732310379115

Rutakumwa, R., Mugisha, J.O., Bernays, S., et al. (2020). Conducting In-depth Interviews with and without Voice Recorders: A Comparative Analysis. *Qualitative Research*, 20(5), 565–81. doi:10.1177/1468794119884806

Ryan, G.W., & Bernard, H.R. (2004). *Social Research Methods: Qualitative and Quantitative Approaches*. London: Sage.

Salmons, H. (2015). *Online Interviewing* (2nd ed.). London: Sage.

Sandberg, J., & Alvesson, M. (2011). Ways of Constructing Research Questions: Gap-spotting or Problematization? *Organization*, 18(1), 23–44. https://doi.org/10.1177/1350508410372151

Sandelowski, M. (1995). Sample Size in Qualitative Research. *Research in Nursing & Health*, 18, 179–83.

Sandelowski, M. (1996). One is the Liveliest Number: The Case Orientation of Qualitative Research. *Research in Nursing & Health*, 19, 525–9.

Sandelowski, M. (2011). 'Casing' the Research Case Study. *Research in Nursing & Health*, 34, 153–9.

Sandelowski, M., & Leeman, J. (2012). Writing Usable Qualitative Health Research Findings. *Qualitative Health Research*, 22(10), 1404–13.

Schnell, M.W., & Heinritz, C. (2006). *Forschungsethik: Ein Grundlagen- und Arbeitsbuch mit Beispielen aus der Gesundheits- und Pflegewissenschaft*. Bern: Huber.

Schöngut-Grollmus, N., & Energici, N.-A. (2022) Designing Qualitative Research for Studies in Latin America. In U. Flick, (Ed.), *The SAGE Handbook of Qualitative Research Design*. London: Sage.

Schreier, M. (2014). Qualitative Content Analysis. In U. Flick (Ed.), *The SAGE Handbook of Qualitative Data Analysis* (pp. 170–83). London: Sage.

Schröer, N. (2009). Hermeneutic Sociology of Knowledge for Intercultural Understanding [37 paragraphs]. *Forum Qualitative Sozialforschung / Forum: Qualitative Social Research*, 10(1), Article 40. http://nbn-resolving.de/urn:nbn:de:0114-fqs0901408

Schütz, A. (1962). *Collected Papers*, Vols I and II. The Hague: Nijhoff.

Schütze, F. (1976). Zur Hervorlockung und Analyse von Erzählungen thematisch relevanter Geschichten im Rahmen soziologischer Feldforschung. In Arbeitsgruppe Bielefelder Soziologen (Eds.), *Kommunikative Sozialforschung* (pp. 159–260). Munich: Fink.

Schütze, F. (1977). *Die Technik des narrativen Interviews in Interaktionsfeldstudien, dargestellt an einem Projekt zur Erforschung von kommunalen Machtstrukturen.* Manuskript der Universität Bielefeld, Fakultät für Soziologie.

Schütze, F. (1983). Biographieforschung und Narratives Interview. *Neue Praxis*, 3, 283–93.

Schütze, F. (1984). Kognitive Figuren des autobiographischen Stegreiferzählens. In M. Kohli & G. Robert (Eds.), *Biographie und Soziale Wirklichkeit: neue Beiträge und Forschungsperspektiven* (pp. 78–117). Stuttgart: Metzler.

Seidelsohn, K., Flick, U., & Hirseland, A. (2020). Refugees' Labor Market Integration in the Context of a Polarized Public Discourse. *Qualitative Inquiry*, 26(2), 216–26. https://doi.org/10.1177/1077800419857097

Seitz, S. (2016). Pixilated Partnerships, Overcoming Obstacles in Qualitative Interviews via Skype: A Research Note. *Qualitative Research*, 16(2), 229–35. https://doi.org/10.1177/1468794115577011

Shaw, I., Ramatowski, A., & Ruckdeschel, R. (2013). Patterns, Designs and Developments in Qualitative Research in Social Work: A Research Note. *Qualitative Social Work*, 12(6), 732–49.

Sheller, M., & Urry, J. (2006). The New Mobilities Paradigm. *Environment and Planning A*, 38, 207–26. http://dx.doi.org/10.1068/a37268

Sherman, R. (2002). The Subjective Experience of Race and Gender in Qualitative Research. *American Behavioral Scientist*, 45(8), 1247–53. https://doi.org/10.1177/0002764202045008008

Shuy, R. (2001). In-person versus Telephone Interviewing. In J.F. Gubrium, & J.A. Holstein (Eds.), *Handbook of Interview Research* (pp. 536–55). London: Sage.

Silverman, D. (2017). How Was it for You? The Interview Society and the Irresistible Rise of the (Poorly Analyzed) Interview. *Qualitative Research*, 17(2), 144–58.

Skilling, K., & Stylianides, G.J. (2020). Using Vignettes in Educational Research: A Framework for Vignette Construction. *International Journal of Research & Method in Education*, 43 (5), 541–556. doi:10.1080/1743727X.2019.1704243

Skukauskaite, A. (2012). Transparency in Transcribing: Making Visible Theoretical Bases Impacting Knowledge Construction from Open-ended Interview Records [66 paragraphs]. *Forum Qualitative Sozialforschung / Forum: Qualitative Social Research*, 13(1), Article 14. http://nbn-resolving.de/urn:nbn:de:0114-fqs1201146

Smith, L.T. (2012). *Decolonizing Methodologies: Research and Indigenous Peoples* (2nd ed.). London: Zed Books.

Spataro, S.E., & Bloch, J. (2018). 'Can You Repeat That?' Teaching Active Listening in Management Education. *Journal of Management Education*, 42(2), 168–98. https://doi.org/10.1177/1052562917748696

Spradley, J.P. (1979). *The Ethnographic Interview*. New York: Holt, Rinehart and Winston.

Stake, R. (1995). *The Art of Case Study Research*. Thousand Oaks, CA: Sage.

Stake, R.E. (2006). *Multiple Case Study Analysis*. New York: The Guilford Press.

Staller, K., & Chen, Y. (2022). Choosing a Research Design for Qualitative Research – A Ferris Wheel of Approaches. In U. Flick (Ed.), *The SAGE Handbook of Qualitative Research Design*. London: Sage.

Stals, S., Smyth, M., & Ijsselsteijn, W. (2014). Walking & Talking: Probing the Urban Lived Experience. In NordiCHI 2014 Proceedings of the 8th Nordic Conference on Human-Computer Interaction: Fun, Fast, Foundational, pp. 737–46. http://dl.acm.org/citation.cfm?id=2641215

Stephens, C., Burholt, V. & Keating, N. (2018). Collecting Qualitative Data with Older People. In *The SAGE Handbook of Qualitative Data Collection* (pp. 632–51). London: Sage. www.doi.org/10.4135/9781526416070

Stephens, N. (2007). Collecting Data from Elites and Ultra Elites: Telephone and Face-to-Face Interviews with Macroeconomists. *Qualitative Research*, 7(2), 203–16.

Stewart, B. (2017). Twitter as Method: Using Twitter as a Tool to Conduct Research. In L. Sloan & A. Quan-Haase (Eds.), *The SAGE Handbook of Social Media Research Methods* (pp. 251–65). London: Sage.

Stewart, D.M., & Shamdasani, P.N. (1990). *Focus Groups: Theory and Practice*. Newbury Park, CA: Sage.

Stewart, D.M., Shamdasani, P.N., & Rook, D.W. (2009). Group Depth Interviews: Focus Group Research. In L. Bickman & D.J. Rog (Eds.), *The SAGE Handbook of Applied Social Research Methods* (pp. 589–616). Thousand Oaks, CA: Sage.

Stolte, O., & Hodgetts, D. (2015). Being Healthy in Unhealthy Places: Health Tactics in a Homeless Lifeworld. *Journal of Health Psychology*, 20(2), 144–53. https://doi.org/10.1177/1359105313500246

Strauss, A.L., & Corbin, J. (1990/1998/2008). *Basics of Qualitative Research* (2nd edn 1998, 3rd edn 2008). London: Sage.

Stroebe, W., & Strack, F. (2014). The Alleged Crisis and the Illusion of Exact Replication. *Perspectives on Psychological Science*, 9(1), 59–71. https://doi.org/10.1177/1745691613514450

Strube, G. (1989). Episodisches Wissen. *Arbeitspapiere der GMD*, 385, 10–26.

Stryker, S. (1976). Die Theorie des Symbolischen Interaktionismus. In M. Auwärter, E. Kirsch, & K. Schröter (Eds.), *Seminar: Kommunikation, Interaktion, Identität* (pp. 257–74). Frankfurt: Suhrkamp.

Sturges, J.E., & Hanrahan, K.J. (2004). Comparing Telephone and Face-to-Face Qualitative Interviewing: A Research Note. *Qualitative Research*, 4(1), 107–18. https://doi.org/10.1177/1468794104041110

Suh, E.E., Kagan, S., & Strumpf, N. (2009). Cultural Competence in Qualitative Interview Methods with Asian Immigrants. *Journal of Transcultural Nursing*, 20(2), 194–201. https://doi.org/10.1177/1043659608330059

Szala-Meneok, K. (2009). Ethical Research with Older Adults. In D.M. Mertens & P.E. Ginsberg (Eds.), *The Handbook of Social Research Ethics* (pp. 507–18). Thousand Oaks, CA: Sage.

Tausig, J.E., & Freeman, E.W. (1988). The Next Best Thing to Being There: Conducting the Clinical Research Interview by Telephone. *American Journal of Orthopsychiatry*, 58(3), 418–27.

Taylor, S. (2012). 'One Participant Said ...': The Implications of Quotations from Biographical Talk. *Qualitative Research*, 12(4), 388–401.

Thornberg, R., & Charmaz, K. (2014). Grounded Theory and Theoretical Coding. In U. Flick (Ed.), *The SAGE Handbook of Qualitative Data Analysis* (pp. 153–69). London: Sage.

Tight, M. (2022). Designing Case Studies. In U. Flick (Ed.), *The SAGE Handbook of Qualitative Research Design*. London: Sage.

Trinczek, R. (2009). How to Interview Managers? Methodical and Methodological Aspects of Expert Interviews as a Qualitative Method in Empirical Social Research. In A. Bogner, B. Littig, & W. Menz (Eds.), *Interviewing Experts* (pp. 203–16). New York: Palgrave Macmillan.

Tulving, E. (1972). Episodic and Semantic Memory. In E. Tulving & W. Donaldson (Eds.), *Organization of Memory* (pp. 381–403). New York: Academic Press.

UCL (2018). Guidance Paper for Researchers. www.ucl.ac.uk/legal-services/ucl-general-data-protection-regulation-gdpr/guidance-notices-ucl-staff/guidance-researchers (last accessed 22 April 2019).

UKRI (2018). *GDPR and Research – An Overview for Researchers. What is GDPR?* www.ukri.org/files/about/policy/ukri-gdpr-faqs-pdf/ (last accessed 23 April 2019).

Ulrich, C.G. (1999). Deutungsmusteranalyse und diskursives Interview. *Zeitschrift für Soziologie*, 28, 429–47.

Van Maanen, J. (1988). *Tales of the Field: On Writing Ethnography*. Chicago: University of Chicago Press.

Vitale, A., & Ryde, J. (2018). Conducting Individual Semi-structured Interviews with Male Refugees on their Mental Health and Integration. *SAGE Research Methods Cases*. doi:10.4135/9781526444431

Walter, C., Fischer, F., Hanke, J.S., Dogan, G., Schmitto, J.D., Haverich, A., Reiss, N. Schmidt, T., Hoffman, J.-D., & Feldmann, C. (2020). Infrastructural Needs and Expected Benefits of Telemonitoring in Left Ventricular Assist Device Therapy: Results of a Qualitative Study Using Expert Interviews and Focus Group Discussions with Patients. *The International Journal of Artificial Organs*, 43(6), 385–92. https://doi.org/10.1177/0391398819893702

Weger, H., Castle, G.R., & Emmett, M.C. (2010). Active Listening in Peer Interviews: The Influence of Message Paraphrasing on Perceptions of Listening Skill. *International Journal of Listening*, 24, 34–49. doi: 10.1080/10904010903466311

Weiss, R.S. (1994). *Learning from Strangers: The Art and Method of Qualitative Interview Studies*. New York: Free Press.

Weitzman, E.A. (2000). Software and Qualitative Research. In N. Denzin & Y.S. Lincoln (Eds.), *Handbook of Qualitative Research* (2nd ed., pp. 803–20). London: Sage.

Welch, C., Marschan-Piekkari, R., Penttinen, H., & Tahvanainen, M. (2002). Corporate Elites as Informants in Qualitative International Business Research. *International Business Research Review*, 11(5), 611–28.

Weller, S. (2015). The Potentials and Pitfalls of Using Skype for Qualitative (Longitudinal) Interviews. http://eprints.ncrm.ac.uk/3757

Wertz, F.J., Charmaz, K., McMullen, L.M., Josselson, R., Anderson, R., & McSpadden, E. (2011). *Five Ways of Doing Qualitative Analysis*. New York: The Guilford Press.

Whitaker, E.M., & Atkinson, P. (2019). Authenticity and the Interview: A Positive Response to a Radical Critique. *Qualitative Research*, 19(6), 619–34. https://doi.org/10.1177/1468794118816885

Wigfall, V.G., Brannen, J., Mooney, A., & Parutis, V. (2013). Finding the Right Man: Recruiting Fathers in Inter-generational Families across Ethnic Groups. *Qualitative Research*, 13(5), 591–607. https://doi.org/10.1177/1468794112446109

Wilkerson, J.M., Iantaffi, A., Grey, J.A., Bockting, W.O., & Rosser, B.R.S. (2014). Recommendations for Internet-based Qualitative Health Research with Hard-to-reach Populations. *Qualitative Health Research*, 24(4), 561–74.

Willig, C. (2014a). Discourses and Discourse Analysis. In U. Flick (Ed.), *The SAGE Handbook of Qualitative Data Analysis* (pp. 341–53). London: Sage.

Willig, C. (2014b). Interpretation and Analysis. In U. Flick (Ed.), *The SAGE Handbook of Qualitative Data Analysis* (pp. 136–49). London: Sage.

Wilson, S. (2008). *Research is Ceremony: Indigenous Research Methods*. Manitoba: Fernwood.

Witzel, A. (2000). The Problem-Centered Interview [26 paragraphs]. *Forum Qualitative Sozialforschung / Forum: Qualitative Social Research*, 1(1), Article 22, http://nbn-resolving.de/urn:nbn:de:0114-fqs0001228.

Wolff, S. (1987). Rapport und Report. Über einige Probleme bei der Erstellung plausibler ethnographischer Texte. In W. v. d. Ohe (Ed.), *Kulturanthropologie: Beiträge zum Neubeginn einer Disziplin* (pp. 333–64). Berlin: Reimer.

Wolff, S. (2004). Ways into the Field and Their Variants. In U. Flick, E. v. Kardorff, & I. Steinke (Eds.), *A Companion to Qualitative Research* (pp. 195–202). London: Sage.

Wolgemuth, J.R., Erdil-Moody, Z., Opsal, T., Cross, J.E., Kaanta, T., Dickmann, E.M., & Colomer, S. (2015). Participants' Experiences of the Qualitative Interview: Considering the Importance of Research Paradigms. *Qualitative Research*, 15(3), 351–72. https://doi.org/10.1177/1468794114524222

Wood, D., Geoghegan, S., Ramnarayan, P., Davis, P.J., Tume, L., Pappachan, J.V., Goodwin, S., & Wray, J. (2020). Where Should Critically Ill Adolescents Receive Care? A Qualitative Interview-based Study of Perspectives of Staff Working in Adult and Pediatric Intensive Care Units. *Journal of Intensive Care Medicine*, 35(11), 1271–7. https://doi.org/10.1177/0885066619856573

Woodward, S. (2020). *Material Methods*. London: Sage.

INDEX

Abraham, T.H. 354
Abrams, K. 107, 264, 309
abstraction process 325
academic contexts 22
access to potential interviewees 122–5,
    128–34
  in institutions 123–5
  methods of obtaining 128–30
  physical and social 124
  preparatory steps 132–3
active citation 355, 380
active listening 181, 380
Adamson, J. 91, 99
adolescents 155, 224, 226, 271
age classification 155, 158
Aguinis, H. 357, 367
aims of study 44–8
Allmark, P. 147–8, 152–3, 167
Alvesson, M. 24–5, 37, 42, 51, 81
analysis of interview data xvi, 322,
    338–40, 348
  critiques of 371–2
analytic induction 380; see also negative
    cases
anonymity and anonymization 141, 148, 159,
application spotting 81
Archibald, M.M. 309
archiving 319–20, 355, 372
Arshavskaya, E. 275
artificial groups 255
artificially-bound groups 105, 380
assent to research 156
Atkinson, P. 5, 9, 14, 31, 47, 369, 372
Atlas.ti package 320–1
attention deficit hyperactivity disorder
    (ADHD) 90
audio recording 315
avoidance of certain topics 33, 171
axial coding 324–6, 380
Ayres, L. 181

Back, L. 33–4
Baker, S.E. 113, 119
balancing phase 243, 245, 380
Bamberg, M. 220
Barbour, R. 253, 269
Barker, J. 272, 285
baseline positions 87

Bauer, M. 251
Baym, N.K. 288–9
Becker, H. 47, 76, 78, 83, 366
beginning an interview 95, 179–80, 322
benchmarking 347, 380
beneficence 140
Bengry, A. 136
Bernard, H.R. 114
bias in data 172, 258
biographical research 46–7, 157, 380
Birt, L. 353–4
Blaikie, N. 76–7
Block, E.S. 288–9, 309
Bloor, M. 187, 351–2
Blumer, H. 22–3
Bogner, A. 57, 128, 201–2, 208, 210,
    216–17
'bombing' 303
Bondy, C. 136
Bortz, J. 172
Brickmann Bhutta, C. 110
Briggs, C. 348
Brinkmann, S. 28, 41, 76, 180–1,
    197, 350
British Psychological Society (BPS) 144
British Sociological Association (BSA) 144
Brynmawr University 303
Burgess, E.W. 5
Butler, C. 155–6

Caelli, K. 115
Caldera, A. 246, 251
Calderon-Berumen, F. 246, 251
Campbell, J. 157
Canvin, K. 123
Carpiano, R.M. 91, 279
'case' and 'case story', meaning of 126, 326
case-sampling 102; see also sampling
case studies xvii, 6, 13, 79, 83–5, 126, 133
  of one person, institution or
      community 83
  real-world research 13, 41, 52, 92, 110–
      11, 129–30, 145–6, 149–50, 155–8,
      161–3, 177–8, 182–5, 189–90, 203,
      206, 209, 211–12, 226–30, 244, 246,
      258–62, 266, 275, 280–1, 290–5,
      298–300, 303–4, 317, 327–30, 338,
      325–6, 358

'casing' process 84
Cassell, J. 124
categorization 325
Cernat, A. 366
Charmaz, K. 47, 61, 108, 323, 326–7, 335, 347
checklists xvii, 172, 302
Chen, S.-H. 285
Chen, Y. 96, 99
Chicago School of Sociology 5, 380
'child', meaning of 155
children, interviewing of 155–7
Chilisa, B. 9, 10, 61, 67, 91, 110, 119, 148, 167, 191, 247, 338, 353
Christensen, P. 157
chronic disease 42–4, 200, 224–7, 239–43
Clandinin, D.J. 238
Clark, T. 57
classical design of interviewing, extension of 88–94
closed and *close-ended* questions 63–4, 178
co-construction of knowledge 25–6, 34, 39
codas 242
codes of ethics 144
coding of data 84, 323–30, 335, 380–1
    definition of 323
    different forms of 324
    initial and *focused* 326–8
    steps in 323
coding frames 323, 331–3
Coffey, A. 47
'cold calling' 291
combination of different types of interview 46
comic strips 188
communicative validation 381
communities included in data analysis 338
community-based participatory research (CBPR) 10
comparative studies 40, 84–8, 337
    over time 85
complete collections 105, 381
comprehensive collections 105
computer-assisted qualitative data analysis
computer-mediated interaction 50, 288, 321
condensing 243
Conelly, F.M. 238
conferencing platforms 93
confessional tales 359
confidentiality 148, 212
consent forms 156, 179
constant comparison 325
constraints 381
constructed codes 324
constructed knowledge 43
constructing listeners 33–4, 63, 76, 305
constructivism 381

contact with participants, maintenance of 86
content analysis 386
    'narrow' or 'wide' contexts 332
    structuring content analysis 333
content knowledge 202
contextualization 348, 361
convenience sampling 110, 381
    definition of 107
conversation and conversation analysis 28–9 49, 178, 180, 272–3, 336, 370, 381
Copes, H. 186, 197
Corbin, J. 52, 57, 152, 324–6, 330
Covid 19 pandemic 8, 282, 288, 292, 305
Cram, F. 9, 10, 91, 251
credibility xvi, 346–8, 351–3, 364, 381
    of data 122
    of research results 354
Creswell, J.W. 76, 89
Crilly, N. 186
criteria for interviewing 348–9
critical-case sampling 106
critical discussion 5
critical research 246–7
critiques of interviewing 32, 369–72
Cross, T. L. 338
cross-sectional studies 84
cultural differences 26, 31, 75–6, 103, 190
cultural validity 353
Cunsolo Willcox, A. 71, 306, 310

danger, physical 279
data collection xvi, 4, 62–4, 311, 314–18, 387
    structuring and standardizing of 64
data construction 25
data context 26
data management and administration 319–20
data protection 141, 151, 161, 163, 179, 212, 352, 355, 381
Deakin, H. 302, 309
deception, online 161
decolonizing methodologies 26–7, 61, 91
Deeke, A. 200
Deppermann, A. 336
design, concept of 73
design of interview research xvi, 75–80, 88, 96, 163, 174, 376, 381, 386
    complexity of 15
    process of 78–80
    qualitative 76–7
    questions posed by 76–7
    six Fs of 77–8, 102, 111–12, 122, 163, 176, 212–13, 229–30, 244–5, 259, 276–7, 282–3, 298, 334, 339–40, 358–9, 371, 376

in terms of *focusing, framing, selecting*
and *distilling* 77
detailing 243
deviant cases 372, 381
Dhunna, S. 251
dictaphones 291–2
digital platforms 67
directive and *non-directive* counselling 384
digital technologies 92–4, 161
Dingwall, R. 140
discovery 335
discursive psychology 47
distractions 291
documentation 223, 315–16, 319, 354
documents as data sources 89
Döring, N. 172
Döringer, S. 202
double-coding 323
Douglas, J.D. 351–2
Draucker, C.B. 327–8
Drawson, A. 10, 57
Duchesne, S. 260

Economic and Social Research Council
(ESRC) 143
Edge, V. 306
editing of manuscripts 306
education research 187–8
Edward, S. 61, 174
Edwards, R. 113, 119
Edwards, S. 26–7, 37
Eisenberg, M.E. 99
elderly people, interviewing of 158–9
elite interviewing xvi, 65, 105, 128, 194,
209–10, 381
elites, definition of 210
email interviewing 51, 68, 92–3, 287–8,
293–302, 381
practicalities of 296–300
preparing for 298–300
and the research process 296–8
embeddedness 66, 272, 291, 347
emigration 241–2
emoticons 298
empirical material 324
encryption 148
ending of interviews 184, 258
Energici, N.-A. 11, 91, 99
'entertainers' 332
episodes 228
definition of 222
episodic interviews 46, 50, 65–6, 87, 137,
187, 194–5, 213, 220–3, 228–32,
235–9, 271, 276, 291, 381
preparation for and conducting of
222–3, 228–32

types of data in 228–30
episodic knowledge 220–1, 227, 382
epistemology 9, 22–35, 42, 54, 170–3, 355,
361, 382
critical discussion of 31–2
functions in social research 24
Erskine, L. 288–9, 309
ethical dilemmas 160
ethical issues xvi, 4, 54, 117, 134, 137–48,
155, 158–64, 319, 357, 361, 380
codes on 144
country-specific cultures relating to
142–3
definition of 140
preparing and carrying out research on
163–4
principles applied to 143–4, 148
researchers' analysis of 141
and settings for listening 161–3
theory of 140
ethics committees 144–7, 161, 382
ethnographic interviews 271–6, 282–3,
315, 382
ethnography xvi, 8, 10, 48, 88, 159, 194,
235, 370,
and ethnomethodology 382
European Union (EU) 141
evaluating services 13
Evans, J. 91, 278
everyday knowledge 201
everyday language 179–80, 273, 350
everyday life 185, 224, 279–80
exploration of issues 8–9
experience-near and *experience-distant*
concepts 62, 359, 382
expert interviews xvi, 65, 105, 128,
149, 194, 199–217, 235, 271–2, 276,
294, 382
aims of 201
avoidance of failure in 207–8
distinctiveness of 212–13
framework for listening in 203–6
in indigenous research 202–3
interaction in 208
knowledge in 202
participants in 212
preparing for and conducting of 205–8,
211–15
research questions for 204–6
sampling for 204–6
types of data in 208–9
uses of 209
expert knowledge 13, 200–1, 382
experts
definition of 200
identification of 203, 206

explanatory questions 176
explicative content analysis 332, 382
explorative questions 82, 170, 180
extempore narratives 382
extreme-case sampling 106

face-to-face communication 8, 51, 265,
    274, 289, 292, 306
Facebook 264
Facetime 300–1, 382
facts, collection of 63, 65
family interviews 155
fatness, research on 23
feminism and feminist analysis 26, 31,
    41, 52, 60, 246
field notes 278
field research 67, 103, 134, 271–2, 359–60
Fielding, N.G. 88
films 173, 185
finding participants for research 77
first-degree and *second-degree* constructions
    22–3, 382
first-hand knowledge 382
Fischer-Rosenthal, W. 336
Flick, U. (author) xiv, 18, 57, 88, 92, 234,
    285, 322, 342–3, 346, 360, 366
Flynn, L.R. 150
focus groups xvi, 3, 49–50, 67, 88, 194,
    209, 287–8, 303, 335, 382–3
  advantages and weaknesses of 254–5
  contextualization in 262
  interactions within 258, 265
  levels of 253–4
  online 263–5
  participant cancellations 256
  preparing for 255–61
  reasons for use of 263
  recruitment of participants to 264–5
  types of data emerging 258
focus of research 11–12
focused coding 323, 327, 383
focused interviews 5, 65, 172–4, 185,
    257, 383
  objectives of 173
  range, specificity, depth and *personal*
    context of 173
focusing on topics for research 11–12, 77
follow-up interviews 86–7
follow-up questions 170, 176–7, 383
Fontana, A. 67, 254
foregrounding 77
foreign languages, interviewing in 188–90
foreseeing 77
formal and informal interviewing 67,
    159–60
formats for interviewing 60, 63–6

formulating 78
frames of reference 173
framing 77, 172
Frey, J.H. 67, 254
Fuji, L.A. 33

Gaiser, T. 161, 264, 309
gap-spotting 81
Garcia, C.M. 99
gatekeepers 383
Geer, B. 47
Geertz, C. 71
General Data Protection Regulation
    (GDPR) 141–4
generalization of research results 24, 314,
    337, 383
generative questions 170
Germany and German language 46–7,
    142–3, 189–90, 200, 209
Gestalt 239, 243–4, 381
Gibbs, G. 342
Glaser, B.G. 107, 347
go-along interviews 8–9, 92, 160, 235, 272,
    277–9, 383
Gobo, G. 11, 31, 272, 275
Goldsmith, R.E. 150
Goodall, H. 306
Google Hangouts 264
grand tour questions (*typical, specific, guided,*
    task-related or *mini*) 273
grounded theory and GT research 47, 61,
    108, 320, 323–4, 327–9, 346–7, 383
group discussion 67
group dynamics 263, 265
group interviews 67, 170, 195, 235, 253–8
  definition of 254
  development phases 257
  see also focus groups
Guba, E.G. 346, 351, 353, 366, 372
Gubrium, J.F. 24, 31, 289, 372
Guest, G. 114

Hakim, C. 318
Halkier, B. 268, 335
Hammersley, M. 143, 148, 369–370, 379
Hanrahan, K.J. 289–90
hard-to-reach groups 12–13, 125–6, 201,
    290, 300, 383
Harkins, D. 247
harm, avoidance of 144, 153, 163
Harper, D. 185
Harper, S. 306
Harrington, W. 41
Harvey, W.S. 210
headsets 302
health sciences 143

Heinritz, C. 143
Hepburn, A. 47, 370–2, 379
Hermanns, H. 56, 62, 180, 238, 350, 371
heterogeneous groups 255, 383
Heyl, B. 274–5
Hildenbrand, B. 14, 124
Hill, C.E. 338
Hochschild, A. 80
Hodgetts, D. 13, 42, 103, 105
Holstein, J.A. 24, 31, 289, 372
Holt, A. 290
homelessness 12–13, 28, 42, 87, 159, 204,
    208, 212, 226–7, 271
homogeneous groups 255, 383
Hopf, C. 183, 197
Horrocks, C. 78, 83, 153
Huberman, A.M. 128
Hutchinson, S.A. 52
hypothesis-testing 54

implicit knowledge 12
impressionist tales 360
in vivo codes 324, 384
indexing and indexing dates 320, 383
indigenous research 9–10, 110–12, 202–3,
    306, 353, 383
individual interviews 67
informed consent 142–4, 149–52, 156,
    161, 291, 383
  critical issues of 152
  definition of 150
informed outsiders 210
initial coding 326–7, 383
initial questions about stories 240–2
initial state of a process of change 86
instructured and *semi-instructured*
    questions 173
intensity sampling 106–7
intensive interviewing 47, 383
  definition of 61
intercultural skills 275
the Internet, use of 235, 288, 306
interpretation 22, 26, 45, 335, 337, 383
interview guides 63, 65, 88–9, 94–5, 170,
    174–85, 206–7, 222–3, 256, 272, 290,
    294, 296, 333, 349–50, 383
  aims of 174–5
  bureaucratic use of 182–3
interview methods
  dimensions of 61–3
  selection of 121–2, 374
interview questions 179–80
interview research
  doing of, as distinct from understanding
      methodology xv
  framework for 32–4

suitability for the topic 79–80
  working definition of 33
interview schedules 174
  structure of 171–2
'interview society' 5, 9, 17, 18, 31–2, 36,
interviewees
  accessing and recruitment of 122–34
  breaks for 291
  concentration on their life-worlds rather
      than theoretical concepts 371
  contact with 147
  feelings of safety for 176
  inner views of 372
  interaction with 179, 371–2
  non-verbal reactions of 292
  openness for 63–6
  reluctance to take part in research 53–4
  remembering specific situations 224
  stances on particular issues 173
  in their own words 62, 194
  views of 51–4, 172
interviewers
  openness about professional
      backgrounds 153
  role of 27–8, 33, 39, 169, 172–6, 179,
      240, 249, 254, 296, 371
interviewing process
  aims of 5, 39–41
  choice of approach 11, 15–16, 30, 35, 42,
      47–50, 68–70, 170, 194–5, 305–6, 348
  combined with other methods of
      research 15
  complexity of 4
  and epistemological concepts 24–7
  expansion of 7
  expectations about 153
  forms of 4, 6, 9
  in journalism and qualitative
      research 40–1
  knowledge about 15
  long tradition of 4
  origin and development of the
      method 5–6
  for purposes of research as distinct from
      therapy or journalism 1, 313
  specific contexts for 159–61
  stage directions for 350
  use of 23–4
  when *not* to make use of 54
interviews
  kinds of 42
  knowledge produced by 28
  methodological principles underlying
      use of 14–5, 29–31
  precise construction of 171–2
  preparation for 178

problems with 178
reasons for use of 45
as a short-term personal relationship
    14–15
and technology 6–7
used despite the critiques 54
investigative journalism 41
Irvine, A. 291–3
Ison, N.L. 293

Jeffries, C. 187
Jenkins, N. 197
Jenner, B.M. 301
Jerolmack, C. 47
Jones, P. 50, 91, 278
Josselson, R. 60, 220
journal articles 355
journalism 40–1, 314, 384
journals 60, 140
Jovchelovitch, S. 251

keeping to plan 76
Kendall, P.L. 5–6, 65
key informants 210
Khan, S. 47
Khanolainen, D. 188
King, N. 78, 83, 153
Kirk, R. 203
knowledge, construction of 28
Kristensesen, G.K. 133, 136
Kusenbach, M. 8, 50, 57, 92, 277–9
Küsters, Y. 240–3
Kvale, S. 27–8, 180–1, 197, 247, 274, 350

language, *native* and *non-native* 273–4
Lawton, B. 251
layers of discovery 46
learning
    frameworks for 255–8
    from mistakes 178, 373–4
    how to interview 178, 373
LeCompte, M.D. 105, 210
Lee, R.M. 4, 18
Leeman, J. 363–4, 367
legal age 155
LGBT communities 10–11, 69, 266, 377
Lewis, J. 85
life histories xvi, 5, 219, 235, 238–45,
    295, 314
life stories 61, 174, 195
life worlds 62, 178, 180, 350, 371–2, 377
Lincoln, Y.S. 197, 346, 351, 353, 366, 372
line-by-line coding 326–7, 384
listening, framework for xvi, 101–2, 121–2,
    174–6, 313–14, 351, 376
    in episodic interviews 222–8

in expert interviews 203–6
in narrative interviews 240
in online interviews 288–9
listening, settings for 161–3
listening actively 33–4
literature, reading of 206, 240
Littig, B. 210
Lobe, B. 269, 310
local area differences 91
localist positions on interviewing 25
London School of Economics 303
longitudinal research 14, 86–8, 384
    prospective 86–7
    timeframe for 86
Lucius-Hoene, G. 336
Lüders, C. 47, 354
Lugo, M. 246, 251

McCracken, G. 372
McCreanor, T. 10, 26, 91, 99
McDonald, S. 281, 285
McLellan, E. 318
McNaughton, D. 181
McNaughton Nichols, C. 85
Madge, C. 309
Maeder, D.W. 187
Mann, C.S.F. 264, 288
Manokaran, R. 23
Māori people 247
Markham, A. 93, 129
Mason, M. 113
Massey, A. 203
material sampling 102
MAXQDA package 320–1
Maxwell, J.A. 83
May, T. 373
Mayring, P. 331–2, 342
meaning-making 222
meanings in interviewees' own
    words 62
measuring effects 54
Meho, L.I. 296, 309
member checks 351, 354,
    371–2, 384
memos 320, 384
mental health issues 82, 293
Menz, W. 201–2
Mertens, D. 155
Merton, R. 5–6, 65, 172–3, 254
metaphor, use of 27–9, 33
'methodological imperialism' 9
Meuser, M. 213
Microsoft Teams 303
Mikecz, R. 210
Miles, M.B. 128
Mishler, E.G. 220

mistakes
  in interviewing 178, 183–4
  learning from 178, 373–4
mixed-methods research 10, 15, 47, 89–91, 363, 384
Mizock, L. 247
Mji, G. 202–3, 217
mobile interviewing 8, 50–1, 91–2, 160–1, 194, 276–9, 282–3, 315, 384
moderating a group interview 254, 256
Moewaka Barnes, H. 26, 91, 99
Moore, N. 319
Morant, R. 247
Moravcsik, A. 354–5
Morgan, D. 256
Morse, J. 52, 57, 96, 108, 152
multi-angle case construction 126–7
Munz, E. 272
Murphy, E. 140
muting 303
Myers, K.C. 301

Nagel, U. 213
narrative interviews 176, 194–5, 237–49, 295
  analysis of 336–7
  in critical research 246–7
  distinctive features of 249
  preparing for and conducting of 240–5, 248–9
  types of data in 245
narrative meaning 222
narrative questioning 242–3
narratives xvi, 3, 29–30, 42, 45, 58, 60–2, 65–7, 87, 95, 137, 219, 247, 384
  characteristics of 238–9
  online 295
  'research on' and 'research with' 220
  small-scale 222, 235, 237, 301
natural groups, 255, 384
naturally-bound groups 105, 384
naturalistic research 5, 384
Navigator for interview research xviii, 2, 20, 38, 74, 100, 120, 138, 168, 198, 218, 236, 252, 286, 312, 344, 368
Neale, B. 86–7
negative cases 347, 372
neglect spotting 81
neopositivist concepts of interviewing 24–5
Neuman, W.L. 82, 338
Newman, P.A. 269
Nikunen, M. 41
non-direction 4–5, 173
Norman, H. 306
norms, communicative 348
Northway, R. 147
note-taking 5, 315
Novick, G. 289

Oakley, A. 26
observational strategies 47–50, 88–9, 274; see also participant observation
O'Connor, H. 309
off-the-record conversations 154
'one question' interviews 95
online interviewing 8, 50–1, 67, 92–3, 129, 161, 194, 263–5, 284, 287–8, 303–6, 315, 385
  in indigenous research 306
  preparation for and conducting of 304–5
  reasons for 287–8
open coding 324–6, 329, 385
open-endedness 62, 64, 91, 256
open questions 6, 170, 180, 385
open science 357
openness 163, 272
O'Reilly, M. 114–15
orientation of research 68
ownership of interview data 152

paradigm model 325–6
paraphrasing 181, 213, 332, 334, 385
parent–child relationships 157
Parker, N. 114–15
participant observation 5, 43, 45, 88–9, 271, 275, 281, 347, 385
participants in research
  analysis doing justice to 154–5
  experience of 11–12
  making approaches to 4
  numbers of 64
  perspectives of 29, 130–1
  respect for and protection of xvi, 161
  responsibilities of 131
  selection of 6, 102
  sensitivity towards 134
  views of 51–2
  welfare of 145
passwords 303
Patton, M.Q. 47, 49, 67, 105–7, 119, 175, 219–22, 227, 254
Pawlowski, C.S. 91
payment for interviews 154
peer debriefing 347, 352–3, 372, 385
permissive environments for groups 264
Perry, B. 373
personal information 141, 147
perspectives on interviewing 42–4, 48–50
phase designs 89–90
photo elicitation 10, 185–7, 280, 290, 385
photography, use of 280
photovoice 278, 385
planning of research 76, 78, 95–6, 102, 333–4, 357–8
  while it is in progress 76

Platt, J. 4–5
Poland, F. 351
Polkinghorne, D. 222
Porst, R. 11
postcolonial studies 10–11, 149, 190, 327–8, 338–9, 353
postmodernism 28, 32, 385
potential interviewees 54, 68–9, 80
   selection from 6, 102
Poth, C.N. 76
Potter, J. 47, 254, 256, 369–372, 379
pragmatic considerations 47–8
Pratt, M.G. 353, 366
Preissle, J. 105, 210
preparing for research 68
present book, aims of 1, 115–16
presuppositions 83
Priest, J. 76–7
privacy, protection of 141, 144, 147–8, 161–3, 179, 212
probing 5, 95, 152, 174, 179–84, 213, 275, 296, 349, 385
problematization 81
problems with interviewing 179
process knowledge 202, 208, 385
process-oriented research 45
propaganda 173
protocols 315–16, 384
Prout, A. 157
pseudonyms and pseudonymization 141, 148, 385
psycho-diagnostic analysis and categorization 313–14
public opinion 31
Puchta, C. 254, 256
purposive sampling 105–8, 127, 385
Pyer, M. 157

QualBoard program 264
qualitative content analysis 323, 331–4
   process of 331–2
   using *inductive* or *deductive* codes 331
qualitative interviewing 6, 24, 52, 130
   when to make use of 45–6
qualitative research 7, 31, 41, 89, 91, 104–5, 113, 139–40, 155, 170, 174, 179, 200, 247, 289–92, 318–19, 331, 335–7, 340, 346–8, 354–7, 360, 364
   definition of 322–3
quality
   of the interview situation 350–1
   practical aspects of 349–50
quantitative research, dominance of 47
questionnaires 170, 194–5
questions
   to be asked at interview (as distinct from the research question) 95, 350, 383

ethnographic 273
   functions of 89, 170, 180
   to generate narratives 383–4
   preparation of 176, 178
   revision of 179
   types of 170, 173–6, 222
quotes from interviews 361–2

racism 247
Radley, A. 280
Ragin, C.C. 76, 83–4
Rapley, T. 109, 119, 178, 369–72
rapport 25, 60, 179, 263, 272, 302, 348, 385
Ravn, M.N. 131, 136
Ray, S. 247
realist tales 359
reality, construction of 30
recording of interviews 6, 31, 154, 159, 178–9, 213, 278–9, 291, 305–6, 314–16, 351
recruitment for interview research 130–4, 385
reflection and reflexivity 6, 65–6, 79, 174, 239–40, 311, 347–9, 356
   on interactional context 335–6
reflective interviewing 6, 28, 60
reflexive use of questions and interview guides 178–9
reflexivity xvi, 11, 30, 134, 140, 157, 163, 373–7, 385
   endogenous and *referential* 373
   and reflective practice 376
refugee status 82
Reichertz, J. 354
relational approach to interviewing 60
relevance 225, 314, 363
   general and *specific* 79
'repisodes' 229, 385
replicability of research 357, 385
replication crises 355, 385–6
reporting on research 370–1
research
   purposes and expectations of 147
   strategies for 46–7
research fatigue 54, 86
research questions xvi, 4, 12–13, 68, 70–84, 90, 95, 102–3, 176, 179–80, 183, 195, 237–8, 272, 314, 316, 319, 333, 350, 354, 370, 386
   as distinct from interview questions 175
   for expert interviews 204–6
   generalizing or *particularizing* 83
   good or bad 82–3
   and interviewing generally 42–4
   precise formulation of 80
resources needed 95–6
respondent validation 351, 354

'respondents' to research (rather than 'informants') 5
response rates 64
responsive interviewing 60, 386
retrospective research 6, 86, 173, 386
rights and dignity of participants in research 145
risk 225
Ritchie, J. 147, 152
Rizvi, S. 246, 251
Robinson, O.C. 119
Rogers, C.R. 4
Röhnsch, G. 42, 157, 360
role-play 178
'romantic' concept of interviewing 25, 42
rooms for placing cameras in Skype interviews 302
Rosenthal, G. 241, 251, 290, 336
Roulston, K. 25–6, 37, 51–2, 60, 178
Rubin, H.J. and I.S. 45, 60, 79, 289, 348–9
Rugkåsa, J. 123
Russian-speaking groups 189–90
Russon, B. 306
Rutakumwa, R. 315
Ryan, G.W. 114

Salmons, H. 51
sample size 112–13
sampling xvi, 9, 102–17, 128–9, 133–4, 240, 319–22, 354, 361, 386
  with criteria defined in advance 104–5
  decisions on 103
  in expert interviews 204–6
  in indigenous interview research 110–12
  and selection 103–4
sampling plans 104, 111–12, 116–17, 133
Sandberg, J. 81
Sandelowski, M. 84, 119, 363–4, 367
saturation xvi, 73, 113–15, 134, 387
  problems with the concept of 114–15
  theoretical 108
Schnell, M.W. 143
Schöngut-Grollmus, N. 11, 91, 99
Schreier, M. 331–2, 343
Schreiner, A.E. 161
Schröer, N. 190
Schütz, A. 22
Schütze, F. 66, 87, 238–9, 242–3, 290
scientific concepts 175, 179–80
scientific quality of research 144
scope of research 83
second interviews 86
second opinions 353
secondary analysis 318–20, 386
  definition of 318
  sources of data for 319
second-degree construction 386

security of data 148
Seitz, S. 302
selection as an individual for participation in research 130–1
selective coding 324, 326, 329–30, 386
self-reported data 47–8
semantic knowledge 220–1, 227, 386
Semenova, E. 188
semi-structured interviews xvi, 29, 42, 45, 61, 81–2, 91, 137, 170–84, 194–5, 213, 220, 235, 237, 275–6, 290, 294, 301, 386
sensitive topics 154, 289–90, 352
sequencing of questions 6, 171, 183
sexual health 92
shadowing 281, 386
Shaw, I. 98
Sherman, R. 266
short description of each case 328–30
short-term projects 48
shorthand 6
Silverman, D. 18, 31–2, 37, 54, 371–2
simulated interviews 178–9
Skilling, K. 187
Skukauskaite, A. 355
Skype 7–8, 51, 67–8, 264, 287–8, 294, 300–2, 304, 315, 386
  practicalities of 302
  used for talk only 302
small-talk 225, 258
smartphones 315
snowball sampling 93, 109–10, 124–8, 264, 386
social media 8, 51, 93, 129, 141
social research 5, 7, 24, 139
Social Research Association (SRA) 144
socio-demographic data 243–4
software packages 320–1
Solarino, A. M. 357, 367
spontaneous interviewing 67,93
spontaneous reactions 294
Spradley, J.P. 272–6
Staller, K. 96, 99
Stals, S. 91–2
stand-alone method 386
standardization of questions 170
standardized interviews 64
statements not seen as true facts 26
statistical analysis 64
Stephens, N. 292
stereotypical interviews 170
Stewart, B. 94
Stewart, D.W. 256
Stewart, F. 264, 288
Stolte, O. 13, 18, 42, 103, 105
storytelling 381
strangers

learning from 61, 188
  researchers seen as 14
Strauss, A.L. 324–6, 330, 347
stress 163, 184, 267–9, 278–9
Strube, G. 220
structuration 62–5, 170
structured interviews and questions 6, 25,
    63–4, 170–4, 195, 386
Stryker, S. 23
Sturges, J.E. 289–90
Stylianides, G. 187
subjective theory 201, 386
subjectivity 21, 45, 223, 359
sub-questions 170
success factors 16, 35, 55, 97, 118, 134,
    166, 178, 196, 215, 233, 267, 284,
    307–8, 341, 364–5, 378
Suh, E.E. 343
surveys 45, 174
symbolic interactionism 22–3
synchronous/asynchronous communication
    51, 92, 263–4, 295–6, 380
synchronous groups 376
systematic reviews 387

tailoring of interview formats 63
talking, varieties of 377
tape-recording 6, 213, 315
target groups 65, 155–9, 210, 212
targets, contradictory 179
Taylor, S. 167
teamwork for listening 305
technical problems 264, 301–2, 305
technology, use of xvi, 6–8, 202, 208
telephone interviewing 287–93, 300–1,
    315
  cost savings from 289–90
  drawbacks of 292
  practicalities of 291–3
thematic coding 323, 328–31, 387
themes 79
theoretical coding 327–8
theoretical sampling 107–9, 387
  definition of 108
theoretical underpinnings of interviewing
    22–3, 35
therapeutic interviews 33, 387
  as distinct from research interviews 40
Thomas's theorem 23, 222, 387
Thornberg, R. 347
timing of work 96
tools for interviewing 135, 184–5,
    188, 254
topics 77, 79
'trails' 278
training in interviewing 178–9, 183, 384

transcription 32, 96, 152, 179, 213, 278,
    298–302, 305–6, 314–18, 348, 351–2,
    357, 371
translation of research findings 264
translators 188–90
transparency xvi, 349, 352, 354–6, 361,
    364, 370, 374, 387
  definition of 354
  in writing about research 356
triangulation 15, 88–90, 221–2, 387
  used with other qualitative methods
    88–9
Trinczek, R. 208
trust and trustworthiness 53, 60, 346–7,
    353–4, 387
  between interviewer interviewee 129
Tulving, E. 220
Twitter 93–4
typical-case sampling 106

Ulrich, C.G. 349
unexpected events 46
United Kingdom Research Institute
    (UKRI) 142
University College, London (UCL) 142

vaccination 266
validity concepts 353
Van Maanen, J. 359–60, 366
variation sampling 106
verbal and *non-verbal* communication 181,
    314, 351
verbatim interviews 5
verstehen 29, 387
video recording 306, 315
vignettes 187–8, 387
  definition of 187
vulnerability 10–11, 157, 175, 201

Wakefield, K. 302, 309
walking interviews 272, 277–83
walking process 277, 279
Walter, C. 217
Webex 67–8, 264, 287, 303–4, 387
Weiss, R. 14, 40, 45, 61, 188, 347
Welch, C. 210
Wertz, F.J. 155, 337
Whitaker, E.M. 9
Wigfall, V. 125
Wilkerson, J.M. 57
Willig, C. 47, 335
Wolff, S. 356
women managers 266
women of colour 246, 251, 377
women's health 85
Wood, F. 187

Woodward, S. 186
wording of questions 171, 174
writing about research 356–63

xenophobia 333

younger people, interviewing of
155, 157

Zoom 67–8, 264, 287–8, 303–4, 387
zugzwang 387